Equality and Liberty

EQUALITY AND LIBERTY

A Defense of Radical Egalitarianism

KAI NIELSEN

ROWMAN & ALLANHELD
PUBLISHERS

ROWMAN & ALLANHELD

Published in the United States of America in 1985
by Rowman & Allanheld, Publishers
(A divison of Littlefield, Adams & Company)
81 Adams Drive, Totowa, New Jersey 07512

Library of Congress Cataloging in Publication Data

Nielsen, Kai.
  Equality and liberty

  Includes index.
  1. Equality. 2. Liberty. I. Title.
JC575.N45 1984   320.5'3   84-8223
ISBN 0-8476-6758-8

84 85 86 / 10 9 8 7 6 5 4 3 2 1

Printed in the United States of America

6-5-86

Table of Contents

PART V ON LIBERTY REQUIRING EQUALITY: A FINAL WORD FOR EGALITARIANISM

Preface

In this volume I try to develop a comprehensive defense and a nuanced articulation of a form of radical egalitarianism. In the past few years egalitarianism has received a bad press. Radical egalitarianism has often been thought to be at best hopelessly utopian and at worst incoherent. I seek to provide an account of radical egalitarianism that is not subject to any of those alleged defects and that is indeed a plausible and attractive theory which, if such terms are appropriate to normative theories at all, might very well be true. At least I shall defend such an account as the most adequate account we have of justice. (Even if we can't properly speak of truth in ethics, we can speak of one account being more adequate than another.)

If I am going to make such a grandiose claim at all plausible, I must not only show radical egalitarianism's superiority to desert-based claims and entitlement theories (the most thoroughly anti-egalitarian of the alternative accounts of justice), but also to liberal egalitarian theories such as those of John Rawls, David A. J. Richards, and Ronald Dworkin.

When egalitarianism is considered, these liberal accounts are usually thought to be the most egalitarian accounts of social justice it is reasonable to accept. Indeed, conservative defenders, such as Daniel Bell, of something they label the "Old Egalitarianism," regard Rawls' "New Egalitarianism" as too egalitarian. Rawls, they believe, is bad enough, radical egalitarianism is clearly beyond the pale. (I shall, returning the compliment, argue in Chapters 7 and 8 that this "Old Egalitarianism" is no egalitarian theory at all.)

By contrast to the "Old Egalitarianism," I think, as do many others as well, that the Rawls, Richards, and Dworkin type accounts are very plausible indeed, though I try to articulate a more sociologically based egalitarianism that is both more egalitarian than liberal egalitarianism and takes greater cognizance of and is more responsible to thicker sociological descriptions of the world, has a firmer grasp of our social realities (including the way power relations work in our societies), and has a better understanding of what our social alternatives are. [For an approach that methodologically speaking bears a certain resemblance to my own, see Gerald Doppelt, "Rawls' System of Justice: A Critique from the Left," *Nous* 15, no. 3 (September, 1981): 259–307. See also Bernard Williams, "The Moral View of Politics," *The Listener,* June,

1976.] It is far less wedded to a somewhat improved version of the present than is liberal egalitarianism and is, in the appropriate non-conflicting ways, both more utopian and more realistic than liberal egalitarianism. Here the importance of Marx and thinkers and doers who have developed the Marxist tradition should be readily apparent. [For a volume that in diverse ways brings out some of the considerations that need to be brought to the fore here, see Richard C. Edwards, Michael Reich, and Thomas E. Weisskopf (eds.), *The Capitalist System,* 2nd ed. (Englewood Cliffs, NJ: Prentice-Hall, Inc., 1978).] Part II, and particularly Chapters 3 and 5, shall bear the brunt of that discussion, though I shall return to it in altered form, and from a somewhat different perspective, in my final chapter.

I shall also be centrally concerned throughout to argue that there is no general and intractable conflict between liberty and equality. It will be a central burden of this book to argue that liberty, far from being incompatible with equality, requires it, if it is to be at all extensive. *Here* I do not face any *fundamental* opposition from liberal egalitarians, though I do from (a) meritocrats defending what they call the "Old Egalitarianism," (b) desert-based theories of justice, and (c) individualist libertarians.

When I speak of libertarians in this volume I shall be speaking, as most people do, of people such as Milton Friedman, Frederich Hayek, and Robert Nozick who are "individualistic libertarians," i.e., defenders of laissez-faire capitalism and of civil liberties and opponents of anything more than a minimal state. I do not refer to libertarian socialists such as Michael Bakunin, Peter Kropotkin, and Noam Chomsky. Like the conservative libertarians, they defend civil liberties and reject statism, but unlike them they are through and through socialists and egalitarians. The libertarian socialist position on the relation of equality to liberty is fundamentally the same as mine. [For a brief, but incisive discussion of libertarian socialism see Noam Chomsky, "Introduction" in Daniel Guerin, *Anarchism From Theory to Practice* (New York: Monthly Review Press, 1970), pp. vii–xx.]

Part III and Part IV will be devoted to an examination of the rationale for the above-mentioned theories and will attempt to meet their varied and sometimes powerful anti-egalitarian arguments in their strongest formulations. I shall, to anticipate a bit, be concerned in the first place to show that none of these accounts succeed in establishing that egalitarianism is the enemy of liberty and that they do not undermine my claim that liberty requires equality. However, in addition, I shall attempt, in Parts III and IV, to show that there are grave defects in the positive accounts of desert-based theories of justice, the meritocratic accounts of the "Old Egalitarianism," and in entitlement theories (my main stocking horse there shall be Robert Nozick). However, these defects not withstanding, I shall also be concerned to show that there are in those accounts important valid claims concerning justice with which any adequate theory of justice must come to terms. We cannot, as John Rawls and Stuart Hampshire seem at least to want to, banish considerations of desert from our account of social justice, though I shall also be at pains to try to show in Chapter 6 that it has a far more modest place in such an account than traditional beliefs about justice give to understand. Similar things should be said about entitlements and entitlement theories which should, by the way, be distinguished from desert-based theories. And again, a similar thing should be said for meritocratic arguments. A perfectly just or even an imperfectly just society would not be a meritocracy, but, as Chapter 8 shall try to establish, that does not mean that there is no room for considerations of merit in areas such as job placement and the awards of fellowships and the like.

The book will begin by providing some essential stage setting about the nature of equality and by drawing some important distinctions. Chapter 2 will both raise central questions concerning moral methodology and, in the context of discussing those methodological considerations, spring a Nietzschean attack on egalitarianism. An attack of this type, in terms of challenging underlying presuppositions, is the deepest attack on egalitarianism that has any force.

Finally, in Part V, I shall return, with these various critiques of the idea of equality before us, to a final chapter which, while pulling the fugitive elements together, seeks to define and to articulate in a rounded way a radical egalitarianism that would also maximize human liberty for everyone alike without falling into anything remotely like the statism so compulsively feared by conservative "friends of freedom"—"friends of freedom" who never worry about the multinationals or the capitalist order.

If this last remark, and perhaps some others as well, has something of a *parti pris* spirit, it should be remembered that the issues discussed in this volume are not only of academic import, they also touch in important ways our lives together. So it is not unnatural that comments on the various sides of the issues raised here should sometimes have an edge. I would even argue that it is not inappropriate, but the key thing, of course, is the various arguments and their soundness. For, after all, what we want, or at least should want, is to ascertain, if we can, which account, if any, more closely approximates the truth.

Kai Nielsen
October 1984
Calgary, Alberta

Acknowledgments

Many people have contributed to this book in various ways for which I am deeply appreciative. Without their help the book would never have come into existence. Moreover, its virtues, if it has any, would not be what they are without their help. In particular, I would like to thank my students, graduate and undergraduate, for their responses to some of the ideas presented here and for making me see the necessity of taking into account issues which I would otherwise too easily have set aside. Similar thanks go to my colleagues at The University of Calgary and at the Hastings Center. Discussions with them have been invaluable. Parts of this book, in some form or other, have been read to philosophy and social science departments in North America and Europe. I have profited very much from the discussions following those readings. Finally, I would like to thank Merlette Schnell for her cheerful, wonderfully accurate, and prompt typing of the manuscript.

PART I
Laying the Groundwork

1

Egalitarian Justice: Equality as a Goal and Equality as a Right

I

The argument in this chapter will attempt to show that justice should be linked closely to equality and that, so construed, it is not, as conservatives and even some liberals think, the mortal enemy of liberty. I shall also argue that equality, in an important reading, should be regarded as a goal—indeed as a fundamental human good. Moreover, it is something which is both instrumentally and intrinsically good. There is also a reading—a compatible but distinct reading from the reading mentioned above—in which equality is a right. I shall elucidate and also argue for that reading but I shall principally be concerned with arguing for equality as a fundamental goal, a goal essential for justice, which a perfectly just society would realize. In our class societies, and indeed in our dark times, such justice is not in the immediate offing. It is not the sort of thing we are going to achieve in the next decade or so. But such a conception of justice should remain a heuristic ideal in our emancipatory struggles.

In trying to see what is involved here, it will be useful, in this introductory chapter, to start from some very Rawlsian remarks of David A. J. Richards about justice and equality and then move to some central considerations about equality.[1] The chapter will conclude with a re-futation of the claim, made by some ultra-conservatives, that justice, as a backward looking virtue, has nothing to do with equality.[2]

II

Richards starts out his "Justice and Equality" by remarking that re-peatedly in social and political thought "justice has been supposed to involve or implicate the idea of equality."[3] There have been shifts in our beliefs about what equality is or should be, but in reflections about justice it has remained a central issue. Richards is concerned with how the idea of equality should be interpreted and with its role in common-sense reflections about justice and in theories of justice.

He first sorts out a conception of formal justice, namely the idea of treating like cases alike. But this formal conception, though philosophically uncontroversial, is compatible with very very different moral theories and substantive principles of justice, including radically inegalitarian ones. Indeed, even moral sceptics could readily accept that formal conception of justice. They could believe that justice is indeed treating like cases alike, while continuing to believe that "each person's opinion of what makes cases alike as good as any other's."[4]

The formal conception of justice does, however, rest on an idea of equality, for cases are judged to be alike relative to some standard which specifies that the cases are alike. What the underlying task is (or so at least it seems) is to *specify what that standard is*. What we should be looking for is an adequate formulation of a substantive theory of equality in terms of which issues of justice can be properly adjudicated.

In many serious, relatively non-philosophical discussions of justice, the criteria appealed to for ascertaining when like cases are alike are *rights, desert,* or *needs.* But people differ radically about which of these conceptions to appeal to, the interpretation to give to these criteria and the weight to place on them. Herbert Spencer, for example, focuses on desert and repudiates any appeal to needs, while Peter Kropotkin (to take someone at the other end of the spectrum) takes needs to be the only sound grounds for the making of judgments of distributive justice and rejects any appeal to desert as immoral. And apart from the import attached to the different criteria, the various criteria themselves get different readings. Conservatives run a tight ship as to what will count as a right, while left-leaning liberals will have a more expansive conception of rights. They might think, for example, that there is something like a right to work or a right to health care, while conservatives would regard this as a dangerous expansion of rights-talk.[5] Desert will similarly get different readings. Some will only count effort in judgments of desert. Others will count, as well, talent, contribution, and even good fortune. Still others, as we shall see in Part III, will simply count contribution. And what will go on lists of needs, let alone what a need should be taken to be, will again be rather various. The short of it is that there is no general consensus among reflective people about these matters. We are sometimes told that formal justice, understood as treating like cases alike or even as giving each its due, can be interpreted in "terms of common-sense criteria of likeness or oneness (rights or desert or needs), but we find, on examination, that these criteria are extremely controversial, both in the interpretation and the relative weighting of each of them."[6]

III

It is here that Richards thinks philosophical theories of justice can properly enter. His hope is that an examination of the leading ethical theories will not lead us to fall back on a reaffirmation of common-sense moral pluralism. By contrast, I think that neither such philosophical accounts nor moral pluralism are likely to achieve much unless they are integrally linked with a reasonably sophisticated political sociology and a sound critical theory of society. Be that as it may for the present, Richards takes such a fall back to common sense-moral pluralism to be a counsel of philosophical defeat. What he hopes, and expects, is that one of these holistic theories of justice "would afford a useful perspective from which we could clarify both the interpretation and weighting of common-sense criteria."[7] All such theories will in certain respects be counter-intuitive, but he thinks, everything considered, what he calls "contractarian natural rights theory," which for him is a very Rawls-like theory, comes out the winner. For Richards three "substantive applications" provide crucial tests of theories of justice: questions about (1) the distribution of basic goods and resources, (2) the liberal priority of free speech and the right of personal autonomy, and (3) retributive justice issues in sentencing policy. But what seems to me to get lost in this discussion are some fairly straightforward answers to what the appropriate standard of substantive equality is. We lose sight of the central issue, namely the standard for determining when cases are alike so that morality requires that people be treated in the same way.

IV

As everybody knows, equality and egalitarianism are unclear notions. Just for a starter: is equality a right or is it a goal or is it in some complicated way both? Moreover, goal or right, what is equality and what are its criteria? What are we demanding when we demand equality? Many people—perhaps now most people—who are anti-egalitarians believe that people have a right to be treated equally in certain respects. Libertarians, though they detest egalitarianism, firmly believe that there are rights (for them negative rights) that *everyone* is supposed to have and so in that way these rights are egalitarian. Most contemporary moralists and social theorists, including even anti-egalitarian thinkers on the right (Flew, Nozick, Friedman, Lucas, Hayek), share with egalitarians "an assumption of moral equality between persons," though they differ in their interpretations of it.[8] "They agree that the moral claims of all persons are, at a sufficiently abstract level, the same, but disagree over what these are.[9] They all, that is, believe in moral equality but they, of course, radically differ about what this comes to. They try, in some sense, to give equal weight to each person's point of view. People must all be treated as moral persons of equal worth; in that way they must be treated as equals. But, anti-egalitarians are quick to remind us, that does not mean that we must or even should treat them equally and this is surely right, *if* it means (as anti-egalitarians usually assume) to treat them identically. A child and a very old and ill person should not be treated the same. But no egalitarian thinks that they should.

What then is the distinctively egalitarian commitment to moral equality? What reading should the egalitarian give it and what substantive claims does it involve? There are some things that once defined egalitarians but that now are accepted by conservatives as well. They are certainly conditions that would have to be met in an egalitarian society. I refer to equal legal and political rights for all members of a society. It is now well known, though perhaps not sufficiently taken to heart, that there can be, and indeed are, in our societies great substantive inequalities in legal protection and political power even though there is formal legal and political equality—for example any adult citizen can vote or stand for office, all people can have their day in court, and no caste or class or gender distinctions can be made by the courts.[10] Substantive legal and political equality is in reality importantly dependent on economic factors; questions of legal, political or social equality cannot be detached from questions of economic equality. Yet these formal equalities, as insufficient as they are, are not to be despised, for they are the opening wedge in the struggle to achieve equality and they must be a part of any adequate specification of the criteria for equality. For there to be equality, these political and legal conditions must obtain. But we must never lose sight of the fact that though they are necessary they are not nearly sufficient conditions for equality.

There is a historical dimension to egalitarianism. Once the commitment to political and legal equality was something that distinguished the egalitarian from the non-egalitarian. Now, in theory at least, even anti-egalitarians accept legal and political equality as readily as do egalitarians and many, provided they could give their own reading to it, would accept the vague notion of social equality as well. They are not like Aristotle or Nietzsche. That their actual concrete political commitments cut against even these equalities is something else again.

However, for contemporary egalitarians some form of economic equality is central as part of a package with legal, political and social equalities, though again what this will come to has been variously interpreted. Part of our task will be to specify what this will come to, as well as to specify clearly what we are talking about in speaking of social equality. We need to ask whether people have a right to equal portions of certain social goods and if so what social goods?

V

In putting it in this way, we should come back to our question of whether equality is a right or a goal or both. Let us assume, for a moment, that egalitarians have successfully specified the equalities they think it is desirable to attain. Then we need to ask, are these desirable things—also things people have a *right* to—or are they simply things that egalitarians, perhaps quite correctly, take it to be desirable that all people, as far as possible, have? Some egalitarians will not defend equality—or at least all the egalitarian conditions it is desirable to attain—as something people have a right to but simply judge it as desirable (morally preferable) that human beings be treated as being equal in certain respects, beyond what is strictly required to treat them as moral equals. These respects might be that people share equally, as far as is reasonably possible, the benefits and burdens of their society or have equal opportunities for self-development or all equally have the institutional bases for having their basic needs satisfied. (It is also debatable whether justice can be so nonglobal. Its scope, arguably, should be the whole world and not just a particular society.)

It is important to see that to take equality as a matter of a set of rights that people have and to take equality as a goal could be importantly different. If we stick to negative rights (rights not to be interfered with), a system of equal rights will predictably lead to very unequal distributions of wealth, power and well-being. If we admit, as genuine rights, positive rights as well, then, depending on what positive rights we admit, there may not be much of a practical difference between the two conceptions.

VI

I want now to consider equality as a goal, though this is not to say that some equalities are not rights, though how this can be needs, of course, to be elucidated. As a goal, as an ideal state of affairs to be obtained, an egalitarian is committed to trying to provide the social basis for an equality of *condition* for all human beings. The ideal, putting it minimally as a first step, is to provide the social basis for an equality of life prospects such that there cannot be anything like the vast disparities in whole life prospects that exist now.

Suppose we ask, "Why should this be thought to be desirable?" We are, I believe, so close to bedrock here that it is difficult to know what to say. That such a condition is desirable gives expression, to speak autobiographically for a moment, to a root pre-analytical (pre-theoretical) conception of a central element in a good society and to my pre-analytic (pre-theoretical) conception of what fairness between persons comes to.[11] Vis-à-vis fairness/unfairness, I have in mind the sense of unfairness which goes with the acceptance, where something non-catastrophic could be done about it, of the existence of very different life prospects of equally talented, equally energetic children from very different social backgrounds: say the children of a successful businessman and a dishwasher. Their whole life prospects are very unequal indeed and, given the manifest quality of that difference, that this should be so seems to me very unfair. It conflicts sharply with my sense of justice.

My egalitarian ideal is a generalization of that. I can understand someone saying that the existence of such disparities is unfortuante, that life itself in that respect is not fair, but to try to do something about it would be still worse for it would entail an onslaught on the family, the undermining of liberty, the violation of individual rights and the like. That being so, we must just live with these disparities in life prospects. Here we have something we can reason about in a common universe of discourse. But what I do not see, what indeed seems both incredible and morally monstrous, is someone who would honestly think that if none of these consequences obtained, with regard to the family, liberty, rights, and so on, they would *still* not see that there is any unfairness in a society, particularly an abundant society, so structured. There is nothing wrong, they seem at least to think, with such people having such radically unequal life prospects even when something could be done about it without violating anyone's rights or causing a social catastrophe. If someone sees no unfairness here, nothing that, other things being equal, should be corrected in the direction of equality, then I do not know where to turn. It is almost like a situation in which someone says that he sees nothing wrong with racial bigotry, religious intolerance or torturing people to get them to confess to petty crimes. It seems that there are very basic considered judgments (moral intuitions, if you will) being appealed to here and that there is little likelihood of getting back of them to something more fundamental or evident. It seems to me to be an intrinsic good that fair relations obtain between people and that it is intrinsically desirable that at least between equally deserving people there obtain, if that is reasonably possible, an equality of life conditions. Equality seems to me to be an intrinsic good, though surely not the sole intrinsic good.

VII

However, and perhaps more importantly, equality is also a very important instrumental good. Where there are extensive differences in life prospects between people, at least within a single society, where their condition is markedly unequal, where there are extensive income differentials, the better off people in this respect tend to gain a predominance of power and control in society. It is as evident as anything can be that there is a close correlation between wealth and power. If we are reasonably clear-headed, and if we prize liberty and autonomy, and if we prize democracy, we will also be egalitarians. With those inequalities of power and control, liberty and democracy must suffer. Equality, liberty, autonomy, democracy and justice, I shall argue, come as a packaged deal. To have any of them in any secure or extensive manner we must have all of them.

VIII

I also want to argue that a certain kind of equality is a right. That everyone, where this is reasonably possible, is to have his or her needs equally met is an egalitarian *goal;* that people be treated as equals, that in the design of our institutions people have an equal right to respect, that none be treated as a means only, are natural *rights.* That kind of equality is something we .have by right. (By a "natural right" I mean nothing more arcane than rights which need not be legal rights or rights which must be conventionally acknowledged.) It is not that I am saying that a right is a goal. What I am saying is that *a certain condition of equality* is a goal that we should strive toward and that, quite independently of its attainment, there are certain rights that we all have, the covering formula for which is the claim that we all are to be treated as moral equals. This is something that could obtain now, though it is certainly not observed, and it is something that we could and should claim as a right, while the egalitarian goal I speak of is something for the future when the productive forces are more developed and when the productive relations and parallel political and legal formations have been transformed.[12]

The link between such rights-talk and such goals-talk is this: if we believe that we human beings have an equal right to respect and that our institutions should be designed so as to achieve and sustain this, we are also very likely, when we think about what this comes to, to say that all human beings also have an equal right to concern on the part of society.[13] By this we mean that our social institutions should be impartially concerned with all human beings under their jurisdiction. We cannot allow any playing of favorites here. If we get this far, it is a very short step, or so at least we are going to be naturally inclined to believe, to the belief that we must not construct our lives together in such a way that the needs of any human being are simply ignored. Beyond that we will also be inclined to believe that there must be an equal concern on the part of society for the satisfaction of the needs of all human beings. (I am, of course, talking about situations of plenty where this is possible.) No one in such a circumstance can be treated as being simply expendable. Rather, all needs and all interests must, as far as that is possible, be equally considered. What starts as a goal— what in some historical circumstances is little more than a heuristic ideal—turns into a right when the goal can realistically be achieved.

And a just social order, if such is ever to come into existence, must have these egalitarian commitments.

It is not likely that a condition of moral equality between human beings can be stably sustained where there is not something approaching a rough equality of condition. Where people do not stand in that condition, one person is very likely to have, in various ways, some subtle and some not so subtle, greater power than another. Because of this, it will be the case that in some ways at least some will gain control over others or at least will be in a position to exercise control or partial control, and that in turn limits the autonomy of some and works to undermine their self-respect. If we want a world of moral equals, we also need a world in which people stand to each other in a rough equality of condition. To have a world in which a condition of equal respect and concern obtain, we need, where a person's whole lifetime is the measure, a rough equality of resources. If equality as a right is to be secure; that is, if that is a right that people actually can securely exercise, we must attain the goal of equality of condition. That, of course, is something we are not within a country mile of attaining. To think about justice seriously is to think about what must be done to be on our way to attaining it.

IX

Conservatives reject the identification of the doing of social justice with the bringing about of an equality of condition. They, of course, reject egalitarianism. They are firmly set against what they regard as a horror of horrors, namely any attempt to bring about equality of result (outcome), though contemporary conservatives do accept moral equality where this is read as the doctrine that all people are to be respected equally in the sense that "we are all entitled to choose our own ends and to do our own things."[14]

To identify justice, or at least social justice, with the achieving of a certain equality of result, say a certain equality of condition, is profoundly mistaken, they believe, for it takes equality of result, a forward looking notion, and identifies it with justice, a backward looking notion very much concerned with determining what actually happened in the past. To do justice, we must remember, is to render to each his due; and, as we are not all the same, like identical chocolate drops coming out of a candy machine, what is due to us will vary as we are variable and as our circumstances vary. These conservatives reject the equalizing conception of egalitarian justice. Justice, they argue, is not concerned with the future oriented ideal of making us more equal in some favored respect or respects. Its concern with distribution is only to try to make it the case that everyone gets her due which is, tautologically, what she deserves or is otherwise entitled to.

Antony Flew, one of the most extreme of the conservatives, even goes so far as to deny that a liberal egalitarian such as Rawls is concerned with justice at all. To talk about justice, Flew would have it, is to talk about our true deserts and our legitimate entitlements. To treat, identify or link justice and equality is to fail to understand what justice is. What "traditional justice is all about is the securing of everyone's presumably often different deserts and entitlements."[15] It is, Flew claims, the demand that everyone should have their own, their due: *suum cuique tribuere.* That in turn is necessarily a matter of our all securing or being allotted our several and—that definition would suggest—often different deserts and entitlements.[16] This is, it is claimed, what justice is and this plainly is not anything about equality of result.

Flew's claim, in the first instance at least, is a claim about the use of a term presumably common to many languages. Minimally it is a claim about English and an examination of an assortment of dictionaries will make it evident enough that the term is, in many contexts, used, and pervasively used, as Flew says it is.[17] But there are, as well, usages, displayed in some of those dictionaries, that readily allow of a reading that is compatible with a liberal egalitarian or even a radical egalitarian understanding of justice.

In the various dictionaries I consulted, justice is linked with fairness. And to be fair was construed by some of these dictionaries as "the treating of both or all sides alike, without reference to one's feelings or interests"; to be fair, in short, is to be just to all parties, to be equitable. In an important way, fair treatment, some dictionaries tell us, is to put everyone on an equal footing. And this fair dealing is justice.

Now this fair dealing can be understood as giving each his due or giving each what he is entitled to, and in this way it squares with Flew's conceptualization of justice; but there is no mandate in the language requiring us to read it in this way. It can, without any linguistic impropriety, be construed as Rawls and Richards construe it. And there are, as they bring out, theoretical reasons for so treating it.

Specifically, liberal egalitarians such as Rawls, Richards and Hampshire are wary of appealing to the concept of desert. Our social and natural inheritance—that, is what kind of people we are and what our abilities and opportunities are—are in important ways beyond our control and are subject to all sorts of contingencies for which we are not, and indeed cannot be, responsible. It is very problematical, from the point of view of justice, whether we should, where it can reasonably be helped, allow those things to advantage or disadvantage us to the extent they do. Conservatives, such as Robert Nozick and Antony Flew, think that justice requires that we allow the chips to fall where they may, while any kind of egalitarian favors some correction for the imbalances that will result.

Reflection on this might very well incline us not to give any central place, or at least so central a place, as Flew and others like him do, to desert or even to entitlement in our conceptualization of justice.

And if we do find these considerations compelling, as Rawls and Hampshire do, there are resources in our language which enable us, without linguistic legerdemain, to construe fairness and with that, justice, without such reference to desert or entitlement. Doing justice can be to make a certain distribution of benefits and burdens in the society, including, as one possibility, providing an equal distribution of benefits and burdens, allowing deviations for the handicapped and the like. That is an intelligible, though perhaps mistaken, conceptualization of justice. Whether it is mistaken or not and whether a more exacting and nuanced statement of it captures adequately the claims of egalitarian justice is a complicated substantive issue. It cannot reasonably be ruled out right from the start on linguistic or conceptual grounds as Flew seeks to do.

This substantive claim of egalitarian justice will be examined in this book as well as the alternative claims of desert and entitlement, but we cannot, rightly, put a full stop to the whole discussion, as conservatives such as Flew seek to do, by claiming that egalitarians are just not talking about justice.

NOTES

1. David A. J. Richards, "Justice and Equality," in Tom Regan and Donald VanDeVeer (eds.), *And Justice For All* (Totowa, N.J.: Rowman & Littlefield, 1982), pp. 241–63.

2. Antony Flew, "Who Are the Equals?" *Philosophia* 9, no. 2 (July 1980): 131–53; and Antony Flew, *The Politics of Procrustes* (Buffalo, N.Y.: Prometheus Books, 1981).

3. Richards, op. cit., p. 241.

4. Ibid., p. 242.

5. Ibid., p. 243.

6. Ibid., p. 244.

7. Ibid., p. 252.

8. Thomas Nagel, *Mortal Questions* (Cambridge, England: Cambridge University Press, 1979), p. 107.

9. Ibid., p. 111.

10. Richard C. Edwards, Michael Reich, and Thomas E. Weisskopf (eds.), *The Capitalist System,* 2nd ed. (Englewood Cliffs, N.J.: Prentice-Hall, 1978), pp. 292–388; and Gerald Doppelt, "Rawls' System of Justice: A Critique From the Left," *Nous* 15, no. 3 (September, 1981): 259–307.

11. For an important discussion of the central role of pre-theoretical conceptions see Stuart Hampshire's two essays in Stuart Hampshire (ed.), *Public and Private Morality* (London: Cambridge University Press, 1978), pp. 1–53.

12. Kai Nielsen, "Emancipatory Social Science and Social Critique," in Daniel Callahan and Bruce Jennings (eds.), *Ethics, the Social Sciences and Policy Analysis* (New York: Plenum Press, 1983), pp. 113–57.

13. Ronald Dworkin, *Taking Rights Seriously* (Cambridge, Mass.: Harvard University Press, 1977), pp. 182–83.

14. Flew, "Who Are the Equals?" p. 146.

15. Ibid., p. 138.

16. Ibid., p. 136.

17. *The Shorter Oxford English Dictionary* (Oxford, England: The Clarendon Press, 1965), pp. 1075 and 539; *The Gage Canadian Dictionary* (Toronto: Gage Ltd., 1973), p. 449; *Webster's New World Dictionary,* Second College Edition (Toronto: Nelson, Foster & Scott, 1970), pp. 766 and 502; and *The American Heritage Dictionary* (Boston: Houghton Mifflin Co., 1970).

2

Methodological Interlude: Egalitarianism and the Appeal to Considered Judgments

I

Throughout this book I appeal to our considered judgments in what I call, following John Rawls and Norman Daniels, *wide reflective equilibrium*. This method has been both widely misunderstood and much criticized. I want in this chapter to explain this method, elucidate it and offer some defense of it. I shall do this in a way that will both pose a challenge to egalitarianism and bring out the strength of wide reflective equilibrium.

I shall set about trying to do this in the following way. I shall contrast a rather mild form of liberal egalitarianism and a related defence of human rights, on the one hand, with, on the other, a Nietzschean attack on such conceptions—an attack which not only cuts against radical egalitarianism and liberal egalitarianism, but even against a belief in moral equality, a belief shared with liberals and radicals by most contemporary conservatives. This Nietzschean challenge to egalitarianism is thus a more fundamental one. I shall try in this chapter to show something of its force and to show something of what an egalitarian response would be like. I do this with two ends in view: first, to address the issue of the Nietzschean challenge itself and secondly, to illustrate, elucidate, and test a fundamental challenge to the method of wide reflective equilibrium. I want to consider whether reliance on the considered judgments that believers in at least moral equality have, can, if put in wide reflective equilibrium, provide rational grounds for rejecting such very deep Nietzschean challenges to egalitarianism. Or do we have here, at a very fundamental level, just the trading of different intuitions? This discussion will provide both a test for the viability of the method of wide reflective equilibrium and an examination of the strength of the Nietzschean attack on even a minimal egalitarianism.

II

Sections II through V will try to show how there is a problem about the grounding of fundamental rights and why sceptical challenges concerning a belief in natural rights or human rights cannot be so easily defeated or defused as some are wont to believe. Sections VI through IX will consider the extent to which the employment of the method of wide reflective equilibrium could be justifiably utilized to defend a belief in the soundness of a radically egalitarian moral system that has, as an essential ingredient, principles that commit one to an acceptance of human rights as morally fundamental. The method of reflective equilibrium developed here is a distinctive one. Hence the reference to *a* method of reflective equilibrium.

Suppose, for the sake of this discussion, that a right-based morality is, after all, at least as plausible as a duty-based or goal-based morality. Even if this is true, we could still ask about the ground, if you will, the "objective ground," of any right-based theory.[1] This is not unlike asking about the objective grounds for a belief in universal human rights. Ronald Dworkin and John Rawls, and somewhat less evidently, J. L. Mackie, believe that an equality of respect and concern is owed all people irrespective of their social position and even irrespective of any merit or excellence they may happen to have.[2] In this way people are to be regarded as being of equal worth however unequal they may be in merit or in various abilities. This treatment is due them simply in virtue of the fact that they are human beings capable of making choices and forming life plans and of giving justice. In this equal worth of all human beings we find the moral foundation of all rights.

I am, speaking personally, like many others, committed through and through to such a conception of the moral equality of persons. However, I differ from many liberals, such as Berlin, Rawls and Dworkin, in believing that it requires socialist institutions for anything even approximating its implementation. But it is not that argument which I wish to pursue here. I rather want to return to a sceptical challenge, as far as I can see extensively ignored, which I raised some ten years ago about this moral foundation of rights.[3] It was raised in the context of querying the powerful defenses of such a grounding of human rights as given by Vlastos, Wasserstrom, Frankena, Brown, and Hart.[4] Vlastos' account in particular, which I took to be the most perspicacious, was the most persistent target of my questioning. In the respects relevant to my concern, both Rawls' and Dworkin's claims are very similar to Vlastos'. The sceptical questions raised, and the line of argumentation pursued, not without ambivalence, still seem to me apposite at least in the sense of providing a challenge to be faced and non-evasively met by a right-based ethic or indeed by anyone who would try to provide a grounding for human rights. In the last half of this chapter, after I have made evident the full force of this sceptical challenge, I shall show something of how a human rights advocate, including the egalitarian human rights advocate, using a method of reflective equilibrium, might begin to meet this challenge.

Our strongest (most forceful) moral language uses the modal term "must." In taut, often humanly taxing moral discussion in which (at least from the disputants' points of view) momentous matters are at stake, we not infrequently say that there are some things we must do, must forebear from doing, or some things that we must not do under any circumstances. We also feel that there are certain things we have a right to expect or a right to do or to have and that others (including the state) must not interfere with us in these areas or in some instances must actively protect these rights. Sceptics about human rights or such strong natural rights doubt that there is any appeal to fact or any set of rational principles that, independent of the considered convictions or attitudes of people, will establish or show that there is anything that any person anywhere or always has the right to do or be protected from having happen to her/him. Neither reason nor an appeal to the facts will show that there are any such rights. It is tolerably evident that liberty and security are prima-facie rights that justifiably can, in certain terrible circumstances, be overridden even if they cannot be forfeited. But it sometimes has been thought that certain general but still substantive principles are claim-rights which are exceptionless in just this way. Some more or less plausible candidates are the following:

1. All human beings have a right to the protection of their persons and vital interests.
2. All people have a right to be treated as equals, not because they happen to be equal in some particular respect or other, but simply because they are human.
3. All people are of equal moral worth, and have a right to be so treated however unequal they may be in merit, abilities, or even in moral sensitivity.
4. All people have a right to be treated as ends (as something of intrinsic worth) and never merely as means.
5. All human beings, capable of such choices, have an equal right to choose how they shall live.
6. All human beings have a right to an equality of concern and respect, a right they possess not in virtue of birth, characteristic, merit, or excellence, but simply as human beings with the capacity to make plans and give justice.

These six rights-claims—all claims of moral equality—are quite similar and all have been taken as the fundamental rights-claim by some natural rights theorist or proponent of a right-based morality. (I shall refer to them as human rights advocates.) The sixth is Dworkin's fundamental rights-claim and something very close to it is claimed by Rawls as well. The fifth is J. L. Mackie's fundamental right and the third is Gregory Vlastos' fundamental right.[5] The fourth, of course, is Kant, but it is evident, with the possible exception of the first one, that they are all very close in spirit. They suggest a very similar attitude on the part of defenders of natural rights.

III

We need seriously to query what it would be like to know or have a sound reason to believe that any or all of these claims are true or are reasonable approximations of the truth. Generally, with moral utterances it is unclear what it is for them to be true or false, or, even if they could be either true or false, what it would be like to know or have grounds for believing that they are true or even approximately true. "People are afraid of making choices" or "People want the kind of lives in which their range of choice is enhanced" are both utterances for which we know what it is like to have evidence for or against them. We, of course, do not know what it would be like to have conclusive evidence here. But we know what to a degree confirms such claims and what would count as evidence against them. One need not be a positivist or neo-positivist to worry about (for example) "(5) All human beings, capable of such choices, have an equal right to choose how they shall live." Suppose we come up against a kind of Nietzschean iconoclast or someone with a very aristocratic and elitist morality who claims that number 5 is little more than an arbitrary liberal dogma, one of "the idols of the tribe" of modern civilization. Most people, he will maintain, are too frivolous, ignorant, and unreflective to make such choices. They, as the Grand Inquisitor realized, would be better off and indeed happier if such choices were firmly, though unobtrusively, in the hands of an intellectual elite, a concerned and morally sensitive elite, but all the same an elite. I am not at all suggesting that no counter evidence or argument could be offered here. After all, just how unreflective is the plain man and how much of his unreflectiveness is due to a particular kind of mind-numbing socialization that reflects more the control of a certain kind of socio-economic order than anything about the plain man? But I am suggesting that the relation between evidence and moral principle is rather tenuous and that it appears at any rate to be the case that there could be extensive argeement about the empirical facts in the case and still disagreement about whether 5 or its negation or neither is true. It is not that I am insisting on a clear model like "'The cat is on the mat' is true if and only if the cat is on the mat.'" What I am claiming is that number 5 does not even have the determinitiveness and conceptual non-opacity of "Most people are bored with their work" and "Most young couples fight a lot." Moreover, this is equally true of all six of the candidate principles for fundamental rights-claims—rights-claims which are also variant statements of principles of moral equality. The very notion of truth for fundamental moral claims is problematic indeed.

However, it might be responded that those moral statements are true which are required by the moral point of view, i.e., they cannot be consistently denied by someone who is committed to the moral point of view. This makes them, in a way which would gladden the heart of many moralists, into statements that are in some sense necessary statements. Moral claims which are true are in some sense necessarily true. But this "necessity" is of little value, for "the moral point of view" that requires them is neither itself a conceptual necessity, required by the very idea of a morality, nor is it a historical necessity. Only on a rather enthnocentric characterization of "the moral point of view" does it turn out to be a conceptual necessity or something which just must be accepted by those who play moral language-games.

Consider number 6, Dworkin's statement of what he takes to be our most fundamental right. Must anyone who understands the use of moral language and who accepts *the* or any recognizable moral point of view at all accept 6? I think not. Reflect on how Nietzsche would respond to the claim that all human beings have a right to an equality of concern, a right they possess not in virtue of birth, characteristic, merit, or excellence, but simply as human beings with the capacity to make plans and to give justice. He would have thought of it as an expression of a slave morality anathema to the "good and healthy aristocratic consciousness" which "accepts with a good conscience the sacrifice of untold human beings who, for its sake, must be reduced and lowered to incomplete human beings, to slaves, to instruments."[6] This is surely an extreme morality, an "immoral morality," if you like. But, where the contrast is between a "moral code" and a "non-moral code," it surely counts as a part of a distinctive moral code. For someone who accepts it, it is (a) prescriptive, (b) universalizable, and (c) a definitive final, overriding and supremely authoritative action-guide. It is sometimes thought to violate (b), but a little reflection will show that to be false. Such a morality urges the morality of "the higher man," the *Übermensch,* who will and indeed should rule, but whose superiority does not consist in superior physical strength but in strength of character and in the capacity to create values and live by his own creations. This very "revaluation of values," which marks out the "higher man," leads him to feel disdain for "the doglike people who allow themselves to be maltreated" and to feel "contempt for the cowardly, the anxious, the petty, those intent on narrow utility . . ."[7] *Übermenschen* will be noble, disciplined types, capable of non-evasively facing the truth about themselves. They will recognize the pervasiveness of self-deception among the *Pöbel,* their slavish attitudes and hypocritical selflessness. A clear-sighted moralist will espouse an aristocratic morality rather than support an egalitarian morality which rests on the plain falsehood that people are of equal worth and which turns a blind eye on the evident difference between the masses and those who create values, are disciplined and are not afraid to acknowledge an order of rank residing in differential merit. (This moralist, Nietzsche in effect claims, will regard an egalitarian morality as an ideology.) But this iconoclastic moral claim, like any moral claim, is plainly universalizable, for it is giving differential rewards to a *type* of person. Anyone who has *des Übermenschen* characteristics has the rights, duties and privileges of an *Übermensch* and anyone with the characteristics of a slave may be rightly treated as a slave. We are not differentially treating individuals as individuals and thus substituting privilege for morality. Moreover, even if we, as does Frankena, add the non-formal characteristic of "having some kind of social concern" as a further defining characteristic or morality,[8] the Nietzschean moral code can satisfy that condition too, for, on that code, "higher men" will have strict duties to their peers and they will have a conception to how men are to be surpassed and how they are to live together.

Finally, if, like Warnock and Mackie, one sees the function or object of morality as providing a set of constraints on conduct, the Nietzschean morality, as well as the liberal egalitarian morality, does that too. The point of morality, on Nietzsche's account, is to provide "the foundation and scaffolding on which a choice type of being is able to raise itself to its higher task and to a higher state of being."[9] This conception provides both a goal—something we want morality for—and a rationale for constraints on conduct.

In short, extreme as it is, this Nietzschean conception of morality still provides us with an alternative moral point of view. An alternative, that is, to a conception of morality in which some equal rights-claims would be true or justified. Someone who accepts that Nietzschean moral point of view will not accept the truth of Dworkin's principle (i.e., 6), or any doctrine of moral equality, for it clearly not only is not required by that moral point of view but it would be rejected from that Nietzschean moral point of view. Most of us, socialized in the way we have been socialized, would not accept a Nietzschean moral point of view, though some of us would accept, more in the manner of T. S. Eliot, a milder aristocratic moral point of view. But our accepting it is not to the point here, for we can clearly see, from reflecting on the use of "morality," that both the liberal-egalitarian and the Nietzschean articulations of a moral point of view are intelligible moral conceptions. If we define or characterize truth in morals as that which is required or necessitated by the moral point of view, we will discover that we have unwittingly relativized truth in ethics, for these are different moral points of view and whether we accept or regard number 6 or any other moral proposition as true or false will depend on which moral point of view we adopt. And, notoriously, we do not all adopt the same point of view. Nietzscheans adopt one and defenders of natural rights another. Whether any of the propositions is accepted as true depends on how one has been socialized and which moral point of view has a grip on one.

IV

Cannot the defender of natural rights or human rights, however, respond by remarking that his moral point of view is both superior to and more reasonable than the Nietzschean one or any elitist code which would reject number 6? What would it be like to establish either of those claims? Let us turn to talk of reasonability first; for, if the code can be shown to be more reasonable, it will clearly also be shown to be superior.

We need here to digress briefly and say rather skeletally something of what reasonability or rationality come to. These concepts are too troubling and too subject to differing conceptualizations to be left utterly unexplicated in answering the above question. (I am not suggesting that "reasonable" and "rational" have the same use. They do not. But their use is sufficiently close so that for our purposes we do not have to distinguish them.)

To get at reasonability, first let us consider what it is to be a reasonable person. A reasonable person will not without good reasons ignore relevant evidence when a belief of his/hers is challenged or becomes questionable and, where he does ignore the evidence, he must in turn have good grounds (as he sometimes does) for doing so. He will seek a set of beliefs which are free of contradictions, inconsistencies or incoherencies. At least most of his beliefs will be open to the kinds of test appropriate to the type of belief they are and they will all be beliefs which will be held in such a way that they will not resist reflective inspection, namely, attempts to consider their assumptions, implications, and relations to other beliefs. A reasonable person will also act in accordance with rational principles of action. That is to say, he will, *ceteris paribus,* adopt the most effective and efficient means to achieve his ends and take the means which will achieve the greatest number of his compatible ends; where his ends conflict, a reasonable person will choose the ends he, on reflection, wants the most or, where they are equally desired, the compossible subset with the higher probability of being achieved will be chosen. He will, *ceteris paribus,* postpone adopting a plan of action where he is unsure what his ends are, what they involve, or (where he has several ends in mind) which he prefers most. A reasonable person will also seek a rather inclusive cluster of ends. He will try to develop a clear sense of those things he wants most—what he on reflection values highest—and he will then seek plans of action which will satisfy those ends and plans to satisfy his other ends will be adopted in so far as they are compatible with the satisfaction of those ends he values most highly.[10]

I do not mean to give to understand that a reasonable person must be, or even typically would be, the sort of person who will calculate all these things or rehearse such conceptions to him- or herself. Typically nothing so "calculating" will obtain, but on a rational reconstruction of what it is to be a reasonable person such elements will enter as core notions. But "being reasonable" is also something which admits of degrees; and people who get full marks here, or nearly full marks, will also be *enlightened* and *emancipated* people. By that I mean they will be reflective, well-informed people free from superstition or prejudice. They will be people of critical insight who are both knowledgeable about their social world and have reflectively taken that knowledge to heart. They will be self-controlled and autonomous human beings with a good sense of self-identity, a reasonable self-understanding, and a good understanding of other human beings. This means they will have a knowledge of the motivating forces operating on themselves as well as on others and they will, particularly for themselves, and for other situations close to home, have gained some understanding of the probable effects of actions which flow from acting in accordance with those motivating forces. They will have a sensitivity to and an understanding of the evils of the world and of the features of the world contributing to human alienation. They will also have an understanding of human needs and of what are our vital centers of interest and some sense, since both interests and needs not infrequently conflict or compete, of their relative importance. And, with such an understanding, emancipated and enlightened people will have a conception of human good (of a distinctive human flourishing) and they will be capable of fairness, objectivity, and impartiality. (This is not to say that they actually will be fair, principled people. I am assuming nothing about Morality's victory over Prudence.) Finally, such people will be free of ideology; that is to say, they will have extricated themselves from the distorting influences of the historically and culturally given conceptions they have been socialized into accepting and they will be liberated from the various illusions and dogmatisms that fetter humankind.[11]

It is crucial, in reflecting on the partial cashing in of rationality in terms of emancipation and enlightenment, to recognize that rationality admits of degrees. A person who met the criteria of rationality spelled out above would indeed be larger than life. What we are talking about is an *ideal* type. But such criteria are not philosophers' concoctions. We are not giving some specialized conception of rationality perhaps tailormade to suit some tendentious philosophical thesis, but we are reminding ourselves of what our criteria actually are as they are found in the stream of life. People will be taken to be more or less reasonable according to the degree to which they approximate satisfying these diverse criteria. The heuristic ideal—the fully reasonable person, the through and through rational human being—is one which satisfies these criteria fully.

I want now, keeping these diverse criteria of rationality in mind, to ask if it will be the case that all reasonable people will be committed to accepting these fundamental human rights. That is, must such people believe that in some sense, there are such human rights and that something like the fundamental principles of human rights I articulated must govern their conduct? Does *reason* itself require such a commitment?

The fragment of a Nietzschean conception I sketched, which does plainly deny universal human rights and moral equality, and number

6, Dworkin's statement of the fundamental principle of equal natural rights—a principle clearly linking (as they should be linked) natural rights and equality—will, if we consider how we might try to argue for the latter against the former, provide a good test for the claim that reason requires a commitment to natural rights.

The Nietzschean and an egalitarian right-based ethics, such as Dworkin's, come out equally well on the counting principles of rational action. Both can, equally well and without the slightest strain to their systems, adopt the most efficient means to achieve the greatest number of their ends and go after the ends they want the most when they must choose between competing and conflicting ends. They both can utilize the principle of postponement and the like. Nietzsche would no doubt regard all this as obvious and think that the need to articulate these things as "principles of rationality" reveals a shopkeeper's mentality. But all the same, they are background assumptions in his thought and they are, in effect, utilized by him without the slightest inconsistency. There is, in short, nothing to choose from between the two moral postures here. Certainly the Nietzschean cannot, on such grounds at least, fairly be labelled an irrationalist.

What about their beliefs? Must the Nietzschean's be less rational? It is difficult for any system to avoid inconsistencies, but it is not apparent, to me at least, that the Nietzschean is any more burdened in this respect than is such a human rights advocate. If Dworkin had the queer ontological baggage of the traditional natural law, there might be grounds for taxing him with an incoherent conception, but he travels ontologically light and has no such encumbrances. Surely, the Nietzschean does not come off worse here by virtue of the fact that he holds his beliefs less critically, is less willing to hold them up to reflective inspection, though it could be pressed against him, that, when we examine the implications and underlying assumptions of his beliefs, it is clear enough that he does not face questions about how people got to be as different as they are. Even if he is justified in making the judgments he makes about the masses as they now are, he neglects considering and giving due weight to the facts of socialization, e.g., to the kind of society with its class structure, its type of technology and educational apparatus which, very usefully for the ruling classes, "educates" the lower classes to be dumb and imbues in them a slavish sense of their station and duties. He doesn't ask the hard questions about what the possiblities are in a more affluent, technologically more advanced culture with a different pattern of socialization and a commitment to achieving classlessness. Whether people in such a circumstance would be so doglike and so crippled by envy and devoted to mediocrity remains to be seen. At least on Nietzsche's part and on the part of Nietzscheans, there seems to be a failure in criticalness here and thus a diminishment in rationality, though nothing that could fairly be called irrationality or even unreasonableness.

However, isn't there a parallel and comparable diminishment on the part of the human rights advocate? Why, we can ask him, should everyone be regarded with equal concern and treated with equal respect when we know people differ considerably in ability and (if we are willing to use such a conception at all) in merit? Some people are plainly more intelligent, reflective, hardworking, more sensitive, more caring of others, more decent and more deserving than others. Why, then, given these undeniable differences, do we say they all have a right to equal concern and respect?

Because, it is responded, they all have the capacity to make plans and give justice. But that is hardly true of all people if we are being quite literal. And that aside, and more importantly, even among the vast majority of "normal" people, capacities vary greatly. Some can and do work out plans reflecting a network of reflective choices; others live thoughtlessly and sometimes even rather brutishly from day to day. Moreover, we need to recognize that their sense of justice and capacity to respond justly and fairly are even more diverse. Some previous twentieth-century defenders of human rights have said that all people ought to be treated with equal concern and respect because they all experience pain and pleasure and could equally suffer.[12] To this it was pointed out in response that they still vary in their sensitivity to pain and in their capacities for suffering, happiness, and pleasure.[13] The same variability is even more obviously true about their capacities for being just or for making choices and framing life plans.

When we say all human beings have a right to an equality of concern and respect because they all share some common characteristic, we are likely to find that this is, on the one hand, false, or, on the other, that the characteristic in question is of doubtful relevance or (like capacities to experience pain or be just) people have it in various ways and to various degrees which appear, at least on the surface, to be morally relevant.

It appears at least that in not acknowledging, let alone meeting, such objections, the human rights advocate has, at least as much as the Nietzschean, shown a diminishment in rationality. Neither should be called irrational for such a diminishment and it perhaps would be too harsh to say that, in so responding, both show they are captured by an ideology; but all the same such reasoning does not reflect the highest degree of reasonability. Nor does it exhibit that reasonability to respond that people all deserve, regardless of merit, the same concern and respect because, being ends in themselves, they have the same *intrinsic* worth. What is the justification for treating them all as ends in themselves (even assuming we are tolerably clear about its meaning) when they are so very different? Why not reserve this for the creative elites who are genuine creators of value? And is it not arbitrary to say that all human beings have the same intrinsic worth when they are plainly so different in intellectual capacity, merit, moral sensitivity, and goodness? It looks like a carryover in a secular context of a non-rational religious attitude.

V

Instead of putting out "All people are of equal worth regardless of merit" as some kind of mysterious truth-claim which appears in fact to be at best groundless and at worst false, would it not have been clearer and less evasive of the human-rights advocate simply to remark that he starts with a commitment on which he will not bend, namely a commitment to the treatment of all people as beings who are to have quite unforfeitably an equality of concern and respect? It is that sort of world that he or she most deeply desires and it is there that he stands pat. There are other equally intelligible and no doubt equally rational, moral points of view that do not contain such commitments. But it is with such a commitment that he takes his stand. Given that stand, he can justify certain claims or principles in ethics, but, with that principle, justification for him comes to an end.

It appears at least that the human rights advocate or the defender of a right-based ethic who, claiming more than this, claims his account is in some way grounded in reason or in fact or both and is demonstrably more reasonable than the elitist's view, whether in a Nietzschean form or that of a milder elitism, has made a claim that is not justified by reason. This is not to suggest what is also not the case—that the elitists have any stronger justification for their position. At this level, it appears at least to be the case that commitment rather than reason is king.[14]

It is not that our sentiments are opposed to or unaffected by our reason, but that in such situations reason (together with a knowledge of the facts) is not sufficient to provide an answer which would tell us what is the right view of the matter and give us the principles in accordance with which, at least in such circumstances, we should guide our lives. What I think the above arguments point toward is that we have no good reason to expect that a human-rights position or a right-based ethic is necessarily more reasonable than an aristocratic one which would not accept human rights (i.e., the belief that there are some basic rights that all humans have simply in virtue of being human). I think the reason why this human rights account fails and indeed why all such arguments will fail is that they fail to realize that while many different moral codes, moralities, and moral points of view can be *consistent* with reason (with, if you will, the canons of practical rationality) *none are required by reason*. It is a great Kantian illusion, and an illusion shared by some who are not Kantians, to think that there is a morality, if only we can unearth or (perhaps) invent it, which is *required by reason*. The fact is that rationality underdetermines morality. There are many moral points of view that can be equally compatible with or in accordance with the principles of rational action and rational belief. There is no Santa Claus of pure reason, including pure practical reason, which will tell us what we must do or even what we should do or what, through and through, would be the most desirable thing for us to do.[15]

VI

So far, if my arguments have been near to their mark, we have seen that we have no good reason for believing that the fundamental moral principles of the human rights advocate are either true or justified or required by the moral point of view or are necessarily more reasonable than those of an iconoclastic moralist who would reject them. Is there any other way in which they can be shown to be superior?

There is another way, one which is temptingly easy to ridicule and set aside (as R. M. Hare and G. R. Grice have), but which may after all be profitable.[16] Stuart Hampshire has recently utilized it and reminded us that we owe it to Aristotle.[17] John Rawls has made it once more prominent; Jane English has characterized it in a programmatic essay; and recently Norman Daniels, in a series of strikingly impressive articles, has clarified, developed, and defended it.[18] What I refer to has been called *the method of reflective equilibrium* or, in Daniels' hands, the method of *wide reflective equilibrium,* a method in which a subtle appeal to our considered judgments is crucial and unavoidable.

It is a method which, I think, should particularly commend itself to anyone who believes that truth in ethics is problematical, who believes rationality underdetermines morality, who rejects what Hare has called Cartesianism in morals, and who believes (as Mackie does) that there is no objective prescriptivity, or, with Dworkin, that we should favor a "constructive model" over a "natural model" (the latter being a model which regards moral truths or objective moral norms as something existing and somehow to be discovered). It seems to me all of those are reasonable attitudes to hold. That is to say, I believe that it is reasonable to make such rejections and to be sceptical in these ways. I am somewhat tempted to believe something even stronger— something which probably is false—namely that modernity and philosophical sophistication quite unequivocally lead us to those conclusions and that, if there is to be any way of reasonably sorting out diverse moral claims, it must be by the use of this method or something rather like it. (I do not claim that by itself it is sufficient.)

What I want to explore in this chapter is whether (a) the use of a method of wide reflective equilibrium will give us grounds for believing that a morality which commits itself to human rights and to the moral equality of all human beings is superior to one which does not; and (b) whether, in trying to so utilize such a method, so many problems naturally arise about the method itself that it becomes self-defeating to use it in an attempt to show that a human rights egalitarian ethic is superior to any ethic that would deny human rights. I should only add the reminder that to be convinced that (a) is true—that is, that there is a morality committing itself to human rights which is superior to the moralities which deny that—is not necessarily to commit oneself to a right-based theory. It may be the case, as Nanette Funk argued, that a goal-based theory or perhaps some still different theory (perhaps some mixed theory) more adequately justifies a belief in human rights.[19]

VII

My first task is briefly to characterize the method of reflective equilibrium. That completed I shall consider whether the method of reflective equilibrium could be used to show that a human rights theory is superior to elitist theories, including a Nietzschean theory.

John Rawls remarks that "Justice as fairness will prove a worthwhile theory if it defines the range of justice more in accordance with our considered judgments than do existing theories, and if it singles out with greater sharpness the graver wrongs a society should avoid."[20] So the appeal to considered judgments does play a central role in his theory as it did in the theories of Pritchard and Ross before him. It is also important to recognize that he regards his principles of justice— his fundamental moral principles—as both "a reasonable *approximation to* and an *extension of* our considered judgments."[21]

Our considered judgments are not just, or necessarily at all, our received opinions; rather "considered judgments are simply those rendered under conditions favorable to the exercise of the sense of justice, and therefore in circumstances where the most common excuses and explanations for making a mistake do not obtain."[22] They enter and remain in moral discourse "as those judgments in which our moral capacities are most likely to be displayed without distortion."[23] These are judgments made when the moral agent is not in various ways intellectually or emotionally incapacitated, including those situations when he is overcome with self-love. Moreover, the "person making the judgment is presumed . . . to have the ability, the opportunity and the desire to reach a correct decision. . . ."[24] Finally, considered judgments on moral matters, like considered judgments on other matters, for example, when the ice will break up on the lake, will not, Rawls claims, be arbitrary.

However, it is not just our considered judgments that are being appealed to, but *our considered judgments in reflective equilibrium.* How are we to understand this notion of reflective equilibrium? A reflective equilibrium is that state a moral agent has reached after he has, using his sense of justice, weighed various proposed philosophical conceptions of normative ethics (most centrally, moral principles) and social theory against his various considered judgments, including (crucially) those which are most firmly embedded, and has attained a matching between theory and considered judgments either by revising his considered judgments to accord with, or accord better with, one of these conceptions of normative ethics (say justice as fairness or utilitarianism), or by adjusting his principles so that they will match with his considered judgments. This may even, in a rather extreme case, work by his holding fast to his initial considered judgments (convictions) and matching them with whatever, perhaps more or less inarticulate, corresponding philosophical (normative ethical) concep- tions he started with. However, the more typical thing is for these rather crude principles to undergo revision.[25] Thus, more typically, the situation is this: starting with our initial considered convictions, we go back and forth between considered convictions, moral principles, factual considerations, and background theories, modifying a theoretical claim here, pruning a considered judgment there, abandoning a putative principle or background belief here, until we achieve a state of affairs in which our considered judgments, duly pruned and adjusted, match with our principles and theories.[26] When we are in such a state we have attained reflective equilibrium.

In spite of the fact that considered judgments will be just that, i.e., not arbitrary or ill-considered or made under emotional duress, they, Rawls recognizes, will be considered judgments which "are no doubt subject to certain irregularities and distortions despite the fact that they are rendered under favorable circumstances."[27] When, as we have seen, a normative ethical theory is presented to a moral agent, which is an intuitively appealing account of his sense of justice, "he may well revise his considered judgments to conform to its principles even though the theory does not fit his existing judgments exactly."[28] This tendency will very much be strengthened, if the normative ethical theory in question (a) accounts for his shifting from the considered convictions he previously had either to others or to ambivalence, and (b) if the theory provides a replacement for the undermined considered convictions, i.e., yields considered convictions or judgments which he now finds he can confidently accept. So from the standpoint of moral philosophy—or at least Rawls' moral methodology—what is crucial is not a person's sense of justice or the ensemble of his considered moral judgments, but rather that the conception of morality and the moral sensibility he has, after such an examination. What is crucial to obtain is a match between these complex clusters of considerations and his considered judgments. When we have this we have attained reflective equilibrium.

In trying to decide what we ought to do, what, through and through and everything considered, is the right thing to do, is what results from this process of reflective equilibrium. If anything is "moral truth," the *resulting* considered convictions are, including, of course, those that remain unscathed in this trial by fire. What is crucial for us, in the present context, is to see if we can ascertain whether this resultant must be the principles that would be subscribed to by a human rights advocate.

However, before we can most profitably pursue the answering of that question some further characterization of reflective equilibrium should be engaged in. This further characterization, I believe, will be particularly important for what I shall say about the human rights advocate and for the claims I have made above. Rawls in effect points to what Daniels refers to as the distinction between *narrow* reflective equilibrium and *wide* reflective equilibrium and remarks that it is clearly the latter that we should be concerned with in moral philosophy. In *narrow* reflective equilibrium we match philosophical moral principles with our existing considered judgments "except for minor discrepan- cies."[29] In *wide* reflective equilibrium, we are presented with all the possible sets of moral principles "together with the relevant philo- sophical arguments for them." Faced with them, we seek, by shuttling back and forth between such a display of principles and theories and our considered judgments, a match between (a) some appropriate selection from the principles with their corresponding background theories and (b) our considered judgments. Rawls sees narrow reflective equilibrium as leaving our sense of justice pretty much intact, while in the use of wide reflective equilibrium Rawls envisages the realistic possibility that our sense of justice may "undergo a radical shift."[30] In a way that sets him apart from at least most of the intuitionists, he regards moral philosophy as being concerned to achieve a *wider* reflective equilibrium, not a *narrower* equilibrium, though, to be sure, equilibria can be more or less wide and Rawls realistically regards the idea of a full wide equilibrium as a *heuristic* ideal to be approximated.[31]

However, Rawls acknowledges the difficulty, though he does nothing about this acknowledgment, that "perhaps the judgments from which we begin, or the course of reflection itself (or both), affect the resting point, if any, that we eventually achieve."[32] And he also reiterates that our normative ethical theories and conceptions are checked against "a definite limited class of facts," namely, "our considered judgments in reflective equilibrium."[33]

Our moral sensitivities and our overall moral conceptualization of the world, whether we are human rights advocates, Nietzscheans, or what not, will be that scheme of principles that match our considered judgments and general convictions in reflective equilibrium.[34] They are in an equilibrium because our principles and considered judgments coincide; they are "reflective since we know to what principles our judgments conform and the premises of their derivation."[35] However, we should be quite clear that, unlike the intuitionists, Rawls' conception of appealing to considered judgments in reflective equilibrium is, in the spirit of Peirce and Quine, through and through fallibilist and non- foundationalist. Neither considered judgments (not even the firmest) nor general principles, such as his two principles of justice, are regarded as necessary truths or taken to be self-evident, or even as something which is unrevisable. Not even the firmest considered judgments, at least in principle, are taken to be immune from the possibility of revision. Indeed, Rawls believes both that many of them will get revised and that all of them are at least in principle revisable.

Rawls makes it plain in his presidential address that he finds the very notion of moral truth problematical.[36] Justification in moral theory, in normative ethics, is not a matter of discovering moral truths, confirming the truth of the moral convictions we hold or deducing a conception of morality "from self-evident premises or conditions on principles. . . ."[37] Rather, Rawls claims, "justification is a matter of the mutual support of many considerations of everything fitting together into one coherent view."[38] In his presidential address he rejects the criticism made, somewhat variously, and with varying degrees of subtlety, by R. M. Hare, Peter Singer, and G. R. Grice, that his method of reflective equilibrium in effect commits him to a conservative and even ethnocentric appeal to received opinion.[39] Rawls, making perfectly evident his fallibilism and non-foundationalism and his commitment to a very wide reflective equilibrium, remarks:

> It may seem that the procedure of reflective equilibrium is conservative: that is, that it limits the investigations to what people (including myself) now hold. But several things prevent this. First of all, one does not count people's more particular considered judgments, say those about particular actions and institutions, as exhausting the relevant information about their moral conceptions. People have considered judgments at all levels of generality, from those about particular situations and institutions up through broad standards and first principles to formal and abstract conditions on moral conceptions. One tries to see how people would fit their various convictions into one coherent scheme, each considered conviction whatever its level having a certain initial credibility. By dropping and revising some, by reformulating and expanding others, one supposes that a systematic organization can be found. Although in order to get started various judgments are viewed as firm enough to be taken provisionally as fixed points, there are no judgments on any level of generality that are in principle immune to revision. Even the totality of particular judgments are not assigned a decisive role; thus these judgments do not have the status sometimes attributed to judgments of perception in theories of knowledge.[40]

I think it is important to see the use of reflective equilibrium in Rawls, as Daniels sees it, namely, as a method for making progress in moral argument, moving from initial disagreement in *some* of our considered judgments to agreement and a consensus on moral matters, showing a recognizable kind of objectivity by that intersubjective agreement. (It may or may not be the only kind of objectivity we can reasonably aspire to in ethics.)

What we have with the method of reflective equilibrium is a method for rationally fixing moral belief even in a moral world which eschews appeals to moral truth and some objective prescriptivity. We could, in our meta-ethics (if we bother with one), be as subjectivist as J. L. Mackie or Gilbert Harman and still employ wide reflective equilibrium to rationally fix moral belief. Indeed, I am tempted to say, if the method of wide reflective equilibrium can achieve what Rawls and Daniels claim for it, the problems about the objectivity of norms raised by Mackie and Harman in reality drop out of sight and are properly seen as at best ancillary considerations in thinking seriously about morality. For without any theory at all about moral truth or the logical status of evaluative and deontological utterances, the theory construction involved in seeking wide reflective equilibrium gives us a device for increasing our ability rationally to choose between competing moral conceptions.

VIII

The claims against a Nietzschean or a milder form of elitist moralism by a human rights advocate, provide an interesting test of this contention. Can we show, using that Rawlsian method, that rational human beings should commit themselves to one of these moral conceptualizations and underlying principles of action rather than the other? Does—to put the matter somewhat differently—the method of reflective equilibrium, construed in the wide way explicated above, enable us to show, supporting Rawls' own intuition, that a human rights advocacy is a superior moral position to a position which would reject human rights? It has been thought that even if such a method of reflective equilibrium avoids difficulties like those of appealing to received opinion, it is still caught, as Steven Lukes and Richard Brandt believe, in an acutely relativistic problem with its unavoidable appeal to *our* considered judgments.[41] Such a criticism, if it is near to the mark, bodes ill for extricating the human rights advocate by way of an appeal to our considered judgments in reflective equilibrium. By examining how we might use the method of reflective equilibrium in defense of the objectivity of appeals to human rights, I shall both see if this defense works, and hopefully, come to have some enhanced sense of the strength of the relativity challenge concerning Rawls' appeal to considered judgments.

We need to recognize what Rawls and Daniels recognize: that between different peoples there are considerable differences in considered judgments and that perhaps those differences will remain even after—for different people differently situated—reflective equilibria have been attained. Starting, as they do, with different considered judgments, they attain different equilibria points. But, as Daniels points out, there are also wide cross-culture sharings of considered judgments. What is more important, the differences or the similarities? What weight are we to give to which elements? The contrast between the human rights advocate and even a rather mild Nietzschean or elitest moralist is a sharp one, but it has analogs in actual cultural positions in the Western World and it reflects different considered judgments. There is, on the part of most of us, a natural tendency not to treat the Nietzschean seriously, but if the reason (or better the cause) of that reaction is that his considered judgments are not *our* considered judgments, some important questions certainly have been begged. What we need to see is whether, when we put the method of wide reflective equilibrium to work, such Nietzschean considered judgments would be extinguished in reasonable persons who are tolerably well informed.

What I should do, to keep this manageable, is simply to list some of the Nietzschean considered judgments, indicating in subsequent discussion some of their supporting rationale. Though we must remember that these considered judgments sometimes occur at the end points of such normative argument or, rather more typically, at various proximate end points at various levels or stages of argument. We must also keep firmly in mind Rawls' point that people have considered convictions, and we appeal to considered convictions, at all levels of generality and not just concerning specific actions and institutions.

We have seen something of what I have called human rights morality and its considered judgments. At any rate it is familiar to us, perhaps too familiar. It has, in our time, its most impressive statements in Rawls and Dworkin. Nietzschean conceptions seem to us, at least at first blush, foreign, and they will seem to many perversely and outrageously iconoclastic. So much so that they often do not get a fair hearing from "sober minds." (Recall that Nietzsche, as well as Marx, was very ironical about that English sobriety, perhaps epitomized best in Bentham.)

Nietzschean considered judgments include, among other things, statements of general moral principles. Some of them are plainly the more or less exact antithesis of principles playing a similar role in the work of Rawls and Dworkin. I give them first.

1. A morality in which all persons are treated as equals, as persons of equal worth, however different, however unequal in merit and other traits of excellence, is a slave morality anathema to the person of knowledge and integrity.
2. Never make that which is unequal equal. To do so is the termination of justice.

Throughout Nietzsche's ethics, and in Nietzschean-inspired accounts, there is a thorough rejection of the stress on equal human rights and the kind of egalitarianism that is central to human rights. (Recall that their being treated as equals does not require their having equal shares of the various goodies in the world.) Besides this general conception of justice and morality, there are corollary claims also resting on considered judgments and providing a picture of human nature. Some plain corollary claims are the following:

3. One has duties only to one's equals; one may act towards beings of lower rank as one wishes.
4. People, mass men with slavish mentalities, are expendable and they may be sacrificed in the pursuit of knowledge. Such people, to put the point more generally, may rightly be sacrificed for genuinely higher ends.
5. The lives of human beings are rightly sacrificed to the attainment of a higher type of man capable of bringing into being a new civilization.
6. We should have contempt for the cowardly, the anxious, the petty, those intent on narrow utility.
7. Until we are owners and rulers, we should be robbers and conquerors for the ideal of the higher civilization.
8. Pride, courage, and the determination to control for the sake of the higher man, and the civilization he will bring into being, are strategic and indispensable human virtues. They are crucial characteristics of the noble man, who is also the good man.
9. Sympathy and pity are marks of weakness, not of virtue.
10. To be hard of heart, to be severe with others and above all with oneself, is a mark of the virtuous man.
11. A mark of nobility is to have a radical enmity and irony towards selflessness and humility.
12. Power and the control of others is to be sought. Fear is a powerful and desirable element in any morality. The masses should learn to fear and respect the nobler types who by right should control them—and use them for their own purposes.
13. What is fair to one *may* not be fair to another; the requirement of one morality for all is really a detriment to higher men as well as an illusion.

These "corollaries" of Nietzsche's fundamental principles of justice are all aristocratic and through and through inegalitarian in their thrust. They are plainly incompatible with the key commitments and considered convictions of the human rights advocate and with any belief in egalitarian justice or even moral equality. Yet they too express the considered convictions of people—though no doubt a minority of people—and it is not immediately obvious why they too could not be in reflective equilibrium.

There are also claims, canonical for the Nietzschean, which reveal a picture of human nature which is rather different than that of the human rights advocate.

14. There is a distinction in rank between man and man, and consequently between morality and morality.
15. Life itself is essentially appropriation, injury, conquest of the strange and weak, suppression, severity, obtrusion of peculiar forms, incorporation, and exploitation.

This is a morality that I stand against as much as any human rights advocate. It seems to me, while often (though certainly not invariably) subtle in its moral psychology, vicious in its implications. But I am perfectly aware that a certain sort of perfectionist would not see it in that light. He would remind me that I, as well as moralists who have a right-based morality, will, at least on occasion, be prepared to accept the doctrine of the lesser evil when hard choices must be made. He would claim that what I call viciousness is in reality a more systematic and less sentimental application of that doctrine. The Nietzschean conception of morality is as much a moral conception as the human rights one and it does not appear (at least in any essential, non-excusable way) less reasonable. Nietzsche points out that it is a conception of morality which is foreign and irritating to present tastes. But that is not a good reason for rejecting it. Taste aside, I also recognize that the fact that it does not match my considered judgments either in or out of reflective equilibrium, that it does not reflect most of yours either, only seems to have force if the sheer fact of numbers is important. But on the face of it, at least, it isn't, and this "majority consensus appeal" is further weakened when we reflect that there have been periods of history when the majority consensus about considered judgments would have gone the other way at least for some weaker version of such an elitist morality. Perhaps it is the case that the input of considered judgments into the mechanism of reflective equilibrium determines largely what is going to come out. That tail wags the dog in the match that we call an equilibrium.

Let us see if we can use the method of reflective equilibrium (using a wide equilibrium) to show, in a non-question-begging way, that the human rights position is morally superior to a Nietzschean one. The Nietzschean contends that morality is rooted in ideology—a falsifying of reality, a distorting of perspective—when it eschews a perfectionist morality; when, that is, it retreats from defending the values of a healthy aristocracy, to wit an intellectual and moral elite with its self-discipline and severity, for a morality where individuals treat each other as equals. How is such an egalitarian view ideological in Nietzsche's view? It is ideological because it ignores the fact that intellectuality and moral sensitivity are in short supply, that there are enormous differences between people in these respects and that this is likely to remain so. Attempts to achieve greater equality are likely to lead, he believes, as have many lesser elitists since his time, to the hegemony of mediocrity and to a diminution of the powers of those who are the bearers and forgers of civilization. Great civilizations from Ancient Egypt, the Mycenaen and Etruscan civilizations, to modern times were made possible by social hierarchy, marked inequality of life prospects, and extensive exploitation.[42] Without such elites, civilization with its enhancement and heightening of that which makes life good (something of value) would be quite impossible. Without it even now we would probably have not passed much beyond the hunting and gathering stage. Certainly we would not have the arts, science, philosophy, and something of a cultivated self-understanding without also having in place severe social hierarchies with their distinctions of rank, with their control of the masses and without some being at least in effect the slaves or serfs of others, freeing those others for the tasks of being culture-bearers and creators of values. That is the way it has always been and that is how it always will be. A morality that does not square with those facts is a sentimental or evasive moral ideology.

The human rights advocate could and should reply that whatever may have been true in the past, the development of civilization, and particularly of science, has made that inequality unnecessary now or, at the very least, has made it much less necessary. Moreover, even if it is to a certain extent necessary now, it will become increasingly less necessary as our mastery of the world and of ourselves increases. More and more people no longer need to be *unsung* Miltons; their talents can find fulfillment, and that very fulfillment enriches our lives collectively and indeed in terms that Nietzscheans and other elitists can understand and appreciate.

The Nietzschean can respond that all the same there will (a) continue to be very considerable differences between people and that the "higher types" are the ones that really count and (b) that, as science develops, we will need ever more subtle divisions of labor and that that will necessitate, in one way or another, rank, control, and hierarchy. It will require in the social sphere, as elsewhere, expertise and people with command, knowledge, discipline, and self-understanding, who will lead, and it will require a passive group (the great majority) who will be led. Talk of equality, moral or otherwise, is foolishness.

The human rights advocate can and should respond here (a) by first remarking that from the fact, if it is a fact, that there will continue to be great differences between people it does not follow that it is "the higher types who really count," and it does not follow from the fact (or putative fact) of all these very great differences that we have any non-ethnocentric or non-tendentious criteria to identify which are "the higher types." Is it not more likely in a more complex civilization with its higher and more diversified level of general education, that we will come to have still greater human diversity within the population with increasingly diversified interests, skills, and excellences—interests, skills, and excellences which are often incommensurable, so that nothing like "a higher type" emerges but just many different and differently valued types with little need to try to impose a hierarchy.

Perhaps, more importantly, vis-à-vis (a), is the response by the human rights advocate that while in these developed civilizations a social division of labor will certainly require specialization, it will also provide the possibility for far greater leisure and social wealth, making it increasingly possible for many more people, including those very specialists, to become the creative, well-rounded *Übermenschen* that Nietzsche, rightly, so much admired. Many people, if not *Jedermann,* can become *Übermenschen.* The unsung Miltons will not only be fewer but we will have more Goethes, quasi-Goethes, and mini-Goethes. Nietzsche's prize model for the *Übermensch,* at least in some kind of approximation, will not, in our changed environment, be such a rare specimen.

Answering (b) proves a deeper challenge for the believer in human rights, i.e., the person who takes human rights seriously and not just as ideological rhetoric. I think he should immediately concede that modern societies, where the springs of social wealth flow freely, will require much specialization and with that, of course, a division of labor. Though it does not at all follow from that that it requires anything very like a capitalist or statist authoritarianly structured division of labor. The link between specialization and rank and hierarchy can perhaps be broken. There can be, as the anarchists stressed, many natural authorities respected and honored and in certain domains deferred to without there being a political or social authority with its rank, power, and privileges and with the social stratification and social hierarchy that results. I normally defer to my dentist about the care of my teeth, while I in turn might teach him about the social contract. We both, in turn, defer to a properly trained mechanic about our cars, to mountaineers about how to climb the Eiger, and to experienced trout fishermen about what fly to use on a given day. We do not need order and rank and it is through and through unclear whether we need any experts on how to order *social life.* There are certainly *technical aspects* of social issues that would profit from expertise, but wider social assessments need no authorities other than the authority of what can be made out by force of argument; and here, for our social health, as J. S. Mill and Jürgen Habermas have stressed, we need citizens educated to act intelligently as citizens and not as passive creatures to be manipulated. The need for specialization and a division of labor does not require such specialization here. Moreover, even if there is something like a genuine expertise here, the bad side-effects of such dominance are well known. That we need, in a technological age, scientific expertise and a considerable specialization does not entail or even weakly establish that we need technocrats or philosopher-kings directing our social existence. The very fact of greater leisure and more education make that an increasingly undesirable alternative.

The Nietzschean could in turn respond that it is simply assumed in the above response that it is possible to attain something approximating a classless society. But this assumption, he will respond, is at best ingenuous and at worst harmful. People are plainly quite different in their abilities, their moral sensitivity, and in their capacity and their drive to accomplish something. Even if we attach no non-instrumental value to award according to merit, concluding that we no more deserve our abilities than our eye-color, still such awards have considerable utility for us all. No egalitarian redistribution, as Hume recognized, could long prevail unless there were repeated forced re-distributions. The moral cost of providing the wherewithal to achieve and maintain equality, even an equality in human rights, is just too high. With culture and civilization hierarchy and rank and inequality have always existed and it exists fiercely and pervasively today in both our capitalist and "state socialist" societies. There is no good reason to think that the equality of person required by a human rights advocate is possible, or, if possible, once we are aware of the costs, should be taken to be desirable.

The human rights advocate has, at a minimum, another inning. He can respond that, given an end to the conceptual ambiguities in which classes and strata are confused, and in which classlessness is identified with an absence of all differentiation and with a breakdown of any division of labor, it is by no means evident that classlessness is unachievable.[43] And it isn't so evident, as elitists believe, that it is undesirable.[44] Natural authority—the authority of talents—will remain in an egalitarian society. People will continue to be appreciated for their talents and excellences and these abilities can be put to good use without implying that some will or should control others, that there will be social stratification with its ranking and control, and that there will be socio-economic classes with the consequent domination of the weaker, underprivileged classes by the dominant class. And with greater abundance, there need not be the possessive individualist scramble for more, a scramble that would repeatedly upset those egalitarian patterns necessary to secure an equality in human rights, which in turn are needed for an equality in concern and respect, for an equality in self-respect, and for an equal chance for all people to choose how they shall live.

IX

The dialectic of this argument between the elitist or Nietzschean, on the one hand, and the human rights advocate, on the other, need not and should not end here. Indeed, sometimes directly and sometimes more indirectly, we will see in this volume something of how it can be played out. I have merely, in this methodological chapter, given some sampling of the argument in order to exhibit concretely the role considered judgments and wide reflective equilibrium play here. Recall that the question was posed whether the use of wide reflective equilibrium should lead reasonable people to go in one direction rather than another here. What I think this discussion shows is how it could favor the defender of human rights. I advisedly said "could," for whether it would or not would require the actual careful and self-conscious employment of that method to this problem, i.e., the articulation of the full argument, revealing the structures of alternative normative ethical theories embedded as they are in larger social theories. What I think I have shown is that we have no *a priori* or even strong empirical reason to think that such normative-cum-sociological arguments must lead us to an impasse where we simply find ourselves in a Sartrean situation where we just have to choose. I do not think we are faced in such normative arguments with such a breakdown: with, that is, the sociological fact of opponents with conflicting or incommensurable considered judgments, still as adamantly and as rationally irresolvably apart as before they employed reflective equilibrium. I do not deny that people can be and often are bloody-minded, obstinately and irrationally standing pat on grounds they should recognize to be indefensible. Unfortunately, we all, from time to time, get ourselves into such predicaments. What I am questioning is whether we should think that in applying wide reflective equilibrium we are still left with rationally irresolvable disagreements in which all we can do—no matter how reasonable we are being—is to pit different and conflicting considered judgments, like different conflicting intuitions, against each other.

The situation may be more accurately characterized in a way that is very analogous to the situation in science. We see a developing argument, often with telling but not typically conclusive specific arguments, that can, but perhaps won't, end in a rational consensus. We are not in a situation in which each person relies on received opinion or what he takes to be considered judgments. Rather, the considered judgments appealed to are always or at least typically embedded in a sociology, a social theory and a conception of human nature. The considered judgments we make and the considered convictions we have are typically not held independently of those social theories but are quite dependent on them. And, whatever we might want to say about "moral truth," there is plainly room in such social theories for truth of an unproblematic sort, for evidence, and various tolerably straightforward arguments to the best explanation. Sociological assumptions and these background social theories, in this case theories of a rather rudimentary sort, were very much in evidence in our sample argument. Considered convictions were, of course, involved but they did not at all function like an appeal to isolated intuitions but were an integral part of a social account. The moral element reflecting the considered convictions and the social account were so much of a piece that they could only be artificially (if at all) pried apart.

Someone might still respond that all the same, in such moral arguments, the weighting given by a Nietzschean or human rights advocate to certain empirical and social theoretical considerations (because of the distinctive considered judgments they just happened to have, no doubt, as a matter of non-rational socialization) will certainly be quite different; and with that difference there will be a skewing of their social theories in certain distinctive ways. People will dismiss, count heavily, take seriously, readily discount, override, hold as a last resort, etc., various bits of empirical evidence, theoretical claims, empirical possibilities, conceptual difficulties, depending on what deeply embedded considered convictions they start with and, in that initial situation, hold most firmly. In short, the whole baroque argument, characterized as the use of the method of wide reflective equilibrium, is a fantastically elaborate rationalization for believing what one wants to believe in morals.

This sometimes could be so. Sometimes I very much fear it nearly always is, but I still think that there is room for scepticism about that scepticism. Surely some people, dishonestly, wittingly, or honestly yet still ideologically unwittingly, will so use the method of reflective equilibrium. But this is a misuse, and I see no reason to think all uses are likely to be misuses. (*Perhaps* this is even a conceptual impossibility.) What does seem perfectly possible is that it can be used non-ideologically, as Rawls and Daniels intend it, in order to make progress in moral argument and in moral theory and, more generally, moral progress. We will not know whether such a method is endemically subject to defeating rationalization until we carefully and repeatedly apply it in laying bare the structure, including most importantly the interlocking substantive moral conceptions, to which our various considered convictions are attached. We need to compare them with alternative structures and carefully assess and develop the background social theories appealed to or simply assumed. Moral philosophy, when it is any good, will become a part of critical social theory. It will be much less pure than traditional normative ethics.[45] We will display the structrue of moral theories with their background social theories, but, utilizing wide reflective equilibrium, we will also use them in substantive moral argument. I have tried to show, unless we wish simply to be ideologues, why we should take sceptical arguments against a belief in human rights seriously. It is important to know, if one can, whether one's deepest commitments are non-rational or ideological. I have argued, or in some cases simply assumed (e.g., as against natural law theories), that the standard defenses are not adequate.[46] I have tried to show that we can give some reasonable, but at this stage at least far from conclusive, grounds for thinking by appealing to our considered judgments in reflective equilibrium a rational consensus might tip things in favor of the human rights advocate.

Whether it actually would or not, will, I believe, depend on two things: (1) whether we can actually develop a moral-cum-social theory which will be able to establish a rational consensus on topics of the *type* I discussed in my sample argument, and (2) whether we can clarify adequately the conception of wide reflective equilibrium and show it to be an adequate method of ethical reasoning, a method which will do the work Rawls and Daniels assign to it and will show how moral progress is possible. I think we have some reason to be hopeful on both counts. (Perhaps this only shows that I am a child of the enlightenment?)

One might, with a certain Kierkegaardian irony, make light of what seems at least to be my underlying assumptions in arguing, as I have above. I seem to be talking as if human rights totter while we wait for a grounding moral theory, an account which may or may not be available. Not everything a reasonable person believes or commits him- or herself to is believed or committed to for a reason. Belief in human rights may, after all, be a groundless belief, a matter of here I stand though I could do other. But one need not give it up for all of that. Justification does come to an end.[47] Perhaps the belief that all human beings have a right to an equality of concern and respect, irrespective of merit or other excellence, is just such a belief. With it we can justify other moral beliefs but it cannot itself be justified. It is, from one moral point of view, a crucial point where justification comes to an end.

I have tried to show that this is perhaps not so for such a belief in human rights—and in moral equality—and that perhaps it can have a grounding in a moral-cum-social theory, utilizing the method of wide reflective equilibrium. If this is so, it would have the advantage that such a justification does not require a belief in self-evident natural moral laws or even a belief in moral truth or objective prescriptivity or some foundational account of morality. One could even accept John Mackie's sceptical meta-ethics and accept such an objective grounding of rights.[48] Human rights and a conception of egalitarian justice have not been objectively grounded yet, but with the development of ethical-cum-critical theory we might find or devise such a grounding.[49] And this tentativeness—to turn to Kierkegaard's little fable at the expense of Hegel—does not mean we must live in a moral shack while we await the philosophical edifice that will ground, or give an adequate rationale for, rights.[50]

NOTES

1. J. L. Mackie, "Can There be a Rights-Based Moral Theory?" *Midwest Studies in Philosophy* 3 (1978): 350–59; Ronald Dworkin, *Taking Rights Seriously* (Cambridge, Mass.: Harvard University Press, 1977), pp. 171–77.

2. Ronald Dworkin, op. cit., pp. 180–83; John Rawls, *A Theory of Justice* (Cambridge, Mass.: Harvard University Press, 1971), p. 511.

3. Kai Nielsen, "Scepticism and Human Rights," *The Monist* 52, no. 4 (October 1968): 575–94.

4. Gregory Vlastos, "Justice and Equality," in *Social Justice,* Richard Brandt, ed. (Englewood Cliffs, N.J.: Prentice-Hall, 1962), pp. 31–72; Richard Wasserstrom, "Rights, Human Rights and Racial Discrimination," *The Journal of Philosophy* 61, no. 20 (October 1964): 628–41; William Frankena, "Natural and Inalienable Rights," *Philosophical Review* 64, no. 2 (1955); Stuart Brown, "Inalienable Rights," *Philosophical Review* 64, no. 2 (1955); and H. L. A. Hart, "Are There Any Natural Rights?" *The Philosophical Review* 64, no. 2 (1955).

5. Ronald Dworkin, op. cit., p. 182; John Rawls, op. cit., p. 511; J. L. Mackie, op. cit., p. 357; Gregory Vlastos, op. cit., pp. 36–39 and 71.

6. Friedrich Nietzsche, *Jeneits von Gut and Böse* (Leipsig, 1886). Page references are to the English translation by Walter Kaufmann, *Beyond Good and Evil* (New York: Random House, 1966), p. 202.

7. Nietzsche, op. cit., pp. 202 and 204–5.

8. W. K. Frankena, *Perspectives on Morality* (Notre Dame, Ind.: University of Notre Dame Press, 1976), pp. 125–32, and G. J. Warnock, *The Object of Morality* (London: Methuen & Co., Ltd., 1971).

9. Nietzsche, op. cit., p. 200.

10. I have elaborated this conception of rationality in "Principles of Rationality," *Philosophical Papers* 3 (October 1974): 55–89; and in "The Embeddedness of Conceptual Relativism," *Dialogos* 11, no. 29/30 (November, 1977): 85–111.

11. I have developed this non-instrumental conception of rationality in "Rationality, Needs and Politics," *Cultural Hermeneutics* 4 (1977); and in "Reason and Sentiment," in T. Geraets, ed., *Rationality Today* (Ottawa, Ont.: The University of Ottawa Press, 1979).

12. Vlastos, op. cit., pp. 44–47.

13. Kai Nielsen, "Scepticism and Human Rights," *The Monist* 52 (October 1968): 590–91; and Joel Feinberg, *Social Philosophy* (Englewood Cliffs, N.J.: Prentice-Hall, 1973), pp. 88–94.

14. This notion has been ably developed by Henry Aiken in his *Reason and Conduct* (New York: Alfred A. Knopf, 1962). See particularly Chapter 4.

15. See Kai Nielsen, "Reason and Sentiment," op. cit.

16. R. M. Hare, "Rawls' Theory of Justice," in Norman Daniels, ed., *Reading Rawls* (New York: Basic Books, 1975), pp. 81–107; G. R. Grice, "Moral Theories and Received Opinion," *The Aristotelian Society,* Supplementary Volume 52 (1978): 2–12.

17. Stuart Hampshire, *Two Theories of Morality* (Oxford: Oxford University Press, 1977).

18. John Rawls, *A Theory of Justice,* op. cit., pp. 20–21, 48–51. See as well his presidential address, "The Independence of Moral Theory," *Proceedings of the American Philosophical Association* 48 (1974–75), pp. 5–22; Norman Daniels: "Wide Reflective Equilibrium and Theory Acceptance in Ethics," *The Journal of Philosophy* 76 (1979); "Moral Theory and the Plasticity of Persons," *The Monist* 62, no. 3 (July 1979); "Some Methods of Ethics and Linguistics," *Philosophical Studies* 37 (1980); and "Reflective Equilibrium and Archimedean Points," *Canadian Journal of Philosophy* 10, no. 1 (March 1980).

19. Nanette Funk, "A Sketch of a Theory of Rights in Socialism," *Radical Philosophers' Newsjournal* 10 (Spring 1978): 31–40. For some general remarks about Marxism and rights, see Ljubomir Tadic's "The Marxist and Stalinist Critique of Right." It occurs in English translation in Gerson S. Sher, ed., *Marxist Humanism and Praxis* (Buffalo, N.Y.: Prometheus Books, 1978), pp. 161–74. For a quite different defense of a goal-based account see T. M. Scanlon, "Rights, Goals and Fairness," in *Public and Private Morality,* ed. Stuart Hampshire (Cambridge, England: Cambridge University Press, 1978), pp. 92–111.

20. John Rawls, *A Theory of Justice,* p. 201.

21. Ibid., p. 195. Italics supplied.

22. Ibid., pp. 47–48.

23. Ibid., p. 47.

24. Ibid., p. 48.

25. Ibid.

26. Ibid., p. 20.

27. Ibid., p. 48.

28. Ibid.

29. Ibid., p. 49. In an important article, "Nature and Soundness of the Contract Arguments," in *Reading Rawls,* David Lyons raises some significant issues concerning narrow reflective equilibrium. He points out that "our shared, considered judgments cover but a limited range of cases, alternative explications are always possible and no clear rules can tell us which are best" (p. 146). Lyons goes on to claim that, given this indefiniteness, considered judgments will hardly provide a decisive test for the adequacy of normative ethical theories. Moreover, how can such a method, appealing as it does to our shared sense of justice, test whether any proposed set of principles of justice are valid principles of justice or indeed even show that there can be such things? (p. 146). In establishing a match between principles and considered judgments, we seem at least to move "in a circle, between our current attitudes and the principles they supposedly manifest" (p. 146). We "test" moral principles by comparing them with current firm considered convictions but we also test the considered convictions by the

principles. And we still can wonder whether the considered convictions express any more than arbitrary commitments or sentiments that we just happen now to share. "To regard such an argument as *justifying* moral principles thus seems to assume either a complacent moral conventionalism or else a mysterious 'intuitionism' about moral 'data'" (pp. 146–47).

It is surely tempting to argue as Lyons does. I have done so myself in the past, but, all the same, such an argument fails to take sufficiently into consideration the way wide reflective equilibrium works. Considered judgments, even the firmest, are themselves up for test. We do not simply consider the considered judgments of our tribe. Our net has a wider sweep. We do not just see which moral principles, embedded in which ethical theories, are most congruent with our considered judgments, but we use those principles and theories, along with complicated background theories from the social sciences, to test and weed out our considered judgments. The ones that at a given time are decisive are those that we would still stick with—the ones that would not be extinguished— when we have carefully reflected, have a full knowledge of alternative considered judgments together with their varied rationales, a knowledge of alternative normative ethical theories and of relevant social theories and have cooly taken the whole matter to heart. We are not treating as bottom line and unassailable—irrefragable as Sidgwick would put it—the convictions we just happen to have before we engage in such a reflective inquiry.

30. John Rawls, *A Theory of Justice,* p. 49.

31. Ibid., pp. 49–50.

32. Ibid., p. 50.

33. Ibid., p. 51. Presumably it is wide reflective equilibrium that is being referred to. It is also the case that there emerge here the problems concerning cultural relativism vis-à-vis our considered judgments, problems that I have elsewhere pressed and that Steven Lukes presses. Kai Nielsen, "Our Considered Judgments," *Ratio* 19, no. 1 (June 1977): 39–46; and Steven Lukes, "Relativism: Cognitive and Moral," *Aristotelian Society,* Supplementary Volume 48 (1974): 165–88; and his "An Archimedean Point," *Observer,* June 4, 1972. It is important to recognize that Rawls sees himself as operating with what he takes to be the core method of classical moral philosophy at least down to and through Sidgwick. See page 51 of *A Theory of Justice* and the long footnote there.

34. John Rawls, "The Independence of Moral Theory," p. 7.

35. John Rawls, *A Theory of Justice,* p. 20.

36. John Rawls, "The Independence of Moral Theory," p. 7.

37. John Rawls, *A Theory of Justice,* p. 21

38. Ibid.

39. The references to Hare and Grice are given in note 16. Peter Singer, "Sidgwick and Reflective Equilibrium," *The Monist* 58 (July 1974): 490–517. But see Frank Snare, "John Rawls and the Methods of Ethics," *Philosophy and Phenomenological Research* (1976): 100–112.

40. Rawls, "The Independence of Moral Theory," pp. 7–8.

41. Steven Lukes, op. cit.; and Richard Brandt, *A Theory of Good and Right* (Oxford: Clarendon Press, 1979), Chapter 1.

42. Grahame Clark, *World Prehistory in New Perspective* (Cambridge, England: Cambridge University Press, 1977).

43. Kai Nielsen, "On the Very Possibility of a Classless Society," and C. B. Macpherson, "Class, Classlessness and the Critique of Rawls," both in *Political Theory* 6, no. 2 (May 1978). See also Mihailo Markovic, *The Contemporary Marx* (Nottingham, England: Spokesman Books, 1974), pp. 128–39.

44. Kai Nielsen, "Class and Justice" in *Justice and Economic Distribution,* eds. John Arthur and William H. Shaw (Englewood Cliffs, N.J.: Prentice-Hall, 1978); and my "Radical Egalitarian Justice: Justice as Equality," *Social Theory and Practice* 5, no. 2 (Spring 1979). See also the arguments developed in detail in Parts II and III below.

45. See Kai Nielsen: "For Impurity in Philosophy," *University of Toronto Quarterly* (January 1974); "The Role of Radical Philosophers in Canada," *Committee on Socialist Studies Annual* 1 (1978); and "Reason and Sentiment," op. cit.

46. I have criticized them in "An Examination of the Thomistic Theory of Natural Moral Law," *Natural Law Forum* 4 (1959) and in "The Myth of Natural Law," in *Law and Philosophy,* ed. Sidney Hook (New York: New York University Press, 1964). I have criticized some contemporary accounts that are in a way descendents in "Conventionalism in Morals and the Appeal to Human Nature," *Philosophy and Phenomenological Research* (December 1962); and in "On Taking Human Nature as the Basis of Morality," *Social Research* 29 (Summer 1962).

47. Ludwig Wittgenstein, *On Certainty* (Oxford: Basil Blackwell, 1969); Georg von Wright, "Wittgenstein on Certainty," in *Problems in the Theory of Knowledge,* ed. Georg von Wright (The Hague: Martinus Nijhoff, 1972); Norman Malcolm, "The Groundlessness of Belief," in *Reason and Religion,* ed. Stuart C. Brown (Ithaca, N.Y.: Cornell University Press, 1977); and Kai Nielsen, "On the Rationality of Groundless Believing," *Idealistic Studies* 11, no. 3 (September 1981).

48. J. L. Mackie, *Ethics: Inventing Right and Wrong* (Harmondsworth, Middlesex, England: Penguin Books, 1977).

49. I have further developed this critical defense of the method of wide reflective equilibrium in "Considered Judgments Again," *Human Studies* 5 (1982): 109–18; and in "On Needing Moral Theory," *Metaphilosophy* (1982).

50. Joseph Raz, in "The Claims of Reflective Equilibrium," has raised a number of issues about the appeal to wide reflective equilibrium that deserve careful comment. He probes ambiguities in it and raises critical claims about its central theses. I shall, on some other occasion, try to come to grips in some thorough way with Raz's critique of the method I employ. But here, briefly, and sounding far more dogmatic than I actually am, I shall say this. I construe the method of wide reflective equilibrium as a holistic, anti-foundationalist method which works from agreement and does bypass epistemological and meta-ethical problems. I seek to show what would constitute a rational consensus and I in no way rely on the notion of moral truth. (Indeed, such a notion may be a Holmesless Watson.) Raz mistakenly thinks that Rawls thinks that the study of the "main conceptions found in the tradition of moral philosophy and in its leading representative writers" can be detached from an appeal to considered judgments. What we do is shuttle back and forth between them, mutually testing them until we get a coherent fit concerning which there is a wide consensus. Joseph Raz, "The Claims of Reflective Equilibrium," *Inquiry* 25, no. 3 (September 1982): 312–14.

PART II

In Defense of Egalitarianism

INTERLUDE AND PROEM ONE

In Part II, I shall characterize and defend radical egalitarianism. Building on the preliminary remarks made about equality in Chapter 1 and utilizing the method of wide reflective equilibrium explicated and defended in Chapter 2, I shall state, explain, and defend two principles of radical egalitarian justice. I shall contrast those principles of justice with Rawls' two principles of justice and try to establish that (a) they are more egalitarian than Rawls' principles, (b) more adequate, and (c) provide a better rationale for a commitment to equal basic liberties for all. I do not seek to show that my principles are more rational than Rawls' ("more rational" in the sense that any intelligent, fully informed person, when reasoning impartially, would choose mine rather than his), but I do try to show, in Chapter 3 and again more extensively in Chapter 5, that they are as rational as Rawls' principles and square better with our considered judgments in wide reflective equilibrium than do his principles. Thus we, in a very fundamental sense, use the same method, i.e., the method of wide reflective equilibrium, although I do not use the contractarian method and I do not draw the sharp division Rawls does between ideal and non-ideal theory.

Utilizing the method of wide reflective equilibrium, I seek, in Chapter 4, to deflect some anti-egalitarian arguments against a position such as mine— anti-egalitarian arguments more moderate, though perhaps less incisive than Nietzsche's, and consequently acceptable to more people. In doing this I shall expand further my analysis of radical egalitarianism. (I think that these standard anti-egalitarian arguments—Flew's are paradigmatic—reflect pervasive ideological currents in our society. Nietzsche's work, by contrast, has a way of being both exciting and threatening.)

In Chapter 5, I introduce more extensively than in Chapter 3 the notions of class and power and attempt to show, if these notions answer to what Marx and others on the left think they answer to, that my radical egalitarian principles provide a more adequate defense of our basic liberties than do Rawls' principles and would, rather than his or David A. J. Richards' similar principles, be more adequate fundamental principles for a perfectly just society. It should be evident here, if my arguments are near to their mark, that an adequate moral philosophy requires a political sociology.

Finally, I should add that in Part II I introduce the notion of socialism and argue that only in a democratic socialist society could these radical egalitarian principles of justice be satisfied and that only in such a socialist society could Rawls', or for that matter J. S. Mill's prized situation of equal basic liberty for all be realized. Perhaps it will not come about even with socialism, but, I shall argue, it will not come about in advanced industrial societies without socialism.

3
Radical Egalitarian Justice: Justice as Equality

I

Put somewhat crudely and oversimply, my intention in this chapter is to explicate and defend an egalitarian conception of justice both in production and in distribution that is even more egalitarian than John Rawls' conception of justice. I shall argue that such a conception of justice requires, if it is to be anything other than an ideal which turns no machinery, a socialist organization of society. It is clear that there are a host of very diverse objections that will immediately spring to mind. I shall try to make tolerably clear what I am claiming and why, and I shall consider and try in some degree to meet, some of the most salient of these objections.

I shall first give four formulations of such a radical egalitarian conception of justice: formulations which, if there is anything like a concept of social justice, hopefully capture something of it, though it is more likely that such a way of putting things is not very helpful and what we have here are four conceptualizations of social justice which together articulate what many on the left take social justice to be. I shall follow that with a statement of what I take to be the two most fundamental principles of radical egalitarian justice.

FOUR CONCEPTIONS OF
RADICAL EGALITARIAN JUSTICE

1. Justice in society as a whole ought to be understood as requiring that each person be treated with equal respect irrespective of desert and that each person be entitled to the social conditions supportive of self-respect irrespective of desert.[1]
2. Justice in society as a whole ought to be understood as requiring that each person be so treated such that we approach, as close as we can, to a condition where everyone will be equal in satisfaction and in such distress as is necessary for achieving our commonly accepted ends.[2] (We must recognize that we cannot achieve this for the severely handicapped and for people in analogous positions and we cannot do that for people with expensive tastes. The latter are not so worrisome, but even for

them, in conditions of great abundance, we should work towards such a state.)
3. Justice in society as a whole ought to be understood as a complete equality of the overall level of benefits and burdens of each member of that society.[3] (This should be understood as ranging over a person's life as a whole.)
4. Justice in society as a whole ought to be understood as a structuring of the institutions of society so that each person can, to the fullest extent compatible with all other people doing likewise, satisfy her/his genuine needs.

These conceptualizations are, of course, vague and in various ways indeterminate. What counts as "genuine needs," "fullest extent," "complete equality of overall level of benefits," "as close as we can," "equal respect" and the like? Much depends on how these notions function and in what kind of a theory they are placed. However, I will not pursue these matters in this chapter. These conceptualizations, in any case, should help us locate social justice on the conceptual and moral map.

The stress and intent of these egalitarian understandings of the concept of social justice is on equal treatment in various crucial respects of all humankind. The emphasis is on attaining, in attaining social justice, some central equality of condition for everyone. Some egalitarians stress some prized condition such as self-respect or a good life; others, more mundanely, but at least as crucially, stress an overall equal sharing of the various good things and bad things of the society. And such talk of needs postulates a common condition of life that is to be the common property of everyone.

When egalitarians speak of equality, they should be understood as asserting that everyone should be treated equally in certain respects, namely that there are certain conditions of life that should be theirs. What they should be understood as saying is that all human beings should be treated equally in respects $F_1, F_2, F_3, \ldots F_n$, where the predicate variable will range over the conditions of life which are thought to be things that it is desirable that all people have. Here equality is being treated as a goal. To say, where "X" refers to "human beings," "All X's should be treated equally in respects $F_1, F_2, F_3, \ldots F_n$" can be expressed, for those who go in for that sort of thing, in the logically equivalent form of the usual universal quantification, "For anything, if it is X, then it should have $F_1, F_2, F_3, \ldots F_n$." This is to say that each person should have them, but this is not to say, or to give to understand, that each person, like having equal amounts of an equally divided pie, should have identical or uniform amounts of them. Talking about identical or uniform amounts has no clear sense in such matters as respect, self-respect, satisfaction of needs or attaining the best life of which a person is capable. The equality of condition to be coherently sought is that they all have $F_1, F_2, F_3, \ldots F_n$. Not that they must all have them equally, since for some F's this does not even make sense. Even in speaking of rights, as when we say that everyone has a right to respect and to an equal respect in that none can be treated as second-class people, this still does not mean, or give to understand, that in treating them with respect you treat them in an identical way. In treating with equal respect a baby, a young person, or an enfeebled old man out of his mind on his death-bed, we do not treat them equally, i.e., identically or uniformly, but with some kind of not very clearly defined proportional equality.[4] (It is difficult to say what we mean here but we know how to work with the notion.) Similarly, in treating an Andaman Islander and a Bostonian with respect, we do not treat them identically, for what counts as treating someone with respect will not always be the same.

I want now to turn to a statement and elucidation of my egalitarian principles of justice. They are principles of just distribution, and it is important to recognize at the outset that they do not follow from any of my specifications of the concept of social justice. Someone might accept one of those specifications and reject the principles, or conversely accept the principles and reject any or all of those specifications, or indeed believe that there is no coherent concept of social justice at all but only different conceptualizations of justice that different theorists with different aims propound. But there is, I believe, an elective affinity between my principles and the egalitarian understanding of what the concept involves specified above. I think that if one does take justice in this egalitarian way one will find it reasonable to accept these principles.

I state my principles in a way parallel to those of John Rawls for ease of comparison and I will briefly compare them with his principles and show why I think an egalitarian or someone committed to Ronald Dworkin's underlying belief about the moral equality of persons, as both Rawls and I are, should opt for something closer to my principles than Rawls'.[5]

PRINCIPLES OF EGALITARIAN JUSTICE

* 1. Each person is to have an equal right to the most extensive total system of equal basic liberties and opportunities (including equal opportunities for meaningful work, for self-determination and political and economic participation) compatible with a similar treatment of all. (This principle gives expression to a commitment to attain and/or sustain equal moral autonomy and equal self-respect.)

  2. After provisions are made for common social (community) values, for capital overhead to preserve the society's productive capacity, allowances made for differing unmanipulated needs and preferences, and due weight is given to the just entitlements of individuals, the income and wealth (the common stock of means) is to be so divided that each person will have a right to an equal share. The necessary burdens requisite to enhance human well-being are also to be equally shared, subject, of course, to limitations by differing abilities and differing situations. (Here I refer to

different natural environments and the like and not to class position and the like.)

PRINCIPLES OF JUSTICE AS FAIRNESS

1. Each person is to have an equal right to the most extensive total system of equal basic liberties compatible with a similar system of liberty for all.
2. Social and economic inequalities are to be arranged so that they are both:
    (a) to the greatest benefit of the least advantaged, consistent with the just savings principle, and
    (b) attached to offices and positions open to all under conditions of fair equality of opportunity.[6]

I shall start with a comparison of Rawls' principles and my own, setting out a brief critique of Rawls' principles as I go along.[7] We both, as a glance at our respective *first principles of justice* makes clear, have an equal liberty principle, though I do not claim the strict priority for mine over my second principle that Rawls does for his. Over the statement of the equal liberty principle, there is no serious difference between us and I am plainly indebted to Rawls here. The advantage of my principle is that it makes more explicit what is involved in such a commitment to equal liberty than does Rawls' principle. They both give expression to the importance of moral autonomy and to the equality of self-respect and they both acknowledge the underlying importance of a commitment to a social order where there is an equal respect for all persons and where the institutions of that society show an equal concern for everyone. This must show itself in seeing humankind as a community in which we view ourselves as "a republic of equals." This, at the very least, requires an acceptance of each other's moral autonomy and indeed equal moral autonomy. There can be no popes or dictators, no bosses and bossed. The crucial thing about the first principle is its insistence that in a through and through just society we must all, if we are not children, mentally defective or senile, be in a position to control the design of our own lives and we must in our collective decisions have the right to an equal say. (The devices for doing this, of course, are numerous and the difficulties in its implementation are staggering. It is here that demanding, concrete socio-political-economic thinking is essential.)

The sharp differences between Rawls and myself come over our *second principles of justice.* My claim is that, in terms of our mutual commitment to equal self-respect and equal moral autonomy in conditions of moderate scarcity (conditions similar to those in most of North America, Japan and much of Europe), equal self-respect and equal moral autonomy require something like my second principle for their attainability. There are circumstances, Rawls' intentions to the contrary notwithstanding, where Rawls' second principle is satisfiable where equal liberty and equal self-respect are not obtainable. In short,

I shall argue, his first and second principles clash. Rawls would respond, of course, that, given the lexical priority of the first principle over the second, that this just couldn't obtain; but he, in his interpretation of the second principle, allows inequalities which undermine any effective application of the equal liberty principle.

Rawls would argue against a radical egalitarianism such as my own by claiming that "an equal division of all primary goods is irrational in view of the possibility of bettering everyone's circumstances by accepting certain inequalities."[8] The difference principle tells us that if the worst off will be better off—better off in monetary terms (more generally they will have more goodies)—they should accept the inequality. Justice and rationality conspire to require it. The rub, however, is in Rawls' understanding of "better off" or "improving the position" of the worst off. He cashes it in, at least in the first instance, in purely monetary terms. This prompts the response that either, on the one hand, this is too narrow a notion of being "better off" or of "improving your position" or, on the other, we are not justified in believing that rational agents, who have a tolerably adequate conception of fairness, will always give first priority to being "better off" or "improving their position." They might very well, in conditions of moderate scarcity, recognize other things to be of greater value. Concerning these alternatives, it is well to remark, as Wittgenstein might, "Say what you will, it still doesn't alter the substance of the matter." Either "being better off" is being construed too narrowly by Rawls or it does not always have first priority in deliberations about what is desirable. Indeed Rawls' own notion of the good of self-respect provides us with a jarring conception of what can, in circumstances such as ours, be a conflicting assessment of what is most desirable. Self-respect is for Rawls the most important primary good and it is something the basis of which is to be shared equally. We cannot in Rawls' system in situations of moderate scarcity (relative abundance) trade off a lesser self-respect for more goodies. But the disparities in power, authority and autonomy that obtain, even in welfare state capitalism, to say nothing of its cruder forms, and are not only allowed but justified by the difference principle, undermine, for the worst off and for many others as well, their self-respect. Certainly it does not make for a climate of equal self-respect.

Rawls recognizes this as an "unwelcome complication" and tries to show that self-respect need not be undermined or even diminished by the disparities in power and authority allowable in his system by the difference principle. But he concedes that if they did so undermine self-respect, the difference principle should be altered.[9] He argues that a well-ordered society, in which his difference principle is in operation, would not be a society in which these inequalities in power, authority and the ability to direct your own life, would, for the worst off, and for the strata which are near relatives to them, be particularly visible: thus they would not have the effect of diminishing self-respect.[10] There would be, as Rawls puts it, a "plurality of associations in a well-ordered society, with their own secure internal life. . . ."[11] The more disadvantaged strata will have their various peer groups in which they will find positions that they regard as relevant to their aspirations. These various associations, Rawls remarks, will "tend to divide into . . . many non-comparing groups," where "the discrepancies between these divisions" will not attract "the kind of attention which unsettles the lives of those less well-placed."[12] This itself is a tendentious sociological description of life in contemporary class societies. It is in particular very innocent about the nature of work in those societies. Such a view of things could hardly withstand reflection on the facts about work in the twentieth century brought out (for example) in Harry Braverman's *Labor and Monopoly Capital.*

However, even if that were not so and even if Rawls' account here is in some way a "telling it like it is," it still reflects both elitism and paternalism. People are to be kept in ignorance and are to moderate their own aspirations and to accept their stations and its duties with their respective roles—roles which often will not bear comparing, if self-respect is to be retained. However, they can, if they are so deceived, retain self-respect and society will not be destabilized by their agitation. They will not make comparisons and will unreflectively accept their social roles. Here we not only have elitism and paternalism, we have the ghost of aristocratic justice. Rawls' "realism" here has driven him into what in effect, though I am sure not in intention, is a crass apology for the bourgeois order.

However, Rawls does not retreat here for he sees it as the only acceptable way in which self-respect can be preserved. The equality of self-respect must be preserved or achieved in this way, for we cannot rationally go for a levelling of wealth and status—an alternative way of achieving equal self-respect—because it would be irrational to undermine the incentive value of those limited inequalities of wealth which will produce more goodies for all including the worst off. But that appeal, even if the motivational hypothesis behind it is true, begs the question. Some would say—and there are conflicting elements in Rawls' theory which would support them—"Better a greater equality in self-respect than more goodies." Even if—indeed particularly if—that claim is made by the worst off in conditions of moderate scarcity (relative abundance), that claim, as far as anything Rawls has shown, is neither irrational, nor is it even less rational than his worst off chaps sticking with the difference principle. (Even with the links stressed by Rawls between self-respect and liberty, and given the priority of liberty, this is also what he should say. Indeed, given Rawls' and Dworkin's own deeply embedded belief that there should be equal respect and concern across persons, it would seem here that the response "Better a greater equality in self-respect than more goodies" would be, morally speaking, more appropriate. For reasons that Bertolt Brecht has made unforgettable, we must never forget that we are, in making such a claim, talking about conditions of relative abundance.)

Rawls might counter that he was not talking about our societies but, operating from within his ideal theory, about an "ideal type" called a well-ordered society, where, by definition, there would not be such disparities in authority and power and effective control over one's life. But he also claims that his account is meant (a) to be applicable in the real world and (b) even to some forms of capitalism. But, my point was, his difference principle sanctions inequalities that are harmful to the sense of self-respect of people in the worst off strata of any capitalist society, actual or realistically possible. They simply, if they are being rational, must accept as justified disparities in power, wealth and authority which are harmful to them. Indeed they attack their self-respect, through undermining their moral autonomy; they, in such social conditions, do not have effective control over their own lives. Thus his difference principle, in a way my second more egalitarian principle is not, is in conflict with his first principle and, given Rawls' doctrine of the *priority of liberty,* should be abandoned.

Rawls tries to square his two principles and provide moral and conceptual space for both liberty and socioeconomic inequalities by distinguishing between liberty and the *worth* of liberty. Norman Daniels, in an impressive series of both internal and external criticisms, has, I believe, demolished that defense.[13] So I shall be brief and stick with the simplest and most direct points. Even allowing the coherence and non-arbitrariness of the distinction, it will not help to say that the socioeconomic disparities effect the *worth* of liberty but not liberty itself, for a liberty that cannot be exercised is of no value and, indeed, it is in reality no liberty at all. What is the sense of having something, even assuming it makes sense to say here that you have it, which you cannot exercise? "A liberty" that we cannot effectively exercise, particularly because of some powerful *external* constraints, is hardly a liberty. Certainly it is of little value. If I have a right to vote but am never allowed to vote, I certainly do not have much of a right. Moreover, rational contractors, or indeed any thoroughly rational person not bamboozled by ideology, would judge it rational to choose an equal *worth* of liberty, if he judged it rational to choose equal basic liberties. To will the end is to will the necessary means to the end. It is hardly reasonable to opt for equal liberty and then opt for a difference principle which accepts an unequal worth of liberty which, in turn, makes the equal liberty principle inoperable, i.e., it makes it impossible for people to actually achieve equal liberty.

I want now to return to Rawls' arguments that equal self-respect in class societies can be had by the inequalities remaining invisible or at least invisible to those who are on the deprived side of the inequality. This hardly accords with Rawls' insistence that the principles of justice are "principles that rational persons with true general beliefs would acknowledge in the original position."[14] As Keat and Miller aptly remark, "a theory is not acceptable if the stability of a society, based upon it depends upon the members of that society not knowing its principles and the way in which it is organized."[15] There is, as they continue, something morally distressing—they actually say abhorrent—about a theory of justice relying on "the worse-off members of society continuing not to compare their position with that of the better off. This narrowing of reference groups, and the concomitant lowering of expectations, is something which should be a main object of criticism for any theory of justice which claims, as Rawls' does, to be 'democratic' and 'egalitarian.'"[16]

My arguments above—as well as those of Keat and Miller and Daniels—should push Rawls, if they are near to their mark, in a more egalitarian direction. Specifically, they should require either an abandonment or an extensive modification of his second principle. If the preservation of self-respect is regarded as a conception at the heart of any theory of social justice and is taken, as Rawls would take it, to be directly relevant to questions about the just distribution of primary goods, then it seems that we would be forced to adopt more egalitarian principles of just distribution than Rawls adopts.

II

However, to go in a more egalitarian direction, is not, of course, necessarily to bed down with my principles. There are other alternatives. I shall now directly examine my egalitarian principles starting with an elucidation of my second principle (pages 48–49) and then proceeding to a consideration of some of the criticisms that would naturally be made of it. Additional criticisms and alternatives will be examined in the next chapter.

A central intent of my second principle of egalitarian justice is to try to reduce inequalities in primary social goods or basic goods. The intent is to reduce inequalities in goods that are the source of or ground for distinctions that will give one person power or control over another. All status distinctions should be viewed with suspicion. Everyone should be treated equally as moral persons and, in spite of what will often be rather different moral conduct, everyone should be viewed as having equal moral worth.

The second principle is meant as a tool in trying to attain a state of affairs where there are no considerable differences in life prospects between different groups of people because some have a far greater income, power, authority or privilege than others. My second principle argues for distribuing the benefits and burdens so that they are, as far as is compatible with people having different abilities and needs, equally shared. It does not say that all wealth should be divided equally, like equally dividing up a pie. Part of the social product must be used for things that are public goods, e.g., hospitals, schools, roads, clean air, recreation facilities and the like. And part of it must be used to protect future generations. Another part must be used to preserve the society's productive capacity so that there will be a continuous and adequate supply of goods to be divided. However, we must beware— coming out of an economically authoritarianly controlled capitalist society geared to production for profit and capital accumulation and only secondarily to meet needs—of becoming captivated or entrapped by productivism. We need democratically controlled decisions about what is to be produced, who is to produce it and how much is to be produced. The underlying rationale must be to meet, as fully as possible, and as equally as possible, allowing for their different needs, the needs of all the people. Care must be taken, particularly in the period of transition out of a capitalist society, that the needs referred to are needs people would acknowledge when they were fully aware of the various hidden persuaders operating on them. And the satisfaction of a given person's needs must, as far as possible, be compatible with other people being able similarly so to satisfy their needs.

A similar attitude should be taken toward preferences. People at different ages, in different climates, with different needs and preferences will, in certain respects, need different treatment. They all, however, must start with a baseline in which their basic needs are met—needs that they will have in common. (Again what exactly they are and how this is to be ascertained is something which needs careful examination.)

Rawls' primary goods captures something of what they are. What more is required will be a matter of dispute and will vary culturally and historically. However, there is enough of a core here to give us a basis for consensus and, given an egalitarian understanding of the concept of social justice, there will be a tendency to expand what counts as "basic needs." Beyond that, the differing preferences and needs should, as far as possible, have equal satisfaction, though what is involved in the rider "as far as possible" is not altogether evident. But it is only fair to give them all a voice. No compossible need should be denied satisfaction where the person with the need wishes its satisfaction when he/she is well-informed and would continue to want its satisfaction were he/she rationally to deliberate. Furthermore, giving them all a voice has, as well, other worthwhile features. It is evident enough that people are different. These differences are sometimes the source of conflict. Attaching the importance to them that some people do, can, in certain circumstances, be ethnocentric and chauvinist. But it is also true that these differences are often the source of human enrichment. Both fairness and human flourishing are served by the stress on giving equal play to the satisfaction of all desires that are compossible.

So my second principle of justice is not the same as a principle which directs that a pie be equally divided, though it is like it in its underlying intent, namely that fairness starts with a presumption of equality and only modifies a strict equal division of whatever is to be divided in order to remain faithful to the underlying intent of equal treatment. For example, two sisters may not both be given skates— one is given skates, which is what she wants, and the other is given snowshoes, which is what she wants. Thus both, by being in a way treated differently, are treated with equal concern for the satisfaction of their preferences. Treating people like this catches a central part of our most elemental sense of what fair treatment comes to.

It should also be noted that my second principle says that each person, subject to the above qualifications, has a right to an equal share. That is, they will have, where sufficient abundance makes this possible, an equal right to the resources necessary to satisfy their needs in a way that is compatible with others likewise satisfying their needs. But this does not mean that all or even most people will exercise that right or that they will feel that they should do so. This is generally true of rights. I have a right to run for office and to make a submission to a federal regulatory agency concerning the running of the C.B.C. But I have yet even to dream of exercising either of those rights, though I would be very aggrieved if they were taken away; and, in not exercising them, I have done nothing untoward. People, if they are rational, will exercise their rights to shares in what Rawls calls the primary goods, since having them is necessary to achieving anything else they want, but they will not necessarily demand equal shares and they will surely be very unlikely to demand equal shares of all the goodies of the world. People's wants and needs are simply too different for that. I have, or rather should have, an equal right to have fish pudding or a share in the world's stock of jelly beans. *Ceteris paribus,* I have an equal right to as much of either as anyone else, but, not wanting or liking either, I will not demand my equal share.

When needs are at issue something even stronger should be said. If I need a blood transfusion, I have, *ceteris paribus,* a right equal to anyone else's. But I must actually need it before I have a right to an equal share or indeed to any blood plasma at all. Moreover, people who need blood have an equal right to the amount they require, compatible with others who are also in need of having the same treatment; but, before they can have blood at all, they must need it. My wanting it does not give me a right to any of the common stock, let alone an equal share. And, even for the people actually getting the blood, it is unlikely that a fair share would be an equal share. Their needs here would probably be too different.

How does justice as equality work where it is impossible to give equal shares? Consider the equal right to have a blood transfusion. Suppose in a remote community at a given time two people both need, for their survival, an immediate transfusion and it was impossible to give them both a transfusion at that time. There is no way of getting blood of the requisite type in time, and in order to live each person needs the whole supply of available plasma—thus it cannot be divided. There can, at least for people who are being even remotely reasonable, be no equal division here. Still are not some distributions just and others unjust? If there are no relevant differences between the people needing the plasma, the only just thing to do is to do something like flipping a coin. But there almost always are relevant differences and then we are in a somewhat different ball game.

It might be thought that, even more generally in such a situation, the radical egalitarian should say: "In such a situation a coin should be tossed" but suppose the two people involved were quite similar in all relevant respects except that A had been a frequent donor of blood and B had never given blood. There is certainly a temptation to bring in desert and say that A is entitled to it and B is not. A had done his fair share in a cooperative situation and B had not, so it is only fair that A gets it. (We think of justice not only as equality but also as reciprocity.) Since "ought" implies "can" and, since we cannot divide it equally, it does not violate my second principle or the conception of justice as equality to so distribute the plasma.

I would not say that to do so is unjust, but, given my reservations about giving a central place to the category of desert (something I shall discuss in Part III), I would hesitate to say that justice requires it. But the central thing to see here is that such a distribution according to desert does not violate my second principle or run counter to justice as equality.

Suppose, to take a different example, the individuals involved were an A′ and a B′. They are alike in all relevant respects except that A′ is a young woman who, with the transfusion would soon be back in good health and who has three children, and B′ is a woman ninety years of age, severely mentally enfeebled, without dependents and who would most probably die within the year anyway. It seems to me that the right thing to do under the circumstances is to give the plasma to A′. Again it does not violate my second principle for an equal division is rationally impossible. But it is not correct to say A′ deserves it more than B′ or even, in a straightforward way, needs it more. We can, however, relevantly say, because of the children, that more needs would be satisfied if A′ gets it than B′. This is bringing in utilitarian reasoning here; but, whatever we would generally say about utilitarianism as a complete moral theory, it seems to me perfectly appropriate to use such reasoning in this context. We could also say—and notice the role universalizability and role reversal play here—that, after all, B′ had lived her life to the full, was now quite incapable of having the experiences and satisfactions that we normally can be expected to prize and indeed will soon not have any experiences at all, while A′, by contrast, has much of the fullness of her life before her. Fairness here, since we have to make such a horrible choice, would seem to require that we give the plasma to A′ or, if "fairness" is not the correct notion here, a certain conception of rightness seems to dictate that, everything considered, that is the right thing to do.

Let me briefly consider a final pair A″ and B″. Again they are alike in every respect except that A″ is the community's only doctor while B″ is an unemployable, hopeless drunk. Both are firm bachelors and they are both middle-aged. B″ is not likely to change his ways or A″ to stop supplying needed medical services to the community. Here it seems to me we again quite rightly appeal to social utility—to the overall good of the community—and give the plasma to A″. Even if, since after all he is the only doctor, A″ makes the decision himself in his favor, it is still something that can be impartially sustained. Again my second principle has not been violated since an equal division is impossible.

I think that all three of those cases—most particularly the last two with their utilitarian rationale—might be resisted because of the feeling that they, after all, violate not only my second principle, but, more generally, that they also run against the underlying rationale of justice as equality by not giving equal treatment to persons. B, B′ and B″ are simply treated as expendable in a utilitarian calculation. They are treated merely as means.

This response seems to me to be mistaken. B, B′ and B″ are no more than the As simply being ignored. If the roles were reversed and they had the features of the A they are paired with, then they should get the plasma. They are not being treated differently as *individuals*. We start from a baseline of equality. If there were none of these differences between them, if there were no other relevant differences, there would be no grounds to choose between them. We could not, from a moral point of view, simply favor A because he was A. Just as human beings, as moral persons or persons who can become capable of moral agency, we do not distinguish between them and we must treat them equally. In the limiting case, where they are only spatio-temporally distinct, this commitment to equality of treatment is seen most clearly. Morality turns into favoritism and privilege when this commitment is broken or ignored. *Within* morality there is no bypassing it; that is fixed by the very language-game of morality (by what the concept is, if you don't like that idiom).

III

I want to turn now to what is plainly a perfectly natural criticism to make of my radical egalitarianism. Mihailo Marković, in his *The Contemporary Marx,* while defending a socialist egalitarianism, argues against what he calls "radical egalitarianism."[17] He points out, quite rightly, that

> Marx was quite well aware of natural differences among individuals and of
> the fact that these will increase in importance when institutions that favour
> social discrimination and inequality disappear. He is very far from conceiving
> communism as a rigid egalitarian society in which all individuals would be
> equally paid and cultivate a uniform style of life.[18]

Marković then adds—again correctly and importantly—that Marx's conception of equality is focused on "the demand to abolish class exploitation, that is to abolish capital and wage labour, in the last instance
to overcome commodity production and the market as the basic regulator
of production."[19] The sensible demand for an equality of condition, he
argues, is the demand for the abolition of classes and differentiation
by social status. But what, at the end of a historical process, this
classless society would look like, Marković remarks, was left by Marx
"in a very vague, general form, susceptible of all kinds of interpretation,
misunderstanding and controversy."[20]

Marković tries to say something a little more precise about this and,
at the same time, to distance his egalitarianism more clearly from what
he calls radical egalitarianism. He points out that in every society—
including the future classless society—"there will be differences among
individuals in their abilities, character, gifts, etc."[21] Radical egalitarianism, as he understands it, would impose a uniformity which is
"incompatible with the aspiration for individual self-realization that
remains the very basic objective of all humanist thought, including a
Marxist humanism."[22] Such radical egalitarianism, he claims, is destructive of individual freedom: "the realization of different individual potential capacities . . . is incompatible with conditions of life that are
the same for all."[23] It is, Marković argues, utterly wrong-headed and
unMarxist to think that even in a classless society there will not be
some inequalities in the way of there being differentiations, not of rank,
but of social role and natural capacity. These will continue to exist
for they arise naturally out of different abilities and proclivities. It is
impossible to avoid them. But, even if it were not, it would be undesirable
to do so. What we must avoid, however, are inequalities which involve
any form of domination or economic exploitation, though we must also
realize that in a classless society there will remain different social roles.
There will remain, and valuably, differentiation and inequality in the
kind of role; what must be overcome or avoided in a perfectly just
society is this differentiation in social role becoming or remaining as
well a form of social stratification (an inequality in rank) and particularly
a stratification (endemic to complex class societies) involving a political
or economic hierarchy.[24] Differing social roles have in the past brought
with them privileged status and with that power, wealth and domination.
But this, he argues, need not continue to be so with a socialist
organization of society, though something of the length of time it takes
can be seen from the class struggles in China starting in 1947 and
continuing up to the present.[25]

Marković departs from Marx and Engels in claiming that the abolishment of class differences, while necessary for the achievement of equality, is not in itself sufficient. Social stratification (inequalities in rank) on the basis of different social roles is very persistent and has affected hitherto both socialist and capitalist societies. Various kinds of managers, technocrats and intelligentsia, given the role they play in social life, gain status, prestige and power. There is a tendency for them to become new elites with a very considerable power in their hands. A fully egalitarian society would not only be classless, it would also be without social stratification. But it would not be a society without differentiation on the basis of social roles and it would have people who, as Bakunin put it, would have a kind of natural authority on the basis of sensitivity and understanding and (if this doesn't come to the same thing) on the basis of their moral and intellectual qualities. This would not be a source of political power or control over people; they would, in Marković's terms, only be an "elite of spirit, of moral authority, of taste."[26] Any other kind of elite is as unacceptable to an egalitarian as is class society or elitist political and economic control. But this egalitarianism, Marković continues, is quite distinct from a rigid radical egalitarianism which, in "the distribution of goods," would insist on "strict equality of share" and would advocate "conditions of life that are the same for all."[27] In a fully developed classless, strataless society—the communist society of the future—goods are not distributed according to equality or on the basis of work (some form of merit or entitlement) but according to need.[28]

It should be evident enough that Marković and I are at cross-purposes here. We use the term "radical egalitarianism" in different ways and for our own purposes, but labels apart, our egalitarianism is substantially very similar. I stress, in a way he does not, equal division *of wealth with adjustments for differences in need and in nonsocioeconomic circumstance* and I am a little more nervous than he is, recalling the cultural role of charismatic figures, about even his "elites of the spirit," but I do not deny that there can be such people and, when they are genuine and flanked by entrenched democratic institutions of a socialist sort, they are desirable elites (if that is the right word for them). But the last difference in particular is a very minor difference. On the major issues a glance at my two radical egalitarian principles should make it evident that I do not want to reduce people to a uniform sameness of condition, such that they all get the same things, do the same things, have the same interests and in general behave in the same way. That is not what my conception of equal wealth aims at or would result in. I stress the importance of recognizing differences in need and stress that they must be catered to by an equal distribution principle. This is built into the formulation of my second principle. I also stress that, where we have full abundance, need should be a criterion of distribution, though not the sole criterion. I only claim that, once allowances are made for human differences and the like, in a world of moderate scarcity, each individual should have a right to an equal share of the available resources where, of course, such sharing is possible.

What I am *most* concerned to avoid, and I expect Marković is too, is not income differentials but inequality in whole life prospects between members of different classes and strata. With such differences, there exists control, domination and privilege by one group over another. It is a control etc. that makes the lives of some groups quite arbitrarily better and more autonomous than those of other groups. Since this is so, there must be, to achieve social justice, a levelling such that a society will come into existence that has neither classes nor strata. This I call a *statusless* society. Essential for the existence of such a society—not the whole of it but something without which the rest is impossible—is an equality in political and economic power. It is essential for equal autonomy and equal autonomy in turn provides the rational basis for equal self-respect. This in turn is necessary if there is to obtain a situation in which there is an equal respect for all human beings.

However, I also argue, in a way Marković does not, that in a socialist reconstruction of society, where the society is one of relative abundance and tending toward classlessness, the underlying general conception should be that of everyone having a right to an equal share, where there is something like an equal need, of the available resources that can be shared.

We should start with this presumption, a presumption showing an equal concern for all human beings, and a belief—rooted in that equal concern—that there should in the normal case at least be an equality of the overall level of benefits and burdens. Departures from that initial presumption must be justified first on the basis of differing genuine needs and differing situations (where differences in rank do not count as being in a different situation) and secondly on differing preferences where the first two are satisfied or irrelevant. The case of handicapped people is an obvious case where some adjustments must be made. But plainly this is not the normal case, and a theory of social justice set for the design of a just society must first set itself out for the normal case and then add the qualifications necessary for the exceptional cases. This, as I have already shown, in a very literal sense, is not to treat everyone the same and it avoids what I believe is one of the most persistent criticisms of radical egalitarianism, namely that it advocates, or would result in, a grey, uniform world of sameness where human freedom, creativeness and diversity would be destroyed.

NOTES

1. David Miller, "Democracy and Social Justice," *British Journal of Political Science* 8 (1977): 1–19.

2. Ted Honderich, *Three Essays on Political Violence* (Oxford: Basil Blackwell, 1976), pp. 37–44.

3. Christopher Ake, "Justice as Equality," *Philosophy and Public Affairs* 5, no. 1 (Fall 1975): 69–89.

4. Sidney Hook, *Revolution, Reform and Social Justice* (Oxford: Basil Blackwell, 1975), pp. 269–87.

5. Ronald Dworkin, *Taking Rights Seriously* (Cambridge, Mass.: Harvard University Press, 1977), pp. 150–83; Kai Nielsen, "Class and Justice," in *Justice and Economic Distribution,* ed. John Arthur and William Shaw (Englewood Cliffs, N.J.: Prentice-Hall, 1978), pp. 225–45.

6. These are, of course, Rawls' principles of justice. See John Rawls, *A Theory of Justice* (Cambridge, Mass.: Harvard University Press, 1971), p. 302.

7. See also Kai Nielsen: "Class and Justice," in *Justice and Economic Distribution*; "On the Very Possibility of a Classless Society," *Political Theory* 6, no. 2 (May 1978): 191–208; and "The Priority of Liberty Examined," *The Indian Political Science Review* 11, no. 1 (January 1977): 48–59.

8. John Rawls, op. cit., p. 546.

9. Ibid.

10. Ibid., p. 535.

11. Ibid., p. 536.

12. Ibid., pp. 536–37.

13. Norman Daniels, "Equal Liberty and Unequal Worth of Liberty," in *Reading Rawls,* ed. Norman Daniels (New York: Basic Books, 1975), pp. 253–81.

14. Rawls, op. cit., p. 547.

15. Russell Keat and David Miller, "Understanding Justice," *Political Theory* 2, no. 1 (1974): 24.

16. Ibid.

17. Mihailo Marković, *The Contemporary Marx* (Nottingham, England: Spokesman Books, 1974), Chapter 7.

18. Ibid., p. 130.

19. Ibid.

20. Ibid., p. 131.

21. Ibid., p. 132.

22. Ibid., p. 132.

23. Ibid., p. 137.

24. Ibid., p. 132.

25. Charles Bettelheim, "The Great Leap Backward," *Monthly Review,* July–August, 1978, pp. 57–130.

26. Marković, op. cit., p. 133.

27. Ibid., p. 137.

28. Ibid.

4

Impediments to
Radical Egalitarianism

I

In the previous chapter, I explicated and defended in an initial way
a radical egalitarian conception of justice.[1] In deliberate contrast with
Rawls' account, I have argued for two radical egalitarian principles of
social justice and a conception of social justice I call *justice as equality*.
I have attempted, against conventional wisdom and the mainstream of
philosophical opinion, to argue that a radical egalitarianism is not only
coherent, it is also reasonable. It is not the case, I have argued, that
Rawls' account of justice is the most egalitarian account that can
reasonably be defended. Justice in society as a whole ought to be
understood as a complete equality of the overall level of benefits and
burdens of each member of that society with adjustments for people
who are handicapped and the like. What we should aim at is a structuring
of the institutions of society so that each person can, to the fullest
extent compatible with all other people doing likewise, satisfy his/her
needs. We should seek a "republic of equals" where there will be a
fundamental equality of social condition for everyone. I articulated
these two principles which should govern that conception of justice
as equality.

1. Each person is to have an equal right to the most extensive total system
   of equal basic liberties and opportunities (including equal opportunities
   for meaningful work, for self-determination and political and economic
   participation) compatible with a similar treatment of all. (This principle
   gives expression to a commitment to attain and/or sustain equal moral
   autonomy and equal self-respect.)
2. After provisions are made for common social (community) values, for
   capital overhead to preserve the society's productive capacity, allowances
   made for differing unmanipulated needs and preferences, and due weight
   is given to the just entitlement of individuals, the income and wealth
   (the common stock of means) is to be so divided that each person will
   have a right to an equal share. The necessary burdens requisite to enhance
   human well being are also to be equally shared, subject, of course, to
   limitations by differing abilities and differing situations. (Here I refer to

different natural environments and the like and not to class position and the like.)

In asking about justice as equality, three questions readily spring to mind: (1) Why is a greater equality in the conditions of life desirable? (2) Is anything like my radical egalitarianism something that could actually be achieved or even be reasonably approximated? (3) Given the steep inequalities that actually exist, if they (or at least most of them) are eradicable, are they only so at an unacceptable cost? In short, is the cost of equality too high?

There is no complete answer to (1), (2), and (3) which is entirely independent. There is, that is to say, reason for not considering them in utter isolation. In the previous chapters, I sought to give an answer to (1). A short answer to (1), an answer that encapsulates something that was at the heart of the previous chapter, is that a greater equality is desirable because it brings with it greater moral autonomy and greater self-respect for more people. It isn't, as some conservative critics assume, so much equality *per se* which is so desirable but what it brings in the way of human flourishing, though there is in such egalitarian thinking the assumption that the most extensive equal realization of that is an end devoutly to be desired. What I argued for in the previous chapters I shall assume here, namely, that equality, if its costs are not too high, is desirable. I shall assume, that is, that (1) has a positive answer at least when it is not considered in relation to (2) and (3). But, as (3) asks, are the costs of this equality, after all, just too high? Many conservative critics claim that they are.[2] I shall, before I turn to (2), consider (3), as it is more closely linked to (1).

It is pointed out by conservative critics that we cannot in our assessments of what is just and what is unjust start from scratch. Goods to be distributed do not come down, like manna from heaven; they come with entitlements. Certain people have produced them, bought them, been given them, inherited them, found them, struggled to make them and to preserve them. To think that we can override their entitlements in setting out ideal distributive patterns is to fail to respect people. It is to be willing to run over their rights in redistributing goods—to treat some people as means only. A society in which a state or a class can take from people what is rightfully theirs cannot be a just society. The ideals of equality and the ideals of justice are different ideals. Equality is a forward looking virtue concerned, some conservative theorists claim, with seeing that it is the case that people have their various and not infrequently unequal entitlements.[3] Justice will be done in a society when people have what they are entitled to. The idea isn't to establish a certain distributive pattern, but to protect people's entitlements. Because this is what justice really is, rather than anything about equality, it will sometimes be the case that an individual, a family, or even a class will quite justly achieve certain advantages on which the rest of the society can have no proper claim. Our maxim

for justice should *not* be "Holdings ought to be equal unless there is
a weighty moral reason they ought to be unequal," where the burden
of proof is always to justify unequal treatment. Rather, our maxim
should be "People are entitled to keep whatever they happen to have
unless there is a weighty moral reason why they ought to give it up."
The burden of proof has now shifted to the redistributivist to justify
a redistribution.[4] The normal situation will be that people will be
entitled to what they have properly acquired. These entitlements are
rooted in the particular situations and activities of people. They cannot
in the typical situation be equal. Fairness doesn't come to distributing
things equally, even with allowance for differing needs, but to *not*
taking from people what they are entitled to. Particular entitlements
can be challenged, but if anyone with a passion for justice sets out
"systematically and at a stroke to devalue the lot, in the interests of
a new strictly forward-looking distribution, he is, by this move, abandoning the whole notion of justice in favour of another alternative
ideal."[5]

I shall return to this objection in a moment. However, even if it is
the case that some distinction between social justice and individual
justice or justice in distribution and justice in acquisition should show
this criticism to be mistaken, there are still two related objections that
remain in place and again have to do with the value of individual
autonomy. (It is the three together which seem to me to constitute a
formidable cluster of objections.) Firstly, it is claimed that if we treat
social justice as equality, we will repeatedly have to use state intervention
to keep the pattern of distribution at the requisite level of equality,
for people in their ordinary transactions will continually upset the
pattern whatever the pattern may be. But such continual intervention
constitutes an intolerable interference in the lives of people. No one
who cares about individual liberty and moral autonomy could support
that. Secondly, in a democratic society people would not support with
their votes a redistributive policy that was egalitarian, let alone the
radical egalitarianism that I propose. It would have to be imposed
from above by some dictatorial elite. It will not be accepted in a
democratic society. Again, its costs would be too high because it could
only be achieved by abandoning democracy.

I shall start with the last objection for that one seems to me the
weakest. It seems to me that it is not at all a question of imposing
or trying to impose egalitarianism on anyone. In the first place, it is
unrealistic because it cannot be done; but, even if it could and such
a procedure were not self-undermining, it still would be undesirable.
Justice as equality is set out as an ideal of social justice which, radical
egalitarians argue, best captures what is fundamental to the very idea
of justice. The thing is, by moral argumentation in "the public sphere,"
to use Jürgen Habermas' conception, to convince people of it. There
is no question at all of imposing it or of an "egalitarian clerisy"

indoctrinating people. Whatever the morality of it, it is impractical to try in such circumstances to impose equality or such an understanding of justice. The only road here is through patient and careful social argumentation to make the case for egalitarianism.

Socialists are well aware that the consciousness industry will be turned against radical egalitarianism and that there will be a barrage of propaganda directed against it, some (depending on the audience) subtle and some unsubtle. It will not get a fair hearing, but there is nothing else to be expected from a class society in the hands of a class who must be deeply opposed to egalitarianism. But this is just a specific application of the general political problem of how social change can be achieved in an increasingly managed class society. This is one of the deep and intractable social problems of our time—one of the problems Max Horkheimer and Theodore Adorno anguished over—and, particularly for those of us in developed capitalist societies, it is a very puzzling and intractable problem indeed. But whatever we should say and do here, it will not be the case that we intelligentsia should try to impose egalitarian ideals on an unwilling working class. Until the working class—the vast majority of people—see fit to set about the construction of a genuinely egalitarian society, the role of the intellectual can, and should, be that of someone who through the employment of critical analysis and ideology critique makes attempts at consciousness raising in his society. (This is, of course, also perfectly compatible with an unflinching search for truth.)

II

I want now to consider the second objection, namely, the claim that any patterned distribution, and most particularly the patterned distributions of radical egalitarianism, would require such continuous and massive state intervention that it would undermine individual liberty and the moral autonomy essential for the good of self-respect.

This objection uncritically makes all the background assumptions of laissez-faire capitalism—a social order which has not existed for a long time and probably could not exist in our contemporary world. But a society committed to radical egalitarianism would also be a genuinely socialist society and would have very different background conditions. The objection just unrealistically assumes a genuinely free market society where people are busy, possessive individualists devoted to accumulating and bargaining and are concerned very centrally with protecting their private property. It simply assumes that human beings, independently of the particular type of socialization they have been subject to, have very little sense of or feeling for community or cooperativeness, except in the form of bargaining (again the free market being the model). But a society in which radical egalitarianism could flourish would be an advanced socialist society under conditions of considerable abundance. People would not have a market orientation. They would not be accumulators or possessive individualists, and the aim of their economic organization would not be profit maximization but the satisfaction of the human needs of everyone. The more pressing problems of scarcity would have been overcome. Everyone would have a secure life, their basic needs would be met, and their level of education, and hence their critical consciousness, would be much higher than it is now, such that, in their situation, they would not be committed to Gomper's dictum of "more." Furthermore, the society would be thoroughly democratic and this would mean industrial democracy as well as political democracy. That would mean that working people (which would include all able-bodied adults) would control—collectively control in a fair democratic manner—their own work: that is, the production relations would be in their hands as well as the governmental functions of the society, which in this changed environment would have become essentially administrative functions. In fine, the institutions of the society and the psychological motivations of people would be very different than those implicitly appealed to in the objection. Under these conditions, the state, if that is the best thing still to call it, would not be the instrument of class oppression and management that it now is. People would democratically manage their own lives and the design of their society in a genuine *gemeinschaft* so that there would no longer exist structures of class domination interfering with people's liberties. People would be their own masters with a psychology that thinks in terms of "we" and not just, and most fundamentally, in terms of "I," where the protection of my rights is the crucial thing. Moreover, now the society would be so organized that cooperation made sense and was not engaged in just to avoid the "state of nature." The society would be a secure society of relative abundance. (Communism and radical egalitarianism are unthinkable in any other situation.) It would be a society in which the needs of everyone would be met. Since the society would be geared, within the limits of reasonable growth, to maximize for everyone, and as equally as possible, the satisfaction of their needs, a roughly egalitarian pattern would be in a steady state. It would not have to be constantly tinkered with to maintain the pattern. People would not, in such a secure situation, have such a possessive hankering to acquire things or to pass them on. Such acquisitiveness would no longer be such a major feature of our psychologies. Moreover, given the productive wealth of the society, there would be no need to worry if in practice distributions sometimes swayed a little from the norm of equality. Everyone would have plenty and have security; people would not be possessive individualists bent on accumulating and obsessively concerned with mine and thine. There would, moreover, be no way for anyone to become a capitalist and exploit others and indeed there would be precious little motivation to do so.

If, in spite of this, an elite did show signs of forming, there would be firmly in place democratic institutions sufficient to bring about the demise of such deviations from the norm. This should not be pictured as an impersonal dictatorial state interfering with people's liberties, but as the people acting collectively to protect their liberties against practices which would undermine them. Yet that things like this would actually happen—that such elitist practices would evolve—in such a situation of abundance and cooperation is rather unlikely. In such circumstances, the pattern of distribution of justice as equality would be stable and, when it did require adjustment, it would be done by a democratic government functioning to protect and further the interests of everyone. This patterning would not upset liberty and undermine moral autonomy and self-respect.

III

I will now turn to the first objection—the objection that justice is entitlement and not anything even like equality. (This is also a thesis that I will probe from another direction when I examine libertarianism in Part III.) It may be that justice as entitlement is that part of justice which is concerned with justice in initial acquisition and in transfer of what is initially justly acquired and is not distributive justice at all, the justice in social schemes of cooperation. It may be that these are two different species of justice that need capturing in some larger overall theory. Be that as it may, the challenge of justice as entitlement seems, at least on the surface, to be a very real one. Entitlement theorists certainly have a hold of something that is an essential part of justice.[6]

I shall in Parts III and V attempt to sort these issues out, but here I believe I can, skirting that task for the time being, give a practical answer which will show that such a challenge is not a threat to justice as equality. In doing this I want to show that such a conception of justice is consistent with the rights of entitlement. Recall that a radical egalitarian will also be a socialist. He will be concerned with justice in the distribution of products, but he will be centrally concerned as well with justice in production.[7] His concern with the justice to be obtained in production will come, most essentially, to a concern with transforming society from a society of private ownership and control of the means of production to one of a social ownership and control of the means of production, such that each worker—in a world of workers—will have an equal say in the disposition and rationale of work. (Control here seems to me the key notion. In such new production relations, the very idea of ownership *may* not have any unproblematic meaning.) It will, that is, be work which is democratically controlled. The aim will be to end class society and the dominance of an elite managerial stratum. Justice as equality most essentially requires a society with no bosses. The demand for equality is most fundamentally a demand to end that state of affairs and to attain a situation of equal moral autonomy and self-respect.

These considerations are directly relevant when we consider that entitlement conceptions of justice are most at home in situations where a person has mixed his labor and care with something, say built and lovingly cared for a house or built up a family farm. It would, *ceteris paribus,* be wrong, plainly unjust, to take those possessions away from that person and give them to someone else. But a radical egalitarian is not challenging entitlements of this type. Socialists do not want to take people's houses or family farms from them. In a Communist society there are consumer durables and there is individual property, e.g., people can own their own car, house, family farm, family fishing boat, and the like. The private property socialists seek to eliminate is private ownership and control of the major means of production. This is the private property that is the central source and sustainer of class divisions, of the great power of one person over another and the great advantages of one group over another. This form of private ownership is at the root of much existing exploitation and injustice. This is most crucially true of the great industries controlling vast resources and employing wage labor. Family farms and family fishing boats, as long as they do not sprout into empires employing many wage-laborers, are not the problem.[8] The equality aimed at by radical egalitarians is that of a classless, statusless society. But in such a society the type of personal entitlements that we have been speaking of can perfectly well remain intact. And it is just such entitlements that are allowed for in the articulation of my second principle of justice. It is over entitlements of this last sort that our moral convictions remain firmest.

The entitlement theorist will surely respond by saying "If the person who builds a house or works a farm up out of a wilderness is entitled to it, why isn't a capitalist who, through his own initiative, creativeness, and dogged determination, creates an industrial empire entitled to keep his property as well?" They both are the effect of something we prize in human nature, namely, we see here human beings not merely as satisfiers of desires but as exercisers of opportunities. At least in some cases, though less and less typically now, they can be his hard-earned and creatively-struggled-for holdings.

This creates a presumption of entitlement, but only a presumption. (Alternatively, we can say it creates an entitlement but a defeasible one that can be rightly overridden.) We have, as is not the case with the house or the family farm, very good grounds indeed for overriding this presumption and requiring a redistribution. Remember the conservative principle was "People are entitled to keep whatever they happen to have, unless there is a weighty moral reason why they should relinquish it." Well, in this situation, there are weighty moral reasons, entirely absent in cases like that of the fishing boat, family farm or house. First, in our historical circumstances, such capitalist ownership and control of the means of production causes extensive misery and impoverishment that could otherwise be avoided. Secondly, it gives capitalists and a small managerial elite (who are often also capitalists themselves) control over people's lives in such a way as to lessen their effective equal citizenship and undermine their self-respect and moral autonomy. Moreover, these are not inevitabilities of human life but the special and inescapable features of a class society, where there must be a dominant capitalist class who owns and controls the means of production. But they are not inescapable features of the human condition and they have not been shown simply to be something that must come with industrial society.

Someone determined to defend laissez-faire capitalism and an entitlement theory of justice might tough it out and claim that the error in the above entitlement theorist's conduct of his case is in stating his account in such a conditional way, namely, that "People are entitled to keep whatever they happen to have, unless there is a (weighty) moral reason why they ought to relinquish it." It should instead be stated as "People are entitled to their holdings if the initial acquisition was just and any transfer from it just; the initial acquisition, in turn, was just if it accords with the Lockean proviso that it was taken from unclaimed land and if the initial appropriation left enough in kind for everyone else." This principle of justice is designed, in the way the first entitlement account was not, to normatively block any attempt by the state or any group of people to justifiably compel any transfer, under any circumstances not specified in the above formulation, of any holdings to satisfy any redistributive scheme. Any person, quite categorically, may justifiably and justly hold on to whatever he initially justly acquired, no matter what the consequences. There is the obvious point that we do not know how to go about ascertaining whether in fact the patterns of holdings now in effect result from just acquisitions via just transfers. But this obvious point aside, such a categorical entitlement account has plain defects. To take such a right of property to be a moral absolute is unduly to narrow even a right-based moral theory. A society organized with that as its fundamental moral principle— a principle of justice which could never rightly be overridden—would lead to the degradation of large numbers of people. They would, in circumstances such as our own, have the *formal* rights to acquire property but in actuality they would have little or no property and their impoverishment and loss of autonomy and self-respect would be very great indeed. To hold on to an unqualified right to property in those circumstances would be not only arbitrary and morally one-sided, it would be morally callous as well. Moreover, it is not a commitment that clearheadedness and a devotion to rationality dictates. What such a one-valued absolutism neglects is that we are morally obliged to respond to suffering. On such an entitlement theory we would not be obliged to relieve the suffering of another even when we could do so without serious loss to ourselves. What it gains here in categoricalness, it *loses* in moral coherence. To have an understanding of the moral language-game, to have an understanding of what morality requires, we need to understand that we cannot be indifferent to the sufferings of others. Are we morally justified in holding onto even a *miniscule* bit of our property, say food which could be shared with a starving person, when sharing it could be done without any serious inconvenience to ourselves? To think that, morally speaking, our options are open in such a situation is not only to exhibit moral callousness, it is also to reveal a failure even to understand what it is to take a moral point of view. To avoid harming others and violating their rights is, of course, as this entitlement account stresses, central to morality, but morality requires—taking a moral point of view requires—that, under certain circumstances, preventing or alleviating or remedying the misery of others is also part of our duty. The recognition of such duties undermines such a categorical commitment to entitlements to private property. Sometimes we are morally compelled to redistribute. Anything else would be grossly unjust and immoral. Whether we feel compassion or not, the relief of human misery, where this is reasonably within our capacities, is something that is morally required of us. What we otherwise would be entitled to, we can hardly be entitled to when we could, by sharing it, save the life of another and (to put it concessively and minimally) not cause any great distress to ourselves. My last remark can easily be misunderstood. It is not so much demands placed on individuals within an unjust social system that are crucial but a commitment on the part of individuals to alter the social system. In a period of political stagnation, to demand of a tolerably well off suburbanite that he greatly diminish his holdings and send a not inconsiderable sum of money to the Sahel comes too close to requiring him to be a Don Quixote. What needs to be altered is the social system. To maintain that severe sacrifices are required of individuals when there is little prospect of turning the society around is to ask them to be martyrs if, by so acting, there is not a chance for significant social change. Still, morally speaking, there has to be redistribution, and where we genuinely could relieve misery to not acknowledge that such a *sharing* is required of us is to fail to grasp something very essential to morality. Failure here is as much a moral failing as an intellectual one and no amount of cleverness can get around that.

IV

I want now to turn to the second general problem about radical egalitarianism I mentioned at the beginning of this chapter. Some critics of egalitarianism maintain that however abstractly desirable egalitarianism may be, it still is an impossible ideal, for it is impossible to achieve or even reasonably to approximate.[9] Such a criticism would apply doubly to my radical form of egalitarianism. We must just come to recognize, so the criticism goes, that inequality is inevitable and erect our account of justice in the light of this inevitability.

Are there any basic features or functional prerequisites of society or human nature that make inequality inevitable in all societies or at least in all industrial societies? I shall limit my answer to remarks about industrial societies and consider the claim that classes, bureaucracies (with their hierarchical social relations) and social stratification are inevitable. The inevitability of any of them would ensure that any future industrial society would also be to some degree a status society with a ranking of people, and not just a society with differentiations, according to social roles. With these inequalities in status there would be the differences in power and authority that have plagued societies in the past and continue to plague our societies.

It has been claimed that inequalities are functionally necessary to any industrial society. There will be a division of labor and a differentiation of social roles in those societies. Since certain social roles are functionally more important than others—being a doctor at the Crisis Center is functionally more important than being a ski instructor—and since suitable performance in these more important roles requires suitable training and discipline, it is necessary to induce with adequate rewards those with the appropriate talents to delay gratification and take on the required training—the long years of struggle in medical school, graduate school, or law school. This is done by assuring them that at the end of their training they will be rewarded more highly for their sacrifice in taking on that training. This requires the inequalities of differential incentives. People, the argument goes, simply will not make the sacrifice of going to medical school or going to law school unless they have very good reason to believe that they will make much more money than they would by selling cars or running a little shop. To stream people into these functionally necessary occupations, there must be differential rewards and with those rewards social stratification with its concomitant inequalities in prestige, power, and authority. Moreover, we must do this to make sure that the most talented people will continue to occupy the most functionally important positions and to work at their maximal capacity. The very good of the society requires it.

The first thing to note is that all this, even if sound, does not add up to an inevitability. Still, some might say that it is all the same a "rational inevitability," given that it is a functional prerequisite for the proper functioning of an industrial society. But is it actually a functional prerequisite? Again, like some of the previous criticisms of egalitarianism we have examined, it simply uncritically assumes something like contemporary capitalism as being the norm for how any industrial society must operate, but there is no reason why the additional training should be a form of sacrifice or even be regarded as a sacrifice. It too much takes the ideology of the present as an accurate depiction of social reality. In an egalitarian society, by contrast, everyone would be materially secure and there would be no material loss in remaining in medical school, law school, or graduate school. Once that becomes so and once the pace is slowed down, as it really could be, so that students are not rushed through at great stress and strain, it would be, for many people at least, far less of a sacrifice to go through medical school than to be a bank-teller, rug salesman, or assembly line workman all day. For many people, perhaps for most people of normal intelligence, the work both during their school years and afterwards would be more rewarding and challenging than present-day routine jobs. There is no need to provide special incentives, given other suitable changes in society, changes which are quite feasible if we do not continue to take a capitalist organization of society as normative. It is a particular social structure with its distinctive value scheme (scheduling of values) that requires such incentives and such attitudes towards incentives—not anything in the nature of industrial society itself. (I leave aside whether we can, for a whole range of cases, and not just in some obvious cases, identify, in a non-ethnocentric manner, what the functionally important positions are. Are ministers more important than garage mechanics? Are lawyers more important than dental technicians? Are marriage counsellors more important than airline stewardesses?)

A more interesting argument for the inevitability of inequality is Ralf Dahrendorf's claim that the very concept of a society is such that, when we think of its implications, we realize that there could not— logically could not—be a society without inequalities.[10] A society by definition is a moral, as distinct from amoral, community. We might say of a way of life of a society that we deeply disapprove of that it is an immoral society. It makes sense to say (that is, it is not a deviation from a linguistic regularity to say) "Swedish sexual morality is immoral," but it makes no sense to speak of an amoral society. In that sense every society is a moral community. It will have a cluster of norms, tolerably integrated, which regulate the conduct of its members. More-over, these norms carry one or another kind of sanction which ensure their obligatory character by providing rewards for conforming to them and penalties for deviation from them. Dahrendorf concludes from that that "the sanctioning of human behaviour in terms of social norms necessarily creates a system of inequality of rank and that social stratification is therefore an immediate result of the control of social behaviour by positive and negative sanctions."[11] But, given the very idea of what it is for a mass of people to be a society, there could not be a society without such norms; but, if there are such norms, then there must also be a schedule of inequalities.

Steven Lukes, quite succinctly, exposes the crucial mistakes in Dahrendorf's influential argument.[12] "It does not follow," Lukes argues, "from the mere existence of social norms and the fact that their enforcement discriminates against those who do not or cannot (because of their social position) conform to them that a society-wide system of inequality and 'rank order of social status' are 'bound to emerge.'"[13] From the fact that a society, actually to be a society at all, must have norms, spelling out what it is right and wrong to do, and that it must apply sanctions to assure general compliance, it does not follow that these norms are the sort of norms that would provide a social stratification with a hierarchy of power, status, and authority. An egalitarian society would have norms and the associated sanctions too, only they would be far less oppressive and pervasive. As Lukes nicely puts it, "Dahrendorf slides unaccountably from the undoubted truth that within groups norms are enforced which discriminate against certain persons and positions . . . to the unsupported claim that, within a society as a whole, a system of inequality between groups and positions is inevitable."[14] Dahrendorf gives us no grounds for believing that all societies must, because they have various norms carrying sanctions, be organizations which have a system of stratification, either implicit or explicit, in which their various norms and behavior are ranked within a single system of stratification.

V

I now turn to what I, at least, take to be the most troubling arguments about the inevitability of inequality in industrial societies. They turn on the claim that the empirical evidence, when linked to reasonable theories and arguments, shows that a status society is inevitable under the conditions of modern life. There is no way of making industrial societies free of bureaucracy with the cluster of privileges and differential power and authority which go with such inegalitarian structures.

It is reasonable to argue that there are, when we look at the various modern societies (including Russia, China, Cuba, and Yugoslavia), no classless societies, or what is more relevant, and from a leftist perspective more disturbing, no societies which are clearly tending in the direction of classless societies. Given this, isn't radical egalitarianism implausible? Would it not be better, given these empirical facts, to opt for a more modest egalitarianism with principles something like Rawls'? We must not tell ourselves Marxist fairy tales!

The above argument rests on reasonable empirical data and, unlike Dahrendorf's, does not involve a transcendental argument. (Wherever we find anyone making anything very crucial turn on a transcendental argument we ought to be suspicious.) It is certainly anything but clear that there are any complex societies which are moving in the direction of classlessness. Occasionally, we do see some hopeful indicators: Mozambique, Zimbabwe, the Chile of Allende, some developments in Spain, France, and Italy, but they are but fitful and very uncertain indicators. It is anything but evident what will develop in those atmospheres, though we can be cautiously hopeful. Rather than put all, or even most, of one's eggs in that historical basket, it is theoretically more useful, I believe, to note certain general facts, and on the basis of them to develop a theoretical argument.

First the facts. We have not had any proletarian revolutions yet, though we have had revolutions made in the name of a very small and undeveloped proletariat.[15] We have yet to have a dictatorship of the proletariat—a society controlled by the proletariat and run principally in its own interests. The state socialist societies that exist are not socialist societies that developed in the conditions that Marx said was propitious for the development of socialism but (East Germany and Czechoslovakia aside as isolated exceptions) in economically backward societies that had yet to experience a bourgeois revolution. It is also a fact that these socialist societies (if that is the right name for them) are surrounded by strong capitalist societies which are, naturally enough, implacably hostile to socialism.

If these are the facts, as I believe they are, then it is very unlikely that a classless society will begin to emerge out of these societies until those empirical situations radically change. There is a further fact that should be noted. In the bourgeois democracies there is not yet good evidence for a rising class consciousness. The masses do not seem to be on the verge of being radicalized. In North America a proletarian class consciousness seems to be almost non-existent. It is slightly stronger in Europe, though Europe's industrial giant (West Germany) shows very little of it and in Japan it is, as well, very weak. Again, in these circumstances, a movement in the direction of classlessness is hardly evident.

Yet most of these countries have troubled economies. If the instability of monopoly capitalism increases and if the Third World remains unpacified, conditions in the industrially developed capitalist countries may change. A militancy and a sense of class may arise and class conflict may no longer be merely a muted and disguised reality. That could lead to the first social transformation by an actual proletarian class, a class developed enough, educated enough, numerous enough, and strong enough to democratically run things in its own interests and to pave the way for a society organized in the interests of everyone, namely a classless society. I do not maintain that we have good grounds for saying that it will happen. I say only that that scenario is a coherent possibility. Minimally I do not believe that anyone has shown this to be a mere dream, a fantastic bit of utopianism. If it is also, as I believe it to be—everything considered—a desirable possibility, it is something to be struggled for with all the class conflict that that will involve.

VI

However, even if all this is so, there remains another worrying objection which tends to engender the anxiety that a statusless radically egalitarian society may still be pie in the sky by and by. Suppose we can achieve a strictly classless society, that is, a society in which there is no structural means by which a historically extendable (intra-generational) group, by means of its social role, can extract surplus value from another group because all remuneration is according to work and there is no land-rent or profits from shares and the like. However, even in such a society, as Mihailo Marković observes, and as we discussed in the previous chapter, there still could be political elites or at least bureaucratic elites.[16] These elites could come to exert considerable domination over other people and, even if there was only a bureaucratic elite and that bureaucratic elite had little political power, something which is actually not very likely while it remained an elite, still their high status would make for considerable social inequality and would plainly be harmful to the egalitarian commitment to equal self-respect and to equal moral autonomy. Thus, even though in a strict sense classes were no more, it could be the case that a status society of rank and privilege could still exist with a rather sharp social stratification which would still contain considerable differences in whole life prospects. Differences which are clearly incompatible with a radical egalitarianism.

Marković is no doubt right in saying that it is at least "theoretically conceivable how the emergence of a hierarchy of power may be prevented."[17] Marković's prescription is like Marx's and Mao's. There is "democratic election, replaceability, and vertical rotation for all functions of social management."[18] While there will continue to be a division of labor, the persistent aim is to prevent the formation of a group of professional managers and to break down the class-impregnated and status-engendering traditional distinction between mental and manual labor. This will also cut down at least the extent of the bureaucracy. There will under such conditions be no persistent and stable group of people who alone will know how to manage the society and who can claim a kind of technical expertise in management that must simply be accepted and taken as authoritative and which will lead to a high status and, very likely, again to political power. The power of occupational roles and particularly of bureaucratic occupational roles is both understandable in an industrial society and threatening to egalitarianism and moral autonomy.

It surely is not known that status society can be overcome. It is simplistic wishful thinking to say that we know that it will be overcome. But it is also a too easy *realpolitik* to claim that we know that conditions cannot arise in which a society other than a hunting and gathering or an agricultural society could come into being and flourish which had no such elites. Whether it is probable that such a society is on the historical agenda is hard to say. Indeed it is not evident what, if anything, is on the historical agenda, but as far as I can see, it has not been shown not to be a reasonable historical possibility. Similar considerations obtain to those we noted in discussing class. The facts about the conditions under which state socialist societies emerged make the existence of status distinctions under such conditions practically speaking unavoidable. That they emerged is surely hardly surprising. It is those factors that can, when we reflect on them, make us prematurely pessimistic. But what would emerge out of a socialist revolution in an advanced industrial society, with an established bourgeois democratic tradition, is another thing again. Surely the bourgeoisie, and particularly the haute bourgeoisie who run our societies, would like us to be cultural pessimists, would like us not to believe in the possibility of "the art of the impossible." But what is reasonable to hope for, and to struggle for, should not be so culturally defined, defeating our hopes for a more human future. Given a humanistic conception of what sort of society is worth bringing into being, such a hope, given the stark alternatives, is not an unreasonable hope of human beings who are not blind to social reality.

NOTES

1. Kai Nielsen, "Class and Justice" in *Justice and Economic Distribution,* eds. John Arthur and William Shaw (Englewood Cliffs, N.J.: Prentice-Hall, 1979), pp. 225–45; and Kai Nielsen, "On the Very Possibility of a Classless Society," *Political Theory* 6, no. 2 (May 1978): 191–207.

2. Robert Nozick's *Anarchy, State, and Utopia* (New York: Basic Books, 1974) is the best known current example of such a conservative critique. But it has also been developed by Robert Nisbet in his "The Pursuit of Equality," *The Public Interest* 35 (Spring 1974): 103–20 and in his "The Costs of Equality" in *Small Comforts for Hard Times,* eds. Michael Mooney and Florian Stuber (New York: Columbia University Press, 1977), pp. 3–47; and Irving Kristol, "About Equality," *Commentary,* November, 1972.

3. Nozick, of course, argues this, but it has most intransigently been argued by Antony Flew in two articles: "Equality or Justice?" *Midwest Studies in Philosophy* 3 (1978): 176–94; and "A Theory of Social Justice" in *Contemporary British Philosophy,* ed. H. D. Lewis (New York: Humanities Press, 1976), pp. 69–85.

4. Flew, "Equality of Justice?" p. 183.

5. Ibid., p. 186.

6. Thomas Nagel, in his *Mortal Questions* (Cambridge, England: Cambridge University Press, 1979) and in his discussion of Nozick, indicates how entitlement conceptions and distributive conceptions may in reality mesh as complimentary parts of a coherent conception of justice. See Thomas Nagel, *Mortal Questions* (Cambridge, England: Cambridge University Press, 1979), pp. 106–27; and his "Libertarianism Without Foundations," *Yale Law Journal* 85, no. 1 (November 1975): 136–49.

7. Ziyad I. Husami, "Marx on Distributive Justice," *Philosophy and Public Affairs* 8, no. 1 (Fall 1978): 27–64; Gary Young, "Justice and Capitalist Production: Marx and Bourgeois Ideology," *Canadian Journal of Philosophy* 8, no. 3 (September 1978): 421–55; Allen Buchanan, "The Marxian Critique of Justice and Rights," *Canadian Journal of Philosophy,* Supplementary Volume 7, pp. 269–306.

8. Nancy Holmstrom, "Exploitation," *Canadian Journal of Philosophy* 7, no. 2 (1977): 353–69; Allen Buchanan, "Exploitation, Alienation and Injustice," *Canadian Journal of Philosophy* 9, no. 1 (March 1979), pp. 121–39.

9. Ralf Dahrendorf, "On the Origin of Social Inequality" in *Philosophy, Politics and Society: Second Series,* eds. Peter Laslett and W. G. Runciman (Oxford: Basil Blackwell, 1962), pp. 83–109.

10. Dahrendorf, op. cit.

11. Ibid., p. 107.

12. Steven Lukes, "Socialism and Equality" in *The Socialist Idea,* eds. Leszek Kolakowski and Stuart Hampshire (London: Weidenfeld and Nicolson, 1974), pp. 74–95.

13. Ibid., p. 92.

14. Ibid., p. 93.

15. Irving Fetscher, "Karl Marx und die 'Marxistischen' Revolutionen," *Neue Züricher Zeitung,* September 30, 1977, pp. 35–36.

16. Mihailo Marković, *The Contemporary Marx* (Nottingham, England: Spokesman Books, 1974), pp. 128–39.

17. Ibid., p. 133.

18. Ibid.

5
Class and Justice

I

In the previous two chapters I have tried to make something of the case for a radical egalitarian conception of justice and to refute or deflect certain conservative criticisms. In the course of defending this radical egalitarian conception of justice, I contrasted it not only with conservative anti-egalitarian accounts of justice, but with liberal egalitarian accounts of justice such as John Rawls' and Ronald Dworkin's. The present chapter will extend that last contrast in two ways. It will attempt to refute the claim that an account like Rawls' is the most extensive form of egalitarianism that it is reasonable to defend, and it will try to show that a key issue between a liberal form of justice such as Rawls' and a radical egalitarian account such as my own turns, to a very considerable extent, on the truth of a claim in political sociology concerning the possibility of classlessness. If classlessness is impossible, then something like Rawls' account is the more reasonable form of egalitarianism, but if classlessness is a reasonable future possibility, then something like my own account is the more reasonable option. I shall here try to make a case for the possibility of classlessness and to reinforce and deepen the argument made in Chapter 3 that if classlessness is a reasonable possibility then our sense of justice should carry us beyond liberal egalitarianism to a form of radical egalitarianism.

II

It has been argued, not implausibly, against those who would tax John Rawls with reflecting a conservative/liberal ideological bias, that his account of egalitarian justice is the most egalitarian form of justice it is reasonable to defend.[1] In arguing against this claim, I shall attempt to articulate in skeletal form a socialist conception of justice, in which liberty and equality are treated as indivisible, a conception that is more egalitarian and at least as reasonable as Rawls' form of egalitarianism.[2] Indeed, it is my belief that if it were to become a core conception guiding the design of our social institutions, it would guarantee more adequately than Rawls' own account the very values (so important to

Rawls and indeed to any reflective human being) of equal self-respect, equal liberty, and moral autonomy.

In *A Theory of Justice* Rawls unreflectively, and without any supporting argument, makes certain problematic assumptions about classes and the possibilities of classlessness. Only if those assumptions are justified will it be the case that Rawls' account is as egalitarian as it is reasonable to be. My argument shall be that these assumptions are not justified. Rawls has an inadequate conception of what classes are and what classlessness would be. When taken in conjunction with his theory of the primary social goods and the assumptions he makes about human nature, they lead him to adopt a theory of justice which has not been shown to be the uniquely rational one for contractors in the original position to adopt or for fully informed rational and moral agents to adopt after the veil of ignorance is lifted. It is not at all evident, as I argued in Chapter 3, that his *difference* principle provides us with enough equality or, more surprisingly, that his two principles together afford sufficient effective liberty to provide the underlying structural rationale for a perfectly just society.

In this section of the present chapter I shall pose problems about the possibilities of classlessness and its relation to egalitarianism. In section III I shall discuss, working with a paradigm, class and moral autonomy and Rawls' *difference* principle, while in section IV I shall discuss liberty and equality and probe the extent and nature of Rawls' commitment to egalitarianism. Finally, in section V I make an additional direct argument for a more radical egalitarian conception of justice, requiring classlessness, which views equal liberty as being dependent on equality.

Even in societies that Rawls would regard as well-ordered, in which his two principles of justice were satisfied, there could be, as we have seen, considerable differences in the life prospects between the more advantaged strata of the society and the least well off. Indeed, it may very well be that even in a society where the means of production are socially owned, differences in the whole life prospects of people will persist because of the differences in income, status, and authority which remain even after capitalism has been abolished or died the death of a thousand unifying expansions. With differences in status, authority, and income remaining, different groups, differently affected, may find that their whole life prospects are still very different indeed.

We plainly seem to require something very like an industrial society to feed, cloth, etc. our vast and, for the immediate future at least, growing world population. I speak now just of meeting subsistence needs. I do not speak of making the springs of social wealth flow freely and fully. That seems to require a division of labor and with *that* division of labor, divisions of people along class lines which deeply effect their life prospects. I would argue that it is by no means certain that this outcome of the division of labor is inevitable, particularly

when the time comes when there is no longer any private ownership
or control of the means of production. It is not unreasonable, however,
to believe that some division of labor is an inevitable feature of
industrially developed societies. Yet it is also not unreasonable to
believe that the division of labor could be altered in various ways from
what it is under capitalism and that it could be reduced. We could
and should be able to bring along far more versatile, many-sided human
beings doing more varied work and standing in many different social
roles, and we should and could, as well, develop various social devices
to ameliorate the inequalities and inequities resulting from the present
forms the division of labor takes. It is at least not inconceivable that
a state of affairs could develop where there was a genuine social
ownership of the means of production, with democratic control through
workers' councils, with the gradual transformation of state power into
a governmental structure which, as Marx puts it, would come to have
only administrative functions.[3] In that sense the state could wither
away and the exploitation of others could end, because, with such
social ownership and control of the means of production, there would
be no *structural* means of transferring to oneself the benefits or the
powers of others. No class or anything replacing a class would be in
a position to exploit. Thus, in that very important sense, there would
be no classes, i.e., people who are at higher and lower levels, where
the higher levels are the result of or the means to exploiting others,
extracting from them surplus value. It is in this way and in this sense
that class divisions and the existence of classes most deeply and
pervasively effect us.[4] It is because of the existence of classes of this
sort that the most appalling and extensive inequalities and injustices
arise and persist in our social structures. It is vital to know whether
in this sense class divisions are inevitable. If the assumption that they
are can be successfully challenged, it makes room for the possibility
of a more radically egalitarian form of justice than anything Rawls
regards as a reasonable option.

In seeking to articulate the principles of social justice and to attain
an Archimedean point for appraising basic social structures, Rawls does
not face the questions raised by the existence of social classes. I do
not mean to suggest that he regards our actual class-divided societies
as basically just or even well on their way to social justice. He eschews
the making of such political judgments, but he does think that some
capitalist societies with their unavoidable class divisions can still be
well-ordered societies which are plainly just societies and he would
thus be committed to regarding societies in which class divisions and
exploitation, in the sense characterized above, are inexpungeable features, as still societies which could be perfectly just societies.[5] Rawls
takes the existence of classes to be an inevitable feature of social life
and he, quite naturally, regards justice as something compatible with
that unavoidable social condition. There can be capitalist societies,
Rawls maintains, which are just and perfectly well-ordered societies.

In thinking about justice and class two general facts are very important. The first is that in capitalist societies there are deep class divisions, and the second is that, barring some worldwide catastrophe, the trend to complex industrial societies appears irreversible. This makes classlessness a problematic matter. Yet the very existence of exploiting classes as an integral part of a capitalist order poses evident problems for the attaining of social justice in capitalist societies. I shall argue that because of his unjustified assumptions about classes Rawls (a) takes certain disparities in life conditions between different groups of people to be just, although these disparities have not been shown to be just and appear at least to be very unjust; and (b) he too easily accepts the belief that capitalism with its class relations can in some forms be just.

Capitalist societies are and must remain class-divided societies. Talk of "people's capitalism" is at best fanciful. Rawls is right in seeing class divisions as an unavoidable feature of capitalist societies, but he is mistaken in uncritically accepting the conventional wisdom which maintains that all industrial societies must have class divisions. Rawls, unfortunately, does not examine classes or exploitation. But he does assume, as I remarked initially, the inevitability of classes at least in the sense to be specified in the next two paragraphs.

There is an important sense of "class," developed in the Marxist tradition, concerning which it is by no means evident that classes are inevitable. Rawls largely ignores that conception and generally talks about classes in the way most bourgeois social scientists do, where "class" and "strata" are roughly interchangeable terms. Indeed, Rawls is not clear about what he thinks classes are, but it is evident that he believes that institutionalized inequalities affecting the whole life prospects of human beings are inescapable in complex societies.

My counter is that it has not been shown that it is impossible to have a complex society without functional groupings which determine broad life prospects and that thus Rawls unnecessarily limits the scope of his egalitarian claims. (This is one rather non-Marxist characterization of what classes are.) Rawls seems principally to think of a class-divided society as a society with social strata in which there are differences in status, authority, income, and prestige. He believes, plausibly enough, that some such differences will persist in any society and thus assumes that classes are inevitable. But such a belief's persuasiveness is tied to the identification of class and strata. If, alternatively, we either, on the one hand, think of classes as a Marxist does, essentially in terms of the relationship of people to the means of production, or, on the other, more generally as segments of society between which there are considerable differences in income, prestige, or authority, and, consequently, in whole life prospects, it is not in either case safe to assume, as Rawls does, that classes are inevitable.

It is not, however, clear that Rawls is committed to denying the possibility of a society without classes in the Marxist sense. After all, he admits that it is possible that societies can be both socialist and just. But he does take it to be an inescapable fact that there are and will continue to be classes in the sense that there are and will continue to be institutionally defined groups whose whole life-prospects are importantly different. We cannot design and sustain a society where that will not obtain.

I shall argue that it has not been established that such class divisions are inevitable or that classes in the Marxist sense are inevitable. With these commonly assumed inevitabilities no longer secured, we are not justified, if we believe as Rawls does in the equal moral worth of all people, in qualifying egalitarianism and justifying inequalities in the way he does. But there are many challengeable propositions here that require establishment in a somewhat less conditional manner. It is to this that I now turn.

III

Rawls argues that for conditions of moderate scarcity, the principles of collective action that rational persons would accept in circumstances in which they were disinterested, uninfluenced by a knowledge of their own particular situation, their natural endowments, their individual life plans or aspirations but in which they did have *general* social science and psychological information about human nature and society are (in order of priority) the following:

(1) Each person is to have an equal right to the most extensive total system of equal basic liberties compatible with a similar liberty for all and
(2) social and economic inequalities are to be arranged so that they are both
(a) to the greatest benefit of the least advantaged, consistent with the just savings principle, and
(b) attached to offices and positions open to all under conditions of fair equality of opportunity.[6]

Now (a) above (the *difference* principle, i.e., the principle that inequalities to be just must benefit the least advantaged) has been thoroughly criticized, but it remains a distinctive and crucial element in Rawls' account and indeed an element he has continued to defend in writings subsequent to *A Theory of Justice*.[7] I do not want to return to that dispute but to consider a far less decisive, yet morally and politically more significant counter-example, which, I shall argue, exhibits how very intractable moral disputes can be. Knowledge and rationality are far less decisive in moral disputes than Rawls and a great many moral philosophers suppose.[8]

Rawls argues that in sufficiently favorable but still only moderately affluent circumstances, where his two principles of justice are taken to be rational ordering principles for the guidance of social relations, it could be the case that justice, and indeed a commitment to morality, would require the acceptance as just and as through and through morally acceptable a not inconsiderable disparity in the total life prospects of the children of entrepreneurs and the children of unskilled laborers, even when those children are equally talented, equally energetic, and so on. If conditions are of a certain determinate sort, a just society, he claims, could in such circumstances tolerate such disparities.

It seems to me that such a society could not be a just society, let alone a perfectly just society.[9] There might, under certain circumstances, be pragmatic reasons of expediency for grudgingly accepting such inequalities as unavoidable. In that way there could, in those circumstances, be *justified inequalities*. When people, whose only relevant difference is that one group had entrepreneurs as parents and the other had unskilled laborers as parents, have, simply because of this difference, life prospects so different that one group's entire life prospects are considerably better than the other's, then that difference is unjust.[10] By contrast, Rawls does not direct moral disapprobation toward a society or moral scheme of things which accepts such disparities, not only grudgingly as unfortunate expediencies necessary under certain distinctive circumstances to maximally improve the lot of the most disadvantaged, but as disparities which even a just, well-ordered society could accept. He believes that such a society could still protect our basic liberties and could still be a just society (perhaps even a perfectly just society). For me, however, the witting acceptance of such disparities, where something could be done about them, particularly when that something would not undermine our basic civil and political liberties, just seems evil. It may be an evil that we might in certain circumstances have to accept because we realize that under those circumstances the undermining of that state of affairs will bring about a still greater evil. But it remains an evil all the same. The moral ideal embedded in a conception of a just and truly human society—a perfectly just society—must be to eradicate such differences.

Rawls or a Rawlsian could reply that in making such judgments I am being unnecessarily and mistakenly sentimental and perhaps a little irrational, or at least confused, to boot. It is bad enough that such inequalities in life prospects must exist, but it is still worse by narrowing them to make the children of the unskilled laborers even worse off.[11] It is better and indeed more just to accept the considerable disparities in life prospects and to apply the *difference* principle. Otherwise, in absolute terms, these children of unskilled laborers will be still worse off. It can never be right or just to knowingly bring about or allow that state of affairs where it could be prevented. To achieve greater equality at such price is to do something which is itself morally indefensible.

It might in turn be responded that Rawls is, in spite of himself, being too utilitarian here. Talk of increasing the advantages of such a group with lower life prospects is not the only thing which is morally relevant, even in those circumstances where, as Rawls would have it, his principles of justice are to hold in their proper lexical order.[12] Even when it is to their advantage, the working class people in such a circumstance, both children and adults, have had, by the very existence of this extensive disparity, their moral persons assaulted and their self-respect damaged. This will have happened even if in terms of income and wealth the inequality of condition itself and the consequent disparities in life prospects will make them better off than they would be in a capitalist society that did not apply Rawlsian principles. That that talk of assault and damage is not just rhetoric, envy, or resentment can be seen from the fact that they suffer, among other things, with such a loss of equality, the loss of effective equal citizenship.[13] Their continuing to have these formal rights is cold comfort. Moreover, their effective moral autonomy is undermined by such disparities in power, in their inability to control their life conditions, and in their inability (situated as they are) to obtain meaningful work.[14] Moreover, it is important to recognize that these disparities are inextricably linked to the different life prospects of children of working class people and the children of the capitalist class and the professional strata whose loyalties by and large are to the capitalist class.

Rawls, it might be thought, could in turn respond that there is no actual conflict with his account even if this is so; for if such conditions obtain, his equal liberty principle would be violated and his principles of justice would not be satisfied after all. For he does claim that "the basic structure is to be arranged to maximize the worth to the least advantaged of the complete scheme of equal liberty shared by all."[15]

However, that there is in reality no conflict with his theory is not so clear, for I had in mind the *effective* rights of equal citizenship and the *effective* moral autonomy of people, while Rawls seems at least to be talking about something which is more *formal* and which could be satisfied in such a circumstance. By utilizing his putative distinction between liberty and the *worth* of liberty—a distinction effectively criticized by Norman Daniels—Rawls tries to account for what I have been talking about under the rubric "the worth of liberty" and not under the equal liberty principle. But, as Daniels' criticisms have made clear, it is far from evident that anything like this can successfully be maintained.[16] Rawls might further respond that, in arguing as I have above, I have not given sufficient weight to (a) his insistence that fair opportunity requires not only that no one be formally excluded from a position to which special benefits attach, but also that persons with like talents and inclinations should have like prospects of attaining these benefits "regardless of their initial place in the social system, that is, irrespective of the income class into which they were born," and (b) that part of his second priority rule specifies that "fair opportunity is prior to the *difference* principle" and that any "inequality of opportunity must enhance the opportunities of those with lesser opportunity."[17] Rawls, with a fine moral sense and a thorough integrity, seeks to make perspicuous a requirement (a requirement which is also bedrock for me) "which treats everyone equally as a moral person."[18] Moreover, it might further be responded that I am failing to take into consideration Rawls' recognition that certain background institutions are necessary for distributive justice. In particular I am forgetting that we need institutions concerned with *transfer* and *distribution.* The institutions concerned with transfer will guarantee a social minimum to the most disadvantaged and will honor the claim to meet basic needs. Taxation will be used by this institution to prevent a concentration of wealth and power which would undermine political liberty and equality of opportunity. Rawls stresses that for principles of justice to be fully satisfied there would have to be a redistribution of income, a wide dispersal of property, and the long-run expectations of the least advantaged would have to be maximized in a way compatible with the constraints of a fair equality of opportunity and with the constraints of equal liberty. To achieve these things we need institutions of transfer and distribution employing taxation and the like.

Yet right there, with the very conception that there will, in a well-ordered, perfectly just society, be a *social minimum,* there is the acceptance of class divisions as just, where the life expectations of some groups are quite different than that of others. While Rawls has the welfare state ideals expressed in the previous paragraph, he also believes that there can be capitalist, and thus class-divided societies, which are well-ordered and in which his principles of justice are fully satisfied. Yet it is just such societies which have exploitative classes and which, as Rawls himself admits, have class differences which make for the substantial differences in life prospects that we noticed between the children of entrepreneurs and unskilled laborers. Rawls thinks such class differences are unavoidable, and he thinks that his principles of justice can be satisfied even when they obtain. But then it is difficult to see how, in such a circumstance, the constraints of a fair equality of opportunity, on which he also insists, could possibly be met. How (or even whether) Rawls' theory can make a coherent whole here is not evident, but what is evident is that he is applying the *difference* principle and claiming an inequality is a just one when that claim is very questionable indeed. Nor is it evident that a person committed, as Rawls is, to a belief in the equal moral worth of all persons, should not opt for a more radical form of egalitarianism.

There surely is merit in the claim, pressed by Ronald Dworkin, that Rawls seeks to translate into a working conception of distributive justice the ideal that everyone be treated equally as moral persons, but there is also—and at least equally evidently—the stress in his theory that such disparities as I have discussed could be justified even in a just, well-ordered society.[19] Rawls' writings on this topic are reflectively self-conscious of objections and are often so qualified that it is difficult to make sure how the various parts go together. But there is the line of argumentation that my counter-example addresses itself to in Rawls. Moreover, such an argument provides an account of the scope of the *difference* principle that will provide a reasonably determinate application. What I have tried to do so far is to show how very much this line of argument conflicts with some tolerably deep sentiments (intuitions, considered judgments) about justice (including, as we have just seen, some of Rawls' other considered judgments). If my arguments in Chapter 2 about the centrality of the appeal to considered judgments in wide reflective equilibrium and Rawls' similar methodological arguments have force, then this is a very important consideration indeed.

However, without trying further to sort this out, I think that Rawls has available a still more fundamental reply, namely, the reply that *such* class divisions are *inevitable* and that, since rational principles of justice, whatever they may be, must be compatible with the "ought-implies-can-maxim," such disparities in life prospects must simply be accepted as something which is in the nature of things in a way not dissimilar to the way differences in natural endowment exist in the nature of things. We can hardly reasonably complain about them as unjust when it is impossible to do anything about them. One might as well say that the cosmos is unjust.

There is an inclination within me to say that if those are the alternatives, then one should say that the cosmos is unjust. More seriously and less tendentiously, one can reasonably follow C. B. Macpherson and Benjamin Barber in questioning whether Rawls has done anything more than uncritically and unhistorically to assume the inevitability of there being classes determining differences in whole life prospects.[20] There is, as I remarked earlier, in spite of the length of Rawls' book, no supporting argument at all for this key assumption and yet it is a governing one in his work and it is the basis for appealing to the ought-implies-can-maxim in this context.

It may well be, as Ralf Dahrendorf argues, that a certain social stratification is inevitable—that there will be in any complex society some differences in prestige, authority, and income—but there is no good evidence, as I argued in the previous chapter, that these differences must result from or result in institutionalized differences in power—including ownership and control of the means of production—which will serve as the basis of control and exploitation, creating crucial differences in whole life prospects.[21] It is where such differences obtain that we have the reality of exploitative classes; but Rawls has done nothing at all to justify, or even to make unproblematic, the assumption that such class differences and the concomitant differences in life prospects are inevitable—and hence not unjust.

Let us imagine a slight twist in the case I have been considering and let us take it that neither disputant thought there was much prospect of achieving classlessness but that one still takes the more egalitarian posture I took and another the Rawlsian position. (Full equality, for the radical egalitarian, now becomes a heuristic ideal to try to approximate.) Yet, given those assumptions about classlessness, is not the Rawlsian position more reasonable and more just? It is, of course, true that there are greater inequalities if we reason in accordance with the *difference* principle, but the *proletarian* or *lumpenproletarian* in such a circumstance is still in a certain plain sense better off. People in such a position have, it is claimed, the chance, given the way the primary social goods hang together, to achieve a greater self-respect due to the fact that they will have larger incomes and—in that way— more power than they would otherwise have.[22]

However, in another and more crucial way they would have less power and not as great a realization of certan of the primary social goods articulated by Rawls, including most fundamentally the good of self-respect. That can be seen if we reflect on the following. In terms of income and power (mostly buying power) that the income provides, it is true that in the more egalitarian society the most disadvantaged could be still worse off than they would be in the less egalitarian society in which Rawls' *difference* principle is satisfied. But it is also true that there would still be, in the greater equality that that society provides, more in the way of effective equal citizenship and in that way a more equal sharing of power and thus a greater basis for realizing the good of self-respect and moral autonomy than in the Rawlsian well-ordered society. In a society in such a circumstance, ordered on Rawls' principles, the least advantaged would have more power *in the sense of more wealth*—more income—than they would have in the more egalitarian society. In the more egalitarian society they would have more power in the sense that their greater equality would make it the case that no one person would have power over another by virtue of his greater wealth and greater consequent control of society. In determining how things are to be ordered, everyone in a radically egalitarian society would stand in common positions of power or at least in more nearly equal positions of power.

I am not, of course, claiming that as a matter of fact the worst off will, even in the narrowest of economic terms, benefit by a regime of private ownership. Like other socialists, I do not think that at this historical stage capitalism benefits the most disadvantaged. Indeed I think it is plain that it does not. In fact I would go beyond that and argue that it hardly can benefit more than 10 percent of the people in societies such as ours. However, even if some trickle-down theory were correct and it could be shown that the worst off would have greater material benefits under the regime of private ownership of the means of production than in a socialist society, that still would not be sufficient to establish that the capitalist society would be the better society or the more just society. In the previous paragraphs I attempted to give some of the reasons for believing that to be so. (I am, of course, speaking, as Rawls is as well, of societies in conditions of moderate scarcity.)

I suspect that in reflecting on these two possible social orders, some would be more than willing to trade their equal power and consequent equal effective citizenship for greater wealth and some would not. But particularly given Rawls' own moral methodology—a moral methodology which is close to my own—there seems to be no conclusive argument to push one in one way rather than in another. Reflective and knowledgeable people go in both directions: it appears to be the case that what is the right and through and through just thing to do in such a situation cannot be objectively resolved. And this suggests, and partially confirms, the belief that justice is an essentially contested concept.[23] However, this relativism may be premature. We shall examine in the next section of this chapter whether the argument can be pushed a little further. Perhaps the disagreement about justice is not all that intractable.

The belief that justice is an essentially contested concept could survive a clear recognition on the part of both parties to the dispute that it is unfair that such differences in life prospects exist. This is so because it is plain that there are no morally relevant differences between the children of such entrepreneurs and the children of such unskilled laborers; but the Rawlsian, utilizing the *difference* principle and taking what is in effect a rather utilitarian turn, is committed to saying that this unfairness in such a circumstance does not, everything considered, create an overall injustice; for if the *difference* principle is not in effect, it will be the case that in such a society, for such people, still more harm and a still greater injustice will result.

IV

Rawls' bedrock argument here is that the inequality in question is just if the equal liberty principle and the fair equality of opportunity principle is not violated and the existence of such inequalities between the sons or daughters of unskilled laborers is to the advantage of the most disadvantaged stratum of society.

Suppose these children of unskilled laborers are part of that most disadvantaged stratum. Rawls, as we have seen, could argue that indeed their life prospects, given their situation, are already unfortunate enough and then rhetorically ask whether, given that situation, it is right or just or even humane to make them still worse off by narrowing the inequality and in doing that, however unintentionally, do something which is not to their advantage. Isn't doing that to add insult to injury? This plainly utilitarian argument has considerable force. Yet one can still be inclined to say that such inequalities remain unfair, indeed even somehow grossly unjust. We have two children of equal talent and ability and yet in virtue of their distinct class backgrounds their whole life prospects are very different indeed. One can see the force of the utilitarian considerations which would lead the parents of such children or the children themselves to be resigned to the inequalities, to accept them as the best thing they could get under the circumstances, but why should we think they are *just* distributions?[24]

In a way parallel to the way Rawls himself argues against simply accepting a maximizing of average utility as the most just arrangement, it is possible to argue against Rawls here. Rawls says to the utilitarian: it is a requirement of fairness to consider the interests of everyone alike even when doing so will not produce the greatest balance of average utility. To fail to do that is to fail to be fair. I am inclined to respond to Rawls in a similar way by saying that we should—indeed morally speaking must—reject such acute disparities in life prospects as unfair and unjust even though they do benefit the most disadvantaged. Are not both arguments equally good or equally bad? If we are justified in rejecting utilitarian reasoning in one case, why are we not justified in rejecting it in the other?

It is not, as Rawls claims, envy that is operative here, for one can have the appropriate sense of injustice even if one is not a member of the oppressed and exploited class. One might even be a part of the ruling class—as Engels was—and still feel it. The point is that it offends one's sense of justice. Or perhaps I should say, to give fewer hostages to fortune, it offends my sense of justice and I know it offends the sense of justice of some others as well. I am inclined to say that Rawls' principles here do not match with my considered judgments and the considered judgments of at least some others. Rawls might well counter that they would if we got them into wide reflective equilibrium. That is, Rawls might claim that if I considered all the facts, the alternative theories, and the principles of rationality, my considered judgments would not be what they are now. It is irrational *not* to accept these inequalities as just or at least as justified.[25]

Such considerations push us back to the basic questions in moral methodology we discussed in the first chapter. If there is anything to the above parallelism, it would appear at least to be the case that both arguments are equally good or equally bad. But just when we clearly recognize that, we still of course want to know which they are. Are they both good or are they both bad arguments? Here our considered judgments come into play and, speaking for myself, even when I have utilized the devices linked with what Rawls calls "reflective equilibrium," it remains the case that my moral intuitions are not firmly settled on this issue, though perhaps I have not pushed the method of wide equilibrium far enough. I am drawn by the teleological "utilitarian" considerations: why not, where we can, act in such a manner that we are likely to diminish as much as possible the occurrence of misery and maximize the attainment of happiness or at least (if that does not come to the same thing) the satisfaction of desire? What else, everything considered, could in such a circumstance be the better, the more humane thing to do? But I am pulled in the other direction as well, for I also find myself asking: but are we to do this when this commits us to doing things which are plainly unfair, i.e., when we in effect either ignore or override the interests of certain people when their interests would not contribute toward maximization, or we simply accept as justified, as "all right," given how things are, vast disparities of life prospects between the children—often equally talented and equally intelligent—of entrepreneurs and unskilled laborers when the *difference* principle and an equal opportunity principle are satisfied? There is another twist here, however, which does not put the *difference* principle in such a bad light. We need to ask whether, as a matter of empirical fact, it could be satisfied if these conditions obtained.

Even on reflection, with the facts and the consequences of both sets of strategems before me, vividly and fully, it still strikes me as grossly unfair so to treat the disadvantaged. Yet I can also see the humanity and indeed the rationality in "utilitarian reasoning" here: why allow any more misery or unhappiness than necessary? If closing up the gap between the classes at some determinate point in history results in that, then do not close it. Still I am also inclined to come back against such "utilitarian reasoning" concerning such a case with something (vague as it is) about fairness, human dignity, and being in a better position to control one's own life (effective moral autonomy). Moreover, it is not clear that happiness should be so set in opposition to human dignity and a control of one's life as if being happy were independent of these things. But the concept of happiness also has its more familiar sides as well. Perhaps it too is an essentially contested concept?

I think that what is happening here is that very deeply embedded but, in this context, conflicting moral sentiments are being appealed to, and our conflicting considered judgments are being matched with these conflicting sentiments.[26] On the side of a socialist conception of justice, more radically egalitarian than Rawls', we have a clearer recognition of and accounting for the danger to liberty of inequalities of economic power and the effects of concentrated wealth and power under capitalism (particularly modern monopoly capitalism) on the moral autonomy and sense of moral worth of such disadvantaged people. There is the recognition that given the realities of social life we are not justified in believing, as liberals do, that we can rightly treat as separate the political and economic spheres of life, that we can still serve best each person's human welfare or flourishing by maximizing political freedoms while tolerating extensive economic disparities. Moral autonomy for all, the socialist believes, is simply not possible under such circumstances.

In such circumstances of moderate scarcity Rawls believes we can and should act in accordance with the *difference* principle while still acting in accordance with the equal liberty principle, i.e., the principle laying it down "that each person has an equal right to the most extensive scheme of equal basic liberties compatible with a similar scheme of liberties for all."[27] But talk of the priority of the equal liberty principle over the *difference* principle should not obscure the fact that in such circumstances reasoning in accordance with the *difference* principle, even when placed in its proper lexical order, will make for less moral autonomy—and in that crucial sense, less liberty—than will reasoning in accordance with the more egalitarian socialist principles. That is so because the latter always aims at diminishing morally relevant inequalities, inequalities in the primary social goods or in basic human goods. With fewer such inequalities, there would be less control of one group over another and thus there would be greater moral autonomy. By contrast, Rawls' *difference* principle has the unfortunate unintended effect of limiting the scope of his equal liberty principle.

This greater moral autonomy afforded by the socialist principles would most plainly obtain if classlessness, or something far closer to classlessness than Rawls allows, were possible. Most crucially, that should be taken to mean the possibility of there being a complex society in which there are no extensive differences in life prospects between different groups of people because some have far greater income, power, authority, or prestige than others. Where there is such a class society there will be less moral autonomy than in a classless society where the more radically egalitarian socialist conceptions can be satisfied. Moreover, in spite of what Rawls may think, what we speak of here is not something which goes "beyond justice," for such considerations concern the fairness of distributions and relations between human beings. So some justification of Rawls' assumption that classlessness is not possible becomes crucial. However, *if* the existence of classes is indeed inevitable, then perhaps for those who find pure libertarian entitlement theories morally unacceptable and utilitarianism unattractive, a Rawlsian egalitarianism may be the best thing that can be had, if one cares about liberty (particularly equal liberty), equality, and human well being. But, given the choices, we ought to be tolerably certain that classlessness is impossible.

Is Rawls justified in assuming that institutional inequalities rooted in class structures are inevitable? What one must do, to establish that classlessness is impossible or unlikely, is to show that it is impossible or unlikely that an industrial society can come into existence where there are only rather minimal differences in income and authority and where none of the differences that do exist result from or are the means to exploiting others. (Note: Given its characterization, it is a conceptual impossibility that such an egalitarian society would be authoritarian.) That is, as C. B. Macpherson would put it, the society would be so organized that there would be no way to transfer "to oneself for one's own benefit some of the powers of others."[28]

Whatever we may want to say about the division of labor it is plainly not necessary that there be private ownership of the means of production. Yet it is the private ownership of the means of production which is the principal source of one human being able to extract for his own benefits some of the powers of others. Such exploitation is unavoidable in a capitalist organization of society, but there is nothing necessary, given our position in history, about the continued existence of a capitalist social order. *Perhaps,* as Dahrendorf believes, some social stratification is inevitable, but that is another matter. What we have no good grounds for taking to be a fixed feature of human life is the sorting of human beings into socioeconomic classes in which one class will exploit the other. Unless it is a mistake to believe that it is these socioeconomic class divisions (or something rather like them in statist societies) which are *a,* and perhaps *the,* principal cause of such radical differences in life prospects, there is good reason to believe that a form of egalitarianism more radical than Rawls' is both feasible and morally desirable and that the principal human task will be to struggle to attain classlessness.[29]

V

I want, at this juncture, to make a disclaimer. I do not claim for these views a support in Marx or the Marxist tradition, though I do hope that they are compatible with that tradition. What Marx's or Engel's views are on these matters is subject to considerable debate.[30] They do not systematically treat this subject and indeed they sometimes talk, when justice-talk is at issue, derisively of ideology or false consciousness.[31] To develop any kind of explicit Marxist theory here would require extensive injections of rather contestable interpretation. I will only remark that my radical socialist egalitarianism is in accord with Engel's claim, in a famous passage on the subject in his *Anti-Dühring,* that "the real content of the proletarian demand for equality is the demand for the *abolition* of classes." Significantly, he then goes on to remark that a "demand for equality which goes beyond that, of necessity passes into absurdity," thereby in effect rejecting what have become straw-men forms of "radical egalitarianism" easily knocked about by philosophers.[32] Neither Marx nor Engels were complete egalitarians in the sense of believing that all human beings should be treated exactly alike in every respect. No thoughtful person, egalitarian or otherwise, believes that everyone old and young, sick and well, introverted and extroverted, should be treated the same in every respect: as if all people had exactly the same interests, aspirations, and needs.

In this chapter, I do not attempt to specify fully, let alone extensively defend, the form of "socialist justice" or, as I would prefer to call it, radical egalitarianism that I have argued is at least as reasonable as Rawls' account, though the whole book should be read as an effort to do just that. In fact, I would go further than that and contend that it is a superior conception for societies of considerable wealth, at least for someone who starts out with moral sentiments similar to those of Rawls, in that it squares better than Rawls' theory, both with what we know about the world (particularly with what we know about the need for meaningful work and the conditions of moral autonomy) and with some of Rawls' deepest insights—insights which led him to reject utilitarianism and to set out his conception of justice as fairness. Here I have in mind his Kantian conception of human beings as members of a kingdom of ends, the weight he gives to moral autonomy, self-respect, equal liberty, and moral community. My contention has been that such things are not achievable under even a liberal capitalist order with its resultant class divisions. Given the way political and economic phenomena interact, liberty and moral autonomy cannot but suffer when there are substantial differences in wealth.[33] It is not only, as is now becoming more generally recognized and apologized for (see the Trilateral Commission's Task Force report: *The Governability of Democracies*), that capitalism is incompatible with equality, it is also incompatible with equal liberty and moral autonomy for all humankind.[34] Equal liberty is impossible without all people of normal abilities being masters of their own lives, but with the differences in power and control between classes within capitalism, this is impossible for most people. Furthermore, given the control of the forces of production by one class and the consequent authoritarian allocation of work, meaningful work must be extensively limited under capitalism. Meaningful work, as Andreas Eshete well argues, must be autonomous, though this does not mean that it cannot be cooperative; it must, that is, bear the mark of our own making in the sense of our own planning, thought, and our own decisions about what is worth doing, making, and having.[35] But this is only possible where there is effective, cooperative, democratically controlled workers' social ownership and control of the means of production. For anyone who sees the plausibility of Rawls' Aristotelian principle or thinks about the conditions of self-respect and thinks carefully about the role of work in life, it should be evident that under a capitalist organization of production these values and with them full moral autonomy are not achievable.

It is a very deep moral assumption of both Rawls' account and my own that all human beings have a right to equal respect and concern in the design of social (including political and economic) institutions. We must, that is, if our normative ethic is to be adequate and our reactions as moral agents are to answer to that theory, treat all human beings with an equal moral respect. We must regard it as morally required that equal moral concern be given to everyone. What sort of principles of justice do we need to match with that underlying moral assumption and with the related conception that a good society will provide the basis for equal self-respect for all people? Rawls sees that it is true that in bourgeois societies, such as those in North America and Western Europe, relative wealth, to a very considerable degree, provides for most people the psychological basis for self-respect. (No claim need be made that these are the only societies so affected.) Given his belief that classlessness is unattainable and that important differences in wealth and power will remain and indeed are important in providing incentives for the accumulation of material wealth, which in turn will better everyone's circumstances, Rawls understandably tries to break the psychological connection between wealth and self-respect. I have argued here and in Chapter 3 that there is a tight link between wealth, power, and autonomy and that equal moral autonomy cannot be sustained without something like a very near equality of wealth and power. It is a simple corollary of that to see that equal self-respect cannot be achieved without equal moral autonomy. If that is right, and Rawls is right in assuming that classlessness is impossible, one should draw some rather pessimistic conclusions about the very possibility of a genuine moral order.[36] However, I have argued that we do not have good grounds for rejecting the empirical possibility of classlessness. Given the fundamental moral beliefs that Rawls and I share, I think that in looking for the basis for stabilizing—indeed making it something that could socially flourish—equal self-respect and equal moral autonomy, we should look again at a principle of justice which would stress the need for an equal division of wealth.

My more radically egalitarian principles of justice (particularly my second principle) captures that. I stated them in a somewhat Rawlsian manner for ease of comparison, though I am not particularly enamoured with their formulation, and I am confident that if there is anything in them at all, they will require all sorts of refinements, clarifications, and (no doubt) modifications. Moreover, I do not offer them as candidate eternal principles of justice, *sub specie aeternitatas,* but rather as principles of social justice for conditions of relative abundance (comparable to conditions in present-day Sweden or Switzerland). This still fits in the upper end of Rawls' situation of moderate scarcity, where conditions of distribution would still be important.[37] For conditions of full abundance, as Marx stressed, questions of distribution would be very secondary indeed.[38]

What I want to capture in some rough initial way with my second radical egalitarian principle of justice, the second principle stated at the end of the first paragraph of Chapter 4, is a distributive principle committed to *equal division with adjustments for differences in need.* I am under no illusions about its being a magic formula, and much of its plausibility (if it has any) would depend on the reading given to its various constituent elements.

I am making no claims about priority relations between my two radical egalitarian principles of justice. I am saying that in a perfectly just society, which is also a relatively abundant society, these two principles will be fully satisfied. It shall be the burden of my argument to show that such principles can only be so satisfied in a classless society where, in Marx's famous phrase, the free development of each is the condition of the free development of all. Furthermore, such principles require democracy for their realization, taken here to mean "the people's self-determination in political, economic, and social affairs" and such a democracy, it is plain to see, requires socialism.[39]

Even in the circumstances where this principle can have a proper application, it is not the case that this is the conception of justice that any rational person would have to adopt who was constrained to reason impartially about what principles of action are collectively rational. I do not believe that my principle, or any other principle including justice as fairness or average utility, can attain such an atemporal rational Archimedean point.[40] I do not think that it can be established that there is a set of principles of collective action which are uniquely rational, even in a determinate historical epoch. *A Theory of Justice* is just the latest in a long line of distinguished failures to achieve such an Archimedean point.

What I think can be shown is that in the situation described, for persons with certain moral sentiments, a conception of justice of the type formulated above would be the rational choice. The sentiment I have in mind is the one that leads Rawls to what Ronald Dworkin regards as his deepest moral assumption underlying his commitment to justice as fairness, namely, "the assumption of a natural right of all men and women to an equality of concern and respect, a right they possess not in virtue of birth or characteristic or merit or excellence but simply as human beings with the capacity to make plans and give justice."[41] I do not know how anyone could show this belief to be true—to say nothing of showing it to be self-evident—or in anyway prove it or show that if one is through and through rational, one must accept it.[42] As I was at pains to show in chapter 2, a Nietzschean, a Benthamite, or even a classist amoralist who rejects it cannot thereby be shown to be irrational or even in any way necessarily to be diminished in his reason. It is a moral belief that I am committed to and I believe Dworkin is right in claiming that Rawls is too. What I am claiming is that in the circumstances I described if one is so committed and one has the facts straight, reasons carefully, and takes these reasons to heart, one will be led not to utilitarianism or to justice as fairness or even to a form of pluralism, but to some such form of radical egalitarianism.[43]

NOTES

1. Ronald Dworkin, "The Original Position," *University of Chicago Law Review* 40, no. 3 (Spring 1973): 533; and Thomas M. Scanlon, "Rawls' Theory of Justice," *The University of Pennsylvania Law Review* 121 (1973): 1064.

2. It tries to capture something of what Marx had in mind with his conception of a classless society in which the free development of each is the condition of the free

development of all. An account, at core very close to my own but given a more political and historical expression and closely related to the contemporary political scene, is given by Martin J. Sklar, "Liberty and Equality and Socialism," *Socialist Revolution* 7, no. 4 (July/August 1977): 92–104. Evan Simpson, "Socialist Justice," *Ethics* 87, no. 1 (October 1976) argues much more abstractly to similar conclusions, but I find his argumentation, as distinct from his conclusions and depiction of the liberal/socialist division, obscure.

3. Irving Fetcher, "Karl Marx on Human Nature," *Social Research* 40, no. 3 (Autumn 1973): 461.

4. I am here indebted to the work of C. B. Macpherson. His own important critical essays on Rawls have unfortunately been neglected. C. B. Macpherson, *Democratic Theory* (Oxford: Clarendon Press, 1973), Chapter IV; and "Rawls' Models of Man and Society," *Philosophy of the Social Sciences* 3, no. 4 (December 1973). I have in my own "On the Very Possibility of a Classless Society: Macpherson, Rawls, and Revisionist Liberalism," *Political Theory* 6, no. 2 (May 1978): 191–207, attempted to elucidate and critically assess the force of Macpherson's critique of Rawls. Elizabeth Rapaport, "Classical Liberalism and Rawlsian Revisionism" and Virginia McDonald, "Rawlsian Contractarianism: Liberal Equality or Inequality," both in *New Essays on Contract Theory*, eds. Kai Nielsen and Roger Shiner (Guelph, Ontario: Canadian Association for Publishing in Philosophy, 1977), have extended and developed, essentially along Macpherson's lines, a socialist critique of contractarianism.

5. Wesley Cooper has spotted some of the inadequacies in Rawls' conception of a perfectly just society. Wesley E. Cooper, "The Perfectly Just Society," *Philosophy and Phenomenological Research* 10 (1977): 46–55.

6. John Rawls, *A Theory of Justice* (Cambridge, Mass.: Harvard University Press, 1971), p. 302. That there is, or even can be, such general knowledge of society is challenged by P. H. Nowell-Smith, "A Theory of Justice?" *Philosophy of the Social Sciences* 3, no. 4 (December 1973); and Robert Paul Wolff, *Understanding Rawls* (Princeton, N.J.: Princeton University Press, 1977), Chapter 13. A powerful theoretical underpinning for the kind of claim made impressionistically by Nowell-Smith and Wolff is brilliantly articulated by Charles Taylor, "Interpretation and the Sciences of Man," *The Review of Metaphysics* 25, no. 1 (September 1971).

7. Robert Paul Wolff, op. cit., pp. 67–71; Brian Barry, *The Liberal Theory of Justice* (Oxford: Clarendon Press, 1973), pp. 50–51; David Copp, "Justice and the Difference Principle," *Canadian Journal of Philosophy* 4, no. 2 (1974); and the essays by R. M. Hare, David Lyons and Benjamin Barber in *Reading Rawls*, ed. Norman Daniels (New York: Basic Books, 1975). John Rawls, "Social Unity and Primary Goods," in *Utilitarianism and Beyond*, eds. Amartya Sen and Bernard Williams (Cambridge: Cambridge University Press, 1982), pp. 159–85.

8. I have, in various ways, argued this against Rawls in several different contexts. Kai Nielsen, "The Choice Between Perfectionism and Rawlsian Contractarianism," *Interpretation* 6, no. 2 (May 1977); "On Philosophic Method," *International Philosophical Quarterly* 16, no. 2 (September 1976); "The Priority of Liberty Examined," *The Indian Political Science Review* 11, no. 1 (January 1977); and "Rawls and Classist Amoralism," *Mind* 86, no. 341 (January 1977). It has also been argued in various ways by Steven Lukes, "An Archimedean Point," *Observer,* June 4, 1972; and in his "Relativism: Cognitive and Moral," *Aristotelian Society Proceedings,* Supplementary Volume 48 (1974); Andreas Esheté, "Contractarianism and the Scope of Justice," *Ethics* 85, no. 1 (October 1974); and William L. McBride, "Social Theory *sub Specie Aeternitatis,*" *Yale Law Journal* 81 (1972).

9. It is clear enough that Rawls would regard such a society in conditions of moderate scarcity as a well-ordered society if certain conditions were met. Whether he would say it is a perfectly just society is less clear, though there is at least one passage (p. 102) that suggests that. Cooper, op. cit., brings out very well the inadequacy of Rawls' conception of a perfectly just society.

10. Joel Feinberg expresses clearly the standard and, as far as I can see, a perfectly adequate rationale for such a belief as follows: "Let us consider why we all agree

. . . in rejecting the view that differences in race, sex, IQ, or social 'rank' are the grounds of just differences in wealth or income. Part of the answer seems obvious. People cannot by their own voluntary choices determine what skin color, sex, or IQ they shall have, or which hereditary caste they shall enter. To make such properties the basis of discrimination between individuals in the distribution of social benefits would be to treat people differently in ways that profoundly affect their lives because of differences for which they have no responsibility. Differences in a given respect are relevant for the aims of distributive justice then, only if they are differences for which their possessors can be held responsible; properties can be the grounds of just discrimination between persons only if those persons had a *fair opportunity* to acquire or avoid them." Joel Feinberg, "Economic Justice" in *Ethics in Perspective,* eds. Karsten J. Struhl and Paula Rothenberg Struhl (New York: Random House, 1975), p. 421.

11. Brian Barry, op. cit., convincingly argues that there are good empirical reasons to doubt whether the narrowing of such inequalities would in fact have the effect of making the worst-off parties still worse off.

12. Yet it is clear enough that Rawls is not insensitive to these problems. John Rawls, *A Theory of Justice,* pp. 298–301.

13. Rawls makes far too much play with envy here. Besides envy and jealousy, the disadvantaged, as Rawls recognizes himself, could feel "resentment from a sense that they are unfairly treated." Ibid., p. 540.

14. Andreas Eshete, "Contractarianism and the Scope of Justice," *Ethics* 85, no. 1 (October 1974).

15. John Rawls, *A Theory of Justice,* p. 205.

16. Norman Daniels, "Equal Liberty and Unequal Worth of Liberty" in *Reading Rawls,* ed. Norman Daniels (New York: Basic Books, 1975).

17. John Rawls, *A Theory of Justice,* pp. 73–74, 275–79, and 512.

18. Ibid., p. 75.

19. Ibid., pp. 98–102, 511–12, 530–41 (most particularly 534, 536, 537 and 539). See also John Rawls, "Distributive Justice" in *Philosophy, Politics and Society,* eds. Peter Laslett and W. G. Runciman, Third Series (Oxford: Basil Blackwell, 1967), pp. 66–70. For a perceptive discussion of this see C. B. Macpherson, *Democratic Theory* (Oxford: Clarendon Press, 1973), pp. 88–92.

20. C. B. Macpherson, op. cit. and Benjamin Barber, op. cit.

21. Ralf Dahrendorf, *Essays in the Theory of Society* (Stanford, Cal.: Stanford University Press, 1968), pp. 151–78.

22. Benjamin Barber powerfully probes whether they do so hang together. Barber, op. cit.

23. This leads us back to the literature cited in note 8.

24. Paul Taylor, "Utility and Justice," *Canadian Journal of Philosophy* 1, no. 3 (March 1972), has very forcefully argued, in a manner plainly influenced by Rawls' root conception of justice as fairness, how distinct questions of justice are from those of utility.

25. John Rawls, *A Theory of Justice,* p. 546. Rawls, as some have thought, seems to have confused "just inequalities" with "justified inequalities." It may not be just to sanction such inequalities but it may still be justified on utilitarian grounds. It may be one of those cases, *pace* Rawls, where considerations of utility outweigh considerations of justice and where what we should do, through and through, is not identical with what justice requires. To claim this would require a rather considerable change in Rawls' system, but it would give him a rather more plausible justification for his *difference* principle.

26. I have discussed problems about matching here and problems of Rawls' conception of reflective equilibrium in "On Philosophic Method," *International Philosophical Quarterly* 16, no. 3 (1976): 358–68.

27. John Rawls, "Some Reasons for the Maximum Criterion," *The American Economic Review* 64 (1974): 142.

28. C. B. Macpherson, "Rawls' Models of Man and Society," *Philosophy of the Social Sciences* 3, no. 4 (December 1973): 341.

29. The conception I use of statist societies is clarified, applied, and defended by Svetozar Stojanovic in his *Between Ideals and Reality* (New York: Oxford University Press, 1973), chapter 3.

30. William L. McBride, "The Concept of Justice in Marx, Engels, and Others," *Ethics* 85, no. 3 (April 1975); Lucien Goldmann, "Is There a Marxist Sociology?" *Radical Philosophy* 1 (January 1972); Derek Allen, "The Utilitarianism of Marx and Engels," *American Philosophical Quarterly* 10, no. 3 (January 1973); George Brenkert, "Marx and Utilitarianism," *Canadian Journal of Philosophy* 6, no. 3 (September 1976); Robert Tucker, *The Marxian Revolutionary Idea* (New York: W. W. Norton, 1969), chapter 3; Allen Wood, "The Marxian Critique of Justice," *Philosophy and Public Affairs* 1, no. 3 (Spring 1972); Michael P. Lerner, "Marxism and Ethical Reasoning," *Social Praxis* 2 (1974); Kai Nielsen, "Class Conflict, Marxism and the Good-Reasons Approach," *Social Praxis* 2 (1974); Derek Allen, "Is Marxism a Philosophy?" and Marlene Gerber Fried, "Marxism and Justice," both in *The Journal of Philosophy* 71, no. 17 (October 1974); Nancy Holmstrom, "Exploitation," *Canadian Journal of Philosophy* 7, no. 2 (June 1977); *Marx, Justice and History*, ed. Marshall Cohen *et al.* (Princeton, N.J.: Princeton University Press, 1980); *Marx and Morality*, eds. Kai Nielsen and Steven Patten (Guelph, Ontario: Canadian Association for Publishing in Philosophy, 1981); and Allen E. Buchanan, *Marx and Justice* (Totowa, N.J.: Rowman and Littlefield, 1982).

31. We need in this context to face questions which arise about moral ideology. See here W. L. McBride, "The Concept of Justice in Marx, Engels, and Others," *Ethics* 5, no. 3 (April 1975); Andrew Collier, "Truth and Practice," *Radical Philosophy* 5 (Summer 1973); and "The Production of Moral Ideology," *Radical Philosophy* 9 (Winter 1974); Tony Skillen, "Marxism and Morality," *Radical Philosophy* 8 (Summer 1974); Peter Binns, "Anti-Moralism," *Radical Philosophy* 10 (Spring 1975); Philip Corrigan and Derek Sayer, "Moral Relations, Political Economy and Class Struggle," *Radical Philosophy* 12 (Winter 1975).

32. F. Engels, *Anti-Dühring* (New York: International Publishers, 1939), pp. 117–18. For one recent such effort to refute egalitarianism, splendidly made into a straw man, see H. J. McLoskey, "A Right to Equality?" *Canadian Journal of Philosophy* 6, no. 4 (December 1976). Other such efforts include: Robert Nisbet, "The Pursuit of Equality," *Public Interest* 33 (1974); Isaiah Berlin, "Equality" in *The Concept of Equality*, ed. William Blackstone (Minneapolis, Minn.: Burgess Publishing, 1969); and Hugo Bedau, "Radical Egalitarianism," in *Justice and Equality*, ed. Hugo A. Bedau (Englewood Cliffs, N.J.: Prentice-Hall, 1971).

33. Evan Simpson, op. cit., p. 2.

34. The provisions and ideological transformations of the concept of democracy are interesting to observe in the literature of the Trilateral Commission. See, for example, *The Governability of Democracies*, ed. Samuel Huntington *et al.* and the Trilateral Commission's publication *Trialogue*, particularly the summer issue, 1975, the winter issue, 1975–76 and the spring issue, 1976. Note particularly the writings of Huntington, Crozier, Watanuki, Dahrendorf, and Carli. For trenchantly critical remarks about the Trilateral Commission, see Noam Chomsky, "Trilateral's Rx for Crisis: Governability Yes, Democracy No," *Seven Days*, February 14, 1977, pp. 10–11.

35. Eshete's comments on work are particularly important here. See Andreas Eshete, op. cit., pp. 41–44.

36. These conclusions are drawn about the attainment and sustaining of genuine moral relations in *class-divided societies*. See the references to Lerner and Nielsen in note 30 and to Collier, Skillen, and Binns in note 31. The steadfast and probing recognition of this is captured in a profound way in the work of Bertolt Brecht.

37. A rejection of (a) the possibility of attaining such eternal principles and (b) an argument that they are unnecessary for attaining a basis for rational social critique is made by William L. McBride, "Social Theory *sub Specie Aeternitatis*," *Yale Law Journal* 31 (1972); Andreas Eshete, op. cit.; and Boris Frankel, "Review Symposium of *Anarchy, State, and Utopia*," *Theory and Society* 3 (1976): 443–50.

38. See Marx's *Critique of the Gotha Programme*. For a perceptive discussion of issues arising from this and of Marx's slogan "From each according to his ability and

to each according to his need," see Edward and Onora Nell, "On Justice Under Socialism" in *Ethics in Perspective,* eds. Karsten J. Struhl and Paula Rothenberg Struhl (New York: Random House, 1976).

39. Martin J. Sklar, op. cit., pp. 96 and 103. The arguments in the above paragraph, as well as Sklar's essay, should make it evident why my two principles require socialism. We cannot have industrial democracy of the type characterized or classlessness with any kind of capitalist organization of society. There simply will not be democracy in the workplace under capitalism. People will have to sell their labor and they will be controlled by others in their work.

40. My articles cited in note 8 were, in part, directed to establishing this point.

41. Ronald Dworkin, op. cit., p. 532.

42. My "Scepticism and Human Rights," *The Monist* 52, no. 4 (October 1968) was meant to go some of the way toward establishing this. For two more general theoretical arguments to provide a theoretical underpinning for such type arguments, see my "Why There is a Problem About Ethics: Reflections on the Is and the Ought," *Danish Yearbook of Philosophy* (1968) and "Principles of Rationality," *Philosophical Papers* 3, no. 2 (October 1974).

43. In this last section I have speculated from, and turned to my own purposes, points often made in different contexts and for different purposes by Martin J. Sklar, op. cit.; Andreas Esheté, op. cit.; William L. McBride, op. cit.; Henry Shue, "Liberty and Self Respect," *Ethics* 85 (April 1975); Lawrence Crocker, "Equality, Solidarity, and Rawls' Maximin," *Philosophy and Public Policy* 6, no. 3 (Spring 1977); and Derek L. Phillips, "The Equality Debate: What Does Justice Require?" *Theory and Society* 4 (1977): 247–72.

PART III

Desert, Merit and Meritocracy

INTERLUDE AND PROEM TWO

I have set out in Part II my basic defense of radical egalitarianism and with it something of the grounds for my underlying claim that such a conception of justice and equality, far from being in conflict with liberty, is necessary for its full flourishing. In Part III (Chapter 6), I shall first consider justice as desert as an alternative to justice as equality. In the course of doing this, I shall first try to show why many—among them John Rawls and Stuart Hampshire—are reluctant to appeal to criteria of desert as criteria for justice. However, I shall also go on to attempt to show, these difficulties not withstanding, why such a conception has been repeatedly appealed to, why it is necessary to make such an appeal, and what the criteria of desert are.

I shall argue, in attempting to do that, that, Rawls and Hampshire to the contrary notwithstanding, there must be in any adequate and full account of justice a place for desert, though not nearly so central a place as traditionalists have taken it to be. Moreover, or so I shall argue, even in an utterly deterministic world, if such it is, there are sound reasons for accepting some appeals to desert and, even in such a world, there remains a fair but diminished niche for considerations of desert in setting out a design for a just society, even a perfectly just society.

Building on my arguments about desert, I go on in Chapters 7 and 8 to discuss meritocracy and meritocratic accounts of justice. I seek to follow through the logic of meritocracy showing both its appeal and how finally, if thoroughly pressed, it ends in absurdity. In the course of doing this, I examine the defense, erected by the "Old Egalitarianism," of a "meritocratic egalitarianism," a defense which places a heavy stress on equality of opportunity and which seeks to undermine the "New Egalitarianism's" stress on equality of result. I shall resist such a weight being given to equality of opportunity. Alternatively, I shall argue (1) that equality of opportunity can only be attained to a limited extent and (2) that talk of equality of opportunity is little more than a cruel joke unless a concern to achieve equality of opportunity is wedded to a concern to achieve some substantial equality of condition. Indeed, if not so linked to equality of condition, it can only come to the formal right, no matter how disadvantaged the person may be, to be at the starting line in various meritocratic races for positions of prestige and power.

I shall, however, conclude Part III with an argument for retaining in certain areas of our social lives merit assessments while thoroughly rejecting meritocracy and its fetish about equality of opportunity without anything like an equality of condition.

6

Justice and Desert

I

Some believe that John Rawls and, to a lesser extent, Robert Nozick have failed to provide a proper place for what is really central to justice, namely, desert and merit. Justice quintessentially is the treating of each person in accordance with her deserts. Justice, put simply, is getting what one deserves. In thinking about the rightness of any distributional scheme or the justice of any social arrangement, it is vital that we do not leave out of consideration *giving individuals what they deserve.* No account, it is often felt, which leaves desert or merit out of account can be an adequate account of justice. People should have certain benefits or burdens because they deserve to have them. Certain things they did in the past or are doing now make it the case that justice requires that they be treated in a certain way. Social justice, as well as individual justice, requires that a certain treatment be accorded them.

I will return to that claim and to an examination of its underlying rationale in the next section, but I want first to exhibit something of the rationale for discounting considerations of desert. I shall do this by taking up some remarks of Stuart Hampshire's which go even further down the road to rejecting such an approach than do Rawls'.[1]

Hampshire argues that we should "reject altogether the notion of deserving as having a place in a rational and systematic ethics."[2] His argument occurs in the course of a discussion and criticism of Rawls. Hampshire starts from a by now oft quoted passage from Rawls.

> Perhaps some will think that the person with greater natural endowments deserves those assets and the superior character that make their development possible. Because he is more worthy in this sense, he deserves the greater advantages that he could achieve with them. This view, however, is surely incorrect. It seems to be one of the fixed points of our considered judgments that no one deserves his place in the distribution of native endowments any more than one deserves one's initial starting place in society. . . . Character depends in large part upon fortunate family and social circumstances for which he can claim no credit.[3]

Hampshire, pushing this, asks:

> Is there anything whatever that, strictly speaking, a man can claim credit for, or he can properly be said to deserve, with the implication that it can be attributed to him, the ultimate subject, as contrasted with the natural forces that formed him? In the last analysis, are not all advantages and disadvantages distributed by natural causes, even when they are the effects of human agency?[4]

Rawls, Hampshire points out, is not trying to characterize justice in terms of getting what one deserves. He operates with a principle of equality in which a human being is to receive a certain treatment merely in virtue of being a human being, open to reason and with a sense of justice. He does not operate with the meritocratic conception that a person should have a certain treatment because of his/her ability, effort, achievement or contribution (the traditional desert bases).

Hampshire accepts some formulation of the Rawlsian principle of equality and then goes on to claim that it also becomes a principle of fairness, a fundamental principle of justice, when one thinks, as Hampshire believes one should, of all advantages as unearned and undeserved. We should say that, he contends, not only of naturally acquired advantages but of socially acquired ones as well. We go into the "poker game of social competition" set out with a certain character and a set of dispositions which are our lot, and not something we could choose or be responsible for. We come to be what we are from the turn of "genetic roulette and the roulette of childhood environment." We all, at least up and into the present, come into a social world "determined by largely unknown historical forces." In the last analysis our characters are set for us and not by us. And if that is so, we can hardly be said to deserve the characters we have. Any praise or blame that is directed at us as a result of our acting, as people with the characters we come predictably to have should act, is not something for which, except in a purely pragmatic sense, we can properly be praised or blamed. If we reflect carefully on how it is we became the kinds of people we are, we will, Hampshire claims, reject altogether the notion of desert as a moral category. It may sometimes be a useful pragmatic tool with a utilitarian rationale, but we, morally speaking, cannot properly say that anyone deserves anything whatsoever, whether it be good or ill. To do so is not to be properly reflective about the sources of character formation.

Rawls is perfectly right in saying that "no one deserves his place in the distribution of native endowments any more than one deserves one's initial starting place in society." If we reflect dispassionately on this, we will not use desert as a moral category or at least as a fundamental category of moral appraisal and we will not characterize justice as getting what one deserves.

II

The above argument plainly has its appeal. Yet there are surely not a few who would say that still in some way an adequate account of justice must make room for desert. We should not, as Hampshire would, utterly reject it as a moral category. Whatever we might say about in "the last analysis" or about what we would attribute to a human being as an "ultimate subject"—whatever exactly or even inexactly that means—still in workaday moral and social appraisal an appeal to desert continues to have a point and indeed a point that can survive scrutiny. There is a place, some will claim, for distributing economic goods, or more generally benefits and burdens, according to how much they are deserved. Where a person works hard and makes some significant contribution to his society, doesn't he deserve some reward? Is it just that the lazy chap or the chap who makes no special contribution or effort at all should receive the same as someone who has worked very hard indeed and made a contribution?

I particularly want to think about desert in this economic context and put aside questions of retributive justice. James Rachels has perceptively argued that, whatever we might say about the ultimate springs of character formation, desert, as measured by work completed, should continue to serve as *a*, though not, of course, as *the*, basis for the distribution of economic benefits.[5] There must, that is, in a fully adequate account of distributive justice, be some weight given to merit, some focussing on what a person has done to deserve his allotment, rather than an exclusive focussing on his needs or on what kind of person he is, e.g., his "moral excellence." (Indeed it is questionable whether the latter category should come up for consideration at all.)

The stress here must be on *what the person has actually done,* for simply to determine desert by *effort* can hardly be right because, aside from being hard to measure, just the fact that someone tried hard but accomplished little seems no more a basis for desert than is an ability which is only minimally utilized. If A has the ability to do y but repeatedly underachieves and only does z (something needed and on a continuum with y but not quite as desirable as y), while B does not have the ability to do y but by straining his capacities to the utmost succeeds in doing z, it would hardly be right to say that A deserves more in the way of reward than B. If anything we would say that of B. But if C tries very hard but accomplishes almost nothing at all, many would be reluctant to say he would be deserving of much, if anything, in the way of a reward. About all we could say was that it was a good try and respect him for his effort.

There seems to be something morally callous about saying that and yet that can't be quite right either, for on reflection it is plain that anything more than respecting him for his effort would not, everything considered, be fair. We need something like *ability plus effort for desert.* But even that does not seem to be sufficient, for it hardly necessarily adds up to work completed or achievement. We need, as well, to add something like contribution or actual achievement. Where people are in some position of fair equality of opportunity (something in reality we do not have and perhaps can only approximate), achievement and contribution seem an appropriate desert base for pecuniary rewards. (We will in the next two chapters see what a difficult notion the notion of "fair equality of opportunity" is and how difficult it is to even approximate it.)

We might simply try to determine desert in terms of contribution. We might fly under some such banner as "From each according to his ability and to each according to his contribution." There is here, of course, the familiar problem of how we are to measure, in even a remotely objective sense, the contribution to society of various occupations or activities. We can, if we wish to be fair, hardly let market considerations settle a person's contribution or achievement, for it would only show a person's worth to others in certain domains and that only after certain desires for things had been manipulated by advertising techniques and the like. People can make contributions, say that of an artist or a scientist or simply as a person who is very friendly and open to children, which have very little market value. But all the same how do we, with some reasonable objectivity, determine the worth of contributions or of work completed? It is, however, important not to exaggerate the difficulties involved here. We can make some not unreasonable intuitive estimates about the comparative contributions conscientious members in various occupations make to society. Surely dentists, welfare workers, and members of the Salvation Army score higher than advertising agents, circus barkers, and script writers of T.V. commercials.

However, the problem of measurement is not the only problem about such a criterion. There is also the fact that morally irrelevant fortuitous circumstances often keep one person or class of persons from making the same or even comparable contributions to those of another person or class of persons. If A is born in Harlem of a husbandless welfare mother and B is the child of professional parents in Scarsdale, A's chance, to put it mildly, of making a contribution equal to B's is very slight indeed. Before we can use contribution as a basis for desert we at least would have to make sure that a condition of fair equality of opportunity had been attained or reasonably approximated. (How we could even approximate this in a society like ours is something which is anything but obvious.)

We go from the frying pan into the fire if we substitute a conception of a person's overall moral worth as the criterion for desert rather than ability, effort, achievement, contribution or some combination thereof. These latter notions are indeed difficult enough to determine, but how we would determine comparative overall moral worth would be very chancy indeed. We can, of course, distinguish between Hitler and Hammerskjüld. But appeal to paradigm cases will be of little help in trying to use moral worth as a criterion for desert. Appeal to such paradigms will give us guidance in extreme situations, but there remain the great mass of cases with respect to which we are quite at sea.

Still before we throw out desert as a hopelessly woolly notion, it is well to remind ourselves again of the following bit of common sense: if A is plainly not mentally defective or hopelessly perverse and neurotic, but still, after a good education in comfortable and supportive surroundings, does the very minimum at a job that is interesting, socially significant and for which he is plainly qualified, while B works hard and does an excellent job at that same job making a considerable contribution to his society, then, *ceteris paribus,* it is just that B should receive some reward that A does not and indeed to treat them the same, where there is some shortage of desired things for reward, would be unfair and to reward A over B would be grossly unjust.

So it would seem that there must be some link between justice and desert. Justice plainly is not just getting what one deserves but it is also the case that in deciding what justice is we cannot rightly just ignore desert either. Moreover, Rachels must be right in claiming that people's past actions are crucially relevant here.[6]

Rachels also points out that in making judgments about what is just and unjust as well as in the wider class of judgments about what we ought not to do, we need to give reasons for the making of such judgments. Certain reasons are relevant to the claim that something is unjust and certain reasons are not. That something is unfair or that it would override someone's rights is a reason, though, in the latter case, not necessarily a decisive reason, for saying that it is unjust. It is, however, incorrect to believe, as Nozick apparently does, that something is unfair and unjust, only if it violates someone's rights. It may not violate someone's rights if a person does not get a certain thing but it may nonetheless be unjust, for another reason. Indeed another reason for saying something is unjust is that people are not treated as they deserve to be. Suppose that I have my own business and I wish to hire a lawyer to take care of the legal matters arising from my business. Suppose A and B both apply for the job and that A is more able than B, that he has worked very hard to qualify himself for the job, has gone to night school at great sacrifice; while B, who always has had a golden spoon in his mouth, has remained well off and is rather a loafer, but still minimally meets the specified qualifications for the job. Suppose, though I am fully in possession of these facts and do not question them, I still prefer to hire B and do in fact hire B. Suppose I, for no assignable reason, just happen to like him better, though it is not the case that I dislike A. It appears at least as if my preference is not very rational but all the same I have not violated A's rights in hiring B instead of A. But all that notwithstanding, I have, though acting within my rights, treated A unfairly and thus unjustly in not hiring him if I agree that he is the more competent of the two and recognize that he clearly is the more deserving candidate. Violating someone's rights is not the only way of treating someone unjustly, and someone can act within his/her rights and still act unjustly. A just person would, where other things were equal, hire the candidate who most deserved the job. Still, in normal circumstances, I do not violate A's rights in not hiring him, though I do treat him unjustly.

Similarly, if A, through inheritance, gains a fortune he has done nothing to deserve, while others, in other ways no different than A, have nothing, that state of affairs is, *ceteris paribus,* unjust. If one of them is B, then it is unfair, at least on the face of it, that A has all that wealth and B has nothing. Still people, if they legitimately own property, have, in many circumstances, a right to make a gift of that property. Again, if they make that gift, no rights need be, or typically would be, violated; but, to repeat, that is not the only relevant consideration in judging the justice of a distribution. That "some people have more than others, without deserving it, also counts against the justice of the distribution."[7]

There are competing claims for what is just here, with their competing rationales, and it is perhaps not evident in this last under-described case which claim or which reason is the more stringent, but what is evident is (1) we cannot conclude from the fact that a given distribution D is just, that, if G arises from D, by a process in which no one's rights were violated, that G is therefore also just; and (2) that a relevant reason for the claim that a distribution is just (unjust) is that it is deserved (undeserved). However, with respect to (2), we should also not forget that that relevant reason *may* be outweighed in a particular circumstance by some other more stringent reason. Sometimes that more stringent reason may be a claim about needs and sometimes it may have to do with people's rights, though, again, neither of these reasons are always overriding.

By what general criterion, if any, do we make judgments of desert? Rachels claims that "the basis of all desert is a person's own past action."[8] It must, however, be an action which is done knowingly and without coercion. What one deserves depends, Rachels claims, on what one has done and what one will do. If A and B are competing for a promotion and if A has worked more diligently, efficiently, and effectively than B and has been more willing than B to do a greater share of the work, helping out when there have been difficulties when B has not, then A is more deserving of the promotion than B, though, of course, other reasons may in a particular circumstance outweigh considerations of desert. What we can say is that, if other things are equal, since A deserves the promotion more than B, A rather than B ought to have it and that it would, in such a circumstance, be unjust to give it to B rather than A.

III

Going back now to what in effect are Hampshire's and Rawls' arguments, it is natural to ask, as Rachels does, if a person does not deserve things "in virtue of being naturally talented or intelligent or fortunate in some other way, how can he deserve things by working for them?"[9]

In a key passage Rachels gives his answer and with that answer his grounds for claiming that past actions are the *only* bases of desert.

> A fair amount of our dealings with other people involves holding them responsible, formally or informally, for one thing or another. It is unfair to hold people responsible for things over which they have no control. People have no control over their native endowments—over how smart, or athletic, or beautiful they naturally are—and so we may not hold them responsible for those things. They are, however, in control of (at least some of) their own actions, and so they may rightly be held responsible for the situations they create, or allow to exist, by their voluntary behavior. But those are the only things for which they may rightly be held responsible. The concept of desert serves to signify the ways of treating people that are appropriate responses to them, given that they are responsible for those actions or states of affairs. That is the role played by desert in our moral vocabulary. And, as ordinary language philosophers used to like to say, if there weren't such a term, we'd have to invent one. Thus the explanation of why past actions are the only bases of desert connects with the fact that if people were never responsible for their own conduct—if hard determinism were true— no one would ever deserve anything, good or bad.[10]

Recall that "deserts may be positive or negative, that is, a person may deserve to be treated well or badly," punished or rewarded.[11] For things over which we have control—and some of us at least have some control over some things—we may be held responsible without unfairness. We have control over some of our own actions in a way we do not have over our natural endowments or our *initial* social position or class, and we can thus be held responsible for them and some of the things that flow from them. It is because of this that they, and they alone, give us the basis for making ascriptions of desert. Thus we may deserve things, say special benefits, by working for them in the way we cannot deserve them by simply being naturally talented, intelligent or lucky.

Still we might wonder how it can be that if a person does not deserve anything on account of his intelligence or natural abilities, he can deserve anything on account of his willingness to work, his steadfast industriousness. Isn't Rawls plainly correct in treating as thoroughly problematic the claim that "a man deserves the superior character that enables him to make the effort to cultivate his abilities"?[12] His character, no matter what it is like, is not something which he initially determined or indeed could have initially determined. Due to circumstances beyond his control, he may be a person endowed with the sort of character in virtue of which he will make the effort, but, equally, he may, again through circumstances beyond his control, be the sort of person who will not make the effort. Which sort of person he is "depends," as Rawls puts it, "in large part upon fortunate family and social circumstances for which he can claim no credit."[13]

Rachels tries to meet this objection by first pointing out that people deserve the rewards they get not on account of their willingness to work but "only on account of their actually having worked."[14] *The bases of the desert is not a character trait of any kind; the basis of the desert is only the person's past actions.* It may be that not everyone has the capacity for hard work but there are, among those who have that capacity, some who choose to work hard and others who could so choose but who do not. All the members of this class—the class that has the capacity for hard work—are *able* to strive conscientiously. Some members of this class *choose* to strive conscientiously and some do not. The first group deserve some special consideration that the second does not. The first group are the ones more deserving of success and promotion.

Still, whether or not a person will actually make these choices depends, at least in the final analysis, on circumstances beyond his control. If he has one kind of character, he will and if he has another kind of character he won't. However, as J. S. Mill remarked, our characters are not entirely set for us and, at least sometimes some of us, within limits, can, if we will, in certain respects alter our characters. Those of us fortunate enough to be in such circumstances, and within those limits, can alter our characters and so it makes sense to hold us, to some degree, responsible for them. Because of this, we are, for good or for ill, deserving of punishment or reward for at least some of the things we choose to do. Still (a) whether we have the will to make such choices is not in our control and (b) whether we have a character which we can in any significant sense alter is also not in our control. This being so, can we ultimately be said to deserve anything we get as a result of our past actions?

This can be an unsettling question, but we should in this context remember the rather common-sense consideration that working is simply using whatever assets we happen to have. It is this distinctive feature of work which may explain how the concept of desert is tied to work in the way it is not tied to intelligence or talents.

Desert and entitlement, as Feinberg, Nozick, and Sterba have stressed, are distinct.[15] Yet, if we ask why people ought to be treated according to their deserts, we will come to see their close relation. The reason why a conscientious worker ought to be "promoted is precisely that he has earned the promotion by working for it."[16] In earning it, he is entitled to it. Rachels remarks of this: it "is a full and sufficient justification for promoting him, which does not require supplementation of any sort. If we want to ask why he should be treated in that way, that is the answer. It is not easy to see what else, by way of justification, is required."[17]

Still, as Rachels himself points out, justification need not come to an end here.[18] If we value, as most people do, at least in theory, the treating of people as autonomous beings, we can point out that it is plainly true that treating people as they deserve to be treated is a way of treating them as autonomous beings who, being autonomous, are responsible for their own conduct. We, by so viewing human beings, see them as responsible agents meriting approval or resentment.[19] In so viewing people, we must come to recognize that they deserve certain things and do not deserve others. And unless other more stringent considerations override these considerations, an injustice occurs if people do not get what they deserve.

To say that desert never matters, that we should jettison the whole notion, would be to "leave all of us impotent to earn the good treatment and other benefits which others have to bestow, and this would deprive us of the ability to control our own destinies as social beings."[20] To drop the concept of desert from our universe of moral discourse would also be to deprive ourselves of our conception of ourselves as autonomous moral agents who can actively and intelligently intervene in the world and who can sometimes shape our own destinies with intelligence and foresight. But is that comforting moral picture enough to sustain such a conception if in reality it is myth-eaten? But is it myth-eaten? Do we, Hampshire and Hayek to the contrary notwithstanding, even have any tolerably clear conception of what it means to say that it is?

IV

Note that Rachels has in effect attempted to provide an answer to Hampshire's rhetorical question, whether there is anything a person, strictly speaking can claim credit for or properly be said to deserve. Quite simply, Rachels argues, one can, as an autonomous agent, claim credit for what one has done in the past and what one is doing now. Whether that credit should be granted depends on what one has done or is doing and with what intentions. It can justifiably be attributed to him, in Hampshire's words, as an ultimate subject, if he is a rational person who has the ability and the opportunity to do the thing in question and does it because, all things considered, he wants to do it, when the "all things considered" include a reflective second-order desire (a desire which takes another desire as its object) to act in accordance with what it is he wants to do.[21] If these conditions obtain and the person in question is in a rational frame of mind, this remains true no matter what other causal stories we tell or how firmly we remain in the determinist camp. This remains true even though we accept unblinkingly that in the last analysis all advantages and disadvantages—our rationality, our capacity for choice, our self-control, the innermost niches of our personality—are determined by natural causes. (No doubt "natural causes" is pleonastic.)

The issues that divide those determinists who are incompatibilists (hard-determinists) and those who are compatibilists (soft-determinists) surface here. Determinists, of all stripes, believe that for every event and for every action there are antecedent sufficient causes. For any event or action there is a temporally prior set of occurrences and conditions sufficient for the occurrence of that event or action. This is, as J. L. Mackie has argued, an empirical thesis and not a presupposition of science. Determinism would be falsified "if there were two antecedent situations which were alike in all relevant respects but had different outcomes."[22]

Neither hard nor soft-determinists will claim to have established determinism if they are at all sensible. We certainly do not know if it holds for all or even most human actions. Yet its denials are very mysterious indeed and, quantum particles apart, determinism seems a reasonable and to many a quite compelling assumption to make. Still, it is important to keep firmly in mind Mackie's point that it should be viewed as an empirical thesis, open to confirmation and disconfirmation. "We make," as Mackie puts it, "progress towards confirming it in so far as we find what appear to be satisfactory causal explanations of more and more kinds of occurrence."[23]

Hard-determinists (incompatibilists) believe that if determinism is true, freedom is an illusion and that in the deepest sense we can never be justified in blaming or punishing anyone or holding anyone responsible for what they do or for rewarding anyone or for claiming that they are truly deserving (or for that matter non-deserving) of anything. Such vocabulary cannot, they claim, have anything other than some limited pragmatic sense, if determinism is true.

Soft-determinists (compatibilists), by contrast, while remaining as firmly deterministic as hard-determinists, believe that the dispute over whether we ever act as free and responsible moral agents has nothing to do with the controversies over the truth or falsity of determinism. We are free if we are rational creatures who have the ability and the opportunity to do what we want to do and can reflect on our desires dispassionately and form reflective second-order desires about what to do and then can in fact, in accordance with both our first-order and second-order desires, do what we, on reflection, most want to do.[24] Where by contrast we act under constraint or compulsion, are driven by forces we cannot understand and in any way control, we are unfree. The opposite of freedom is not determinism but compulsion or constraint. And it is something which admits of degrees. We are free to the extent that we can reflectively assess our desires and then act on those desires which are not extinguished by such reflection. Determinism or no determinism, we have, in varying degrees, this rational capacity and we have, again in varying degrees, the ability and sometimes the opportunity, to act on those desires, and to that extent—an extent which will vary from person to person and from society to society—

we are free. Under optimum conditions this extent can be considerable and it can be indefinitely extended; all this can obtain, soft-determinists (compatibilists) argue, in a perfectly deterministic universe.

Hard-determinists (incompatibilists) will respond that this does not push the question far enough, for it still does not face the question of the determination of our wants, including our second-order reflective wants and our rational capacities to act on our wants and to take the most effective means to achieve what we on reflection desire. People's capacities vary considerably here. Many of us can be rather self-defeating in this respect and there are Dostoevskian undergroundlings who are both extremely intelligent and extremely perverse and self-destructive. We need to ask whether all of the following are determined by factors (genetic, otherwise variously biological, environmental and most of all by early conditioning or socialization) over which we have no control: (a) *what* we want to do, (b) whether we have the ability or opportunity to do what we want to do, (c) whether what we want to do is done in accordance with our reflective second-order desires or volitions.

It is not unnatural to believe that when we reflect on this and take it to heart, we will hardly give much moral weight to questions of desert, to reward or to blame, if we can be dispassionately rational. Whether we act rationally and fairly or perversely and immorally will, if determinism is true, be determined by factors, some of which are beyond our control. And this will remain true even if, à la Harry Frankfurt and David Zimmerman, we accept an hierarchical account of motivation.[25] Some people can, by reflecting on their actions and taking this reflection to heart, alter their behavior in significant ways and come to act as generous principled human beings, and others can be usefully affected by various normative pressures such as praise or blame; but others will go on in their perverse, irrational or largely amoralist ways. The point, hard-determinists insist, is not just to note those varying abilities and opportunities but steadfastly to recognize that whether we have them or not, whether we can make the effort to change them or not, and with what success, is determined by factors beyond our control. Whether we can pull ourselves up by our own bootstraps is a matter of our own good or ill fortune.

Even if strict determinism does not hold but there is, as Mackie puts it, "some close approximation to it," it is reasonable to believe that our early conditioning, our environment—physical and cultural— and our biological inheritance, are all deeply determining factors in the kind of persons we are and will develop into. With such an understanding, talk of desert and merit will have a hollow moral ring. Perhaps in some narrowly pragmatic sense it is necessary to keep such conceptions to ward off, "the war of all against all," but this will be a matter of what is perhaps a morally justified expediency, but it will not carry the deep moral conviction that some really deserve to be punished for their wickedness or tardiness and others rewarded for their virtue or conscientiousness.

In thinking about the just distribution of economic benefits and burdens according to desert, in arguing that achievement and work done justify departures from an equality of benefits and burdens, where— let us assume—a fair equality of opportunity has been established, we need to keep firmly in mind that, given different innate endowments and a different socialization, there will be different levels of achievement. Perhaps this means that our assumption is unrealistic and that we can never achieve fair equality of opportunity. Whatever we want to say about that, do we not have reason to believe that there will be different levels of achievement which are determined by, if determinism is true, causal inputs some of which cannot be controlled by the individuals affected? And in any event, whether determinism is true or not, are not these levels of achievement still largely determined by conditions that cannot be controlled by the individuals affected? How then can they be rightly held responsible for them or justly receive rewards for their achievement? That A can pull himself up by his own bootstraps and B cannot is determined by, or at least strongly conditioned by, factors that neither A nor B can control. That one person makes the effort and succeeds, another makes the effort and fails and still another cannot even make the effort, is determined by factors that the individuals in question do not, and cannot, control. Where then is the justice of holding them responsible for their actions or the justice of distributing benefits and burdens according to achievement or work done? Justice cannot, we are inclined to say when we reflect on that, be giving everyone what they deserve.

V

It is considerations such as these that give force to Rawls' and Hampshire's claims about desert, though perhaps here I have put in the mouth of the hard-determinist a stronger response than anything Hampshire, let alone Rawls, would wish to make. Still it appears at least as if such a response is strongly rationally and morally motivated. Yet there remains, as there always is with a deeply entrenched philosophical conception, another side to the story, another twist to the dialectic. After reflecting on the arguments of the previous sections, we will still very likely feel compelled to respond, as we are likely to feel compelled to respond to Rawls and Hampshire on desert: "But doesn't what we do, what we strive our utmost to achieve, count for anything?" A hard-determinist picture or any picture that leaves desert out of account must be demeaning, dehumanizing, alienating: it cannot but be a view of life which will, for a reflective and sensitive person convinced by it, be undermining of his self-respect, the very good which Rawls takes to be the chief human good. Here Nozick's remarks about Rawls are apposite:

So denigrating a person's autonomy and prime responsibility for his actions is a risky line to take for a theory that otherwise wishes to buttress the dignity and self-respect of autonomous beings; especially for a theory that founds so much (including a theory of the good) upon a person's choices. One doubts that the unexalted picture of human beings Rawls' theory presupposes and rests upon can be made to fit together with the view of human dignity it is designed to lead to and embody.[26]

Yet, how can we, ostrich-like—again touching on, from a different angle, a matter of human dignity—not accept such an account when we face non-evasively the plausibility of determinism and the facts of our genetic make up, conditioning and socialization? Our most paradigmatic intentional actions—the actions we are most unproblematically said to be responsible for—are both the object of and the causal product of the same desire; and that desire, as all desires, has causes and these causes still further causes, causes which must finally be external to the agent. We should not only heed Nozick's remarks here but Mackie's as well when he remarks that the "facts have to be determined by empirical evidence, and our thinking has then to conform to the facts, not the facts to our thinking."[27] Whatever we say about the "is and the ought," a normative ethical theory which must require, for its viability, a false or an incoherent account of what the facts are cannot, no matter how attractive and encouraging to our hopes that theory is, be an adequate moral theory. The thing we need to ask is about the truth or the comparative plausibility of what Nozick calls the "unexalted picture of human beings Rawls' theory presupposes" and hard-determinism makes quite explicit.

What soft-determinists have tried to do, and what Rachels tries to do, is to develop a picture of responsibility and desert which is compatible with determinism and clearly shows that we do not need to be driven to hard-determinism. One way is to argue, as Mackie does, that we have no need for any conception of "absolute freedom" or "ultimate responsibility" "which is transferred backwards along causal chains, and which would therefore escape to infinity if we accepted a strict causal determinism."[28] Such a view, Mackie claims, presupposes the incoherent Kantian conception of a noumenal self, "the incoherent demand that the 'I' should be able to make that same 'I,' itself at that moment, different from what it is," a belief in an "absolute identity of persons through time" and a commitment to an objective prescriptivity.

It seems to me that this move is too easy. I do not see that the hard-determinist worries require any such commitments. The difficulties for desert-based conceptions of justice I have been considering, as well as the difficulties Rawls and Hampshire bring to the fore, do not require any of these conceptions and could very well rest on a thoroughly naturalistic account of man and morality.[29] What it does rest on is (1) taking determinism seriously and (2) reflecting carefully on the sources of character formation.[30]

What might remain as a recalcitrant suspicion here is the hunch that the hard-determinist, in arguing as he does, must be operating with some, perhaps unacknowledged and implicit, conception of "*ultimate* responsibility" and a linked conception of desert. The thing to do, the compatibilist could plausibly claim, is to proceed, as Rachels does, with humdrum workaday conceptions and show that they will enable us to say everything we want to say without making any appeal to "ultimate responsibility," without rejecting determinism and without raising any of the issues I have discussed in the last two sections.

Whatever we should say about the conditions of character formation and socialization, we have a reason in most job situations to promote someone who has worked hard and we do not have a similar reason (a desert-based reason) to promote someone who has not. Whatever the truth about character formation and determinism, such striving is, in most contexts, though surely not all, an admirable human trait. It isn't puritanism but a fair-mindedness that sees a value in earning one's own way and doing one's own share and sees disvalue in freeloading. If a department has only one graduate fellowship left to give out and only two candidates to choose from, A and B, and A is hard working, brighter than B and more likely to make a greater contribution to his discipline than B, while B is both less talented and rather lazy, A deserves the fellowship more than B; and, if other things are equal, justice requires that A get it rather than B. The same thing obtains, even in an altered circumstance in which the only relevant difference between A and B is that A *has* worked harder than B. And indeed the same judgment would remain in place, even if we knew that if B received a fellowship he would mend his ways and come to work as hard as A. But A still ought to get the fellowship rather than B. This reflects how much moral weight we give in determining desert, and through desert the fair thing to do, both to effort and to what one has actually done. Moreover, this is a considered conviction that moral reflection and a knowledge of psychology would not extinguish.

Note in making these rather firmly held judgments—backed by considered judgments, and indeed, as far as I can see, considered judgments in wide reflective equilibrium—these judgments are made without making any commitments about determinism and can, and should, be readily made in a recognition that A's and B's desires are as equally causally determined as are everyone's, if determinism is true, and are not finally determined by conditions and occurrences they could possibly control or even influence. But that condition they share equally with all humankind, yet there still are differences between A and B in virtue of which we are, in normal circumstances, justified in asserting that it is just that A receive the fellowship rather than B, because A deserves it more. In making ascriptions of desert, we should not ask what makes people what they are but simply ask (a) about what they have done and likely will do and the value of that, and (b) consider what effort or lack thereof has gone into what they have done.

It is a common considered judgment of hard-determinists and soft-determinists alike that it is unfair to hold people responsible for things over which they have no control. People, on any reasonable theory, plainly have no control over their native endowments; but, on any account, it is the case that they at least sometimes have some control over some of their own actions and dispositions. We cannot properly ascribe desert to people for things over which they have no control, because they are not things for which they could properly be said to be morally responsible. But where people have control over their own actions, as they sometimes do, they can be held responsible for these actions and ascriptions of desert can reasonably be made concerning these actions. And it is in fact the case, hard-determinism to the contrary notwithstanding, that sometimes people do have control over their own actions. (What the proper analysis of this is is a difficult matter, but the crucial consideration here is that they sometimes in fact have such control over their actions. This is a given for analysis.) Moreover, we will want to make such ascriptions, if we are clear-headed and reasonable, because we need a rationale, once basic needs are equally met, to have reasonable grounds for awarding scarce benefits when not all can have them.[31] This need for a rationale remains in the face of determinism and its probing picture of human socialization and conditioning. But this is precisely what we found when we recognized the above relevant differences between A and B, the truth of determinism notwithstanding. Such differences provide us with a ground, a much needed ground, to give the fellowship to A rather than B. That ground is in what A did and the effort he made. This only works on the assumption that his actions were under his control in the way his intelligence, general appearance, strength, initial social position are not.

The hard-determinist will challenge this on two grounds: he will (1) assert that in the last analysis none of these things are under our own control, that is to say, neither what we will do, the effort we will make, our social situation nor our native endowment are under our control, and (2) and more proximately, he will contend that there is only a difference in degree between the control that people have over their actions and the control they have over their endowments and their class position. Our first acts are not very much more in our control than are our starting I.Q., strength, weight or social position. Moreover, we can gain or lose weight, become more or less athletic, sometimes shift our social class or social position and perhaps even alter our intelligence. Yet the initial determining conditions for these things— things which must be *sufficient* to bring them about—are all external to us and beyond our control.

The question returns like the repressed; how can we be said to be responsible for some of these things and not for others? If we say we are responsible for them all, we must assign desert a much wider role than we would usually, on reflection, want to. Alternatively, if we are responsible for none of them, then responsibility becomes a Holmesless Watson and desert drops out entirely. As Rachels puts it himself, "*if* people were never responsible for their own conduct . . . no one would ever deserve anything, good or bad."[32] That a person is industrious, that he actually works, as well as being willing to work, is determined by a chain of causes of which some of the earlier are external to him and not under his control. We say that certain past actions occurred which justify our saying that A deserves the promotion and B does not. A and B have had the same opportunities but A's actions were different than B's because of A's industriousness. But Rachels agrees that we cannot rightly say that that character trait or any other was deserved. The desert-base is rather, he argues, the relevant *action*. But, if determinism is true, it is also true that the relevant actions of A, which are distinct from those of B, occurred because of A's industriousness. They (or most of them) would not have occurred if the industriousness were not there; but, if that is the case, then such actions can no more justify the desert than the character trait, for the actions were the causally inevitable result of character traits and a character trait is not something which is in A's control, since they result from external determining conditions that A could not have controlled. (Is this true? Is it not sometimes possible for a person to alter conditions which in turn will alter his personality?) Whether A in the past, present or future will or will not do certain things depends ultimately on circumstances which are beyond his control. (How crucial is this the qualifier "ultimately" here?)

However, all that notwithstanding, plainly some people have a capacity to make something of their lives and some do not. Still, whether or not they have this capacity is determined by conditions some of which are external to them. Even when we are considering only those who are able to strive conscientiously, it remains the case that they, as well as those who cannot so act, still have causes, exterior to themselves, over which they have no control which occasion that behavior. Perhaps by rewards and punishments, we can condition people who in the past have not been industrious to behave more industriously in the future, but that is different from holding them responsible for their past actions, which must have been the result of a chain of sufficient conditions the earlier members of which they could not have controlled and which, if determinism is true, are causally sufficient for the occurrence of the later members. There are indeed non-culturally deprived, rational people, some of whom choose to work hard and others do not. But their choices are themselves determined, if determinism is true, by conditions some of which are external to them and which they do not, and indeed cannot, have under their control. Industriousness can indeed be developed but whether it will be developed is determined by conditions external to the agent. Industriousness (willingness to work) may be, as Rachels remarks, a "super-asset" essential for all others, but it is still an asset, like all other assets, in having initial determining conditions beyond the control of the agent who is fortunate enough to have this super-asset.[33]

However, if we drop all ascriptions of desert, this would deprive us, it could be argued, of our ability to control our destinies as social and moral beings. If it is generally recognized that people cannot properly be said to be deserving of anything whatsoever, if they cannot properly be held responsible for what they do, then they also cannot intelligibly be regarded as autonomous, moral beings or as rational agents in control of their own lives. To drop ascriptions of desert is to drop, as well, where the matter is thought out, ascriptions of moral agency and any kind of normative conception of our own humanness. (Is this really so manifestly the case? Moral agency, autonomy, and rational agency would not come to all of what it means to us, but it is not so clear that these concepts would have no sense.)

Clearly something must have gone wrong in the hard-determinist analysis, for there are in reality differences between people both with respect to their rationality and in the degree of control they exercise over their own lives. There are quite unproblematical, important and obvious differences in degree here. There are differences resulting from class differences, differences between people in different regions of the world, differences caused by different sex role identifications and from individual psychological differences as well. There are plainly people who have been so physically deprived, say from severe early malnutrition, and/or so culturally deprived, say from severe poverty or from mind-numbing work, that they are no longer able to make anything of their lives. Prisons and reform schools often do this to people. There are all sorts of cripples, psychological and otherwise, and the extent to which, in some plain ways, their autonomy is impaired is sometimes tolerably evident. But it is also evident that some people have far more control over their own lives than others and it is only a little less obvious that some life-styles are more autonomous than others. It is also the case, and relatedly, that some ways of organizing society make for greater autonomy than others. Yet all human behavior, if determinism is true, is equally determined; the same story in each case can and should be told about how actions and choices result from determining conditions (causes sufficient for their occurrence) some of which are beyond the person's control. Yet some people exhibit, in a quite unproblematic sense, more autonomy, more rationality, and more re-sponsibility than others and this in a way that is, in part at least, distinct from our talk of their behavior being determined.[34] For one thing their autonomy admits of degrees while it makes no sense to say that something is more or less determined. It is either determined or it is not. Again soft-determinism begins to look plausible and again it looks as if there may be a reasonable place for talk of justice and desert.

There are some related considerations which further support such a compatibilist account and which also support the finding of some place for considerations of desert in reflecting on arguments about what is and is not just. My previous remarks have made it sound as if conditioning always diminished and could never enhance our autonomy. But conditioning—a certain kind of socialization—can make us more autonomous than we otherwise would be. Acting on one's choices is not sufficient to attain autonomy. If we could rid our world of sex discrimination tomorrow, still a not inconsiderable number of women would continue, at least for a time, to choose to remain in dependent and subordinate roles to males. On *simple* soft-determinist conceptions of freedom, they would be acting freely because they would be doing what they wanted to do, what they, without coercion or constraint, chose to do. Indeed some of them would have deliberated first and consciously put their first-order desires in line with their second-order desires. Still they could have consciously opted for domesticity and an auxiliary status. They would characteristically have reasons for their choices and they could correctly be said to have acted upon them rather than to have acted impulsively or thoughtlessly. So in a plain way they would be said to have acted both rationally and freely. Yet, given the distinctive socialization of our sexist (male-dominated) societies, we will not regard such behavior, such rigid sex role following, as fully autonomous or fully rational. Such choices are not enlightened choices or marks of emancipation. Women making such choices exercise less control over their lives than they otherwise could.

Autonomy is not just the freedom to do what you want to do, it also is closely linked with rationality, with, that is, a self-understanding, an enlightened attitude and an ability to look critically at one's desires and preferences and to not being a slave to convention or to a doing of the thing done. Again this is something which always is a matter of degree, but we acquire greater autonomy as we learn to scrutinize critically the values—the mores—we have acquired through our socialization, though notice that this itself is a further, and liberating, socialization. We must, as Irving Thalberg well puts it, "have learned from someone to question folkways and received opinions."[35] It is the acquiring of a critical tradition but it is also something which is liberating and gives us greater autonomy. To have this to any considerable extent is to have the ability to assess rival ideologies, to see how much ideology there is in one's own society and, with a reasonable store of vital information, to be able critically to assess this deeply embedded ideology. We can hardly be doing any of these things without also scrutinizing our dominant attitudes and other reasons for action.

The regular exercising of a capacity for critical assessment required for full autonomy—something which may only be a heuristic ideal—goes beyond a scrutinizing of our dominant attitudes to the attainment of a clear understanding of our very situation, something which itself necessitates a critical understanding and assessment of rival ideologies. Such an ability, even in politically or religiously coercive situations, creates for individuals, who have gained such an awareness, a wider array of options, and such people are plainly freer—determinism or no determinism—than people who do not have such a wider array of options.

I am not claiming that it is natural for people to become autonomous. My belief is that autonomy arises from complex and culturally distinctive forms of socialization that are themselves explicable along determinist lines; but a recognition of this, hard-determinism to the contrary notwithstanding, does nothing to diminish autonomy. We see rather how the conditioning that goes with socialization can be liberating, if it is a certain sort and occurs in certain circumstances. The cases that have previously been focussed on—the ones hard-determinists stress—are indeed fettering. But the above reflections on socialization show how it also can be autonomy-making in certain fortunate circumstances. The sex role conditioning that has led women to choose and indeed in a plain sense want to be, in some instances even reflectively to want to be, in conditions of dependence and subservience where their very identity is derived from their husbands, is a conditioning which undermines personal initiative, the ability to control one's own life, and thus to be autonomous. This results from a conditioning for heteronomy. But there can be conditioning for autonomy as well. We can make fettering choices as well as liberating ones; in doing what we want, we do not always act autonomously because sometimes in doing what we want we close off an awareness of alternatives, including an awareness of a range of identities we could otherwise have chosen from, i.e., the different people we might have become. By doing what we want, given a certain socialization, we can limit our options, thus lessening our freedom. That is what women who opt for *kinder, küche, kirche* do. But in a society normatively characterized as truly human the socialization would go in the opposite direction. It would unlock options and enhance self-direction and thus autonomy.

Autonomy, to be full-fledged, does require being able generally to do what you want to do where that doesn't harm others, but what you want to do must also be what you reflectively would want to do when your knowledgeability had scrutinized your wants and had a vivid awareness of and a capacity to reflectively choose from a full range of alternatives and when your choice was such that it would increase your control over your own life; i.e., your actions would be more self-determined, reflecting your own initiative and a greater control over your own affairs. (I do not mean here, in stressing individual self-determination, to opt for individualism. An autonomous person is a self-directed person with a sense of his own identity, but this does not exclude human solidarity, cooperation, reciprocity, and trust.)

A hard-determinist might respond that this self-determination is impossible, if determinism is true, for no matter what you do there are sufficient conditions for your doing it which are external to you and over which you have no control. It is, as Holbach argued long ago, our ignorance of or our own failure to take notice of the causal chains that link our present behavior with the past that gives us the persistent illusion of self-direction.

If we are determinists, there can be no denying such causal chains, though it does not follow from that that we must assent to talk about "the illusion of self-direction," but it is still false to deny that many women, and indeed many men as well, would be far more independent than they are now were it not for their sex role conditioning. No matter what is the case about determinism, women who are socialized to depend on men, to find their identity in a husband and who are so conditioned that they can find "fulfillment" only in devotion to him, to his career and to what they think of as his offspring, have less self-direction and control over their own lives than women who have a profession, have a sense of their own identity and can find fulfillment both in their own achievements and in activities with others without male or parental dominance. This latter group of women have a greater control over their own lives and thus are more autonomous.

This is the proper contrast between autonomous behavior and heteronomous behavior. This is a specification in a certain context of what it is to act autonomously, to be self-directive. There actually are such differences in the styles of life of people and this is not touched by the fact (if it is a fact, as I believe it is) that on both sides of that contrast the lifestyles that people have sufficient conditions for their occurrence over which the agents in question have no control. Both autonomous and heteronomous lifestyles have such sufficient conditions. But we can see concretely, in the contrastive situation I have characterized, which are more autonomous and which are less autonomous ways of living. This can be readily generalized and extrapolated to other situations. And accepting this distinction, and accepting the fact that, even in societies such as ours, some people have some autonomy and that some people have more autonomy than others, no position need be taken on the coherence, truth, or probable truth of determinism. Even in a completely deterministic universe such autonomy could be in place.

VI

What does such a specification of autonomy—a specification compatible with compatibilism—imply for justice and desert? First, and negatively, it would appear at least to weaken the claim that if we drop ascriptions of desert our autonomy would be undermined. Our unpacking of autonomy went on without reference to desert. The key note to the concept of autonomy was rational (enlightened, emancipated) self-direction. Our autonomy is tied up with control of our own lives, with rationality, self-awareness, self-control, responsibility, a clear under-standing of our situation, the making of enlightened choices, eman-cipation, moral sensitivity, acquiring a critical tradition, having an awareness of the ways ideologies work and having the ability not to be captivated by them, having a wide awareness of human and social options and having the capacity reflectively to choose between those options. The stress here plainly is not on desert. Only the concept of responsibility makes any clear link with desert: a link to the social practices of reward and blame.

With autonomy, as I have characterized it, the link with responsibility, which is only one feature of autonomy among many, is more with the stress on seeing oneself as a self-directive being who takes responsibility for his/her own life. There is no need at all in talking about autonomy to consider punishment or holding someone responsible or rewarding him for his responsibility or giving him his due because he has been responsible and has done what he is supposed to do and made his contribution. All this talk, and the social practices that go with it, could drop out, and there still would be a place for autonomy and responsibility as I have, nonstipulatively and non-arbitrarily, charac-terized them.

To claim that if talk of justice in terms of desert goes, our autonomy will be undermined with it, unless we are massively self-deceived, is, perhaps, quite parallel to saying that if talk of sin and a sense of sin goes we will no longer, unless we are massively self-deceived, have any sense that anything is through and through morally wrong and not to be done. But that, as the development of our moral sense shows, is plainly wrong. There are plenty of people with an acute sense of moral evil and a capacity to stand against it who regard talk of sin as little more than a carryover from a superstitious age. What I am suggesting is that an acknowledgement of autonomy, a prizing of it, and an ability to achieve it, might be quite in place even for someone who had jettisoned the concept of desert or for whom it played no crucial place in his moral universe. This is implicit in the explication I gave in the previous section on autonomy and in the listing of some of its key elements which I have above.

To be autonomous we must be self-directive and in control of our own destinies and have a sense of what it is to have a destiny. This would require besides self-awareness, an awareness of one's situation, self-control, and an ability to see through the idols of one's tribe and other tribes as well. It would involve an awareness of many options and a capacity to make several of them one's own, if one chose to do so. But it would also involve an understanding of what it is to have a destiny, and this would involve a moral sensitivity, a sense of what a human life could come to be and what it was to give or to find a sense in life. Thus we could hardly in any very full sense attain autonomy without having some considerable moral understanding and without having the capacity to respond as a sensitive moral being. But desert, talk of rewards and punishments, and getting one's due need not have any place, or at least any prominent place, in an understanding of what it is for us to be autonomous beings and to live in a society where autonomy is respected.

What I am saying could readily be misunderstood. We could not have an autonomous society in which people could not properly be said to be deserving of anything at all. They must in such a society be respected as moral beings, members of a kingdom of ends, whose rights are respected and whose basic needs are met, where this is possible, and whose condition of life is an object of concern. They must, in an autonomous society, be treated as beings deserving of being treated as persons. They must, that is, be taken to be members of a Kantian kingdom of ends. But this does not entail that we have the social practice of punishment or that we distribute economic or other benefits as a reward for desert. This may be a desirable thing to do but it is not clear that justice requires it, much less that our moral autonomy would be undermined were that social practice not in place.

The second point to consider is this: we have developed a compatibilist account of autonomy. Even in a completely deterministic universe there is, if such an account is on the mark, a coherent distinction between autonomous and non-autonomous behavior. Some people in certain circumstances of life are much more self-directed, have a far greater control over their lives than other people. Some are in a far better position to assume responsibility than others and do act with far greater self-direction and with more responsibility than others. Yet this is all quite compatible with determinism and, if determinism is true, their actions, desires, and volitions are all determined and indeed, to be pleonastic, equally determined.

This means that it is not conceptually incoherent, even if determinism is true, to make judgments of desert, to assert that because of so and so A deserves to have Z while B does not. We can say, that is, that A deserves to get the fellowship, and justice requires that he receive it, while B does not. That there is nothing incoherent in such talk does not mean, of course, that we should go on making such judgments and that we should continue using such moral conceptions. Perhaps, like the concept of sin for many of us, the concept of desert and getting your just deserts should drop out of our moral vocabulary and reflective moral thinking.

The question is, should it? I shall argue that it should have a place, though a rather reduced place, in our moral thinking. No human being can ultimately be responsible for being the sort of person he is. External factors—social and historical situation, class position, family and teachers as well as one's genetic inheritance and physical environment—combine in various ways to mold one into a particular kind of person.

Our wants (first-order and second-order), our second-order volitions, our rational capacities, our irrational and non-rational proclivities, our needs, our very human nature itself are all determined in the strict sense I have specified. There are conditions external to us which are sufficient to bring about all the things that we do and all the things that happen to us, so that if conditions of exactly that kind were to be repeated in exactly that type of situation things of exactly the same type as happened before would happen again. *What* we want to do, whether we can do what we want to do, whether what we want to do is in accordance with our reflective second-order desires and how ethnocentric and ideologically distorted our reflective second-order desires are, are all, like everything else, determined. Nonetheless, as we have seen, it is widely believed that we can claim credit—credit based on desert—for what we have done, are doing, for the effort we make, for our achievements and for our contribution to society. Justice requires that we get what is due to us, that we receive some kind of reward or notice for certain things that we have done, for certain intentional achievements on our part. (What, more exactly the proper form of reward or notice is will depend on the context and what it is we have done in what social setting.)

The determinist story we have sketched above, entails, if it is true, that whether we can do those things or not, or even make the effort to do them, is determined by external factors that are not, finally, in our control. There is a chain of causes the earlier members of which are sufficient conditions for what happens later and the earliest of these members must be conditions we do not control. In this way our behavior is controlled by external forces. Neither what we do nor the effort that we make are ultimately under our control. Yet, as we also have seen, some of us have greater autonomy than others and some act with more responsibility than others.

There is, however, an important ambiguity in the above remark that what we do is not under our own control. I have, with my explication of determinism, in effect shown the way in which no one could do otherwise than what he in fact does do. There is a very strong sense of "could"—a "no-one-could-ever-have-done-otherwise-than-he-did"-*could*—which hard-determinists have at the forefront of their minds and which is at work in the above determinist statements. But there is also a weaker, perfectly ordinary employment of "could" that soft-determinists usually have in mind, which is "the-possession-of-an-ability-plus-the-absence-of-duress"-*could*. It is at work in the following utterances: "Hans lectured on Kant but he could have lectured on Hume if he had chosen to," or "James stayed at home but he could have gone hiking if he had chosen to." To say here that someone could have done something is to give to understand that he had the ability, the opportunity and was not forced to do something else instead. In this way, many of us, in many situations, could have done otherwise than what we did in fact do, though this does not mean that we could have *categorically* done otherwise than what we in fact did. But what we do or the efforts we make are sometimes in our control in the sense that we do not do what we do under duress and we have the ability and opportunity to do something else instead. Thus I could have written here about moral obligation but I chose to write about desert. I have the ability to write about moral obligation, the opportunity is here and no one is forcing me to write about desert. In this perfectly mundane way I could have done otherwise than I did. Similarly it is possible that B could have worked as hard as A but the fact is he didn't. In such ways some people, perhaps everyone to some degree, have some things under their control. However, even though in that non-categorical way they could have done otherwise, it does not follow that they categorically could have done otherwise than they in fact did. That is to say, if exactly the same type of situation were presented to them again, then they would do just the same sort of thing again. (To say they could have learned from the experience of the first occasion is to say that it is not the exact same type of situation.) In that strong way, no one has anything under his control, if determinism is true. But this kind of not "having anything under your control" is very different from the situation and lack of control of the deeply neurotic individual who cannot even bring himself, no matter how much he wants to, to get out of his room and look for a job, in comparison to the situation of two other individuals, one of whom looked for a job and found one he likes and the other who could have looked for a job but simply preferred instead to live off the money his parents gave him. But they both, unlike the above neurotic, could have looked for a job, if they had wanted to and had chosen to, and they even could have chosen to in the same way I could have written about moral obligation if I had chosen to, and I could have chosen to if I had wanted to. Our neurotic is in a very different situation indeed. He wants to look for a job but is immobilized by unnamed fears and compulsions.

The difference between A, who studied hard for the fellowship and B who did not, might be very like that of the two non-neurotic chaps, one of whom preferred to look for a job and the other who did not. If it is (and it could be), there is a straightforward sense in which they both had their act under control and both could have done otherwise than what they did. A made the effort and studied hard and B did not, though they both had roughly the same abilities and same opportunities. Though they both had the capacity to make something of their lives, A chose to exercise that capacity in a way that B did not. They are both quite unlike a person so damaged by severe early malnutrition or by cultural deprivation or by psychosis or neurosis, that he cannot make anything of his life, cannot be self-directed. But these inabilities are not the result of determinism but of certain very distinctive socializing and conditioning factors, just as A's and B's abilities and opportunities to act in certain ways are the result of certain definite autonomy-making conditioning and socializing conditions.

There is an important sense in which at least some individuals in certain favorable social conditions, within certain parameters, can control their levels of achievement. What they will do, with what success and what efforts they will make, is partially, in a proximate way, in their own control. And their achievements can be affected by conditioning, by rewards and punishments, by instruction and by a "telling it like it is." For these individuals in such situations certain things are under their control and they can rightly claim credit for what they have done, are doing and for their effort and contribution. Thus if a high school student has worked hard and passed his final year's courses and exams, he deserves to get his diploma. To not give it to him would be unjust. A worker who has worked hard and met the work quotas deserves the extra week's vacation promised him. Anything else would be unjust. And concerning our two graduate students, A and B, who are the sole competitors for the only remaining fellowship, if A has higher qualifications than B, then, *ceteris paribus,* A deserves the fellowship and it would be unjust not to give it to him.

This last case is particularly apposite for the place of desert within a scheme of justice. When conditions of fair equality of opportunity have been met, or approximated as much as it is reasonable to expect that they can be approximated, then certain positions and the like, should, if more stringent moral considerations do not intervene, be given to the people who deserve them the most. It is, indeed, much more central in the design of just social institutions to aim for a state of affairs, under conditions of abundance, where the basic needs of everyone can be equally met. The aim of egalitarian justice is the equal well-being for all persons at the highest possible level of well-being. But in achieving that there will also be a place for desert. Without it the highest level of equal well-being could hardly be achieved.

This gives a real place, though a subordinate place, for considerations of desert in a scheme of justice. Justice is not just, or even primarily, getting what one deserves, but in a morally adequate scheme of social justice (a conception Hayek thinks makes no sense), we could not overlook or simply discount getting what one deserves, though in many circumstances getting what one deserves would be outweighed by other moral considerations, including other considerations of justice.

So, even in an utterly deterministic world, what we have accomplished through integrity, struggle and perseverence does count. We can rightfully claim credit for achievements and that credit must (morally speaking "must") be accorded where it is due, and indeed, under certain conditions, where certain things have been done to a certain effect, it is due. This is plainly a fair way to treat people—it squares with our considered judgments in wide reflective equilibrium—and it has an evident social utility and pragmatic validity as a device for dividing the surplus, after basic needs have been met, and for awarding positions such as jobs so that such distinctions will generally be in the interests of everyone alike. This is a plain, morally justifiable rationale for rewarding conscientiousness, achievement and contribution. There is a social value in doing one's share rather than freeloading and sometimes rewarding the desirable propensity and discouraging the undesirable one will increase the extent of the former and decrease the latter, and, where the people involved are free responsible agents, such a furthering of the general good is not unfair.

In making ascriptions of responsibility, it is crucial to determine whether the people of whom the ascriptions are made are autonomous agents and, roughly, to what degree. Where they are reasonably autonomous persons in situations where they can exercise their autonomy, we, in making ascriptions of desert, should not ask what makes these people what they are but ask instead (a) what they have done and likely will do and the value of that, and (b) consider what effort or lack thereof has gone into what they have done. Particularly when effort, achievement and contribution line up together, with achievement being the most central consideration, the persons in question exhibit desert and, where everything else is equal, justice requires that they receive their due reward.

However, considerations of desert should have, as I have remarked, a subordinate place in a scheme of social justice. The reasons that Rawls and Hampshire give for discounting desert are part of the reason as are the hard-determinist arguments about autonomy as well. And Hayek gives further, interestingly distinct, important reasons for such discounting. Still those of us whom genetic and social roulette have treated kindly do have a certain autonomy. Some of us more so than others—it is always a matter of degree. Some of us have, by that good fortune, some capacity to make something of our lives. Some of us, if we are very lucky, have achieved a rather considerable autonomy; we are part of a critical tradition, have a tolerably unblinkered appreciation of our situation, have developed a keen appreciation of ideological distortions, a reasonably clear-headed appreciation of our options and an ability to choose in a clear-headed and dispassionate way from among those options. But our having such an ability is itself not something that we can rightly claim credit for, anymore than we can claim credit for our native endowments or our starting social position. We are just very lucky indeed to be in such a situation. Others, with a whole range of lesser social and genetic fortunes, are less and less lucky as we go down the scale of that continuum. But our position here, whatever it is, is hardly anything for which any of us can reasonably claim credit. Hampshire's roulette metaphor is indeed an appropriate one.

When we see all this clearly and take it to heart, we will, I believe, be loath to give a high priority to desert in establishing just distributions.

Where abundance makes it possible "To each according to his needs" is much more attractive, as is a concern to provide equal conditions for freedom and development. But even in a world of incredible material abundance, where basic human needs, as well as what Brecht called "the little extras," are abundantly satisfied, there would still be—though there would be less of this—a scarcity of certain important and interesting positions—not everyone, for example could regularly make extensive T.V. commentaries. Desert seems a reasonable and a fair way of distributing these scarce positions, even if no one can take credit for the social and genetic start that made such abilities possible.

With a steadfast recognition of "the luck of the draw" with these endowments, we should see, if our concern is with justice, these abilities more, though still not entirely, as social assets. With such an awareness, we will recognize the fairness of people getting certain things not only for what they did but for what, given their background, they did not and could not do. We will see this both as an attempt at compensation for them and their children for deprivations they have suffered. But we will also, and more importantly, see it as part of a complex strategy to achieve or at least approximate human equality: to wit the equal well-being of all persons at the highest possible level of well-being. With this ideal in mind, we must realize that sometimes people deserve more for what they have done, but as well, sometimes people deserve more for what they haven't done and could not do.

NOTES

1. Stuart Hampshire, "A New Philosophy of the Just Society," *New York Review of Books* 24 (February 1972): 36–39.

2. Ibid., p. 37.

3. Ibid., p. 38, quoting Rawls.

4. Ibid., p. 36.

5. James Rachels, "What People Deserve" in *Justice and Economic Distribution,* eds. John Arthur and William H. Shaw (Englewood Cliffs, N.J.: Prentice-Hall, 1978), pp. 150–63.

6. Ibid., p. 150.

7. Ibid., p. 154.

8. Ibid.

9. Ibid., p. 156.

10. Ibid., p. 157.

11. Ibid., p. 154.

12. John Rawls, *A Theory of Justice* (Cambridge, Mass.: Harvard University Press, 1971), pp. 103–4.

13. Ibid.

14. Rachels, op. cit., p. 158.

15. Joel Feinberg, *Social Philosophy* (Englewood Cliffs, N.J.: Prentice-Hall, 1973), pp. 98–119; Robert Nozick, *Anarchy, State and Utopia* (New York: Basic Books, 1974), chapter 7; and James P. Sterba, *The Demands of Justice* (Notre Dame, Ind.: University of Notre Dame Press, 1980), chapters 4 and 5.

16. Rachels, op. cit., p. 158.

17. Ibid., p. 159.

18. Ibid. Rachels seems to be making a reversal here, taking away with the one hand what he is giving with the other. Contribution does not seem, after all, to be a full and sufficient justification for awards according to desert or for making such awards at all.

19. Ibid.

20. Ibid.

21. Harry Frankfurt, "Freedom of the Will and the Concept of a Person," *Journal of Philosophy* 68 (1971): 5–20; and David Zimmerman, "Hierarchical Motivation and Freedom of the Will," *Pacific Philosophical Quarterly* (October 1981).

22. J. L. Mackie, *Ethics: Inventing Right and Wrong* (Harmondsworth, England: Penguin Books, 1977), p. 216.

23. Ibid.

24. Frankfurt, op. cit., and Zimmerman, op. cit.

25. Ibid.

26. Nozick, op. cit., p. 214.

27. Ibid., p. 219.

28. Mackie, op. cit., p. 225.

29. I am construing "naturalism" here as it is used by John Dewey and as the term would be correctly applicable to David Hume. "Naturalism" is not defined, as G. E. Moore characterizes "ethical naturalism," as a view which attempts to *define* moral terms in terms of non-moral terms and attempts to derive an "ought" from an "is." Rather it is a view which rejects all supernatural and transcendental conceptions and in talking of morality talks of human desires, interests, or needs.

30. Mackie, op. cit., pp. 223–26.

31. I do not mean to imply that that is the only reason for making such ascriptions.

32. Rachels, op. cit., p. 157.

33. Ibid., p. 158.

34. It is not unnatural, but I think very problematic, to then wonder if this is not in effect to deny determinism.

35. Irving Thalberg, "Socialization and Autonomous Behavior," *Tulane Studies in Philosophy* (December 1979), p. 25.

7

"The Old Egalitarianism" and the Primacy of Equality of Opportunity

I

I argued in the previous chapter that any adequate theory of social justice must find a place for desert, though I also claimed that it should be a subordinate place. The traditional stress on desert has, of course, been a traditional impediment to egalitarianism. The previous chapter in effect sought to show that in reality it is no impediment. Desert claims are not sufficiently central to justice to undermine the claims of egalitarian justice. However, there are still central meritocratic conceptions and arguments about the primacy of equality of opportunity that need to be discussed. They stand as impediments to the rational acceptance of radical egalitarianism.

In this chapter I shall discuss the closely related but still distinct doctrines of meritocracy and "the old egalitarianism." Central to them both is a commitment to the primacy of equality of opportunity where issues of equality are at stake. By "meritocracy" I mean simply and crudely, as a first approximation, the doctrine that societies should be run principally on norms of efficiency and productivity by a genuine natural elite of talent and conscientious drive, selected by a fair principle of equal opportunity, and that the benefits and burdens in the society should be distributed strictly in accordance with overall contribution to productivity.[1] (A somewhat weaker, but, to my mind, a rather more plausible version, gesturing more in the direction of the welfare state, would say that the burdens and benefits should be so distributed only after a minimally conceived set of basic needs had been met across the whole of the society.)

Meritocrats would claim that the formula, even for an advanced industrial society of considerable wealth, should not be "From each according to his ability to each according to his need," but "From each according to his ability and to each according to his ability." The whole society, on the meritocratic conception, would be hierarchically stratified where those with greater abilities (measured primarily in terms of intelligence), who also made the most effective effort, would function as a dominant class or at least a ruling elite—a natural aristocracy, to use Jefferson's conception. They would receive the greatest awards and would have the predominant say in the ordering of the society. It would be a society in which the natural and the social aristocracy would be identical. After them, other strata would be awarded benefits and burdens, prerogatives and powers, in accordance with merit, operating under conditions of fair equality of opportunity. Merit, on such a conception would be measured principally in terms of intelligence and effort or, alternatively, in terms of ability and contribution.

In speaking of equality of opportunity, I am speaking of the ideal of making opportunities for the various cherished positions in society completely open to free competition in which anyone can compete for those prized positions in society (positions which afford very different life-chances) and where they are awarded according to talent and achievement and not on the basis of social position, class, race, sex, friendship, or patronage. This conception, as John Schaar has put it, "emphasizes the need for an equal opportunity among men to develop and be paid for their talents which are of course far from being equal."[2]

Both of these notions at least appear to be dependent on an acceptance of the coherence of and the moral legitimacy of some conception of desert, though one could, and some do, accept the moral legitimacy of desert without being believers in meritocracy or believers in the primacy of equality of opportunity.

Meritocracy, rightly I believe, is seen as a mortal enemy of egalitarianism. I think this is also true of those who defend what I have called the *primacy* of equality of opportunity, though like Rawls I believe a place for fair equality of opportunity must be found in any adequate theory of social justice. However, this is not how the defenders of a "just meritocracy" and of such a primacy see it. They distinguish sharply between something they take to be commendatory, "the old egalitarianism," which stresses such a primacy, and something, in their view at best muddled and mistaken and at worst dangerous, called "the new egalitarianism," paradigmatically exemplified by John Rawls and Christopher Jencks. (Presumably my "radical egalitarianism" would be seen as an extreme version of "the new egalitarianism," way beyond the pale of reasonability.)

II

Charles Frankel, in "The New Egalitarianism and the Old," gives something of the rationale for the old egalitarianism giving such weight to equality of opportunity, but he is not very clear in characterizing the differences between the two egalitarianisms.[3] Daniel Bell, who takes the difference to involve a fundamental conflict, at once normative and semantical, about how the vague term "equality" is to be defined, is more successful in characterizing the differences.[4] (The article by Frankel and two overlapping articles by Bell as well as a later article by John Bunzel should be studied together as paradigmatic statements of what Bell calls a "just meritocracy."[5])

Developing out of the political struggles in the between-wars-period in North America, and in the context of the Great Depression, the "ideal of a just situation [for the Old Egalitarianism] was simply one in which the obstacles to one's ascent, if one wanted to ascend, were not rigid," in which no privileged group, simply in virtue of their social station, wealth, or race, must be deferred to and accepted as having a preponderate authority in political life. "The Old Egalitarianism assumed that social stratification is inevitable and that if it is based on ability it is fair."[6] A commitment to equality meant to undertake a commitment to the struggle for opportunities for all sorts of people who had in various ways been discriminated against. The idea was to provide them with a chance to fairly compete for their place in the sun, e.g., to give them a chance to go to a university and to become professionals or politicians, if they wanted to and if they had the ability and drive. It was an abstract expression of the American dream.

The old egalitarianism, the egalitarianism Frankel, Bell, and Bunzel think we should return to, stressed the centrality and the importance of an equality of opportunity—a fair chance at excelling—in a social system which will be—and quite properly so—socially stratified with differential rewards and unequal positions of authority and wealth. The thing is to give us all an equal starting point to run in the same race, but equality, on such a reading, says nothing about guaranteeing any results. *It is an equality of opportunity not of results.*

"The New Egalitarianism" finds its most rigorous, systematic, and powerful form, Frankel contends, in the work of John Rawls.[7] It is, he claims, a "redemptive egalitarianism" which he takes to be deeply and harmfully mistaken. What Frankel regards as the basic belief of this new egalitarianism—indeed its very *raison d'être*—is the belief that "whenever there are inequalities in society, these are justifiable if and only if they are to the long term benefit of the least favored members of society."[8] It is not enough for the new egalitarians to believe and to act on the belief, as many conservatives as well as the old egalitarians do, that "those who are better placed and educated owe it to others to be useful. . . . " For the new egalitarians what must be done instead, in economic circumstances such as ours, is to strive to design our social institutions so that they are both efficient and operate in the best long-term interests of the worst off strata of society. This is Rawls' democratic conception of equality and it is a fundamental conception of welfare state liberalism and of what Daniel Bell, whose views are very like those of Frankel's, regards as Rawls' socialism. (Like Hayek and Friedman, Bell uses "socialism" in a very extended sense. Any welfare state capitalist society on such a conception becomes a socialist society. Clearly this is an example of a standard trick with persuasive definitions.) It is the core conception of what Frankel, Bell and Bunzel take to be the new egalitarianism.

What the old egalitarians find so objectionable in the new egalitarianism is the egalitarian view that social advantages and disadvantages be distributed, under conditions of fair and equal opportunity, so as to maximally advantage the most disadvantaged strata of society. Frankel sees this stress of the new egalitarianism as rejecting considerations of merit and desert except to, in a rather utilitarian fashion, acknowledge them as social assets to be recognized when they further the good of everyone alike.[9] This new egalitarianism, in his view, leaves out of account the common-sense view of justice "that distinctions should be made among people, and rewards and burdens distributed, in proportion to individual efforts and achievements."[10] Such distinctions based on such desert-based principles are, in turn, regarded by the new egalitarians as morally arbitrary. No one, as we saw Rawls and Hampshire arguing in the last chapter, deserves the greater advantages that their superior talents or character afford them. We do not, as Rawls has put it, deserve our "place in the distribution of native endowments, any more than we deserve our "initial starting place in society." Where we stand in the natural lottery is just a matter of luck. Fairness, Rawls argues, requires us to distribute in such a way that the worst off strata are compensated for disadvantages for which they cannot rightly be held responsible.

Frankel wants something to be given to help the worst off too, but he believes the new egalitarians generally, and Rawls in particular, take too much of a God's eye view of justice and neglect to balance their concern for the poor with a recognition of the just deserts of the meritorious. The new egalitarianism neglects what is due to "the representative person of twenty, in possession of a superior character that enables him to cultivate his abilities. . . . "[11] Frankel remarks that such a person has "usually done *something* to produce this character," though he very often will have had favorable circumstances to help him along as well. But there usually, where the accomplishment is considerable, has been hard work, inner discipline and sometimes even a lacerating struggle as well. Justice requires recognition of this, and this the new egalitarianism overrides or at least utterly neglects. A just society "must notice, approve, or reward outstanding gifts, particularly when the individuals who have these gifts have played some part in developing them."[12]

In the previous chapter, I argued that it is a mistake to discard altogether the notion of desert in a theory of social justice. The serious question is what weight to give it? It is not clear to me why Rawls's account, and even more evidently something as flexible as "the new egalitarianism," could not find a place for considerations of desert, particularly when we keep in mind that the key questions here would be about individual justice and not social justice. Thus in thinking about individual rewards and recognition, Frankel's point that "quite large numbers of people with superior characters came out of inner-city slums, and Scarsdale has been known to produce its quota of feckless types" could be accepted as being utterly unexceptionable though also as utterly obvious.[13] But when we are thinking, as Rawls is and as I am, of the design of just social institutions, such a point has a rather minor import and considerations of what effects different social environments have on representative people in those environments becomes very crucial. So we need something like the Rawlsian *difference* principle and considerations of desert are not in the forefront.

The old egalitarianism needs to give us reasons for putting desert in the forefront. Its proponents would, no doubt, defend a rather more meritocratic system than that of the new egalitarianism. But they need to give us some grounds for believing it to be a juster or in some other way a morally more adequate social system.

The scheme of social justice the old egalitarianism advocates, as we have seen, includes the protection of civil liberties, including of course the protection of legal and political equalities, the achievement and sustaining of equal opportunities, the *ceteris paribus* equal distribution of hardships (e.g., conscription, food or gas rationing in an emergency), the achieving and sustaining of a society in which, in Rousseau's phrase, "no citizen is wealthy enough to buy another and none poor enough so he need sell himself." These conditions of equality must be achieved and protected if we are to have a just society. It will also have an anti-aristocratic cultural style. It isn't a person's royal or noble lineage that matters or his manners, but, from whatever class he comes, it is the kind of person he is, and what he does, that matters. Its cultural ambience is such that it has a faith in the common man and the common man's capacity to achieve excellence—Lincoln and Chaplin are paradigms—and it is irreverent about claims of social position. Yet it is not so levelling, so insistent on uniformity, that it will not see the value of "things which create differences, partisan fellings, and stratification in society" and it will recognize "the need in every society to give public recognition to things noble and excellent lest everything in the society's culture be regarded as disposable."[14] Such considerations, Frankel argues, "set some limits upon the proper range of the principle of equality."[15] Above all, the old egalitarianism, unlike the new, does not rip "the notion of equality loose from its context" and does not see it as a single "first principle but as a member of a family of principles. . . ."[16]

There is something very strange here. Rawls is taken by Frankel and by Bell to be the arch-systematic exponent of the new egalitarianism. It is not clear that such a characterization should be accepted at its face value. In the first place there is nothing in the positive account of the old egalitarianism that Rawls does not accept and is not a functioning part of his system. Even in the more radical egalitarianism that I defend, there is, with the exception of some balking at the remarks about partisan feelings and stratification, nothing I would not advocate as well. Even the remarks about "partisan feelings" and "stratification," if given a *certain reading,* would be acceptable. I recognize the value of acknowledging differences between people and of accepting what Bakunin called certain natural authorities. Thus, if someone is wiser and better informed or more skilled than I am, I am going, in the proper domain, to pay him deference. And even the most radical of radical egalitarians—the newest of the new egalitarians— have not been for human uniformity and they have not taken equality to be the sole fundamental moral value. Only in the caricatures of egalitarianism has such a figure of straw appeared.

If it is said in response that I overlook the point I made myself about Rawls neglecting the importance of considerations of desert, I would respond, as I indicate above, that there is nothing in Rawls' system that would not allow him, without changing anything central in his account, to find a place, though a subordinate place, for desert. And Frankel has given us no grounds for giving such considerations pride of place in a theory of social justice. Indeed, following Rawls, I gave reasons for not doing that. I think it is fair to conclude from an examination of Frankel's account that we have yet to be given any reason for regarding the old egalitarianism as superior to the new or for regarding the two as even clearly distinct conceptions.

III

Daniel Bell, with his tough and sociologically informed defense of what he calls "a just meritocracy," comes closer to producing a coherent contrast to the new egalitarianism than does Frankel. There is less rhetorical slush in his account, though, since so much of it is descriptive, it is, as it is often with Isaiah Berlin, difficult to determine what exactly Bell's own position is. He begins by telling us that the post-industrial society, by which he means to include societies such as our own, is in its logic a meritocracy. It is a society in which achievement has won over ascription: the gaining of elite positions by inheritance or assignment. Power is increasingly matched with intelligence and achievement. Increasingly, "differential status and differential income are based on technical skills and higher education."[17] Fewer and fewer positions are open to those without such qualifications. Even in business the self-made, relatively uneducated but ruthless and hard-driving individualistic *entrepreneur* is becoming an anachronism, except in small businesses which are now in reality quite dependent on larger corporations. But in the larger corporations the talents required are more and more that of highly educated and technically trained professionals who function in managerial positions. (The link between the professions, certain university professionals, and the business community is becoming closer.) New technical elites rise in society. Our post-industrial societies become increasingly hierarchical societies with a complicated variety of technical elites in various positions of power and privilege. It is an increasingly meritocratic society in which the having of educational credentials is essential and in which certification is granted for determinate achievement, increasingly open to people of talent and industry. Good breeding and the correct family connections are no longer enough.

A meritocratic society, given that formal equal legal and political rights are secured, will see an egalitarian and just society as principally a society which will secure *equality of opportunity.* The stress will be to combat arbitrary discrimination against individuals on the basis of race and ethnic background and to create equal educational opportunity for the culturally disadvantaged so that they can fairly compete with those not so disadvantaged for the prestigious and socially desirable and useful places in our credentials society. This is a contemporary expression of the Jeffersonian ideal of meritocracy, a society which Bell sees as being both a just and a rational society, where a fair equality of opportunity means that none, with the requisite native ability, will be excluded from the competitive chance to get on the educational escalator which is the effective entry into the privileged places in society.

This Jeffersonian democratic but still meritocratic ideal contrasts invidiously, Bell believes, with a Jacksonian democracy where each person is thought to be as good as any other and no person is thought to be better than anyone else.[18] While a Jeffersonian meritocrat, like a Jacksonian democrat, would reject the taking on of aristocratic airs and the overriding of equal political and legal rights, he, unlike the Jacksonian democrat, firmly believes, as much as Nietzsche, in a natural aristocracy of intellect and virtue, rooted in conscientious striving and attainment. This group constitutes a cultural elect which should direct the course of development of a society. The proper equality is to be one of careers open to talent and effort, where a fair equality of opportunity underpins this competition for places in the meritocratic hierarchy.[19]

The old egalitarianism, and the classical liberalism of which it is an underpinning, advocates the elimination of "social differences in order to assure an equal start, but it justifies unequal results on the basis of natural abilities and talents."[20] Here, in claims concerning what is just and unjust, there is a plain appeal to desert-based criteria, though there could also be the utilitarian appeal of the incentive system: unequal rewards producing greater productivity and, through greater productivity, benefits trickling down all around. (Friedman and Hayek also make claims of this sort.)

Bell claims that modernity, with the meritocracy that goes with it, involves an uprooting of the old stratified order of aristocracy and wealth by the principle of openness, change, and social mobility with a technocratic elite replacing aristocrats and even capitalists. This springs from the demands of efficiency and results in, and in turn is additionally caused by, equality of opportunity. But this, in turn, and rightly so, produces a new technocratic hierarchy and does not result in anything like an equality of outcome. The aim is to, as much as possible, achieve equality of opportunity, and, *in that distinct sense,* it aims at an equality of condition, but it does not aim at an equality of condition in the sense of resources, income, wealth generally, position, power, or influence in society. It does not aim at equal well-being. The aim of the liberal meritocratic old egalitarianism is to establish equal political and legal rights—the classic civil liberties—and, so far as it is practically feasible, a fair equality of opportunity and to stop there in its drive for social equality. Anything further, they believe, threatens our fundamental liberties and would be deeply unjust. It is envy or resentment, not a sense of fairness or justice, Bell claims, which fuels a demand for a greater equality of condition.

Bell, like Frankel, sees Rawls' account as the most systematic and powerful statement of the new egalitarianism. He takes it as a deeply anti-meritocratic view ultimately committed to a levelling which "requires the reduction of all inequality, or the creation of *equality of result*—in income, status, and power—for all men in society."[21] This, of course, is not, as we have seen, exactly Rawls' position, for his *difference* principle sanctions such inequalities when they will, but only when they will, maximally benefit the worst off strata in the society. But the underlying intent, Bell could reasonably respond, is still a levelling one because we must strive, if we are Rawlsians, to make things as equal as we can, compatible with equal liberties all around, right up to the point where greater equality—equality of result as well as equality of opportunity—would harm the least well off strata of the society. But it is just this kind of levelling—the levelling the *difference* principle commits us to—that Bell thinks is irrational and unjust.

Bell sees the conflict between the "old equality" and the "new equality" as the conflict, in the domain of morality, between individualistic liberalism and socialism. "The claim for equality of result is a socialist ethic (as equality of opportunity is the liberal ethic). . . ."[22] They, Bell would have it, provide alternative pictures of the moral bases of society. In a way that would surprise Rawls, as well as his radical critics, we have in Rawls, according to Bell, a rejection of liberalism and "the most comprehensive effort in modern philosophy to justify a socialist ethic."[23] Bell sees classic liberalism (paradigmatically articulated by John Locke and Adam Smith) as resting on a picture of the unencumbered rational individual, responsible for himself, and seeking his own satisfaction. The satisfaction he will find in life will come in very considerable measure through meaningful work. (The critiques that Herbert Marcuse and Theodore Adorno make of such conceptions should not be neglected.)

Justice is achieved in society when people are rewarded on the basis of their intelligent effort, pluck, and risk, where the aim of each, as a rational utility maximizer, is to maximize his own satisfactions. Bell thinks that with the development of socialism and the new egalitarianism "we have come to the end of classic liberalism. It is not individual satisfaction which is the measure of social good, but redress for the disadvantaged as a prior claim on the social conscience and on social policy."[24] By contrast, the classic liberalism still defended by the old egalitarians "accepts the elimination of social differences in order to assure an *equal start,* but it justifies *unequal results* on the basis of natural abilities and talents."[25] Rawls believes, and I do as well, that to be morally arbitrary and through and through unjust. Here we have a sharp clash between the new egalitarianism and the old. Rawls remarks:

> There is no more reason to permit the distribution of income and wealth to be settled by the distribution of natural assets than by historical and social fortune. . . . The extent to which natural capacities develop and reach fruition is affected by all kinds of social conditions and class attitudes. Even the willingness to make an effort, to try, and so to be deserving in the ordinary sense is itself dependent upon happy family and social circumstances. It is impossible in practice to secure equal chances of achievement and culture for those similarly endowed, and therefore we may want to adopt a principle which recognizes this fact and also mitigates the arbitrary effects of the natural lottery.[26]

To compensate for such contingencies, it is not enough to try to equalize opportunities, we must as well make results more equal. For Rawls, the underlying moral imperative, for all societies and not just for societies in conditions of moderate affluence, is the following: "All social primary goods—liberty and opportunity, income and wealth, and the bases of self-respect—are to be distributed equally unless an unequal distribution of any or all of these goods is to the advantage of the least favored."[27] The thing to do is "to set up the social system so that no one gains or loses from his arbitrary place in the distribution of natural assets or his initial position in society without giving or receiving compensating advantages in return."[28] Some people surely have natural talents which indicate that in one or another culturally prized line they are more valuable to a society than others. For a meritocracy, as it is standardly conceived, justice requires (1) the equal opportunity to put those talents to use or at least the equal opportunity to freely and fairly compete for the chance to use them, and (2) differential rewards for the talented individual who so puts his talents to use. For Rawls, by contrast, the distinctions in talents should not be ignored, but should still be treated as a *social asset.* The basic social structure should be "arranged so that these contingencies work for the good of the least fortunate." Meritocracies, on Rawls' account, are unfair, for they lead to a political and economic domination by a technocratic elite, while the "culture of the poorer strata is impoverished." In short, according to Rawls, a meritocracy would have many of the horrifying and unjust effects graphically depicted in Michael Young's *The Rise of Meritocracy*. In such a society, even if it were to attain Pareto optimality, there would exist, as Rawls puts it, "a marked disparity between the upper and lower classes in both means of life and the rights and privileges of organizational authority."[29] The technocratic elite would increase and stabilize their political and economic domination over the less advantaged strata. "Equality of opportunity," in such a social order, would come to mean "an equal chance to leave the less fortunate behind in the personal quest for influence and social position."[30] These "inequalities of birth and natural endowment are undeserved" and Rawls' conception of justice is such that "undeserved inequalities call for redress. . . ."[31] The underlying idea "is to redress the bias of contingencies in the direction of equality. . . ."[32] And here the equality we are talking about is an equality of result, an equality of condition.

This should have additional force when we recognize that several different distributional schemes can meet the condition of Pareto optimality. Both Rawls' principles and meritocratic ones can satisfy them equally well. We can have both the new equality and efficiency. However, notwithstanding that, Bell sees Rawls and the new egalitarians moving from the meritocratic and classically liberal "From each according to his ability, to each according to his ability" to the socialist (communist) principle of "From each according to his ability to each according to his need." Rawls indeed takes this to be a not inept slogan, but he still regards it as a slogan with all the inexactitude of a slogan. But it is not how Rawls formulates his principles of justice or how he states his underlying rationale for social justice.

What grounds does Bell have for continuing to favor the old "meritocratic egalitarianism," if that is what it should be called, in view of the above considerations that Rawls sets before us and Bell accurately describes? Bell believes that the principles of "merit, achievement, and universalism are . . . the necessary foundations for a productive and cultivated society" and that in Rawls' account, and the new egalitarianism generally, these principles do not get their proper due.[33] Like Hayek, Bell stresses that the institution of universalism—the insistence, built into a social practice, that rules be applied equally to all and the related insistence, again built into a social practice, that there must be no administrative determination between persons—was a great moral and social advance. Moreover, that sort of principled achievement was a victory for egalitarianism. However, Bell believes that with the *difference* principle and Rawls' conception of justice as fairness, we have a regression; for people are in effect, on such a conception, being punished for being wealthy or even comparatively wealthy or for having the capacity for becoming wealthy. Here Bell and Nozick are in agreement. The "wholesale adoption of the principle of fairness in all areas of life shifts the entire society from a principle of equal liability and universalism to one of unequal burden and administrative determination."[34] The new egalitarianism sins against, Bell would have us believe, the evenhandedness and impartiality of universalism. Here Bell's views are very like those that Hayek has extensively developed.[35]

It is also the case, though perhaps not for the reasons that Bell gives, that Rawls' principles of justice and his very fundamental notion of fairness have not been shown to be the conceptions rational persons, with a sense of justice, *must* choose, in or out of the original position. They are *compatible* with reason but they are not *required* by reason.[36] But Bell entirely neglects Rawls' stress on the role of consensus in justification and his appeal to considered judgments in wide reflective equilibrium. With this the addition of a perfectly central part of Rawls' account, we would, methodologically speaking, get something much closer to Bell's own stress on consensus.[37]

Bell gets to something with a little more meat when he argues that our societies now, and in the foreseeable future, are up against problems about the limits of growth. If, because of these conditions, we are not going to have post-scarcity societies in conditions of full abundance, Rawlsian egalitarian ideals become very questionable indeed.[38] If economic circumstances are similar to present-day Western Europe, Canada, the United States, and Japan, and if we view, as Rawls does, societies as cooperative ventures for mutual advantage, it would be both, Bell claims, more rational and more just to scrap the *difference* principle and allow greater incentives for those who can, and with incentives will, expand the total social output and in turn use this increased social output to the mutual, yet differential, advantage of all.

Rawls would surely reply that this is exactly what he does advocate as long as the advantages accruing to the more able accrue solely as incentives to advantage maximally the most disadvantaged strata. Presumably Bell, following Nozick, would move to an attack on Rawls' underlying principle of fairness and ask why the division of the social pie should most favor the worst off? Why not, instead, the far better off or the middle strata or why should not the surplus, once the incentive factors are catered to, be divided equally across the entire population?

Rationality does not require any of these choices but—and here we perhaps come close to rock bottom—our reflective considered judgments, if we would carefully relate them to our theoretical understanding—would, I believe, favor Rawls. If, in societies of our productive capacity, giving these incentives would produce greater abundance, and not lead to crucial political and economic advantages threatening liberty and self-respect, then, where they are to the mutual advantage of everyone in the society, they should be granted. However, it is seldom, if ever, the case that we can assess everyone's advantage; what will maximally advantage one group may not maximally advantage another. Where enough abundance obtains so that basic needs all around are being equally met, we should, where both groups cannot be maximally advantaged, advantage the worst off group. That does not deny Bell's point about the importance of incentives and yet captures what, I believe, is one of our deepest reflective intuitions (considered judgments) about fair distributions and indeed about both fair and humane treatment of people generally. We are justified in allowing differentials in income but only to the extent that it maximally advantages the worst off stratum in the society. This, rather than the market or some criteria of merit, gives us a rough sense of what income disparities justice allows under conditions of moderate scarcity. (In Part IV we will take up the Nozickian position, a position Bell does not advocate, that justice must be silent here.)[39]

Rawls, we should not forget, allows for incentives too. Bell must give some distinct argument why we should abandon Rawls' *difference* principle and allow the market or individual merit or macro-productivity considerations to determine the degree of disparity instead. Bell has not given us grounds for going in another direction here, so he has not given us good reasons, anymore than has Frankel, for rejecting the new egalitarianism and returning to the old.

Bell is indeed correct in claiming that there are many kinds of inequalities, and often the crucial practical choice in a given political situation is deciding which ones are the ones that we should try to reduce in a particular situation where we plainly cannot reduce them all. (It is not clear that Bell does not believe that *some* of them are positively valuable.) There are inequalities in income and wealth generally, but there are, as well, closely related inequalities in liberty and power, in educational and occupational opportunities, in status, in access to medical services and creature comforts, and the like. There is, Bell claims, no one scale of equality and inequality in virtue of which we could characterize a just egalitarian society. What we should seek to achieve instead is "a basic social equality" where "each person is to be given respect and not to be humiliated on the basis of color, or sexual proclivities, or other personal attributes."[40] These are surely key things that an egalitarian society, indeed any kind of just society, would require, but the new egalitarianism attempts to go beyond that limited but still vital part of what social equality would come to.

There are indeed many inequalities and there is perhaps no single scale. There are problems in trying to establish an index of primary social goods; but, beyond Bell's minimal conception of social equality, we have some notion of what if would be like to distribute equally liberty and opportunity, income and wealth, and the basis of self-respect. We, of course, do not have a precise idea but we have, as we have seen in Part II, an idea which gives us some guidance in concrete situations. Moreover, an egalitarian—a new egalitarian, if you like—will take it as a fundamental moral touchstone for social justice that there be, as much as this is possible, an equal consideration of everyone's needs and interests. And while these notions are themselves troublesome, we are not in the position of having no idea of what to expect in a society that distributed with the aim of meeting everyone's needs equally, and, where that was reasonably accomplished, to meet people's compossible preferences equally.[41] This, of course, leaves lots of hard questions unanswered about what to do when not all needs can be met equally or even met at all. But we do have a conception—a heuristic device, if you like—about what ideally to seek in establishing a just society, and that ideal goes far beyond the limited ideals of the old egalitarianism.

Bell believes that some inequalities of result are both unavoidable and desirable. For him the crucial thing is to determine when *inequalities are fair.* But, unlike Rawls, Bell believes that we determine this in terms of desert. We determine which inequalities are fair by determining "which have been earned . . . and which kinds of equalities are necessary to preserve the natural rights of men and the social rights of citizenship."[42] This, I believe, is a grossly unfair and morally insensitive principle of fairness. To bring only such considerations to bear when trying to determine when inequalities are justified is to be neglectful of the fact that at the bottom of society are many people, including children, often in conditions of desperation and despair, who are suffering these deprivations through no fault of their own. This would remain true, though not quite so starkly, even in a modern society which met one of Bell's necessary conditions for a just society, namely, a society in which "each person is entitled to a minimum set of services and income which provide him with adequate medical care, housing, and the like."[43]

Bell might respond that in a genuine meritocracy, where people really have an equal chance equally to compete, there would be nothing unjust here. There would, in such a circumstance, be no people on the bottom of the heap through no fault of their own. But, even if it were possible, as far as social conditions are concerned, to so engineer it that poeple could in those respects start out on an equal footing, they could hardly start out with equal natural endowments unless we engaged in some—to put it mildly—morally questionable and probably not even achievable genetic engineering. (In the next chapter we will see how impossible it is to meet these conditions, thus, in effect, showing how unrealistic Bell's views are here.) Most people can, within certain limits, control some of their own behavior and take responsibility for their own actions; but there is much, including the ability to make sustained and successful efforts at achieving things of some difficulty and value, which human beings cannot invariably control. I do not, as I made plain in the previous chapter, want to rule out all appeal to desert, either on pragmatic grounds or in terms of considerations of fairness, but to give such central weight to it in judgments of fairness, as Bell does, is to unfairly neglect the awful weight, for good or ill, of biological inheritance and early social conditioning.

There is a place in society for meritocratic considerations, that is for positions of earned status and rational authority.[44] *Perhaps* even some institutions—say some universities—should operate largely meritocratically. But from this it does not follow that the whole society should be a meritocracy with the hierarchy, sharp divisions of advantages and disadvantages, and positions of authority and control this involves. We need experts in all sorts of scientific areas but whether in the domain of social life we need or should rationally want, or indeed even could have, "political experts" or "moral experts" is very questionable indeed.[45] We need economic advisors in certain technical domains but we are befuddled by scientistic ideology if we think we need or even could have experts in telling us how to live.[46] A professional political elite, even one selected on meritocratic principles (if that is indeed a possibility), and functioning as a ruling elite in this domain which so deeply touches all our lives, would undermine our moral autonomy by their control of our lives. Moreover, their control would not be rooted in a rational authority grounded in the appropriate expertise, for there is no "moral expertise."

There is, of course, a distinction between power and authority, but while authority, as a "competence based upon skill, learning, talent, artistry, or some similar attribute," has application in scientific, artistic, and legal domains, it is highly questionable whether it does in political-social life. It is not just populist resentment that makes us wary of moral experts and, certain technical domains apart, we have reason to be leery of political experts as well. Political leaders have power: an ability to command, backed up, either implicitly or explicitly, by force. A meritocracy would, by its very divisions, lead to a rule by such an elite.[47] This would turn democracy into a farce and undermine our moral autonomy.

It is not that we would not have natural leaders in such domains whom we would respect and praise and whose advice we would carefully ponder and often follow. Bakunin stressed this as much as Bell and other neo-conservative elitists. What Bakunin resisted, and what radical egalitarians would resist, is putting these natural leaders, or anyone else, in positions of authority and power. Resentment at an elite of intelligence and ability is not the rationale for rejecting meritocracy. Rather, it is a recognition that we cannot have an open society, where people have a genuine control over their own lives, where there is such a hierarchical structure of authority and power.[48] This, together with a recognition that most people have a moral capacity and can, given half a chance, control their own lives without a benevolent and far-sighted Big Brother or Grand Inquisitor, leads to a rejection of meritocracy.

Though there would be much less pressure in that direction there would be room in the new egalitarian society for people to rise to the top in scholarly, artistic, and scientific domains, domains in which expertise has some genuine meaning. But we could, and should, do without "political and moral experts" rising to the top. Indeed, to protect our freedom, and what Jürgen Habermas calls our adult autonomy, it would have to be the case that we have no such top.

It *may* be, as Bell contends, that in every society we have known, and indeed in every extant society, there have been "three fundamental realms of hierarchy—wealth, power, and status."[49] If such hierarchies are *inevitable,* if no classless society can come into being, something Bell has not shown, then we would have to eke out such social justice as we could manage under such constraints. (Here a reference back to the discussion of such issues in Chapters 3 and 5 is desirable.) But this would not keep a classless, statusless society from remaining a heuristic ideal: a picture of what *ideal* social justice would come to if we could obtain the kind of society which would make for the most extensive equal liberty for all and for the most extensive equal satisfaction of interests for everyone. The heuristic ideal of a statusless, as well as classless, society without social stratification does not exclude differentiations between people or a recognition of the worth of intellectual qualities and moral sensitivity and sagacity in the running of public affairs. The central moral impact of such a classless, statusless society is in its making possible, in a way a meritocracy could not, the social conditions for equal moral autonomy, where people are related together as equal members of a kingdom of ends, where there are no masters and servants, no bosses and bossed, thus giving full expression to the ideals of human sisterhood and brotherhood, in short to radically democratic and egalitarian ideals.

NOTES

1. I do not mean by this that "merit" is defined in terms of efficiency or productivity. That is not its ordinary language implication, and there is no reason to believe that it needs to be so defined. However, meritocrats use "merit" in such a way that it has this implication and that is reflected in my characterization of meritocracy.

2. John H. Schaar, "Equality of Opportunity and Beyond" in *Equality, Nomos IX,* eds. J. Roland Pennock and John W. Chapman (New York: Atherton Press, 1967), p. 229.

3. Charles Frankel, "The New Egalitarianism and the Old," *Commentary* 56, no. 3 (September 1973): 54–61, and his "Equality of Opportunity," *Ethics* 81, no. 3 (April 1971): 191–211.

4. Daniel Bell, "On Meritocracy and Equality" in *The New Egalitarianism,* ed. David Lewis Schaefer (Port Washington, N.Y.: Kennikat Press, 1979), pp. 21–52; and Daniel Bell, "A 'Just' Equality," *Dialogue* 8, no. 2 (1975): 1–4.

5. John Bunzel, "Rescuing Equality" in *Sidney Hook: Philosopher of Democracy and Humanism,* ed. Paul Kurtz (Buffalo, N.Y.: Prometheus Books, 1983), pp. 171–87.

6. Frankel, "The New Egalitarianism and the Old," p. 54.

7. Ibid., p. 56.

8. Ibid.

9. Ibid., p. 57–59.

10. Ibid., p. 57.

11. Ibid., p. 58.

12. Ibid.

13. Ibid.

14. Ibid., p. 61.

15. Ibid.

16. Ibid.

17. Bell, "On Meritocracy and Equality," p. 22.

18. Ibid., p. 28.

19. Ibid.

20. Ibid., p. 41.

21. Ibid., p. 29.

22. Ibid., p. 35.

23. Ibid., p. 44.

24. Ibid.

25. Ibid.

26. John Rawls, *A Theory of Justice*, p. 74.

27. Ibid., p. 303.

28. Ibid., p. 102.

29. Ibid., p. 107.

30. Ibid., pp. 107–8.

31. Ibid., p. 100.

32. Ibid.

33. Bell, "On Meritocracy and Equality," p. 51.

34. Ibid., p. 47.

35. Friedrich A. Hayek, *The Constitution of Liberty* (Chicago, Ill.: University of Chicago Press, 1960); and Friedrich A. Hayek, *Law, Legislation and Liberty*, 3 vols. (Chicago, Ill.: University of Chicago Press, 1973).

36. Bell, "On Meritocracy and Equality," pp. 47–48.

37. Ibid., p. 48.

38. Ibid.

39. Something of the distance between Bell and Nozick, in spite of the fact that they are both firm conservatives, can be seen from their exchange in a debate. See the debate between Daniel Bell, Robert Nozick, and James Tobin, "If Inequality Is Inevitable What can be Done About It?" *The New York Times,* January 3, 1982, p. E5.

40. Bell, "On Meritocracy and Equality," p. 49.

41. Amartya Sen, "Equality of What?" in *The Tanner Lectures on Human Values,* Vol. 1, ed. Sterling M. McMurrin (Cambridge, England: Cambridge University Press, 1980), pp. 197–220.

42. Bell, "A 'Just' Equality," p. 3.

43. Ibid.

44. Bell, "On Meritocracy and Equality," p. 50.

45. See the discussion on moral expertise in *Contemporary Moral Issues,* ed. Wesley Cragg (Toronto: McGraw-Hill Ryerson Ltd., 1983), pp. 577–610.

46. Jürgen Habermas, *Toward a Rational Society,* trans. Jeremy J. Shapiro (Boston: Beacon Press, 1968).

47. Steven Lukes, *Essays in Social Theory* (London: Macmillan Press, 1977), pp. 30–51.

48. Jürgen Habermas, *Strukturwandel der Öffentlichkeit* (Neuwied: Luchterhand, 1962).

49. Daniel Bell, "On Meritocracy and Equality," p. 52.

8
On the Logic
of Meritocracy

I

Frankel and Bell are, as we have seen, both defenders of the primacy of equality of opportunity and critics of an equality of result. And Bell, quite explicitly, and Frankel by implication, are defenders of what Bell calls "a just meritocracy." I have tried to show (a) how their central arguments do not work, and (b) how they have not succeeded in showing the new egalitarianism, etiher in a Rawlsian form or in my own more radically egalitarian form, is unsound and not to be morally preferred to their old egalitarianism.

I now want to go on the offensive and show more fundamentally what is wrong with meritocracy, though I will also attempt to show, as I did with desert, that *certain* suitably tamed meritocratic conceptions also have a place in an adequate theory of social justice.

In doing this I begin by following out Bell's suggestion that post-industrial societies, whether corporate capitalist or state socialist, are in their logic meritocratic societies. I shall, beyond anything that Bell and the other neo-conservatives have dared to push, adumbrate what a fully and consistently meritocratic society would look like. Here I shall follow out the core of Michael Young's Swiftian satirical depiction of an imaginary meritocracy developing out of what was once the British Welfare State and the characterizations of meritocracy, along with its critique, in John H. Schaar's classic article "Equality of Opportunity and Beyond."[1] I turn first to these writings for we find here brilliantly devised a certain kind of ramified interpretive description which is at the same time a critique—a negative evaluation—of meritocracy and of a stress on the primacy of equality of opportunity in a society above all committed to as efficiently as possible increasing productivity. Young's and Schaar's strategy is to show fully, and clearly, what is involved in a certain set of practices and in a way of life, that is, a meritocracy. To do this, they believe, is *eo ipso* to show what is wrong with meritocracy. Exhibiting the genuine logical implications of meritocracy shows, parallel to the way in which *a reductio* argument works, the moral untenability of meritocracy. In section III of this chapter, I shall turn to more conceptually based and traditional philosophical arguments which purport to show either that in an important way equality of opportunity is an unachievable or an incoherent ideal. This will pave the way for our final discussion of the adequacy of a "just meritocracy" and of the "egalitarianism," if such it be, of the old egalitarianism, dear to the hearts of certain neo-conservatives.

Meritocracy is on the agenda for the neo-conservatives and Michael Young depicts, in a fantasy with powerful Swiftian strokes, what a consistent meritocracy would come to when it is unfettered by conflicting and importantly modifying moral considerations. (In this way Frankel's and Bell's conceptions are, to their credit, rather impure forms.) Neo-conservatives contend that the "new class"—"men and women with technical or intellectual skills who sell their services and hold jobs"— require *"an ideology which justifies classes."*[2] A meritocracy, which could be shown to be a just meritocracy, would do just that. Most neo-conservative intellectuals do not want to reinstate "the prebourgeois or even the bourgeois state." What is on the agenda for them is meritocracy and the rule of policy professionals. The political practice of this ideology will be "technocratic, elitist, and *dirigiste* in character."[3] With meritocratic rule also goes the desire to establish (re-establish?) an order of civility; what this comes to, for them, is the teaching of "a proper respect for our meritocratic betters."[4] (Students, in public at least, should not refer to the president of their university as "Diamond Jim" and an institute of applied physics should not be called a house of prostitution for the bourgeoisie.) We need, neo-conservatives claim, a society genuinely open to talent, but a society in which an equality of opportunity is still *a genuine opportunity to be unequal in a fair structure of competition.* And we need as well a proper civility which would be the unsullen acceptance by the lower orders of meritocratic hierarchies that result from this competition.

Meritocracy has a natural appeal in competitive capitalist societies or in state socialist societies in their long competitive struggle with capitalist societies. Societies of both types are scientistic and committed to norms of productivity. Both recognize and indeed stress the fact that as a matter of empirical fact human beings are not equal. In both capitalist and state socialist societies there is both the sociological reality of, and the general recognition of, the fact that there are often obvious inequalities among human beings "on virtually every trait or characteristic" and that indeed some of them are ineradicable.[5] Moreover, meritocrats believe such differences justify differential evaluations of those differences. They believe that the search for an equality of result or of condition rests on a mistake. But there is still room in a proper meritocracy for the only equality, they claim, that really counts, namely, equality of opportunity, a generous ideal of an open society which "makes no distinctions of worth among men on any of the factitious grounds such as race, religion, or nationality. . . ."[6] In general it sets no artificial limits on individuals; "on the contrary, it so arranges social conditions that each individual can go as high as his natural abilities will permit."[7] The acceptance of this primacy of competitive equality of opportunity is a key indicator, meritocrats claim, of a fair, open, and generous society.

They see a truly democratic society as one in which talent is in a position to govern and direct the course of society; central to a meritocracy is a belief in the justness of a hierarchy based solely on merit. Where equal opportunity obtains, women and men get what they deserve and justice is essentially getting what you deserve; that is, being rewarded primarily on the basis of talent and industry.

It is not so evident now (1983) as it was when John Schaar wrote "Equality of Opportunity and Beyond" (1965) that meritocratic assumptions still have such a grip on us, though we should not forget the rise in the United States and in the United Kingdom of a neo-conservativism which, when it does not just romanticize the past, is likely to be either meritocratic or libertarian or some uneasy amalgam. Part of the reason for the weakening of meritocratic attitudes among the intelligentsia may have something to do with the widespread popularity of *The Rise of the Meritocracy*. But, be that as it may, there is still, certain intellectual and left wing circles apart, a not inconsiderable ready, often rather unwitting, and certainly uncritical acceptance of meritocratic assumptions. In such a cultural environment, it is even now only a slight exaggeration to say, as Schaar does, that the "argument for hierarchy based on merit and accomplished by the method of equal opportunity is so widespread in our culture that there seems no way to find a reasonable alternative to it."[8]

I think that most of us who live in North America, Western European countries, or Japan will, if we are honest with ourselves, admit to conflicting emotions as we read Young's futuristic fantasy. The dominant emotion will be one of disgust and alarm at such a "utopia." If this, or anything close to it, is what a meritocracy comes to, the notion of a "just meritocracy" is plainly an impossibility. Such a world is an inhuman world that amply justifies the populist revolt it provoked in *The Rise of the Meritocracy*. We hope that such an order of society would be unstable, would be its own gravedigger, as Young optimistically believes. We may have our doubts on this score, but our considered moral judgments are such that we *hope* Young is right. But, I think, if we do not deceive ourselves, we will see that it is also the case that not everything goes against the meritocrat. There is often a rather awful rationality to his arguments, but it is also true that the meritocracy he depicts not infrequently has a point that has *some* moral force. We can, that is, feel the force of the meritocratic considerations. That is what gives Young's satire bite. There is sometimes merit in the meritocrat's case, even in this extreme form, and a shrewd understanding of human nature.

That, however, is a submerged motif; the dominant one is that of rejection. But we also see that if justice and rationality are to be fully served, some place, in the articulation of the very idea of a perfectly just society, must be found for some of these meritocratic conceptions. The hope is that they can plausibly be placed in some overall theory of justice and theory of a good society that is not meritocratic. However, it will be said, by meritocrats or those more tempted toward meritocracy than I, that this begs a lot of questions and may possibly appeal to considered judgments that are not widely shared.

What is this picture of a meritocracy which is relentless in following out "the logic of meritocracy" and is horrifying but still in some way alluring? We see, in such a picture, a social order evolving which is, in the most efficient and uncompromising manner, committed to ever-increasing productivity and the overall maximizing of ever greater totals of what in some plain sense is greater overall social wealth. The meritocracy is wanted because it is thought to be the one way really to achieve progress, where "progress" is, of course, defined primarily in terms of economic growth. For someone clear-headed and truly committed to modernity, the claim goes, there are no other viable alternatives. We live, we are told, in a keenly competitive world where the capitalist countries are all competing with each other and together they compete, though not always without internal conflict among themselves, against the state socialist countries. This competition will force all countries, capitalist and state socialist alike, to subordinate everything to the claims of production—and this, in turn, serves as a great forcing house for merit (page 32). Progress and indeed even economic survival requires the matching of power with intelligence. In such fierce competition for dominance, or even survival, we can no longer afford to condemn talented people of the lower classes to manual work; instead we must do everything we can to facilitate as effectively as possible the rise of people of the lower orders, where they are the best people for the job, into positions of responsibility and control, in which their creative talents can find full scope. When they have the ability, they must be moved up. There must be full upward mobility for those who are both intelligent and hard-working and full downward mobility, unhindered by irrational family protectionism, for those who are not. Both schools and industry must be, without any reservations or qualifications at all, thrown open to merit. Only by doing this in a rigorous and uncompromising way can the full capacities of a society be realized. The objective should be, in all domains of life, to have the best qualified person in every position, and thus to maximize the country's productivity. A person should be in a lower position than his talents would otherwise warrant only if the positions above him are occupied by people still more talented, and no person should ever be in a job when there is another person below him in the hierarchy of positions who is better qualified. Personpower must be used as efficiently as possible without privilege to kith or kin or aristocratic privilege or patronage. To allow such factors to intervene will diminish overall productivity.

We need also to recognize that to use manual labor power to the greatest advantage, we must swell the ranks of the scientists, technologists, artists, and teachers, using all the truly talented people we have. It is, of course, unavoidably the case that "every selection of one is a rejection of many," but civilization does not depend on the labor of the stolid but uninspired, but on the creative minority, no matter from what ranks they may spring. What we need to elicit by careful social selection is an "elite selected according to brains and educated according to desert" (page 21). What we must do really to achieve a society which is both maximally efficient and just is to give the talented a genuinely fair—that is a genuinely competitive—opportunity "to rise to the level which accords with their capacities. . . ." (page 14). After this careful winnowing, the lower classes will consequently be reserved, as is not the case now, for those who are also lower in ability. If someone is in that class he will be there because that is where he deserves to be. In short, moving away from hereditary aristocracy and plutocracy to a natural aristocracy of talent, there must be a realignment of classes in the name of efficiency. We should abandon populist and Jacksonian conceptions of democracy with their dangerous myths of the rule of the people and of "democratic equality" and accept rule, not by the people, but of the "cleverest and most informed people"—a true meritocracy where intelligence wedded to industry reigns supreme. It is such people who must exercise leadership if democracy is not to be a mobocracy or a disguise for plutocracy (page 38). We must never forget the frugality of nature: "for every man enlivened by excellence, ten are deadened by mediocrity. . . ." (page 39). The object of good government is to ensure that the latter do not usurp the place in the social order which rightly should belong to their natural betters (page 40). We must keep a firm commitment to the rule of disciplined intelligence. Such a commitment, such a use of creative intelligence in social engineering and social design, will avoid the waste and impediments to productivity of the old class system (page 25). What could be fairer and what could be more rational where we are committed to norms of maximum productivity?

In the name of productivity, justice, and security, it is necessary to mount an attack on the evils of inheritance in property, jobs, and access to education. To further productivity, these three ills must be obliterated and equality must be achieved not, of course, in condition or result or resources, but in the truly vital theatre of opportunity. When we ask, as we rightly must, "*equality for what?*" the answer must be for the chance equally to compete for positions of advantage and prestige of value to the society—positions to be awarded purely according to talent and industry.

For a meritocracy to stabilize itself and to become an effective working order, the state must come to police the family. The power of the family must be weakened and the school system must be thoroughly rationalized along meritocratic lines. Both the selfish and outmoded attachment to family advancement of (among others) the modern bourgeois and the sentimental egalitarianism of socialism, with its commitment to an equality of condition for everyone, must be undermined and replaced by an equality of opportunity which, given the natural differences between people, is clearly an opportunity for people to end up in very unequal positions. It is not just that equality of opportunity cannot guarantee equality of results. Instead, allowing reasonable empirical suppositions about human nature, it will almost certainly guarantee unequal results which lead to a true hierarchy of merit.

A meritocratic society would require a rationalized school system very different from the system extant in North America. With developed I.Q. tests, we need to screen children at as early an age as our I.Q. tests will enable us to make reliable identifications. Of course, in the interests of both efficiency and fairness, further tests should be administered at regular intervals, together with the subsequent streaming of children upward or downward as the results change. Inaccuracies will occur, particularly in the beginning, and, in the interests of avoiding social waste and lowering productivity, we must correct them.

Exceptional brains require exceptional teaching. In the schools typical of the North American system, the intelligent few are wantonly sacrificed to the many in the name of a sentimental version of equality (page 46). It is indeed true, as socialists will argue, that so to segregate the clever from the stupid "would deepen class divisions," but new meritocratically-based class divisions are necessary for a just and maximally efficient society. By being so segregated, the bright could have their talents stretched to the utmost. Moreover, in this system the stupid would receive training appropriate to their abilities among their peers. By being not constantly in the bright light of comparison with their betters, their self-respect would not be quite so extensively buffeted. The bright students from the lower orders capable of entering the meritocracy must be spotted early and given the appropriate education while they are very young. That is to say, conditions of education must be provided so that they can leave the lower class into which they were born and enter the higher class into which they are fitted to climb. We need to develop a merit-stratified society prepared by habit of mind to recognize a hierarchy of intelligence where it is clearly established on sound educational principles.

In Young's satirical negative utopia, it is because of such considerations that educational psychology assumed such a central place in pedagogy. It perfected I.Q. tests and in its applied branches made an extensive use of them until everyone in the more advanced stages of the meritocracy had an I.Q. identification number indicating their I.Q. Such a device, though disquieting to some romantics, is plainly useful in educational screening and placement, job placement, and indeed even in the attaining of proper intelligenic marriages. Every prospective employer and marriage partner and even every registered marriage counsellor will have access to the relevant information, to wit the relevant person's I.Q. number as well as the I.Q. of his or her parents, grandparents, and great grandparents (should this information be available). However, to ensure fairness as well as efficiency, people are to be retested for I.Q. every five years. Then old I.Q. numbers will be destroyed and only the current ones will be used. The careful scientific development and use of these tests will finally enable us, indeed in tolerably minute and ramified ways, to classify children one above the other and finally thoroughly to lay to rest the absurdly sentimental egalitarian belief that everyone is the equal of everyone else, that one man is as good as any other.

However, the educational psychologists of the meritocracy are not methodological Luddites. They know full well that with their tests they are not assessing all-around intelligence. Perhaps there is no such thing. But what they can do, and that is all that is needed, is to provide tests which could identify the aptitudes needed to enable people to benefit from and to excel at higher education or at least the higher education extant in the meritocracy, an education geared to maximize productive efficiency. Children who perform well on the tests perform well in grammar school—that is all that the meritocracy cares to know or needs to know. Metaphysical disquisitions into what intelligence really is may be put aside as questions not conducive to salvation, i.e., enhanced productivity. But, meritocrats may still argue, it is not just Pareto optimality but fairness which is being served here, for, for the first time in history, the right of everyone to be judged according to his ability was being fully honored. Each person with his National Intelligence Card and with the right to be retested could rest assured that neither man nor child should be judged stupid until fully and accurately proven to be.

It is not only desirable to spend money on brainpower by developing a truly efficient meritocratic school system, it is also essential, for much the same reasons, to extend meritocratic thinking throughout industry. The I.Q. testing must continue throughout adult life. We must avoid having the wrong man or woman in the wrong position simply because they are older or have seniority or we do not want to relieve them of their jobs. We must, to have full productivity, rationalize our promotions and demotions system according to merit. Meritocratic principles developed in the schools should be extended to the working lives of all human beings. If this is to be done rigorously and fairly, we must get rid of the control of society by the gray beards. The seniority principle must be undermined just as the hereditary principle was undermined. Having "the wrong man in a position of power merely because he was of superior age was every bit as wasteful as having the wrong man in a position of power merely because his parents were of a superior class. In an open society the few who are chosen out of the many who are called should be chosen on merit; age is as much an irrelevant criterion as birth" (page 79). In a truly open and productive society competition should last for life. The principle of seniority must yield to the principle of merit. Authority must be thoroughly dissociated from age.

The effect of this, given an ever-improving school system, the growth of knowledge, and more selective breeding resulting from intelligenic marriages, is that the young will continue to outstrip the old. Few people over fifty-five will have full membership in the meritocracy.

However, in spite of its advantages, there is a danger here. Such a rationalized scheme has a dysfunctional, destabilizing effect which must be effectively countered in a meritocracy. There will be a middle-age malaise rooted in a very real fear of dismissal. Some useful work must be found for the middle-aged people—and there will be a not inconsiderable number—whose powers are falling off or just edging off or who are just losing out in the ever-keener meritocratic competition. Through resocialization—good, careful meritocratic moral training— the elderly must learn to reconcile themselves to demotion as their capacities fall off. Managing directors should expect in time to become office boys, judges court clerks, bishops curates, professors library assistants. And through intelligent moral education they will come to see the propriety of these things. The rationale here is not, of course, vindictive or a romantic revolt of the young, but simply the fair and rigorous application of meritocratic principles coupled with a recognition of the need, for the mutual benefit of all, to raise productivity. No one will ever be demoted simply because he is old. The criterion for upward and downward mobility is always merit. It is just that with seniority criteria knocked out, as at an earlier time hereditary, racist, and sexist criteria were knocked out, equal opportunity will finally be fully realized (page 96).

With such use of scientific I.Q. testing and scientific social selection for jobs and positions of responsibility and authority, we will finally have a true modern elite: an elite that truly deserves its elite position. Our society will be more class stratified than ever but the upper class, the 5 percent who really run the show, will need feel no guilt about their position. Like Plato's philosopher-kings, they will know who they really are. They will be a brilliant class of intellect and perseverance, selected on scientific meritocratic principles. They will know that they have the right to rule. Each man or woman can confidently say, secure in his or her position, that I am the best person for the job.

However, just as there are problems with middle-age malaise, there will be problems in such a society with the lower classes. In class societies such as our own workers can rightly criticize the higher orders. Bright workers can perfectly well know that but for certain fortuitous circumstances, they too could be in such advantageous positions with a commodious life. Our upper classes have their share of dullards and wastrels and people who are only in their positions of privilege because of their family connections. This would not obtain where the class structure is meritocratic. Every person would be just in the position they deserved to be in and now the lower classes would have no grounds for complaint. *Inequality of opportunity fosters the myth of human equality* (page 106). But, with meritocratic classes, living by fair principles of equality of opportunity, the lower classes could have no illusions left about themselves: they are at the bottom because they just are inferior. In a developed, effectively functioning meritocracy, it would not be the case, as it is with us, that native intelligence was evenly distributed among the classes. In meritocratic class society the gulf between the classes would actually widen, for we would no longer have classes roughly homogeneous in brains. As Michael Young powerfully and ironically put it:

> Now that people are classified by ability, the gap between the classes has inevitably become wider. The upper classes are, on the one hand, no longer weakened by self-doubt and self-criticism. Today the eminent know that success is just reward for their own capacity, for their own efforts, and for their own undeniable achievement. They deserve to belong to a superior class. They know, too, that not only are they of higher calibre to start with, but that a first-class education has been built upon their native gifts. As a result, they can come as close as anyone to understanding the full and ever-growing complexity of our technical civilization. They are trained in science, and it is scientists who have inherited the earth. What can they have in common with people whose education stopped at sixteen or seventeen, leaving them with the merest smattering of dog-science? How can they carry on a two-sided conversation with the lower classes when they speak another, richer, and more exact language? Today, the elite know that, except for a grave error in administration, which should at once be corrected if brought to light, their social inferiors are inferiors in other ways as well—that is, in the two vital qualities, of intelligence and education, which are given pride of place in the more consistent value system of the twenty-first century [pages 106–7].

Plainly this makes for a severe morale problem among the lower classes. They know that in a *just* meritocracy—that is a genuine meritocracy, for a real meritocracy could not be unjust—they have had every chance; they have been tested again and again and have had every chance to improve their lot. But if they see themselves so clearly as stupid how can they keep their self-respect? What is needed is a new ideology for the lower orders. This has as its centerpiece a new mythos: *The Mythos of Muscularity* (page 109). The thing is to build on the lower classes' addiction to sport and to build up a cult of physical prowess. We should, in the schools for the lower classes, encourage young students to value "physical strength, bodily discipline, and manual dexterity" (page 109). Strongly inculcate it in youth and continue to reinforce it for such people throughout their lives. Gymnastics and games, along with manual training and handicrafts, should be at the core of their curricula (page 109).

Such training, with such a mythos, will serve three purposes: (1) it will give them a new source of self-respect, (2) improve manual labor in society, and (3) will make their leisure more enjoyable. The first and third features will be stabilizing for a meritocracy, for the lower orders will, by these devices, be lulled into an acceptance of their lot. Moreover, with full and fair equality of opportunity in place, they will know that however low their own I.Q., their children or their grandchildren will have some chance (though indeed with soundly based intelligence breeding, not much of a chance) of having a shot at entering the meritocracy. Moreover, there will be a general recognition that these class divisions are fair and this in turn will be stabilizing.

Finally, with the concept of self-respect before our minds, it should be recognized that intellectuals must not ethnocentrically project their possibly romantic reactions to such positions onto the lower orders. What would undermine the self-respect of intellectuals and professionals will not undermine the self-respect of people of dull intellect. The realistic and fortunate fact is that, with their low I.Q.s, they will not even have a glimpse at the grand design, they will not know what is done to them (page 111). They will do their jobs contentedly in unstressful and healthy circumstances, safely insulated, because of class segregation on jobs—meritocratic class segregation remember—from the unsettling influences of the brighter orders. After work they return home contentedly to switch to the First Program on the idiot box to watch sports.

A meritocratic order matches efficiency with justice: Pareto optimality with fairness. Productivity is maximized and everyone gets what he deserves. Finally, in a genuinely rational *Weltanschauung* all loose talk has been laid to rest—talk emanating from both the Judeo-Christian tradition and from socialism—of the equality of man. Human beings are really notable not for their equality but for their inequality of endowment. "Once all the geniuses are amongst the elite, and all the morons amongst the workers, what meaning can equality have? What ideal can be upheld except the principle of equal status for equal intelligence?" (page 115). Our slogan should not be "From each according to his ability, to each according to his needs" but "From each according to his capacity, to each according to his capacity." The central axiom of a modern, intellectually non-evasive, meritocracy is that people are unequal and that, because of that fact, the ensuing moral injunction should be that they ought to be accorded a station in life accurately related to their capacities (page 116). The mentally superior rise to the top and the mentally inferior are lowered to the bottom. It is simply stupid and sentimental to go on believing that one human being is very much like another. And it is a bit of egalitarian moral ideology to believe that no man is worthy enough to deserve service from his fellows (page 122). As technology makes more and more of the mentally less agile people unneeded as productive laborers, they should, to have some productive work, become domestic servants of superior people, so that these superior people do not waste their time doing purely menial tasks. The lower orders can find their self-respect in serving those who do important tasks in business, industry and science. The classes will, as we have noted, be even further apart than in pre-meritorian times, but now everyone will have his appointed station and its duties which everyone can recognize are fully deserved. There is, in this, no injustice or exploitation. The situation is very different than in the capitalist societies we know today. Fairness reigns in a fully functioning meritocracy because everyone recognizes that in such a society "on the strength of sheer individual merit they could rise up the social ladder as far as their ability would stretch" (page 146). Moreover, the springs of social wealth would flow fully in a developed modern meritocracy. A certain social minimum would be set beyond which no one, not even the dullest, need fall; no one need be hungry, without health care or adequate housing; and the minimum, that starting position and ground floor for everyone, would go up as the wealth of the society went up (page 153). But, at any period, no matter what the minimum, there would be an extensive hierarchy of graded incomes or at least access to advantages through expense accounts and the like in which all along those graded incomes and/ or other advantages were matched with merit ratings. Where equality of opportunity is functioning, the fairness of the wage gradations are evident and sentimental twaddle about equality of condition or equality of being will finally be clearly seen for what it is, namely the negation of social justice. In such a meritocratic society, we have an objective basis and an adequate measure, through I.Q. tests, for comparing one job with another. We have finally an objective standard for judging who is or isn't better or worse than someone else. With such a true measure for merit, members of the lower class, or (if you will) the lower strata, could have no rational or genuinely moral objection to inequality as such (page 154). The existence of a meritocratic elite is both rational and just.

II

We are now in a position—the moral of Young's satirical fantasy vividly before us—where we can make a general assessment of meritocracy and its key doctrine of competitive equality of opportunity. I shall start in this section to depict the underlying moral objections to meritocracy with its stress on the primacy of a rigorously competitive equality of opportunity. I shall then move in the next section to certain conceptual criticisms of the very idea of an equality of opportunity.

What these conceptual criticisms attempt to show is that the very idea of equality of opportunity is incoherent. If that is so, if the conception really is incoherent, then the very idea of a meritocracy must be incoherent as well. Meritocracy would then merely be a disguise for a new kind of oligarchy with the power and privileges going to an arbitrarily privileged group (social stratum).

Philosophers love clever arguments designed to show that something, particularly something widely believed to be true, is in reality incoherent. These are, of course, devastating arguments when they actually can be carried through. However, our experience with such arguments should make us rather wary of them, for it is very often the case either that such arguments, when carefully inspected, are either seen to fail, or the allegedly incoherent belief, by an inessential modification, sometimes something which is hardly more than a clarification, can be articulated in such a way that it escapes the incoherency. What has to be done, if much of anything along this line is to be accomplished, is to show here that the incoherency arguments leave us no alternative but to conclude that, on any plausible and important reading, to believe in equality of opportunity is to believe in something which is incoherent. We will inspect some intelligent and forceful attempts to do just that. If nothing else, they will serve to force the defender of meritocracy to characterize rather more exactly what he or she is appealing to in arguing for equality of opportunity.

Following that, I shall, in Section IV of this chapter, look at arguments which are designed to show that, even if they are coherent, arguments for equality of opportunity are utopian; for, in societies such as ours, or indeed in societies that might reasonably be thought to be societies which in the foreseeable future might arise from our societies, anything even approximating equality of opportunity cannot be achieved. If "ought" implies "can," to say "A just society ought to be an equal opportunity society" is, the argument goes, to make a claim that cannot be satisfied. Moreover, it has been forcefully argued, the whole idea that educational psychologists have developed or are likely to develop something called I.Q. tests which measure "native intelligence" or "innate intelligence" and can be used to identify the meritorious and the non-meritorious rests on a myth.

I shall, however, start with the moral arguments against meritocracy. Some of them are variants on what no doubt any reflective person feels after reading *The Rise of the Meritocracy*. (Perhaps I should qualify this to "any reflective person who has been conditioned in roughly the ways most of us have been conditioned.") It is an interesting fact about our intellectual culture that it will be widely felt that such an appeal must be a rather weak or at least an indecisive appeal. It will be widely believed that what we need, to have something really forceful, is to show that "a meritocracy" or at least "a just meritocracy" is an incoherent conception or is in conflict with some incontrovertible fact or theory rooted in such facts. I am far from sharing this belief. I am even inclined to believe that it is one of our cultural myths. But I recognize its attraction and am aware of its currency, and here, without trying to fight it, I shall display the array of considerations, factual, conceptual, and moral, which together constitute, I believe, a powerful case against meritocracy. But I shall, as I have remarked, begin with the moral arguments.

Something of the extent of non-utilitarian elements in our ordinary moral thinking will be revealed in the feeling that the first cluster of utilitarian arguments will not be felt, by many, to be moral arguments at all. In Young's fantasy the meritocracy comes to grief because it breaks down. It generates, when it becomes reasonably developed, opposition from both the new meritocratic class and the new underclass. It is inherently unstable and unworkable. Without a thorough undermining of the family, with, á la Plato, state nurseries and the like, something which would itself cause intractable opposition, many individual members of the upper class will work to subvert the rigorous application of criteria of merit to their own children and, given their power, they cannot be stably contained. And the lower classes cannot be satisfied with their bread and circuses and the mythos of muscularity. They will be discontent and they will revolt, given half a chance. And with the conflict internal to the elite, they will have that "half a chance." Given that a morally adequate way of life must be reasonably stable, a rigorously meritocratic system will not be adequate because it would not be a stable system. It would give rise to social unrest and class conflict and it would undermine the very norms of productivity it was advertised as perfectly meeting. Meritocracies just will not work.

In Young's fantasy both utilitarian moral arguments (utilitarian arguments, if you will) and merit-based arguments are utilized. They are not unscrambled in *The Rise of the Meritocracy,* and no indication is given which are taken to be the more decisive; though, given standard attitudes toward productivity, there is some suggestion that the utilitarian ones are thought to be the finally decisive ones. If that is so, then, if the empirical facts about meritocracies are what Young believes them to be, and they are so unstable and so conflict-prone as to lower productivity beyond what it would be if some other plausible social system were in place, then on plain utilitarian grounds a meritocracy is not a morally acceptable social system.

However, the facts about how meritocracies would work may not be as Young imagines them to be and, even if they were, a meritocrat need not give such overriding importance to considerations of productivity and to utilitarian considerations generally. He could argue that (a) most social systems have dysfunctional and destabilizing features and (b) that it is not evident that a meritocracy must be radically unstable. It is not even evident that it would be more unstable than the traditional societies we are accustomed to. Our actual class societies with their class conflicts still often do manage to contain, in one way or another, class conflicts for quite a long time and in this way remain stable, though not without conflict, over a considerable period of time. Given the force of its merit-based arguments, arguments which a meritocrat could take to be overriding such weak utilitarian counters, and, given the reasonable empirical possibility of a meritocracy, he will continue to accept meritocracy.

What then, utilitarian arguments aside, are the other distinctively moral objections to meritocracy? Most fundamentally, it is a dehumanizing society, dehumanizing beyond what at least most readers of this book will experience in their own societies. It is just too inhuman to have such a constant competition between people in practically all domains, a constant sorting, grading, and rating of people to provide an ever-more efficient and more productive society with every man and every woman with their very own I.Q. identification card marking perfectly their place in social space. Such a world is far too inhuman, a far too icy, rationalistic, calculating way for people to relate to each other. It is a dehumanizing society because it destroys any notion of fraternity or solidarity or even of belonging to a common community of which we are all respected as members: as equal members of a Kantian kingdom of ends. Such a meritocratic society, when we give vivid thought to it, as Young forces us to do, is a nightmare—the very opposite of how we on reflection would want to live together.

We can see, if we reflect, what a horror a meritocracy would be if it were applied within the family. But it would, for similar reasons, make it impossible for any people to be *a people,* to be anything like a *gemeinschaft,* in which people would see themselves as "a people"— to say nothing of seeing themselves as part of the human family. The prized humanistic notion of "the family of man" could have no meaning for a meritocrat. (That it has very little meaning in class societies such as our own is not here to the point.) A meritocracy could not be a truly human society. It could only be a cluster of prudent utility maximizers out to make transactions which would, maximally, given the realities of the world, further what they took to be their own interests. Moral relations—genuinely human relations—between people would become impossible.

Intelligenic marriages are not an extraordinary improvement on sexist "perfect-sex-object" marriages, e.g., a non-neurotic Marilyn Monroe or Rock Hudson in every relevant bed, but clearly they are the thing for a rigorously meritocratic society. In such a society the moral wisdom would be not to trust experience and developing relations with another person but to get his or her I.Q. number and, if possible, that of the parents and grandparents as well. One does not want to risk, if one is bright, or even not so bright but aspiring to upward mobility for one's children, having a less than brilliant child, if one can help it. Such a "transactional society" makes any mutuality or reciprocity (Barth to the contrary notwithstanding) quite impossible.

In a related way, as Rawls stresses, a meritocracy undermines the self-respect of many of its members and militates against moral autonomy as well.[9] In a meritocratic society, equality "means an equal chance to leave the less fortunate behind in the personal quest for influence and social position."[10] Each person would be constantly trying to better himself, enhance his position in the social structure, and prove that he was the best. The anxiety would be that the chap next to him might be a little better or getting a little better and that his own powers might be falling off and thus his own human worth as well, for that is measured solely in terms of intelligence plus perseverance. But your nicely quantifiable score there is determined by how you come out in a competitive struggle with others. In such a society most would be losers and indeed for very many they would be very considerable losers indeed. People's self-respect, one of our very fundamental goods, would be constantly threatened.

People would be valued for what they would contribute and the value of that contribution would be measured in terms of conventional productivity canons. Candy manufacturers would be valued more than dental hygenists for they contribute more—or rather their workers contribute more—to the gross national product. There would be no concern, in such a society, to provide education except as the training of useful abilities. In a meritocracy people would not be so valued that educational expense, even in an affluent meritocracy, would be seen as something to be incurred simply because education enriched the "personal and social life of its citizens, including here the less favored."[11] Such a calculation-addicted society is rightly seen as an inhuman society.

A meritocratic society is also an anti-democratic, paternalistic, and elitist society. There are the few who are truly brilliant and informed, knowing they are on the top because they have the ability and the knowledge, together with a disciplined will. They are the really smart people who deserve the power and control they have. I leave aside, for later consideration, whether we have, or are likely to get, any mechanisms like I.Q. tests to pick out such people or even any acceptable criteria in accordance with which we could try to devise such tests. But assume, for the sake of this argument, that there are such elites of the intellect and will and that their intelligence is relevant in such public spheres—spheres having to do with the general governance of life. And assume further that we have some reliable way of picking them out. In such an eventuality, we would have a very paternalistic society run by elites. The masses of people would have very little autonomy indeed. Their lives would be governed *for* them not *by* them. If we regard moral autonomy and something approaching equal liberty for everyone as fundamental *desiderata,* we will not be for a meritocracy, and if we prize democratic values we will not be for it either. Only so-called "democratic elitism" is compatible with meritocracy.

There is a strong tendency to believe that without hierarchies we would have chaos and anarchy and such inefficiency in our society that everyone would suffer. This being so, there is a tendency to conclude that what we need are hierarchies possessing superior merit and that this is what meritocracy provides us with in the fairest and most efficient form. The alternative to a meritocracy or to a plutocratic or aristocratic hierarchical society is an unstable anarchy which would inevitably lead to tyranny. "Realistic democrats"—people who are not hopelessly utopian—realize that these are the real alternatives with which we are faced. Hierarchies we must have. There is simply no alternative to them. If we are democrats we will opt for a meritocratic hierarchy. What we need is a government of the people by a meritocratic elite springing from the people. In mass democracies such as we have today we must have rule by an elite. We need our Kissingers, Brezinskis, Haigs, and Schultz's.

Shaar rejects the idea that our choice is between anarchy and meritocratic elitism.[12] He grants, what is obvious enough anyway, that politics requires political organization and that with organizations we need *some* hierarchy. But what is of crucial importance is the form this takes and whether there is associated with it "a democratic mentality": a "way of thinking about the relations among men which stresses equality of being and which strives incessantly toward the widest possible sharing of responsibility and participation in the common life."[13] With that democratic mentality—a mentality that is the very antithesis of a meritocratic mentality—one can and will expect and accept specialization of function. Some have a far greater expertise than others about how certain sectors of the economy work and others understand better about what is to be done in agriculture or in fisheries or in elementary education or on the arts scene. But we do not need philosopher-kings or scientific elites to tell us how to order our lives. People of normal intelligence and education can, free from propaganda, come to know what is in their interests and have some idea of how to live their lives without a paternalistic Big Brother telling them what to do. And this ability will be encouraged and strengthened in a genuinely democratic culture where care is taken to enrich and extend the education and culture of all.

The doctrine of competitive equality of opportunity, when operating in a meritocracy, divides persons, and sets them against one another, for its central function is to defend the equal right of every human being to compete against each other to become unequal. By proclaiming that it is a sentimental myth to have a belief in a more robust equality, including any egalitarian belief that all people are in some fundamentally important sense of equal worth, meritocracy destroys community and encourages *hubris.* It encourages either the arrogance and contempt of the powerful toward the poor or a paternalistic condescension toward them. There is, with meritocracy, none of the equality of respect that is owed all human beings. We need not, if we are meritocrats, worry about enhancing the culture of all persons or achieving a common literate culture. Some, depending on their intelligence quotient, may only be fit to serve their betters. What Nietzsche proclaimed is now scientifically established!

Once this step is taken, there is little reason to accept the Kantian injunction that no man may be treated as a means only. Yet that is a very fundamental and a very deeply embedded considered judgment in our belief system. Meritocracy, if not actually incompatible with it, threatens it. If this Kantian conception means much to us, we certainly should not be meritocrats.

A consistently meritocratic society—the meritocracy of *The Rise of the Meritocracy,* not Bell's and Frankel's meritocracy—could not have any deep commitment to equal legal and political liberties. If more efficient productivity were gained by overriding these liberties and if some people are clearly superior to others—some being fit to rule and others only fit to live according to the myth of muscularity—it is irrational to insist that people of such radically different capacities should have the same legal and political rights where productivity is at stake. Attachment to that traditional liberal conception is just another sentimental attachment to the myth of the equality of man. So again, we see how meritocracy, in a fundamental way, conflicts with democracy. If we care about democracy, care about human rights, reject paternalism, see a value in human fraternity and solidarity, and desire a social world in which we come as close as we can to an equality of self-respect and liberty, we will reject meritocracy.

III

In the previous section I gave a miscellany of moral arguments against meritocracies. Many of them are challengeable in certain ways, for they involve contestable assumptions about man and society that need to be fully aired. Though that they are so contestable does not mean that, after all, they are not correct. But it does mean that there is not anything incontestable here that could take no further argument. They all rest, as Rawls would put it, on considered judgments which, while widely shared by many, if not most of us, still have not been universally so widely shared at all times and places. For these arguments to have the weight I attach to them, it is essential that these judgments would also be judgments that would still be made as part of a consensus under the conditions of wide reflective equilibrium or, to use another idiom, under Habermasian conditions of undistorted communication.

Philosophers often believe in magic, and many have an insatiable hankering after a single air-tight argument that will refute or establish some central philosophical claim once and for all. The hankering is for a sound argument from self-evidently true premisses. Surely the above moral arguments, if they achieve anything at all, will not achieve anything like that. What we may have here is a cluster of plausible reasonings which together make a very strong case against the acceptance of meritocratic commitments.

We do not, however, have just these moral arguments. We have conceptual arguments as well. John Charvet and D. A. Lloyd Thomas develop arguments to establish that the doctrine of the equal opportunity is an incoherent one.[14] From this it would, of course, follow that meritocracy must rest on a mistake. Here we have arguments of the traditional philosophical sort which, if correct, would satisfy traditional philosophical longings. What are these arguments and how good are they?

To appreciate their force we must first clarify more than we have done hitherto what we are asserting or denying when we assert or deny that there is equality of opportunity. Both of these authors, as does Onora O'Neill as well, point out that part of the trouble with the doctrine of equality of opportunity is its ambiguity and unclarity.[15] It has plainly meant different things to different people and it is often unclear what is being claimed even when someone, in the spirit of the meritocrats, defends competitive equality of opportunity.

"Equal" is an incomplete predicate. We first have to identify in what respect(s) anybody is to be counted as equal to anybody else before we can say anything about how they should be treated to be treated equally or as equals. (Even these notions need not be the same.) When we ask whether Jill's opportunities are equal to Jack's we need to know what respect we are talking about before we can say anything coherent. We need to know what is relevant to answering the question of whether or not their opportunities are equal.[16]

When we speak of "opportunity" or "opportunities," as in "equal opportunity," we are speaking of the opportunity to do or enjoy some activity or benefit. In speaking of a person having an opportunity, we are speaking of certain things that that person can do or have, if (a) she chooses and (b) if it is something that is generally seen, and typically by the person choosing, as at least to some extent something desirable.

Lloyd Thomas points out that in speaking of two people being in a condition, vis-à-vis each other, of equality of opportunity, we typically do not literally mean they have the same opportunity, like two people having the same opportunity to fish the same trout pool at the same time. Often, indeed typically, people do not and cannot have the very same opportunity, yet we often in such situations would still say that their opportunities were equal. What we should mean to say here is that to have equality of opportunity they must both have an equally valuable cluster of opportunities or that they each have a standard set of opportunities, such as, in our culture, having equal (equally good) educational and occupational opportunities. They plainly could not all have the same opportunities *sans phrase* in all things and or probably not even exactly equal opportunities in all things. What is crucial is that for a certain culturally standard set of prized things, such as education and position, they have equal (equally good) opportunities.[17]

There are, however, as Lloyd Thomas points out, difficulties about this. In trying to capture our intent in saying that people are to have equal opportunities, we could reasonably read it as the claim that people are to have an equally good (though different) set of opportunities. But this, to be applicable, would "require some consensus about an interpersonal standard of comparison for the goodness of opportunities."[18] Lloyd Thomas denies that there is any such standard and so denies that the notion of equality of opportunity, read in this way at least, has any application.

It is true enough that there is no prize that we have all agreed to run for. But there are a number of things, at least within a certain family of societies, such as a certain general kind of education and a certain range of positions with certain linked amenities, concerning which there is, within those societies, a rather wide consensus about their desirability. When we say, in defending equal opportunities, that people are to have an equally good (though different) set of opportunities, it is these things we have in mind. The principle here has a determinate yet still an imprecise application. But, as we have learned from Aristotle, this is exactly what we are to expect.

It is also important that we distinguish between competitive and non-competitive equality of opportunity. In speaking of non-competitive equality of opportunity, we are speaking of opportunities, such as equal access to a certain level of medical and dental care, which, the defender of the equal opportunities in question is claiming, ought to be equally available to anybody if they wish to avail themselves of them. They are not opportunities which are to be competitively striven for. Competitive equality of opportunity, by contrast, refers to those opportunities that must be gained or lost in open and fair competition, such as a directorship of a museum or a certain scholarship. In any society there are opportunities to be distributed (say scholarships) and there are more persons desiring them than there are opportunities.

Where the equality of opportunity is non-competitive, everyone who wants to avail himself of it can have it (say a certain type of health care); where the equal opportunity is competitive (say the scholarship) not everyone can have it, but, like runners starting at the same line, everyone, where equal opportunity obtains, has an equal chance to compete for it. But what people get in the end, where they are competing, is not equal. Some will get the scholarship and some will not. The equal opportunity here has to do with the way competitions are conducted.[19] It consists in the establishing of fair, i.e., equal, competition for scarce opportunities. In competitive equality of opportunity, it is not true, as in the non-competitive case, that if a person has an equal opportunity to x he can do x or have x, if he chooses, but that he has an equal opportunity to compete for the earning of x. There is, in competitive equality of opportunity, an equal opportunity to compete, which each has, but not the opportunity for everyone to enjoy that which is competed for.

It is plainly competitive equality of opportunity that meritocracies stress. For them, though not for everyone, an equal opportunity society is a society with *complete* competitive equality of opportunity. It is not the existence of the ideal but the weight (including the stress on completeness) given it in meritocratic societies that we have been criticizing, but it is this very ideal itself that Charvet and Lloyd Thomas claim is incoherent. I now turn, with these clarifications before us, to an inspection of their core arguments.

What would we have to obtain even to have a society of competitive equality of opportunity? John Charvet remarks of such competitive opportunities:

> If one starts by considering the opportunity to attain superior positions in adult practices, one is rapidly led backward into arguing that the opportunity to obtain the education necessary to attain positions should be equal for all. But one cannot stop at schooling, for the development of abilities begins in the family, and it is obvious that families differ in their ability to provide initial opportunities for development. Entrance into more favored families depends, however, not on merit but on mere accident of birth.[20]

To remedy this we would have to remove children at a very early age from families altogether and bring them up in something like state nurseries. The principle of fair competitive equality of opportunity "requires that everyone be in an equal position in regard to those who help and encourage development, i.e., parents, teachers, friends, etc."[21] If Jill has more access to someone who helps than Jack does or has access to an individual or individuals who are better at helping than Jack, then Jill has a competitive advantage over Jack, and equality of competitive opportunity does not obtain. "Having access to those who help rather than hinder, or help or hinder less, confers an unfair advantage unless the access itself is awarded on merit."[22] But, given the family in anything like the way we understand it in our culture or other cultures, this is not something that it is possible to achieve. Entrance into a family simply results from birth. Only if we had something like I.Q. tests that could be made at birth, and we then distributed the stock of babies into the families with matching I.Q.'s, would we even be approximating it. Leaving aside whatever "moral justification" such a practice could possibly be given, the technology of this is something we do not have in place or even know whether it could be developed. But even if we could develop it, we would still not have competitive equality of opportunity, for the meritocratic formula for merit remains I.Q. + effort = merit. But we have no way of knowing which of the babies will be the ones which have, because of their biological nature, the greatest potentiality for making the greater effort so that we can match them with the families who have not only the appropriate I.Q. but the appropriate industriousness and propensity to help bring that capacity out in babies. We do not even know if it makes sense to talk of a "native propensity to industriousness," let alone know how to measure it so that we could distribute babies at birth according to merit. It will, to understate it, surely be felt by many that such a practice, if it could be established, would be morally outrageous, but I think it is even more important here to see that it is, whatever else we would want to say about it, an absurd fantasy that could not possibly be anything more than a fantasy.

State nurseries would fare no better at establishing a competitive equality of opportunity. There would be different people manning them with different abilities and propensities. All babies could not get the same type of treatment. But even approximating it would still not put people in equal positions to run the "competitive race of life." At most it could come somewhat closer to this ideal. And the price for achieving this would be not inconsiderable.

The only way to establish really equal competitive equality of opportunity, it might be argued, is to give children no help or no socialization at all. They must be completely independent. But this is totally absurd for then it would be impossible for them to become recognizably human at all. They wouldn't even be like the wolf child or the young girl in Portugal raised with and fed like chickens in a chicken coop. Moreover, they would still have their different genetic inheritances, giving them from the very start unequal chances.

John Charvet generalizes his position as follows:

> The principle of equality of opportunity requires that no one be dependent for self-development on any other human being or human practice unless this dependence is equal for all. It is accepted, however, that men's abilities and capacities vary, so that the condition for the satisfaction of this requirement is that no one be dependent on anyone else. But this condition is one of having no society at all, and so no men.[23]

Charvet's chief claim—a claim echoed and built on by Lloyd Thomas—is that the principle of equality of opportunity cannot be "formulated without incoherence or contradiction, for a complete formulation renders it incompatible with any form of human society even while it is being put forward as a principle of a good human society."[24]

Charvet thinks that the putatively substantive moral commitment underlying equality of opportunity is the principle "Opportunities to attain superior positions are to be allocated equally to all." But the same reasoning (deployed above) that shows the principle of competitive equality of opportunity to be incoherent shows this principle to be incoherent as well. It "asserts as a basic principle to govern men's social relations a principle which only makes sense in a condition in which men have no social relations."[25] Where we are dependent on one another there can be no equality of opportunity and "a form of society" in which no one is dependent on any other person is no society at all. It is not just bourgeois individualism gone mad. Men are through and through social beings; insofar as they are recognizably human, they are necessarily dependent on each other. And with these relations of dependence no genuine equality of opportunity is possible.

For competitive equality of opportunity to obtain for a competition x, the possession of all the factors which effect the success, and are subject to human control, must be controlled (manipulated) so that all competitors for x possess all those factors to an equal extent.[26] But, as we have seen, such a condition is impossible to obtain short of making people exactly alike by complicated genetic and environmental engineering. But we should also recognize that it is impossible to do this; moreover, if it were possible, it would then be immoral. Quite apart from that, it would not, if it could be done, allow for competitive equality of opportunity, for, if everyone were identical, there would be no competition because it would be foreordained that the results would be identical. No meritocratic conceptions or policies would make any sense at all.[27]

Even if we believe that genetic engineering is impossible and we say that the differences in performance between Jack and Jill are a result of their having different natural abilities, abilities not appreciably affected by differential enculturation, we still have factors which (a) make their competitive opportunities unequal and (b) are not things they can correctly be said to deserve, such that they can rightly obtain a competitive advantage from them. As Lloyd Thomas rhetorically asks: "But surely one's natural abilities are not due to any credit on one's part; they are not deserved, so why should people receive different rewards on that basis?"[28]

The point of competitive equality of opportunity was to provide conditions in which there would be fair (equal) competition for prized unequal positions. If people were identical or only marginally different, there could be no such competition. The thing is to get people equal at the starting line fairly competing for expected unequal results, carrying with them differential rewards. But that actually makes no sense, for if we really succeeded in getting them equal there could be no competition.

Putting aside for a moment our previous objections, we still need to recognize that competitive equality of opportunity could never be institutionalized. One generation, A and B, let us now suppose, compete equally but they have different native abilities (different I.Q.s or different moral qualities, such as the will to stick to difficult tasks). Given these different abilities different results predictably will follow. Then their children, A' and B', cannot start out equal, given the existence of the family. To keep our situation of equality of opportunity—the situation we had for A and B—we would have to go in for something like state nurseries for A′ and B′ and that, for most people, is too high a price to pay for equality of opportunity. "The prizes won in the competitions of the first generation will tend to defeat the requirements of equality of opportunity for the next."[29] Thus again we have reason to believe, given certain at least plausible empirical assumptions, there is incoherence in the very idea of a competitive equality of opportunity.[30]

I think these arguments show that if one really pushes to get strictly fair (equal) conditions of competitive equality to compete for scarce desired positions, say in education or on the job market, one cannot possibly get them. "Equal competitive opportunity," like "a perfect vacuum," is impossible to obtain, and because of this, a strict meritocracy, whatever its moral desirability would be if it were a genuine possibility, is in reality not a possibility.

However, just as there are conditions which can approach in varying degrees what a perfect vacuum would be, so there are competitive conditions that are less unequal than others. Perhaps competitive equality of opportunity should be taken as an unrealizable *heuristic ideal* and certain realizable approximations of it should be taken as what it is, functionally and practically speaking, to attain equality of opportunity. The thing to go after is a proximity to the heuristic ideal compatible with not undermining related cherished values. Like enlarging the areas of freedom, there would be areas which could be indefinitely enlarged, though, of course, there could be no attaining of a perfect competitive equality of opportunity.

What are these conditions?[31] Some things are, conceptually speaking, reasonably simple. A social adjustment that adjusts in the direction of equal competitive opportunities must allow no legal or even quasi-legal barriers to people in that society having a shot at all educational and occupational opportunities. There can be no barriers in an equal opportunity society based on race, religion, sex, or social background to so competing for advanced educational opportunities and job opportunities. Such a conception of equality of opportunity is not *simply* an extension of liberal equality before the law into the sphere of the economy, for equal legal and political rights are not matters of competitive equality of opportunity but of non-competitive equality of opportunity. But the above equalities are plainly a matter of competitive equality of opportunity. There is, in a determinate sense, an equal right, if such measures were really institutionalized, to compete for jobs and educational placement. There can be, in such a society, no more job discrimination based on race, religion, sex, or social background—the property rights of private employers notwithstanding— than there can be legal or political discrimination on such a basis. There are, as we have seen, ambiguities in such a conception, but there is nothing incoherent about it and, using it, true and false statements can be made about the extent to which equality of opportunity obtains or does not obtain in a given society. Similar things obtain about entrance into schools. Equal opportunity in this specific sense does not obtain if there is any barrier to entry on those grounds. Again true or false statements can be made about the degree to which this obtains or does not obtain. There is no incoherence here.

However, there is here at least one possibile ambiguity. In speaking of there being no barriers, say for a black to go to law school, or for a chicano to get a job as a plumber, what originally people had in mind was a *de jure* statement, namely, that it would be against the law to make discriminations on such a basis. In that plain way there could be no discrimination. No firm or school could have a sign saying "No Indians here" and they could not simply reject Indian applicants on the basis of race. But "any barrier to entry" has a *de facto* more sociological reading as well. While there are no legal barriers, Indians, blacks, or women (the matter is compounded when you are a black or Indian woman) could rightly remark that there are still all sorts of *de facto* barriers. A black could very well apply for law school but deficiencies in earlier schooling, impoverished family and neighborhood backgrounds, racial stereotypes of inferiority about himself, prejudices of teachers in his previous school, even things like diet and health care might make it quite impossible for him to compete equally with most white applicants. So while there are no *de jure* legal barriers there are all sorts of *de facto* barriers to her or his equal access to law school or to a job, barriers which do not so afflict white males or do not afflict them to the same extent. Similar things apply to jobs which often in part depend on educational credentials or at least length of time in school. A high school dropout is in a very different position from someone with an M.A. Things are less dramatic with access to elementary schools, but even here there are powerful and similar *de facto* barriers.

Something could be done about breaking down those *de facto* barriers as well. Stereotypical sexist and racist attitudes could be vigorously attacked in various mass media, extra language training for Chicanos could be provided and, for all underprivileged groups, more active input could come from the schools to compensate for deprived family and neighborhood situations. All of these things, as well as other things like them, could be institutionalized and developed. Where things like this obtained there would be, where other things were equal, more competitive equality of opportunity than what obtained before. There are, of course, some things left indeterminate here, but there is no incoherence.

However, where practical interests to increase equality of educational opportunity were at work, it would soon become apparent, what surely should have been anticipated, that differences in family and neighborhood backgrounds are very crucial for achievement. Children from deprived family backgrounds, growing up in a sea of such backgrounds, will do rather worse in school than children who had non-deprived backgrounds, even when they have the same quality teachers. But again something can be done about this by strengthening the in-school influences and weakening the out-of-school influences. A rather thorough attack on this would involve things like boarding schools for all children. Note here that the objections to this, whether justified or not, would be practical and moral, not conceptual. It would, it would be said, cost too much and invade individual liberty too strongly by overriding parents' rights vis-à-vis their children. But still, what would be done, if such policies were instituted, is understandable enough. Indeed, it is just because it is so plainly understandable (coherent) that many so strongly object to it on moral or practical grounds. But again if these social policies were implemented, equality of opportunity would be considerably increased in the plain sense that it would be more fully approximated. And if boarding schools do not start early enough effectively to counterbalance early family and neighborhood influences, state nurseries could be instituted. And again the key criticisms would be practical and moral, not conceptual. We can show that in certain social situations with certain social practices in place, there is a greater proximity to equality of opportunity than in other institutional settings.

However, as our discussions of Charvet's and Lloyd Thomas' arguments attempting to demonstrate the conceptual incoherence of equality of opportunity bring out, even such social engineering, carried out fully and sensitively, would not establish *absolute* equality of opportunity, for even in the state nurseries it would be impossible to give everyone equal care, and similar things would obtain as long as there was any dependence of one person on another, as long, in short, as there was society. Moreover, all these arrangements leave unchanged the differential genetic components, which must have some effect, though perhaps no independent effect, on people. The above "practical" ways of achieving greater equality of opportunity do nothing to show how we can obtain absolute equality of opportunity. But the converse also obtains: that we cannot obtain absolute equality of opportunity does nothing to show that it is not the case that in society A there can be greater equality of opportunity than in society B, that there can be greater or lesser approximations to equality of opportunity.

Charvet would presumably object that if his arguments are correct—arguments I have not challenged—the principle of equality of opportunity cannot be, in its *complete* formulation, stated without incoherence or contradiction. But if this is so, then it (equality of opportunity) cannot be used at all in any specific application. If p is nonsense, period, it cannot make sense to assert p in circumstance c.[32]

Charvet's error here is twofold. It is first in the "it" of two sentences before this one. "It" can, on the one hand, refer to what he calls the complete formulation of equality or what I called "absolute equality of opportunity" or, on the other hand, "it" can refer to one of the proximate statements of equality of opportunity I have made above.

It is only the first that cannot be used in any specific application but no one is claiming that it can or indeed that it need be. His second error is in assuming that because a belief in complete (absolute) equality of opportunity is incoherent, a belief in proximate equality of opportunity is also incoherent. But that is like saying because the concept of a perfect vacuum is incoherent, one cannot intelligibly say that in one chamber there is more oxygen than in another. We cannot only intelligibly make such statements, we can and do make true statements of that type as well. Exactly the same thing obtains for proximate equality of opportunity.

Arguments such as Charvet's and Lloyd Thomas' reflect the philosopher's penchant for attaching more significance to conceptual considerations than they often warrant. Because complete equality of opportunity is a Holmesless Watson and because we cannot establish the conditions for the satisfaction of complete equality of opportunity, they assume that the concept of equality of opportunity must be incoherent and the whole attempt to obtain equality of opportunity pointless. That belief is both politically naive, by implication (if not intent), conservative (*status quo* defending), and false, though I do not say it is false because it is conservative but false for the reasons I have given above.

The crucial considerations here in the arguments about equality of opportunity are the moral, political, and practical ones and certain factual-cum-conceptual considerations about I.Q. we shall consider in the next section. However, conceptual arguments like Charvet's and Lloyd Thomas' are not entirely pointless, for they force us to state more clearly what we are talking about in speaking of equality of opportunity and they do forcefully make us see that we cannot attain an utterly fair through and through equality of opportunity. Individuals will never be able, no matter how classless our society becomes, to have absolutely equal life chances. Such pure fairness cannot be obtained. But it is politically and morally wise, a wisdom which a steady diet of conceptual preoccupations frequently impedes, to recognize that here degrees are of decisive importance. The equal opportunities for blacks in South Africa and in Cuba are very different indeed.

IV

I have argued above that it is not the case that the doctrine of equality of opportunity is a meaningless doctrine, contradictory or in some other way conceptually incoherent. I have argued that there are vague, somewhat indeterminate readings of it which still are not so utterly indeterminate as to make it quite without truth conditions. However, this is not intended to give aid and comfort to meritocracy or to the old egalitarianism which gives primacy to equality of opportunity. If we think of what it would be like to give equality of opportunity to ghetto children, it will be seen as involving a fairly long-term project to attain a social setting in which something approximating an equality of condition would obtain. For this to obtain, the political and socio-economic changes in the societies with the ghettos would have to be very extensive. And this is merely a dramatic example; there are all sorts of advantages and disadvantages in our societies, some of them subtle, most of them not. To overcome these would require profound changes in our whole socioeconomic system.

The two conceptions (equality of opportunity and equality of condition) can be, and should be, analytically distinguished but the two problems must, unless we desire only ideological effects, be attacked together. And it is hardly possible to approach these problems seriously without raising very serious questions about the justice of our underlying social structure, including, very fundamentally, our economic institutions.[33] Moreover, as Young's *The Rise of the Meritocracy* makes plain, a meritocracy requires such a separation, rejects equality of condition and stresses a need to attain a very precise and ramified measure of merit, so that we can all be placed with optimum efficiency in our proper economic boxes. Here at least some of Charvet's and Lloyd Thomas' strictures about the indeterminateness of equality of opportunity have a point. One would have to be able to establish merit positions very accurately indeed for anything even remotely like this to have a ghost of a chance of being fair. But this we cannot do. Finally, even if we could do it, there remains, as our previous examination of moral assessments of meritocracy brought to the fore, the question of whether we should do it.

However, one of the fundamental reasons for believing that we cannot do it has to do with I.Q. and is, at least in large measure, independent of the perhaps overly arcane arguments previously discussed—arguments designed to show that equality of opportunity is an incoherent conception. In *The Rise of the Meritocracy,* recall that accurate measurements of "native intelligence," at least in some sense appropriately operationally defined, were absolutely crucial for the meritocratic program. Educational psychologists were supposed to have developed such I.Q. measurements in some non-arbitrary way.

The claim that we have any such thing or are likely to come to have it has been very powerfully attacked. If these attacks are in the main well taken, meritocracy collapses, even if the Charvet-Lloyd Thomas type conceptual arguments are shown to be unsound and the moral arguments are shown to be indecisive.

Meritocrats in order to carry out the scientific stratification of society rely on the notion that there is something properly called "native intelligence" that can be, and indeed is, properly measured by I.Q. The distinguished geneticist P. B. Medawar points out that there are well-founded "misgivings about whether it is indeed possible to attach a single number valuation to an endowment as complex and as various as intelligence. . . ."[34] Medawar is of the opinion that it is an illusion, reflecting scientific naivete, to think that we can other than arbitrarily and pointlessly—ideological considerations aside—attach "a single number valuation to complex quantities. . . ."[35] We should say of intelligence what demographers now say of fertility or agronomists say of the field behavior of a soil. They recognize that no single number valuation is feasible for the phenomena depends "on altogether too many variables, not all of which are 'scalar' in character."[36] Educational psychologists who develop these tests are crucial to the meritocratic program, for, if we are to have our I.Q. identification numbers, there must be some way to definitely and non-arbitrarily (since, after all, it is a measure of *merit*) assign us our I.Q., just as we can say definitely that a person is five feet nine inches tall. There must be a scalar quantity that intelligence is. But, as Medawar points out, intelligence is a far too complicated and many-faceted affair to be so characterized. "Among its elements are speed and span of *grasp*, the ability to see implications and conversely to discern *non sequitors* and other fallacies, the ability to discern analogies and formal parallels between outwardly dissimilar phenomena or thought structures, and much else besides."[37] Even here I think Medawar has a bit of a onesided diet. Intelligence is indeed the use of such roughly logical powers but it is also shown in some people's judiciousness and wisdom in handling eruptive emotional disputes between children, the making of a fine canoe, the painting of an imaginative picture, in the moral sensibilities of some people, in the ability some people have to understand and react to the moods of others and in much more as well. I think we should say about "intelligence" what Wittgenstein said about "game": that it does not have an essence, some set of defining properties such that we can give necessary and sufficient conditions for it.

Educational psychologists in reality, as they did fictitiously in *The Rise of the Meritocracy,* have an answer of sorts for this. They concede that I.Q. tests do not show what intelligence is but that these tests do give them an operational specification which enables them to pick out which children will do well in school and go on to do well in business and industry afterwards. But, they claim, a test which will catch that is sufficient for the purpose of "intelligence testing" within a meritocracy, for with such a test we can know which children are worth spending extensive educational resources on, for we will know which ones will be most instrumental in enhancing the society's productivity. (Even here we must be careful about what counts as maximizing a society's productivity.)

Even assuming what is also very challengeable that we can pick out "native" talent here, it is still an argument that deserves the scorn that Medawar and Noam Chomsky heap on it.[38] Intelligence in meritocratic arguments was supposed to be one of two chief elements in determining merit or desert. It was to determine which of the people really deserved entrance into the elite of power and prestige. Now that is dropped in substance. The measure for merit or human worth becomes, on the above reading, what poeple have the capacity to succeed in in a society organized along capitalist lines to maximize profitability. Those who are good at doing that are the ones said to be intelligent and meritorious. Those who are not get scaled down in intelligence and desert to the degree they depart from that norm.

Meritocracy, with its stress on the primacy of equality of opportunity, also stresses the need for not only determining what intelligence is but for determining what *native* or *innate* intelligence is; it is concerned to determine what our intelligence is apart from the special influences of our enculturation. The ability to do this is, of course, essential for assigning us our merit places in a fair way and for providing, in the strong sense meritocrats require, equality of opportunity. There are, however, immense difficulties about designing tests which are not culturally biased; but that difficulty aside, the arguments made in the previous paragraphs should be enough to dash that I.Q. designer's dream. That is not all, however, for if there is no way to unscramble the factors due to nature and nurture, the meritocratic claim is triply dashed. That is just the situation we are in. Here Medawar is again a perceptive and reliable guide. It is indeed likely that intellectual differences are in some degree genetically influenced. What we cannot do, Medawar argues, is attach any exact figure to the contribution of heredity to differences in human intelligence. We simply cannot in any exact way determine the percentage contribution of nature and nurture to intelligence.[39]

Geneticists, such as J. B. S. Haldane and Lancelot Hogben, have pointed out the reasons for this. As Medawar puts it himself: "the contribution of nature is a function of nurture and of nurture a function of nature, the one varying in dependence on the other, so that a statement that might be true in one context of environment and upbringing would not necessarily be true in another."[40] Medawar gives the following instructive example:

> The little brackish water shrimp *Gammarus chevreuxi* is extruded from the brood pouch with red eyes, but usually ends up with black eyes— because of the deposition in them of the black coloring matter melanin. The capacity for forming melanin and the rate at which it is formed and deposited are between them under the control of a number of genetic factors. Coloration of the eye is also affected by a number of other environmental factors: certainly the temperature and probably (though I don't know for sure) the dietary availability of such substances as tyrosine and phenylalanine or their precursors.
>
> Among these various factors temperature is perhaps the most instructive, for it is possible to choose a genetic makeup such that coloration of the eye will appear to be wholly under environmental control: black at relatively high temperatures of development and reddish or dusky at lower temperatures. It is also possible to choose an ambient temperature at which red

eyes or black eyes are inherited as straightforward alternatives according to Mendel's laws of hereditary [sic]. Thus to make any pronouncement about the determination of eye color it is necessary to specify both the genetic makeup and the conditions of upbringing: neither alone will do, for the effect of one is a function of the effect of the other. It would therefore make no kind of sense to ask what percentage the coloration of the eye was due to heredity and what percentage was due to environment.[41]

These difficulties are not the only difficulties that Medawar and others point out educational psychologists run up against in trying first to give a coherent sense and then a measure to the notion of "innate intelligence" or "native intelligence," but they are quite enough to show that meritocrats really have nothing objective to go on in trying to establish merit places in a meritocracy. We have no basis at all to assert, as Richard Herrnstein does, that 80 to 85 percent of the variation in I.Q. amongst whites is due to the genes or make any claims at all that I.Q. scores are in any degree heritable. We have no grounds for distinguishing what meritocrats claim to be a meritocracy from a plutocracy or oligarchy.

V

I have in the previous three sections tried to state much of the case against meritocracy with its exclusive stress on productivity and the primacy of equality of opportunity. I have given moral, conceptual, and factual arguments against meritocracy and its defense of a stratified and in an important way inegalitarian society. Even if all my conceptual and factual or factual-cum-conceptual arguments are in some way mistaken, the moral arguments would still remain in place and it is to them, in the last analysis, that I would give most weight. Though for some who are more "subjectivist" or sceptical than I am about moral arguments generally, or, at least, for such moral arguments, the converse obtains. That is to say, even if the moral arguments are in some important ways problematic or just downright mistaken, the conceptual and factual arguments would be unaffected. I should add that in spite of the weight I give to the moral arguments, these other arguments seem to me to be sufficient to demolish the claims of meritocracy. Either way, meritocracy is very much on the ropes.

However, just as I argued in Chapter 6 that the claims of desert have a modest place in a theory of social justice even though justice is not desert, so I shall now argue that while there can be no such thing as a just meritocracy, it is still the case that in things like job placement considerations of merit and productivity have an important place, though they can, for a variety of reasons, sometimes be rightly (justifiably) overridden.

I think it is evident enough, given that we are in a state of scarcity, that concern to achieve efficiency and productivity is not unreasonable. Indeed, since talk of a post-scarcity society in the foreseeable future is a bad joke, it is morally remiss not to be so concerned. Medawar is, of course, perfectly right in remarking that we should not make productivity everything: treating the GNP as the tribal God of the Western world. It should not be treated as a measure of a society's well being, particularly when that society is an advanced industrial society, but, as I am sure he would not deny, it still plainly is an important element in a decent social order. It is, to put it platitudinously but truly, usually socially desirable to enhance productivity wherever possible. It is also the case that there is something, everything else being equal, just about giving the more capable person the job where this can readily be ascertained and where his/her having the job would enhance productivity.

No matter how sceptical we are about I.Q. tests and talk of innate abilities, and no matter how thoroughly we may reject the idea that we could really establish genuine conditions of equality of opportunity, we can, and indeed should, quite consistently with that, recognize the commonplace that some people have interests and abilities which enable them to perform a given job better than others. *Ceteris paribus* having such abilities and interests superior to anyone else competing for the job provides us with a very strong reason for believing that the person with those interests and abilities should have that job. This is not to say that people so blest should have greater rewards or generally have more power in the society than others not so blest; and it does not commit us to a meritocracy: the sort of thing Young portrays where the whole society makes all its job assignments and social rewards on such a merit basis and where the power and control of the society goes to a meritocratic elite. But we can reject meritocracy while still stressing the desirability of productivity and we can see the justice in most circumstances of job placement on the basis of merit, where that is cashed in, as meritocrats do, in terms of ability plus effort.

Norman Daniels, who is surely no anti-egalitarian or a defender of meritocracy, defends such a partial utilization of meritocracy. I want to follow out the rationale of his arguments.[42]

Given plausible empirical assumptions about the distribution of abilities (I say nothing about "innate abilities") among human beings, it is reasonable to make the meritocratic assumption that the closer we can come, without nullifying other things we deeply prize, to achieving a fair equality of opportunity the closer we will come to maximizing the availability of human abilities. If we also attach importance to productivity, as it is desirable to do, recognizing that human abilities are wasted where fair equality of opportunity does not obtain, we will also recognize the desirability of having such a principle in place even in an egalitarian society. This society differs from a meritocracy in that considerations of efficiency and productivity are, in most circumstances, overridden by distinct considerations of justice and right. A concern for equality, a concern to compensate for past injuries or to reward past service, can well override considerations of efficiency and indeed typically would in a society of moderate wealth.[43] So concern for equality of opportunity, as it is linked in meritocratic thinking to productivity, would be trumped by some other considerations of social justice. It is an important principle but it is not the overriding principle as it is in meritocracies.

It is not the case, however, that the sole value of equality of opportunity is determined by its instrumental link to productivity, for it also, *ceteris paribus,* strikes us as fair, where we can, to come as close as we can, without undermining autonomy or equality of condition, to attaining a fair equality of opportunity. But this gives the principle an important dual value, for it is both instrumentally valuable and intrinsically valuable, i.e., *prima facie* such a distribution is just fair and this value is independent of its utilitarian value.

Daniels also argues that a just society would take over from meritocratic thinking a principle he calls the *principle of productivity.* He argues that all merit claims for job placement are derivations from this principle of productivity. The *principle of productivity* says that "job assignments should be made by selecting the most productive array of job assignments: if that is not possible (because some jobs are already held), then select the next most productive array of job assignments and so on."[44] This principle is normally trumped, for the reasons Rawls and Ronald Dworkin have made familiar, by considerations of justice; but, where there is no conflict with justice or other considerations of right, a good society will in most circumstances operate in accordance with such a principle.

We have then a properly chastened meritorian basis for determining when a given individual merits a job: "An individual may claim to merit one job more than another job, or to merit one job more than another person does, if and only if his occupying that job is an assignment that is part of the assignment selected by the Productivity Principle."[45] It is not just the persons having the ability or making the effort that is relevant but crucially the fact that that person, with that repertoire, plays a certain social role. The merit claim is dependent on the productivity claim. Like Rawls, Daniels focuses on "the relevant abilities because of their utility, not because there is something intrinsically meritorious about having them."[46] Like the meritocrat, his notion of merit is a very special one not to be confused with our ordinary notion of desert.

This productivity principle is a macro principle and should be preferred to a micro productivity principle; though Daniels does qualify this by remarking that in a society such as our own where no attempt is made to calculate the macro productivity of job assignments, the micro productivity principle is plainly a better rule of thumb. But in fundamental considerations about the design of just social institutions, the macro principle is to be preferred.

The following quotation from Daniels shows the rationale for both the macro and micro principles.

> To see why the Productivity Principle is the preferred principle, consider the following case. Jack and Jill both want job A and B and each much prefers A to B. Jill can do either A or B better than Jack. But the situation S in which Jill performs B and Jack A is more productive than Jack doing B and Jill A (S'). The Productivity Principle selects S, not S', because it is attuned to macro, not micro, productivity considerations. It says "select people for jobs so that *overall* jobs performance is maximized."
>   It might be felt that the "real" meritocrat would balk at such a macro principle. The "real" meritocrat, it might be argued, is one who thinks a person should get a job if he or she is the best available person for *that* job. We might formulate such a view as the microproductivity principle that, for any job J, we should select the applicant who can most productively perform J from among those desiring J more than any other job. The micro principle would select S', not S.[47]

The reason, Daniels believes, we should stick with the macro principle, is that the "rationale for treating job-related abilities as the basis for merit claims in the first place . . . is [the belief] that it is socially desirable to enhance productivity where possible. . . ."[48]

Libertarians would divorce merit claims from such a strong link with productivity considerations. Libertarians would often link merit claims with entitlement claims and would treat them as subordinate to entitlement claims. They surely would be fearful that such a macro productivity principle would, if accepted, commit us to some centralized hiring bureau or procedure with the long arm of the state entering intrusively and pervasively into our lives.

Defenders of a strong and centrally placed principle of desert linked closely with merit, as it is in ordinary language, would also be wary of such a productivity principle. However, with such a stress on moral desert there are plain worries about what kind of foundations they could have for their desert claims beyond an appeal to a rather narrow range of intuitions. Moreover, as we shall see in Part IV, similar things should be said about the libertarian. But at any rate, this would not be a meritorian basis for merit claims and it is not the type of rationale for merit claims that either Daniels or I are concerned to work into an egalitarian account of justice. ("The new egalitarianism," if you will.) Note that under the macro principle neither Jill nor anyone else is forced into jobs they do not want at all. It just is not always the case that they get their first choices and sometimes they may not even get their second or third choices. But that they would not get anything that they would choose conversant with their abilities is very slight indeed. Such a way of reasoning flies in the face of Nozickian individualism, but that does not show it to be mistaken.

Any lingering sense of unfairness should be extinguished where Jack and Jill know that the macro productivity principle is operating. In such a situation their sense of legitimate expectations would be different or, at least, should be different than it is and indeed should be in our present situation. (Their considered judgments about what is fair and unfair would predictably be different.) But in societies such as our own, where we would be very lucky indeed if something even remotely like the micro principle were functioning, a sense of unfairness is rightly aroused when the most qualified person does not get the job.[49]

In reflecting about the morality of this, it is important to remember that our obligation to honor merit claims to jobs allocated on the above principles is only as strong as the *prima facie* obligation to satisfy productivity considerations. But this does not mean that other considerations—reverse discrimination considerations possibly—might not, in particular cases, and even as a rule, override considerations of productivity. Justice and rights typically trump *mere* utility (productivity, efficiency). It isn't that we simply forget about productivity but that we can in the name of justice—say to help overcome racism or sexism— weaken our concern with productivity and compromise it by giving greater weight to other considerations.

A meritocracy, as we have considered it, and as it is classically displayed by Young, is concerned not only, as Daniels is and as we have been in this section, with *allocating* job placement on the basis of a productivity principle, but, as well, with establishing a certain schedule of favorable rewards, prestige, and societal control and authority for the meritocrats. We have in such a conception a technocratic, meritocratic society run by elites and subservient to the interests of those elites. But the use of the meritocratic job placement principles that Daniels advocates, while compatible with this elitist social order, is equally compatible with an egalitarian libertarian socialist society.[50] It, by itself, implies no particular system of rewards or motivational assumptions about why men work. It is as compatible with Chomsky's account as Herrnstein's.

It is, I believe, disturbing to recognize, as I think we have to recognize, if we would be non-evasive, that job placement on a meritocratic conception (a) depends in part on a morally arbitrary distribution of natural assets and (b) yet should still be made on a merit-basis. Holding (a) and (b) together disturbs deeply our sense of fairness. I believe that it is considerations of that sort which are behind Rawls' and Hampshire's rejection of an appeal to desert.

The setting out of a system of social justice which will in some way counteract or moderate the effects of the morally arbitrary natural lottery cannot be solved within meritocratic assumptions or by any appeal to desert. Some form of new egalitarianism is, as far as I can see, the only way we might get a picture of justice here that might be morally adequate. Daniels suggests a reading of Rawls' theory, with a certain stress on the *difference* principle, as one possibility and I argued in Part II for a form of radical egalitarian justice.[51] The crucial thing is not to allow the effects of the natural lottery to be used as a basis for distributing significant rewards other than jobs. That will not, of course, *nullify* the natural lottery; as we saw in discussing equality of opportunity, there is no morally acceptable way of doing that. We should work for egalitarian reward schedules while generally accepting meritocratic job placement. This should not lead to a world with the social hierarchies that usually go with such meritocratic job placement. The struggle should be to have fully socialized into our being and structured into our institutions what John Schaar calls a "democratic mentality."

VI

It will perhaps be conceded that meritocracies are without merit, that there are very good grounds indeed for not being a meritocrat. But it might be responded that one dogma does not deserve another and that one thing that meritocratic arguments have smoked out is the absurd populist dogma that human beings are equal, that one man or woman is as good as another, and that they all deserve equal concern and respect. It is nonsense to say that men and women are born equal. Medawar insouciantly comments:

> It is a canon of high tory philosophy that a man's breeding—his genetic makeup—determines absolutely his abilities, his destiny, and his deserts; and it is no less characteristic of Marxism that, being born equal, a man is what his environment and his upbringing make of him. The former belief lies at the root of racism, fascism, and all other attempts to "make nature herself an accomplice in the crime of political inequality" (Condorcet) and the latter founders on the fallacy of human genetic equality ("A strange belief," said J. B. S. Haldane—a longtime member of the CP).[52]

It is hardly a characteristic of Marxism to claim that all men are born equal. Engels argues that demands for an equality that is greater than the equality of classlessness are absurd.[53] But that confusion about Marxism aside, many progressive people, including some Marxists, have thought of human beings as in certain fundamental respects equal, and it is this claim that meritocrats regard as a myth.

Those who are classical liberals, such as Frankel and Bell, would, of course, claim that all persons should have equal legal and political rights (though this was not something that early liberalism believed). But it is one thing to say that in certain fundamental respects human beings have a right to equal treatment and it is another thing again to say that biologically or culturally they are equals. Meritocrats, some will argue, have done us a not inconsiderable service in exposing the latter as a myth and, with the recognition of it as a myth, the hard Nietzschean normative question arises: on what rational basis can we justify the treatment of human beings who are neither biologically nor culturally equals as persons deserving of equal respect and concern?

Perhaps this is nothing more than a baseless bit of egalitarian ideology on our part. That we must show people such equal respect and concern is a deeply embedded belief with us, but is it any more justified than the meritocrat's belief? Is it anything more than a characteristic democratic or perhaps, as well, a Jewish-Christian prejudice? (Recall here our discussion in Chapter 2.)

What is perfectly clear and is not up for reasonable argument is that people in a great variety of ways are very different. Some are short and some are tall, some are agile and some clumsy, some are short-tempered and some are slow to anger, some are cruel and some kind, some are selfish and some are unselfish, some are hardworking and some lazy, some are witty and some are dull, some are unreflective and some reflective, some are intelligent and some stupid. There are hundreds of distinctions like these and between these rather extreme contrasts there are all sorts of gradations. None of this is in dispute though what is in dispute are the causes of it, its extent, the degree to which it must and should remain and (more generally) what we should conclude from a firm recognition of it.

Andrew Hacker in the last section of his "Creating American Inequality" makes the interesting historical observation that over beliefs about whether people are in fact equal—rough equality in character, intelligence, competence—there is a very considerable difference between our contemporary beliefs and the beliefs of many prominent intellectuals in the time span between Hobbes and Jefferson.[54] (Remember that Jefferson was a meritocrat.) Even contemporary socialists and radical egalitarians are very unlikely to believe that people are *in fact* equal. We know too much, we believe, "to be ingenuous about equality."[55] Hacker remarks, justly I believe, that "to claim that everyone is born with brains of 'equal' (or 'nearly equal') quality is something few people in our time can bring themselves to say."[56] But in an earlier era people—including some who were hardly in any normative or political sense egalitarians—said just that. He cites as crucial examples Hume, Jefferson, Babeuf, Rousseau, Hobbes, and Adam Smith. It is hardly surprising that Babeuf and Rousseau are on that list, but such cautious and deeply conservative figures as Hume, Smith, and Hobbes do come as a surprise. It was their common belief "that all of us enter the world with essentially similar capacities."[57] (In all this discussion what is being referred to, of course, is undamaged babies.) Adam Smith, for example, remarked that "the difference of material talents in different men is, in reality, much less than we are aware of." The difference, for example, he goes on to remark, "between a philosopher and a common street porter . . . seems to arise not so much from nature, as from habit, custom, and education."[58] This was not taken by Smith—and there are similar things in Hobbes and Hume—to be a moralizing remark or a remark about how, somehow, human nature ought to be, but it is taken to be an empirical fact about the human condition. They thought we started in the world roughly alike but that it was our very early socialization which made us so different. We all have a common human potential.

However, it seems to me that here these seventeenth- and eighteenth-century thinkers are making just the opposite assumption to that of the Herrnstein's and Jensen's of today and that they are equally caught by Medawar's criticism, though the earlier thinkers are far more excusably. They assume that we can sufficiently well unscramble the nature component from the nurture component so that we can make confident claims about what is environmentally and culturally determined and what is due to heredity.

However, with their stress on what we would now call socialization, there was also a recognition by these seventeenth- and eighteenth-century thinkers (particularly by Babeuf and Rousseau) that many of our human differences are unnaturally stressed and transferred into artificial inequalities created by a class society concerned with rank and power. And it is only when these differences are used as a source of ranking that we get social inequalities. Differences between us there plainly are and we hardly are in a position to say whether by nature or innately we are, surface differences aside, essentially the same or essentially different. If we delete enough detail, then of course we are essentially similar but this was hardly what Hobbes and Smith had in mind. But our manifest human differences only become inequalities when we introduce a ranking system and that, as we have seen, is not justified by any reputable theory of intelligence.

Hacker astutely remarks that a key to the differences between an egalitarian and a meritocrat has to do with how they respond to what are commonly recognized as human individual differences. The meritocrat attaches far greater importance to them and sees them as the rationale for a society of status and rank. The egalitarian does not.

All of us will see some differences just as different traits, temperaments, and skills without any suggestion that one is better than another. We, as individuals, also find certain temperaments and ways of doing things more or less *simpatico* with our own ways of living and responding. But if we are reasonably tolerant and liberal-minded people, we will be on guard against allowing this to be a source of ranking as distinct from a source of friendship.

Our society is a very competitive society, and competitiveness, ranking, and envy are bred into us. This, not infrequently, is exacerbated with intellectuals and takes absurd and sometimes bizarre forms. But it is still something which is deeply and pervasively a part of bourgeois culture. So our concern with ranking is very great, and, again and again and often very artificially, judgments about which people and which roles are better or worse go into our thinking, typically unargued, and unrationalized. We keep forgetting that there are many kinds of talents and that intelligence comes in varied forms. It is true that not everyone has the aptitude to be a neuro-surgeon or play jazz. But not everyone has the aptitude to drive a cab around New York or London either or to tell stories to children or to organize a strike or lead people on a white water float or to train German Shepherds. Special skills need not connote overall betterness—general human worth— and we plainly have no non-arbitrary criteria for ranking people occupations, and roles. Moreover, we have no good reason to be so concerned with such ranking, though in our culture we have a not inconsiderable cause to be concerned. The human cost in doing so is very great and the result, as Chomsky has observed, has been to reward and doubly reward the powers that be.[59]

Perhaps, in the ways that are most important, i.e., in our capacities for reciprocity, compassion, capacities to form life plans, to care for one another and the like, there are no, *a distinctive socialization apart,* significant differences between most people, so that we can say that we are equal here and that consequently each of us is of equal human worth. I think that the stress on this (taking it as a not unreasonable working hypothesis), and a stress on our common capacity to look after our own affairs and our common (community) affairs, is far more important than worrying about whether we are, everything considered, equally talented or equally intelligent. Indeed a stress on it is likely to make it more of a reality if in fact now it isn't.

However, it is still important to recognize that we have no good grounds for any belief that there are heritable differences in I.Q. which could serve as a basis, á la Herrnstein and Shockley, for a hereditary meritocracy; and we have no other grounds, as I have been at pains to argue, for accepting a meritocracy and very good grounds for rejecting it.

There simply is no objective measure of intelligence that would allow us to rank human beings and there is no human or moral need to go in search of such a measure. There are differences between us to be sure. At *the extremes,* there are some among us who are stupid and indeed feebleminded and there are some who are brilliant and there are some who are wise (and they are not always the same as the ones who are brilliant). But the great mass of us bunch together with our diverse talents and our diverse deficiencies, both often plainly related to our interests and to the lottery that selected our parents, our class, and where we grew up. And, as Medawar has stressed, intellectual performance is teachable and deeply affected by training and practice.[60] This plainly means that our, or at least our children's, deficiencies can be ameliorated and our talents indefinitely improved, for our own good and for our common benefit. We can accept our differences and indeed rejoice in them without anxiety about or even interest in the question "Who is better, who is worse?" We have no answer for that question anyway, but we have no need to answer it, even if we could. The fact of our differences and our inability to rank ourselves does not stand as a rational impediment to affirming an egalitarianism.

NOTES

1. Michael Young, *The Rise of the Meritocracy* (Harmondsworth, Middlesex, England: Penguin Books, 1961). (The book was first published by Thames & Hudson in 1958. My references will be to the Penguin edition. And all references to Young's book in this chapter will be given in the text.) John H. Schaar, "Equality of Opportunity and Beyond" in *Equality, Nomos IX,* eds. J. Roland Pennock and John W. Chapman (New York: Atherton Press, 1967), pp. 228–49. See also his "Some Ways of Thinking About Equality," *Journal of Politics* 36, no. 4 (November 1964): 867–95. There is the following exchange about Schaar's account: John Stanley, "Equality of Opportunity as Philosophy and Ideology," *Political Theory* 5, no. 4 (February 1977): 61–74; and Mary C. Segers, "On Stanley's 'Equality of Opportunity as Philosophy and Ideology,'" *Political Theory* 6, no. 3 (August 1978): 369–71.

2. Michael Walzer, "Nervous Liberals," *The New York Review of Books* 26, no. 15 (October 11, 1979): 8.

3. Ibid.

4. Ibid.

5. Schaar, "Equality of Opportunity and Beyond," p. 229.

6. Ibid.

7. Ibid.

8. Ibid., p. 240.

9. John Rawls, *A Theory of Justice* (Cambridge, Mass.: Harvard University Press, 1971), p. 106–7.

10. Ibid.

11. Ibid., p. 107.

12. Schaar, "Equality of Opportunity and Beyond," pp. 240–41.

13. Ibid., p. 241.

14. John Charvet, "The Idea of Equality as a Substantive Principle of Society," *Political Studies* 27 (March 1969): 154–68; and D. A. Lloyd Thomas, "Competitive Equality of Opportunity," *Mind* 86, no. 343 (July 1977): 388–404. See also his "Equality Within the Limits of Reason Alone," *Mind* 88, no. 352 (October 1979): 538–53.

15. Onora O'Neill, "How Do We Know When Opportunities Are Equal?" in *Feminism and Philosophy,* eds. Mary Vetterling-Braggin, Frederick Elliston, and Jane English (Boston, Mass.: Beacon Press, 1978), pp. 177–89.

16. Ibid., p. 177.

17. Lloyd Thomas, "Competitive Equality of Opportunity," pp. 389–90.

18. Ibid., p. 389.

19. Ibid., p. 392.

20. Charvet, "The Idea of Equality as a Substantive Principle of Society," p. 157.

21. Ibid.

22. Ibid.

23. Ibid.

24. Ibid., p. 158.

25. Ibid., pp. 159–60.

26. Lloyd Thomas, "Competitive Equality of Opportunity," p. 394.

27. Ibid., p. 395.

28. Ibid., p. 397.

29. Ibid., p. 398.

30. Ibid., pp. 398–400.

31. O'Neill, op. cit.

32. Charvet, op. cit., p. 158.

33. Samuel Bowles and Herbert Gintis, *Schooling in Capitalist America* (New York: Basic Books, 1976), pp. 88–94.

34. P. B. Medawar, "Unnatural Science," *The New York Review of Books* 24, no. 1 (February 3, 1977): 13.

35. Ibid.

36. Ibid.

37. Ibid.

38. Noam Chomsky, *For Reasons of State* (London: Fontana Books, 1973), pp. 104–50. See also his "The Case Against B. F. Skinner," *The New York Review of Books* 17 (December 30, 1971): 16–24.

39. Medawar, op. cit., p. 14.

40. Ibid.

41. Ibid.

42. Norman Daniels, "Meritocracy" in *Justice and Economic Distribution,* eds. John Arthur and William H. Shaw (Englewood Cliffs, N.J.: Prentice-Hall, 1978), pp. 164–78.

43. Ibid., p. 169.

44. Ibid., p. 160.

45. Ibid., p. 166.

46. Ibid.

47. Ibid., pp. 166–67.

48. Ibid., p. 167.

49. Ibid., p. 168.

50. Ibid., pp. 170–71.

51. Ibid., pp. 174–75.

52. Medawar, op. cit., p. 13.

53. Frederick Engels, *Anti-Dühring,* trans. Emile Burns (New York: International Publishers, 1939), pp. 117–18. First published in 1878. See my "Engels on Morality and Moral Theorizing," *Studies in Soviet Thought* 26 (1983).

54. Andrew Hacker, "Creating American Inequality," *The New York Review of Books* 27, no. 4 (March 20, 1980): 26–28.

55. Ibid., p. 26.

56. Ibid., p. 27.

57. Ibid.

58. Quoted by Hacker, ibid., p. 27.

59. Noam Chomsky, *For Reasons of State,* pp. 104–50.

60. Medawar, op. cit., p. 14.

Libertarianism, Individual Rights, and the Rejection of Egalitarianism

INTERLUDE AND PROEM THREE

In Part IV we shall turn to an extended examination of an arch anti-egalitarian social philosophy, namely, the entitlement theory. We saw something in Chapter 4 of such a conception of justice as well as something of the direction of an egalitarian response. But in Part IV I propose to examine it in its full subtlety and force. I shall, conventionally enough, take Robert Nozick as the key exponent of entitlement conceptions of justice. *Epigoni* such as Eric Mack, Jan Narveson, Tibor Machan, and Antony Flew are little more than Nozick's bulldogs. They do not advance the entitlement theory beyond Nozick's account. It is Nozick's account, in my view, which needs most to be met if radical egalitarianism or indeed even liberal egalitarianism is to make its way with intellectual respectability. Fredrich Hayek and Milton Friedman, who most certainly are neither *epigoni* nor bulldogs, also defend less purified forms of the entitlement theory of justice and are equally arch anti-egalitarians. Moreover, in Hayek's case we have a philosophically learned and reflective theory. But while their background accounts have more empirical adequacy than Nozick's, their defense of the entitlement theory, mixed as it is in their accounts with utilitarian arguments, is much less rigorous than Nozick's and their critique of egalitarianism and productive-distributive theories of social justice less penetrating. So I shall concentrate here on examining Nozick's work.

In doing this, I shall proceed as follows. I shall in the next chapter (Chapter 9) set out Nozick's view in sufficient detail to convey something of its subtlety and force, particularly in those domains where it seeks to show how equality and liberty conflict, show the errors of all distributive theories of justice (including, of course, theories which might defend an egalitarian patterning) and where it presents a defense of individual rights and a critique of what he takes to be socialism. (It should be noted, in passing, that Nozick, von Mises, Hayek, and Friedman—the major libertarians—have a very poor understanding of what socialism is. In their critiques, they, for the most part, attack straw men.) I shall conclude Chapter 9 with some rather straightforward moral critiques of the entitlement theory and then proceed in Chapter 10 to a cluster of what I shall characterize as more "sociological critiques." That concluded, I shall turn in the chapter that follows to more conceptually based critiques. I shall complete Part IV with a direct response to Nozick's rejection of the moral adequacy of egalitarian conceptions.

9

Nozick and Individual Rights

I

Robert Nozick begins *Anarchy, State, and Utopia* with, as he puts it, "a strong formulation of individual rights."[1] The very first sentence of his book tells us that "individuals have rights, and there are things no person or group may do to them (without violating their rights)" (page ix). There are certain actions that even in a state of nature would be morally impermissible (page 7). Here Nozick is appealing to something very like Locke's state of nature. Within the bounds of what Locke regards as the law of nature, individuals in the state of nature are perfectly free to do what they want to do including the disposing of "their possessions and persons as they see fit . . . without asking leave or depending upon the will of any other man." The law of nature, of course, sets bounds on our freedom to do what we will by requiring that "no one ought to harm another in his life, health, liberty, or possessions."[2] There are certain moral constraints—Nozick calls them side-constraints—which, for a theory which takes individual rights as fundamental, quite categorically limits actions in the pursuit of any goal. Morally speaking we are, on such an account, forbidden to violate these moral constraints in the pursuit of any goal. A rights view as strong as Nozick's cannot sanction—accept as justifiable or even as morally tolerable—the violation of a person's rights (say railroading an innocent man) in order to minimize the total amount of the violation of rights in the society (page 22). That kind of teleological reasoning—a form of reason which would sanction such violations—is not morally acceptable. There are moral constraints that cannot be violated in the pursuit of any goal (page 2). The "non-violation of rights" is a constraint placed upon an individual's action. It is not, however, an endstate to be realized but constraint on what ends can legitimately be pursued. Nozick's account is a rights-based and not a goal-based theory; there are, on such an account, no ends or goals to be realized (page 30).[3]

There is a natural objection to such a view that Nozick recognizes he must dispose of to make his individual rights view persuasive. It will be thought by many to be irrational to accept a view which prohibits the violation of a right—one is absolutely, barring some catastrophe, forbidden from violating it—but does not commit itself to the goal of minimizing the violation of such rights. That sounds like a person who accepts an end but refuses to accept the necessary means to that end. But, Nozick argues, so to view the matter is a mistake, for a right is not an end to be achieved but a valid claim which specifies actions we are categorically forbidden from doing. Are there any such actions and is this a plausible view? Nozick puts the objection himself forcefully:

> If nonviolation of C is so important, shouldn't that be the goal? How can a concern for the nonviolation of C lead to the refusal to violate C even when this would prevent other more extensive violations of C? What is the rationale for placing the nonviolation of rights as a side constraint upon action instead of including it solely as a goal of one's actions? [page 30]

Nozick's reply is that such absolute side-constraints reflect a deep Kantian assumption about ethics which he (Nozick), against utilitarians and other teleologists, accepts, namely, "the underlying Kantian principle that individuals are ends and not merely means; they may not be sacrificed or used for other ends without their consent" (page 31). It is this, for Nozick, as for Kant, which is morally speaking, bedrock. It is Nozick's contention that only if we can, from a moral point of view, justifiably reject this central Kantian conception can we, morally speaking, allow the violation of an individual's rights to achieve an overall minimization of rights violations. But Kant, he claims, is right here. So treating people is morally impermissible. We cannot, Nozick argues, take that morally illegitimate means to achieve even that noble end, for we can never rightly, by our actions, treat people as means only. "Individuals are inviolable" (page 31).

In Nozick's account, what we must do in our behavior toward any individual is so to constrain our actions that that individual is not used for any purpose to which he does not *consent.* We may not use others for any ends, no matter how noble, without their permission. We cannot violate a person's rights for what is admittedly the greater good or even to minimize evil, including minimizing the extent of rights violation.

We must realize, Nozick claims, in considering the force of the above arguments, that "there is no social entity with a good that undergoes some sacrifice for its own good" (pages 32–33). There is "no justified sacrifice of some of us for others . . ." (page 33). It is Nozick's root moral idea that "there are different individuals with separate moral lives and so no one may be sacrificed for others" (page 33). Nozick puts it:

> There are only individual people, different individual people, with their own individual lives. Using one of these people for the benefit of others, uses him and benefits the others. Nothing more. What happens is that something is done to him for the sake of others. Talk of an overall social

good covers this up. (Intentionally?) To use a person in this way does not sufficiently respect and take account of the fact that he is a separate person, that his is the only life he has. He does not get some overbalancing good from his sacrifice, and no one is entitled to force this upon him—least of all a state or government that claims his allegiance (as other individuals do not) and that therefore scrupulously must be neutral between its citizens. [page 33]

There is, as Nozick again forcefully puts it, "no moral balancing act [that] can take place among us; there is no moral outweighing of one of our lives by others so as to lead to a greater overall social good. There is no justified sacrifice of some of us for others" (page 33). We are distinct individuals who are not resources for others. The fundamental libertarian side-constraint is that of forbidding aggression against another. The individuality and distinctiveness of people must at all costs be respected. They must be left free to do what they will, to live their lives as they see fit, as long as they do not harm others. We are distinct (separate) individuals, each with our own individual lives to lead. We must be protected from others interfering with our lives both by way of harming us or by way of a paternalistic interference with how we would lead our lives. What we need is a non-aggression pact among individuals in which our material moral inviolability is guaranteed.

Human beings are beings who are rational, *in some sense* have a free will, and are capable of moral agency. We are beings with the ability to regulate and guide our own lives "in accordance with some overall conception we, as individuals, choose to accept" (page 40). We must not be interfered with here unless our actions interfere with others living in the same way.

Nozick, with his characteristic, and often fruitful, pressing of questions he himself cannot answer, asks: "Why not interfere with someone else's shaping of his own life?" (page 50). Nozick's answer is that if our lives are to have meaning we must not be so interfered with. "A person's shaping his life in accordance with some overall plan is his way of giving meaning to his life; only a being with the capacity to so shape his life can have or strive for a meaningful life" (page 50). The further "question," "And why shouldn't my life be meaningless?," surely appears at least to be an idling question (pages 50–51). No one outside of his philosopher's study would ask it and it is not even certain that it is a coherent question.[4]

In thinking of the design of a good society, we will think of "a social environment in which people are free to do their own thing" (page 312). On Nozick's conception of a good society, "there will not be *one* kind of community existing and kind of life led in utopia. Utopia will consist of utopias, of many different and divergent communities in which people lead different kinds of lives under different institutions" (page 312). What is crucial to recognize is that "Utopia is a framework for utopias, a place where people are at liberty to join together voluntarily to pursue and attempt to realize their own vision of the good life in the ideal community but where no one can impose his own utopian vision upon others" (page 312). Individuals in a free society "may contract into various restrictions which the government may not legitimately impose on them" (page 320). Individuals, for example, can contract into a socialist community but a government may not force it on them or require individuals born into that community to accept socialism. A similar thing, of course, should be said for capitalism. By consent people can come to accept restrictions on their behavior that, without their consent, would be a violation of their fundamental natural rights. But—and this should hold everywhere and at all times—it remains the case that "everyone has various rights that may not be violated, various boundaries that may not be crossed without another's consent" (page 325). In a free society, where individual rights are not being violated, we may "attempt to unite kindred spirits, but, whatever their hopes and longings, none have the right to impose their vision of unity upon the rest" (page 325).

The only state authority that is morally tolerable is that of a minimal nightwatchman state which "treats us as inviolate individuals who may not be used in certain ways by others as means or tools or instruments or resources . . ." (pages 333–34). It is a state which must treat "us as persons having individual rights with the dignity this constitutes" (pages 333–34).

So it is plain that it is a central claim of Nozick's that we have individual rights—rights not to be assaulted or killed (if we are doing no one harm), rights not to be coerced or imprisoned (again if we are doing no one harm), rights not to have our property taken or destroyed and rights not to be limited in the use of our property so long as we do not in its use violate the rights of others. These are inviolable rights which may not be transgressed by others or by the state for any purpose whatsoever. Morally justifiable state activity will be limited to protecting people against murder, assault, theft, fraud and breach of contract. Such a state, in extensive contrast with the state we are familiar with, is the classical minimal nightwatchman state. No state, on such a conception, has the right or the legitimate authority to restrict the liberty of some of its citizens or impose burdens on their income or wealth to relieve even a very considerable suffering or deprivation of need of others of its citizens.

For Nozick moral wrongdoing can only take the form of the violation of rights. Where rights are not being violated no wrong is being done to any person. Short of catastrophe, how individuals fare under a social system, whether they are miserable or happy, whether they attain self-respect or self-realization, is not a matter that the state or any persons in the state must rectify if no rights have been violated. That such a state of affairs is allowed to obtain, where it can be remedied, is not to suggest a moral defect of that social system. It is only where rights have been violated that moral wrongdoing occurs. All that seems to matter in Nozick's moral landscape is that rights not be violated. An institution can only show its moral probity by protecting rights. It's only moral vices would be the violating of rights or its failure to protect rights where it has the power to do so. No matter what consequences flow from the exercise of rights they cannot be morally objectionable. There can never be a valid moral objection to the exercising of a moral right.

II

Nozick's severely rights-based theory may be inadequate. It may rest on a slender or implausible foundation but it is not, as some have thought, foundationless.[5] If we do not limit government action in the way Nozick urges, if we do not limit our moral theory to a stringent appeal to a few basic rights, but find a larger sphere for government action and for moral requiredness, we will end up, like the utilitarians, ignoring, or at least not giving adequate weight to, the separateness of persons and will not treat them as inviolable. The inescapable fact of separateness of persons is Nozick's foundation for his conception of the moral life.[6]

Nozick applies this rights-based account to a discussion of justice in a predictable way. He is particularly anxious to meet the claims of welfare-state liberals such as John Rawls and Brian Barry that a more than minimal state is necessary to meet the demands of social justice. In Part II of *Anarchy, State, and Utopia,* Nozick criticizes such accounts of distributive justice and sets out his own thoroughly rights-based conception of justice which he calls an entitlement theory. Justice, in his conception, is, as Bernard Williams has put it, "a pipe for the rightful delivery of rights over any distance. . . ."[7]

We have, Nozick begins by arguing, a mistaken way of looking at questions of justice. We think of justice on the model of an adult distributing a pie to children. We tend to imagine the state, fully in the redistribution business, functioning like the adult with a cake to divide among a group of children. As the adult will frequently have to make last minute adjustments in an attempt to rectify careless cutting, so the state will have to continually make redistributions to retain some ideal pattern. Vis-à-vis our social lives and the benefits and burdens and the various goods and services that exist in a society, what is crucial to recognize is that, unlike the cake situation, there is in reality "no *central* distribution, no person or group entitled to control all the resources, jointly deciding how they are to be doled out" (page 149). In a free society, where there is a respect for the rights of persons, no state or group can proceed in this way. No state or member of the state apparatus has a right to so proceed. Different people have diverse holdings, things that they worked for or that they got in some exchange or as a gift. There is no central distribution agency that has the right to redistribute these things. What Nozick seeks to provide is an integrated set of principles of justice in holdings as a more adequate alternative to various distributive principles. This he calls the *entitlement theory* (page 150).

Nozick rejects the idea that there is any pattern of distribution that justice requires. In that way he, like Fredrick Hayek, rejects *social* justice. Any pattern of distribution can, at some particular time, turn out to be just—including both radically egalitarian and inegalitarian patterns. That is to say, that pattern, whatever it is, will be just if certain conditions obtain. Those conditions are that in the original acquisition of unheld things the acquisition was in accordance with the principle of justice in *original acquisition.* A person who acquires a holding in accordance with that principle is entitled to that holding. Besides justice in original acquisition, a complete theory of justice must also include an account of justice in the *transfer of holdings* to cover voluntary exchanges, gifts and the like. In doing that it must articulate a principle of justice in transfer. A person who acquires her/ his holding in accordance with that principle from someone else who in turn is entitled to the holding transferred is entitled to that holding.

In a world where there has been no previous wrong doing, there are no additional holdings that anyone is entitled to, for all other genuine entitlements must arise from repeated applications of the principle of just original acquisition and the principles of just transfer. (That is the point of William's metaphor about the pipe.) In a world in which no injustice had ever occurred, justice would just consist in the application of these principles. Whatever distributions arose from those steps would be just distributions *no matter what pattern they took.* Any configuration of holdings that results from a legitimate transfer of legitimately acquired holdings is itself just. People, in such circumstances, would have what they are entitled to and only what they are entitled to and so we would have a state of perfect justice in which there was protection for the rights of everyone. This is the whole of the legitimate subject of justice: there is no further question about how things are to be distributed. Here we have an account that is radically different from Rawls' account or the account I have given in Part II.

Such a theory of *justice as entitlement* is what Nozick calls a historical theory. It depends on what actually happened. If things had happened otherwise holdings that people justly hold now would not be justly held. This would be so even if the holdings were in structurally identical patterns. It is not the structure which determines justice. It is not, on Nozick's account, a question of how distributions of holdings in a society must be distributed for it to be a just society or a rational society but a question of how things actually happened in the past (page 152).

How do we determine what is an *original just* acquisition? How do we determine when previously unheld things come to be justly held?

Bernard Williams contends that Nozick "does not really address himself to the issue of what is an originally just holding at all, or of property as (what he requires) a purely moral notion."[8] We do not know, Williams claims, in any systematic or exact way, what the boundaries are between people in the state of nature: boundaries that people may not cross. Recall that a holding is just if it is acquired by a just process from a holding which is itself just. But then we very much need a clear answer to how we could determine what is an initial just acquisition. We need some theory of original entitlement or at least some way of determining when it obtains.

Nozick does say something about this, though it is very sketchy, when he discusses what he calls the Lockean proviso (pages 174–82). Suppose I have a yacht and I come across a previously undiscovered island—an island which is utterly uninhabited. Suppose it is a small island that I could readily farm myself. Suppose I claim the island and proceed to farm it. In doing that I do not, in one plain sense, make you or anyone else worse off than you previously were, though you are now without one opportunity you previously had. There is, that is, a certain way in which you now no longer can improve your situation, i.e. you can't rightfully take over that uninhabited island and farm it. But you are not made worse off by my appropriation of the island in the morally crucial sense that you are now no longer able to use freely (without appropriation) what you previously could (page 176). You are not, in that crucial sense, prevented by my appropriation from doing or possessing what you previously did, as you would be if I appropriated a pasture that both you and I had been freely using and, without your consent, fenced it off and prevented you from using it. By my appropriation in that second situation I have, in the relevant sense, made you worse off than you previously were. But nothing like this obtains in my appropriation of the island (page 176). A previously unheld object comes to be justly held by an original just acquisition, if, in that sense of being made worse off, others are not made worse off than they would be in Nozick's (and Locke's) moralized state of nature in which their individual rights are respected. (The state of nature is the imaginary circumstance in which there is no state, yet the people in Nozick's, though not in Hobbes', state of nature are already moralized beings who, though not unfailingly, respect each other's rights and believe that it is wrong to treat people as means only.)

There is a just original entitlement or original just acquisition when and only when a previously unheld object is appropriated and no one is made worse off than they had previously been before the appropriation. Any original acquisition or, for that matter, transfer or combination of transfers, is illegitimate if others are made, in the appropriate sense, worse off than they previously had been by the acquisition or transfer.

This is not a precise account of justice in original acquisition, and it is difficult to know how to generalize it or how to apply it in many circumstances. Nozick, surprisingly, thinks that in genuine free-market capitalism the Lockean proviso would not be violated and that it would be perfectly plausible to believe that many of the entitlements, in that society were on Nozick's own terms legitimate.[9] (This—showing the high level of Nozick's abstraction from social reality—could only hold for a genuinely laissez-faire capitalism and not for the thoroughly statist enterprise that is contemporary capitalism.[10]) But though Nozick's conceptions here are sketchy, and much work needs to be done on them, it is not the case, as Williams avers, that Nozick does not give us any guidance here at all.[11]

Besides the principle of just acquisition and the principle of just transfer, there is also the principle of *justice in rectification*. We do not, of course, live in a world of perfect justice. People plunder, steal, defraud each other and the like. Many of the holdings that people acquire are not acquired by means of an application of the principles of justice in acquisition or transfer. (Nozick, it should be noted, does not commit himself on the justice of people's holdings in our capitalist society.) The existence of these injustices makes it necessary for us to add a third principle of justice—a principle we would have no need for, if injustice had not occurred—namely, as I remarked above, a principle of *justice in rectification in holdings*. Again a principle of rectification will require historical information concerning previous unjust acquisitions or transfers. Again we have in justice a backward-looking virtue. (Here Nozick is a more subtle Flew.)

These three principles constitute the core of the theory of justice of an entitlement theory. Unlike a theory such as Rawls's or Barry's or my own, we have, in such a theory, a set of historical and unpatterned principles. Justice, on such an account, is a backward-looking virtue essentially concerned with how people came to acquire things. On our accounts, by contrast, an essential element of social justice is that it is forward looking: concerned with what end result and patterned principles a fully just society must have. Nozick, by contrast, is concerned to deny that there is any such end result to be achieved or set of patterned principles, including egalitarian principles, that a just or fully just society must exemplify. Any such required pattern, he believes, would undermine individual liberty and trod on individual rights, and so it could not be part of a just society.

However, as Nozick is well aware, patterned end-state principles of justice are principles of justice which are pervasively held and there are specific ones, such as the ones championed by Rawls or Barry, which are (at least putatively) the principles of justice of the liberal welfare state.

Patterned principles of justice specify a certain distribution that is to obtain along some natural dimension, weighted sum of natural dimensions, or lexicographic ordering of natural dimensions. Distribution according to merit, distribution according to need, usefulness to society, marginal product, effort or I.Q. would all be patterned distributional principles (pages 156–57). A distribution in society is patterned when it specifies that holdings are to vary along with some natural dimension or some combination of such dimensions.

Some of these patterned principles are historical and some are nonhistorical (pages 156–57). Distribution according to I.Q. or need are, according to Nozick, non-historical patterned principles. Distribution according to moral merit or usefulness to society are patterned historical principles. All patterned principles, both historical and nonhistorical, specify some distribution which will vary according to some natural dimension or combination of such dimensions. Those patterned principles which are historical principles will pick out some state of affairs done in the past such as someone making something or doing something with a certain intention. But some patterned principles are not concerned with what happened in the past.

Patterned non-historical principles of justice can be current time-slice principles or ones which apply over a time sequence. For these non-historical principles the justice of a distribution is determined not primarily by how things come about but by how they are distributed— by who has what—as judged by some structural principles of distribution such as Rawls' principles, Barry's principle of reciprocity or my own two principles of justice. They are not concerned—or are not primarily concerned—with how people come to have what they have but with who has what. Where they are concerned, as an egalitarian principle would be, with having structural principles which range over time sequences of many current time profiles, we do not have *current* time slice principles, but we still do have what, in Nozick's terms, are unhistorical principles specifying justice in terms of a certain distributive pattern (a certain complex structure) which makes reference to a certain structure of distribution but makes no ineliminable reference to what happened in the past or happened at any particular time.

To attain justice, on such a conception, is not to secure entitlements but to bring a distinctive social design into being and/or to sustain a social design in which a certain pattern of distribution obtains in society. Such principles of justice are always patterned principles (page 155). To know whether justice in society has been obtained is to know whether a certain patterned structure obtains in society.

It is this conception of justice—a conception I defended in Part II—that Nozick believes to be profoundly mistaken. He believes it is mistaken because he does not believe that any of these principles could function as principles of social design in a society without there being an extensive violation of individual rights and an undermining of liberty. We cannot, Nozick argues, treat "To each according to his _____ " independently of "From each according to his _____ " and still attain justice. Marxists are right, Nozick avers, in not treating production and distribution independently in determining what is just or unjust. Similarly, on the entitlement view:

Whoever makes something, having bought or contracted for all other held resources used in the process (transferring some of his holdings for these cooperating factors), is entitled to it. The situation is not one of something's getting made, and there being an open question of who is to get it. Things come into the world already attached to people having entitlements over them. From the point of view of the historical entitlement conception of justice in holdings, those who start afresh to complete "to each according to his _____ " treat objects as if they appeared from nowhere, out of nothing. [page 160]

Where justice is our topic, it is, Nozick argues, always of moral relevance concerning any holding where it came from or who made it, if it was made. But for Nozick, unlike for Marx, it is, as we have seen, of no moral relevance what pattern of distribution obtains. What is of relevance is how it was acquired, transferred or, if it was ill-acquired or ill-transferred, what rectification is being made. That for Nozick exhausts the subject of justice.

IV

I have argued in earlier chapters that liberty requires equality. Nozick, and Hayek and Friedman as well, maintain just the opposite. For them a commitment to equality is incompatible with a commitment to liberty. An egalitarian society could not, they believe, be a free society.

Given Nozick's entitlement conception of justice and his severely rights-based theory (indeed a purely negative rights-based theory), it is understandable that he would make that claim, but it will be important here to see exactly his grounds for saying that equality destroys freedom or liberty. Radical egalitarian principles such as my own or liberal egalitarian principles such as Rawls's or Barry's or Dworkin's are, as we have seen, patterned end-state (end-result) principles. All patterned end-state principles involve redistributive activity and, where rectification does not come into play, that cannot but result in the violation of individual rights. That is why we must not be egalitarians or accept any end-state patterned principles of distributive justice. (168-9)

Why exactly, according to Nozick, must it be the case that end-state, patterned principles of justice violate individual rights? Liberty, he maintains, invariably upsets patterns and it is particularly obvious that it would upset the egalitarian patterns of justice that would obtain in any socialist or other egalitarian society. In an attempt to establish this Nozick starts by giving us two puzzle cases designed to show how liberty upsets patterns: the Wilt Chamberlain case and the case of the entrepreneur in a socialist society. (161-163)

Let us suppose we have established in some society at a given time T some end-state patterned principle of justice yielding a determinate distribution, let us call it D_1, in that society at that time. Let us further assume, for the sake of simplicity and to make the conflict with egalitarianism sharper, that D_1 is an egalitarian distribution expressing the commitments of an egalitarian society. (This is not actually necessary for Nozick's first case, for it is meant to apply to any D_1 prescribed at any time by any patterned end-state principle. But we shall continue to speak as if D_1 were an egalitarianly specified distribution.)

Now suppose into this egalitarian society comes Wilt Chamberlain. He becomes a basketball idol and is much in demand by the fans. Suppose he makes a contract with a basketball team to play home games only under the following conditions. Twenty-five cents from the price of each ticket goes to him. He is such an idol that the fans cheerfully attend the home games, buying their tickets without any grumbling, each time "dropping a separate twenty-five cents of their admission price into a special box with Chamberlain's name on it" (page 161). They want very much to see him play and regard the total price, including the extra twenty-five cents going to Wilt, as well worth it. And, of course, nobody is forced, even by any kind of social pressure, to go to the games. That is something they voluntarily choose to do. As a result of the fans flocking to see Wilt play, Wilt ends up at the end of the season with a considerable wad of money—let us say $250,000—which surely puts him in a very distinct position in this previously egalitarian society and indeed upsets the egalitarian distribution D_1.

Because of this situation, we have moved from the egalitarian distribution D_1 at T_1 to a somewhat inegalitarian distribution D_2 at T_2. But isn't, Nozick rhetorically asks, the move entirely innocent and morally uncriticizable for anyone who values liberty and respects individual rights? Unless we are irrationally envious of Wilt's good fortune what harm is there in the new distribution? Doesn't everybody get what they want? Has anyone been forced to do anything?

At D_1 at T_1 the distribution was the one favoured by the society. Each person *ex hypothesi,* since this is the just distribution at T_1, was entitled to the control over the resources they held at D_1 and they freely chose to give some of their resources to Chamberlain in turn for the privilege of seeing him play. Each person has his legitimate share under D_1 and they did with it, without harming others, what they wanted to do with it. Wasn't that what it was given to them for? They freely transferred some of it to Wilt resulting in D_2 but that plainly is a just uncoerced transfer and if D_1 was just, as *ex hypothesi* it is, then D_2 must also be just, for the change here was utterly voluntary and no third parties were injured for they all still have their legitimate shares: their shares have not at all changed (page 161). It is not the case, Nozick avers, that anything was taken from those in the society who chose not to see Wilt play. The transactions between Wilt and the fans did not effect their shares. The distribution in the society was changed by the transaction and an inequality established but no injustice was done anyone and indeed an injustice would be done by halting a transaction or by taking away the $250,000 from Wilt to restore the egalitarian *status quo* of D_1. If that was done, people's rights would have been trampled on, for their liberty to dispose of what was theirs in ways that would not harm anyone—would not make them worse off than they were at the time the transaction took place—would have been interfered with.

Similar things should be said about Nozick's second puzzle case: the case of the entrepreneur in the socialist society. Suppose our D_1 at time T_1 obtains in a socialist society. Suppose I am in that society and though my needs are all met I still want things I don't strictly need. Suppose it is a very large record library. To get the extra money for it I melt down some of my personal possessions (possessions I legitimately possess under D_1) and I make several machines that make toothpicks which I intend to manufacture and sell to buy records. I offer you and several others a philosophy lecture once a week for an evening's cranking of my machine to make toothpicks. This is all to be done in our spare time, not during regular working hours. You agree and I am in business. (The wood for the toothpicks is also furnished to me by a chap who under D_1 rightly has the wood. He provides me with the wood for the right to attend the lectures.) The short of it is that each person would, by participating in that process, stand to gain something that that person wants over their allotment under D_1. What would happen is that in our egalitarian socialist society private property in the means of production—and a move to D_2 from D_1—would arise in that society if it did "not forbid people to use as they wished some of the resources they are given under the socialist distribution D_1" (page 165). Again to maintain the pattern, rights would have to be trampled on and freedom interfered with, for to maintain the egalitarian distribution the socialist society would have to "forbid capitalist acts between consenting adults" (page 163).

Nozick generalizes his cases in the following remark:

> The general point illustrated by the Wilt Chamberlain example and the example of the entrepreneur in a socialist society is that no end-state principle or distributional patterned principle of justice can be continuously realized without continuous interference with people's lives. Any favored pattern would be transformed into one unfavored by the principle, by people choosing to act in various ways; for example, by people exchanging goods and services with other people, or giving things to other people, things the transferers are entitled to under the favored distributional pattern. To maintain a pattern one must either continually interfere to stop people from transferring resources as they wish to, or continually (or periodically) interfere to take from some persons resources that others for some reason chose to transfer to them. [page 163]

If you see this plain implication and if you are committed to securing a free society, you will not, Nozick claims, be an egalitarian or hold any patterned end-state conceptions of justice. "Any distributional pattern with any egalitarian component is overturnable by the voluntary actions of individual persons over time; as is every patterned condition with sufficient content so as actually to have been proposed as presenting the central core of distributive justice" (page 164).

Nozick's account is often taken to be a morally intolerable form of bourgeois individualism, but Nozick turns that argument around and directs it against those who commit themselves to patterned end-state principles:

> Apparently, patterned principles allow people to choose to expend upon themselves, but not upon others, those resources they are entitled to (or rather, receive) under some favored distributional pattern D_1. For if each of several persons chooses to expend some of his D_1 resources upon one other person, then that other person will receive more than his D_1 share, disturbing the favored distributional pattern. Maintaining a distributional pattern is individualism with a vengeance! Patterned distributional principles do not give people what entitlement principles do, only better distributed. For they do not give the right to choose what to do with what one has; they do not give the right to choose to pursue an end involving (intrinsically, or as a means) the enhancement of another's position. [page 167]

So such patterned end-state principles are, Nozick claims, incompatible with what is really bedrock in morality, namely a respect for the separateness of individuals and a respect for their rights. Without this respect, a meaningful life for individuals is undermined and a truly human society cannot come into being where every person, if he or she has had the ability, can do (has the right to do) as much as possible of whatever it is that she/he wants to do that is compatible with their behaving in such a way that others are not made worse off than they would otherwise be by their acting in this way. Patterned end-state principles make it impossible for people to live their own lives in the way they would choose to if others did not interfere with them.

Entitlements to holdings are rights to dispose of them. Social "choice must take place *within* the constraints of how people choose to exercise these rights" (page 166). Each person, where Nozick's entitlements are in force, may exercise his/her *rights* as he/she chooses. Within the constraints fixed by these rights, legitimate social choices occur. It isn't that the rights determine the social ordering. Rather they "set the constraints within which a social choice is to be made, by excluding certain alternatives, fixing others, and so on" (page 166). Any legitimate patterning or distribution is constrained by rights and the various historically determinate entitlements that people have (page 166). But "patterned principles of distributive justice necessitate redistributive activities. The likelihood is small that any actual freely-arrived-at set of holdings fits a given pattern; and the likelihood is nil that it will continue to fit the pattern as people exchange and give" (page 168). But then it is hardly possible to maintain a distribution—for a society to be committed to any patterned end-state principle—without the violation of people's rights and with that violation, the undermining of liberty (page 168). If, as Nozick believes, the correct moral conception of the world places supreme value on "each person . . . having a right to decide what would become of himself and what he would do, and as having a right to reap the benefits of what he did," then one must reject end-state theories of justice and accept a strict entitlement theory (page 171). Where end-state principles of distributive justice have social and legal force in a society, each citizen has "an enforceable claim to some portion of the total social product; that is, to some portion of the sum total of the individually and jointly made products" (page 171). This entails that everyone has a claim to the activities and products of other persons whether or not these persons "enter into particular relationships that give rise to these claims, and independently of whether they voluntarily make these claims, and independently of whether they voluntarily take these claims upon themselves. . . ." (page 172). But this just involves an overriding of people's rights and a failure to treat them as ends in themselves. Nozick fleshes this out as follows:

> Whether it is done through taxation on wages or on wages over a certain amount, or through seizure of profits, or through there being a big social pot so that it's not clear what's coming from where and what's going where, patterned principles of distributive justice involve appropriating the actions of other persons. Seizing the results of someone's labor is equivalent to seizing hours from him and directing him to carry on various activities. If people force you to do certain work, or unrewarded work, for a certain period of time, they decide what you are to do and what purposes your work is to serve apart from your decisions. This process whereby they take this decision from you makes them a part-owner of you; it gives them a property right in you. Just as having such partial control and power of decision, by right, over an animal or inanimate object would be to have a property right in it.
>   End-state and most patterned principles of distributive justice institute (partial) ownership by others of people and their actions and labor. These principles involve a shift from the classical liberals' notion of self-ownership to a notion of (partial) property rights in other people. [page 172]

V

In Chapter Eight of his *Anarchy, State, and Utopia,* Nozick meets egalitarian arguments head on. He remarks that vague egalitarian claims are frequently assumed and indeed sometimes appealed to like church dogmas but that they are seldom defended. Indeed he believes that there is a dearth of coherent arguments for egalitarianism. (That should hardly surprise him, for, if his own account of justice is near to the mark, egalitarianism is hardly defensible.)

One important assumption that is frequently operative in egalitarian thinking is the belief "that society (that is, each of us, acting together in some organized fashion) should make provision for the important needs of all its members" (page 234). But why should we as moral agents share that somewhat egalitarian belief? What arguments are there for it? For that ideal to be realized would we not have to have part ownership in each other and isn't that plainly morally intolerable?

In search of an argument, if there is a decent one, we must not only reflect on how things are allocated and who are to be the recipients of goods and services but we must consider how they were produced, who produced them and what the people who produced them or can dispose of them wish to do with them (pages 254–45 and 168). We must consider who has entitlements over them. This would surely seem at least to be the case for service activities, e.g., doctoring or barbering. But in a free society—and an unfree society can hardly be a just society—people, say in doctoring, teaching or barbering, may decide for themselves to whom they will give their services and on what grounds. Because all people have a need for the availability of medical care, it does not follow that society or anyone else has the right to force some doctor or other to provide those services if he doesn't want to. Whether he is going to give his services is, or at least should be, up to him. If he doesn't like someone's looks, race, politics or religion, he shouldn't, Nozick argues, be required to give his services to him if he doesn't want to.

Still, we are, in what Nozick would regard as egalitarian moods, inclined to say that he should do so and that *society should,* where it can, *make provision for the important needs of all its members* (page 234). But this is hardly true by definition and Nozick presses us for a justification of it, particularly when it involves, as it frequently does, requiring someone to provide those services. Must we not secure the person's *consent* first? And must he, if he is to act rightly, give his consent? How can we—or can we—show that he, or at least someone able to provide the services to meet the important need, *must* do so?

Nozick, relying heavily on his entitlement theory and the fundamental premises of his exclusively rights-based ethic, argues that the "particular rights over things fill the space of rights, leaving no room for general rights *to be in a certain material condition*" (page 238; italics mine). Suppose we try to justify the claim that society (where it can) should make provision for the important needs of all its members. If in doing that, we try to maintain that, where the needs can be met, or at least where they can reasonably be met—that its members have a *right* to have their important needs met—we run into just this difficulty about there being a general right to be in a certain material condition.

> The major objection to speaking of everyone's having a right to various things such as equality of opportunity, life, and so on, and enforcing this right, is that these "rights" require a substructure of things and materials and actions; and other people may have rights and entitlements over these. No one has a right to something whose realization requires certain uses of things and activities that other people have rights and entitlements over.

Other people's rights and entitlements to particular things (that pencil, their body and so on) and how they choose to exercise these rights and entitlements fix the external environment of any given individual and the means that will be available to him. If this goal required the use of means which others have rights over, he must enlist their voluntary cooperation. Even to exercise his right to determine how something he owns is to be used may require other means he must acquire a right to, for example, food to keep him alive; he must put together, with the cooperation of others, a feasible package. [page 238]

It just isn't the case that we have any general rights to be in any material condition. What a clear view of what rights are forces us to recognize is that while there are "particular rights over particular things held by particular persons, and particular rights to reach agreements with others *if* you and they together can acquire means to reach an agreement," there is no *such* general right to achieve a goal or be in a certain material condition (page 238).

Equality of opportunity, as we saw in an earlier chapter, is a minimal goal for a modern egalitarian—or at least so the "new egalitarians" argue. It is necessary, such egalitarians argue, to move beyond that to some appropriate *equality of condition.* Something that Nozick claims we cannot have by right. This is an important part of what divides the old egalitarians from the new. We have also seen how difficult it is to show what it would be like to achieve equality of opportunity or even to say clearly what it is we are trying to achieve. But we have also seen that something vague but not utterly incoherent can be said here.

Nozick assumes that something coherent is meant and challenges whether justice requires even equality of opportunity. He tries to show that we have good reason for believing that we have no right, even if it could be achieved, to have equal opportunity with others, such that everyone's opportunity, where this is achievable, would be the same. Here he is a severer—someone would say, more consistent— anti-egalitarian than is Friedman or Hayek. In trying to bring the worst off, in terms of opportunity, up to the level of the best off or even to those whose opportunities are average, we have no right to take the holdings to which others—say the better off—"are entitled . . . even to provide equality of opportunity for others" (page 235).

Still, in many circumstances, inequality of opportunity does seem, where something might be done about it, not only unfortunate but *unfair.* Nozick acknowledges the force of the following rhetorical questions.

Wouldn't it be better if the person with less opportunity had an equal opportunity? If one so could equip him without violating anyone else's entitlements (the magic wand?) shouldn't one do so? Wouldn't it be fairer? If it would be fairer, can such fairness also justify overriding some people's entitlements in order to acquire the resources to boost those having poorer opportunities into a more equal competitive position? [page 236]

There is, as we earlier called attention to, a plain and evident disparity in terms of whole life prospects between the prospects of the child of a doctor and the child of a dishwasher, even when these children are equally intelligent, hardworking and the like. We feel that it is wrong—unfair—that their whole life prospects should be so very different. We tend to feel that, *ceteris paribus,* if something can be done about it, we should strive to make their life chances equal or at least more nearly equal. Not to do so would be unfair. Or so we are inclined to react.

However, we must be careful about how we generalize here, or indeed if we can rely on such considered judgments at all, for at least some people have the Nozickian considered judgments that we may not seize what others are legitimately entitled to to achieve that equality of opportunity (page 235). Moreover, we cannot so readily generalize about the moral appropriateness of providing equality of opportunity. Suppose two males A and B are suitors for the same woman C. If C rejected A and agreed to marry B instead because of B's intelligence, gentleness and considerateness, A could not justifiably complain of unfair treatment on the grounds of a lack of equality of opportunity to compete in this regard with B because A was less intelligent, gentle and considerate. There is no legitimate question of equality of opportunity here and the lack of it. The situation, while a misfortune for A, is not an injustice (page 237).

We are still inclined to think that the cases are relevantly different but it isn't very evident what the relevant difference is and the marriage case should make us even more reluctant to claim any general right that, where possible, people are to be in a condition of equality of opportunity.[12]

VI

Nozick's work has raised strong passions. My central concern with it, and with Hayek's and Friedman's views as well, is whether such work really undermines egalitarianism and an egalitarian conception of justice. Nozick has, as our exposition has made evident enough, a conception of justice that radically conflicts with the one I have defended. For both of us human autonomy has center stage, but for me it requires equality, while for Nozick, beyond a limited repertoire of human rights, it is incompatible, as we have seen, with any egalitarian patterning obtaining over any reasonable period of time. *Justice as equality* would for him, as for Friedman and Hayek, be a travesty of justice; for it would lead, he believes, to an evident and extensive violation of human rights. A free society, on his reading, could not be an egalitarian society.

I want to get, if I can, to the bottom of this. I shall start by trying to see what, if anything, of Nozick's views remain after critical scrutiny. Though admired by many for their ingenuity, clarity, imaginativeness and for their having provided a probing challenge to the standard liberal and egalitarian assumptions, Nozick's views have not had, to put it conservatively, widespread acceptance and with some they have generated contemptuous or ironical and indeed sometimes even patronizing rejection.

There is a range of criticisms of Nozick's views from the most directly political and moral to the very searchingly foundational and methodological. I shall start with the most directly political and moral criticisms—some would call them ideological criticisms. The ones I shall initially be concerned with come from welfare state liberals, even, sometimes, from a left liberal perspective. Fastening on the entitlement theory, and crudely and tendentiously seen, Nozick's view, some would claim, when translated into the concrete, turns into a Goldwater-Reagan style indifference to the poor, to human misery, and into a thinly disguised commitment to the protection of the privileges and the power of the wealthy. Nozick is aware, as is evident in his preface, that his account will put him in some bad company and he clearly is uneasy about it. He commendably wants very much to protect individual rights and he wants to provide an intellectual defense for a world in which people are free to shape their own lives. The last paragraph of his *Anarchy, State, and Utopia* powerfully attests to that. Yet some of the central unsavory elements of Reaganism or Thatcherism seem at least to be the practical implications of central elements of Nozick's theory. Reagan, like many conservatives around the world, is setting out to dismantle much of the welfare state.[13] He is setting himself to turn back what many would call the rather limited gains in the direction of equality and a somewhat greater answering to human need that grew out of the New Deal and which find their rationale in contemporary conceptions of the welfare state. As Rawls provides an underlying philosophical rationale for the welfare state, so Nozick's account provides a philosophical rationale for the dismantling of the welfare state. (Von Mises', Friedman's, and Hayek's accounts even more directly and concretely play such a role.)

The direct moral critique of Nozick's account by some of his liberal critics (Kateb, Wolin, Lukes, Spitz, and Barry are particularly to be noted here), would, if sound, highlight at least some of these defects in Nozick's theory—defects which, as one such critic put it, perhaps over-dramatically, give us a conception of society, with a minimal state and an entitlement theory of justice, that constitutes more a vision of hell than of utopia.[14] The critics I shall be referring to (all philosophically sophisticated social scientists) complain of the political naivete and the actual apolitical character of Nozick's work. (This contrasts with the tendency of rather politically unaware philosophers to think it too political.)[15] A book with political sense or with an awareness of political realities could hardly, they claim, be as blind as Nozick is "to the power element in economic transactions and holdings" or simply, as Nozick does, view our political choices as being between a state which has a "monopoly on violence and an individual endowed with near-absolute rights."[16] Neither could it ignore so extensively the fact of and the rationale for "the ever-growing role of the state within contemporary capitalism" or, with such "ideological innocence," accept "*hommo economicus* as the archetypical form of behavior."[17] It is such phenomena—phenomena brought to our attention by liberal critics— which some Marxist critics have in mind when they see Nozick's book as an exercise in bourgeois ideology.

However, these liberal critics also make direct moral criticisms. One of these critics, George Kateb, sees Nozick as advancing the general conclusion that "only when the rights of persons are respected absolutely are persons respected absolutely. Only when the rights of persons are respected absolutely can persons freely search for, and perhaps find, meaning in and for their lives, and thus be recognized in their distinct individuation."[18] He stresses the point that we have stressed, namely that Nozick will not sanction an individual rights violation even to lessen their total violation in the society. He will not accept any doctrine of the lesser evil or allow that it is morally tolerable to take certain means, means that involve a violation of an individual's rights, even to protect the entire system of rights. But, Nozick's "terrible distortion," as Kateb puts it, in resisting the idea of limitless state power and defending the inviolability of individual rights, in reality functions to narrow "his theory of rights to the right of property" and to make "that right his true absolute."[19] If that right is respected, Nozick believes, persons are respected. To this Kateb perceptively remarks:

> Is it not right to say that in *most* circumstances an almost unqualified right of property will lead—even without deliberate wrongdoing—to the degradation of large numbers of people? Their right to property would be intact, but they would have little or no property. They would barely be persons. Is the England of Shaftesbury and Engels and Marx a fantasy? What permits Nozick to accept a society in which only a few or some would benefit from the protection of an almost unqualified right of property? Certainly his conception of each of us as a person does not.[20]

Given actual political and social realities and indeed any reasonable extension of what they are at present, a Kantian conception of respect for persons—a conception requiring that people be treated as ends and never as means only—is not compatible with an *unqualified* acceptance of an individual's rights to property. The importance of having rights is to protect a respect for us as human beings, as persons who are to be respected and whose autonomy must be defended.[21] Moreover, for this to be possible, there must be a system of rights which qualify each other and which, with the various individual rights forming that system, have various weights.[22]

The idea that we can ever, for any purpose whatsoever, justifiably redistribute anyone's justly acquired property, without their consent, through the coercive activity of the state, seems utterly wrong to Nozick. "Man's freedom is to keep his wealth for himself and use it as he pleases."[23] This freedom, on Nozick's account, can never be rightly overridden. But this, Kateb counters, is in reality a "one-sided absolutism." It is unrealistic, if not incoherent, to assume that property is not a creation of law or, in primitive societies, of something like law but that fact notwithstanding, Nozick simply assumes, without argument, that there can be and indeed is a natural right to property which may or may not be reflected in the law or in law-like social structures.[24] But even accepting this unjustified assumption, to give, as Nozick does, "a natural right to property" such moral pride of place is unjustifiable.

Nozick thinks that a major evil—perhaps the cardinal sin—of the non-minimal state is that it uses its power to promote the economic welfare of the less well off at the expense of the better off. Aside from that being a cruel joke, given the actual behavior of states in Western societies, Kateb challenges whether there is indeed an injustice in taking some of the vast wealth of some to give to those who can hardly meet their subsistence needs, typically through no fault of their own.[25] Nozick thinks that the modern state exploits everyone not on welfare. But again Nozick's political sociology, if we can dignify it with such a label, is off the mark. It isn't for the benefit of the poor that most state activity is carried out in the United States, Canada or Western Germany, but for the benefit of the very rich and, to a lesser extent, for the professional strata and for the (more or less) small business community. Much more tax money "goes to supporting business in the form of subsidies, allowances, and exemptions" than goes into any effort to end or seriously to ameliorate poverty. And the war machine gobbles up much more still. (But presumably this is a necessary protection so that our rights will not be violated!)

The power of the contemporary state is indeed awesome and the way and the extent to which it controls our lives is frightening. (It is the sort of thing that Max Horkheimer and Theodore Adorno late in their lives came to agonize about.) But according to Nozick, it robs us and exploits us, if we happen not to be of the strata who are the worst off, principally by taking our money to give to the poor. The reality of the situation is just the reverse. The state, in capitalist societies, predominantly under the influence of the rich, working with the rich owners and managers of private industry, exploits its other citizens and in the case of states, such as the United States, through imperialism, citizens of other states as well. The state, that is, functions primarily to benefit the rich and the powerful in the society.[26]

Nozick, if he ever came to have a good look at how things actually operate, might come to concede this and argue that two wrongs still do not make a right. Any taxation not consented to is unjust. That contemporary states exploit the poor does not mean that it can rightly take from the rich what they have *justly* acquired. We need, Nozick could argue, a minimal state in a genuine market economy which will not do these things. But how are we in such a market society to keep the state minimal and to keep concentrations of capital, and with that power, from developing which will make use of the state in non-minimal ways?

There may, as Nozick himself admits, be such an extensive case for rectification, given our actual situation, that extensive redistribution would, on his own terms, be justified and indeed be perfectly just. But in such a circumstance the rich would not have justly acquired their holdings. But even where there has been no injustice in original acquisition (assuming we can ever know when this obtains) or injustice in transfers, the resulting concentration of wealth and power may be so great and the resulting poverty so extensive that, even with no rights violations, a transfer of some goods is morally required.[27]

However, it is just this that Nozick insists can never be just or justified. We may not violate or override one person's rights to meet the needs, no matter how vital, of another. But Kateb, and many others as well, see this position as the assumption of a morally arbitrary one-valued absolutism. It is not, Kateb argues, necessarily a passion to equalize income that underlies liberal economic policies but the moral passion "to remedy or alleviate or prevent the poverty, the misery of millions of people."[28]

Nozick's central response here is that he is not against the relieving of misery. Of course misery is a bad thing and kindly disposed persons will want to and indeed try to, where they reasonably can, alleviate it, but, if we are not responsible for the misery, if we, by our actions, have not made people worse off than they were before we acted, then we are not *morally obliged* to relieve the suffering of another even if we could do so without serious loss to ourselves. If we refuse to help, we will show that we are hardhearted, but we still would have—Nozick would have us believe—done no wrong and we cannot be blamed or forced to help, for we have violated no one's rights. There is in his system no duty of mutual aid or obligation to relieve suffering.

It is this doctrine that Kateb, quite firmly, and many others as well— Spitz and Barry very harshly, Nagel rather more gently—take to be not only hardhearted but deeply morally unacceptable as well.[29] Kateb's belief is that in acting in such a hardhearted way we have also done something which is wrong, morally wrong. We not only have duties to protect the violation of rights of property but duties to relieve misery as well. Kateb puts the fundamental moral point forcefully:

> We are obliged to respond to suffering. Let that assertion stand. It would be a mistake to believe that the assertion had to be backed up with reasons, that it needed philosophical justification. Or, to say it more modestly, if any assertion can go unjustified, this one can. Nozick holds, in contrast, that we are obliged only to avoid doing harm to others, violating their rights; in particular, we must avoid physical transgression of the boundary

of another person and his property. Not even Bentham, a main source of thinking about moral problems with economic metaphors, delimited responsibility as narrowly as Nozick. To avoid doing harm to another by direct attack on his person and goods, and to compensate him for harm done, is surely an important component of right conduct; it may even be the most important. It is, however, only one component. The duty to prevent or alleviate or remedy the misery of others is also part of our duty, our strictest duty. We may be compelled to it. There is no suggestion or implication in Nozick's own conception of the person that could have led him away from this sense of duty. Only his obsession with property could account for his awful truncation.[30]

A one-valued moral absolutism is morally arbitrary. Nozick and others have shown this for utilitarianism, but his own account is shown here to suffer from a similar defect. Our rights must be protected, including our property rights and, what *may* be an extension of it, our ability to control our own lives and live as we choose. (Recall, what Kateb may not keep firmly enough in mind in criticizing Nozick, namely Locke's and Nozick's very broad construal of property.) But, while our separateness as individuals must be acknowledged and protected, it is also the case that we do not live alone in the world. Besides a duty not to violate rights, we have, Nozick to the contrary notwithstanding, duties to relieve suffering and there are duties of mutual aid.[31] Nozick has done nothing to show that the protection of property rights is the sole duty or the overriding obligation or that a Kantian respect for persons and a belief that people must never be treated as a means *only* requires, or can even sustain, such a moral weight being given to an individual's right to choose to do what he will with what is his. The very reading Nozick gives to Kant to back up his claim here, as Barry points out, is strained.[32] On rather more natural readings it could not do the work he puts it to. However, in what may be a simpler more direct consideration, Kateb's moral argument is (a) that it is our duty to relieve suffering where we reasonably can and (b) "if we are not prepared freely to discharge it, the state is entitled to compel us."[33] This is a hard doctrine for a libertarian to swallow—indeed he can't swallow it and remain a libertarian—but close moral scrutiny forces it on us.

We, on the one hand, also need to recognize that it is important to assert (a) that, *ceteris paribus,* the state has no right to make some miserable in order to stop the misery of others and (b) that it must, in respecting persons, in respecting our individuality, respect the right, again *ceteris paribus,* of everyone to do what he wills so long as he does not harm others. These are indeed telling moral points—points usually put dramatically but hyperbolically without the *ceteris paribus* clause—but, on the other hand, and these points notwithstanding, to tax a few dollars of one's estate is hardly an assault on the autonomy and integrity of one's person. If I am a millionaire and a few of my dollars are taxed, it is hardly the case that I am being reduced to a means only or simply treated as a means. To claim that I am is wildly hyperbolic. Moreover, it is hardly correct to regard all of the one's dollars as exactly and entirely one's own when the system of property is such a cultural product, so bound up with the activities of others and with the channels and opportunities for activity created by state action or permission. So to view it is an ideologically convenient moral myth. If some dollars are taken to fund a program to meet important needs of others at some minimal cost to the taxed person, that person does not suffer an impairment or a violation of his person. His basic liberties are not being violated as they would be if his freedom of speech were overridden, or he was prevented from hearing or reading an unorthodox thought or deprived of the due process of the law, or his right to worship or not to worship as he pleases was infringed. To say that a millionaire's person is violated and his moral autonomy attacked even when he is minimally taxed to pay for the school lunches of ghetto children is morally irresponsible rhetorical exaggeration.

Any society is a complex of liberties and constraints on liberty.[34] There is no escaping that if we are to live in any social order at all. But the thing that needs to be shown is that the above restriction on property and its use is an unjustified restriction that overrides one's moral autonomy. One's moral autonomy is not overridden every time one is prevented from doing something one wants to do even when doing so does not make others worse off than they otherwise would be. If you require me to make certain religious observances, forbid me to marry or have children or prevent me from immigrating, you assault my person, you show lack of respect for me as a human being, but if I am taxed ten dollars more a year to help feed starving people in the Sahel or I am moderately taxed to help pay for a public school system, my person is not violated.

Brian Barry, whose discussion of Nozick, along with David Spitz's, is the harshest—he takes Nozick's account to be a gimmicked up philosopher's version of Barry Goldwater and William F. Buckley—believes that, if the absurd conclusions of *Anarchy, State and Utopia* are accepted, we would be accepting propositions that would entail that the Elizabethan Poor Law must be repealed and would give a "spurious intellectual respectability to the reactionary backlash" in the United States.[35] What rationalizes such a bitter response from Barry is the taking to heart some of the moral defects (putative moral defects) of Nozick's moral vision—including his conception of moral priorities. (The priorities Barry has in mind are priorities we have already exhibited.)

Barry takes Nozick's rejection of utilitarianism to be well taken, as well as his purely internal critique of Rawls. But Nozick's own entitlement theory is not the only alternative to Rawls and utilitarianism. Moreover, one can agree with Nozick that it is not the case that utility (in any of its various formulations) provides us with the sole principle or the ultimate principle of decision-making without committing oneself to the moral irrelevance of all appeals to consequences. Barry, appealing to his own considered judgments, thinks that the extremity of Nozick's anti-consequentialism and simplistic Kantianism leads him to an absurd and morally repugnant position. One can, and should, reject utilitarianism without:

> Thereby committing oneself to Nozick's extreme anti-utilitarian view that making someone only a little worse off and making somebody else a lot better off is never a reason for coercing someone to do something he would not otherwise do. In fact, I would go so far as to say that it is obvious that there may be circumstances (e.g., a case in which someone would sooner destroy food he does not want and cannot use than give it to someone starving) in which it would be right for anyone who had the power to compel a certain action to do so. (There is thus no need to make special claims for majorities as a source of legitimate coercion in order to justify coercion under some circumstances.) If, as Nozick maintains, it is inconsistent with the principle that each person is to be treated as an end in himself for coercion ever to be applied to someone on the grounds that there would be a large net benefit from his acting in the way demanded, it seems to me that the principle, so interpreted, is one to which no decent person could subscribe. This is not, of course, to deny that the principle might be interpreted in some alternative way that does not have this unacceptable implication.[36]

A "Kantianism" with the conclusions Nozick allows would be morally repugnant—through and through morally unacceptable—to our reflective moral conscience. No decent person, as Barry puts it, clearly understanding what is being claimed and what its implications are, could accept it. (Think what this really means in speaking of Nozick's view!)

Similarly the entitlement theory of justice cannot be what it appears to be and no doubt what Nozick takes it to be, to wit a principle of justice which protects individual rights and basic liberties. The reality of it is that justice, on such an account, is identified with *power.* It is an ideologically disguised appeal to power. As Barry puts it:

> Justice for Nozick, as for Thrasymachus, is the interest of the stronger. Any contract that anyone makes, so long as he is not actually threatened with deliberately produced harm by the person with whom he makes it, is just, even if he is facing a *de facto* monopoly seller of goods, a *de facto* monopoly buyer of labour, or a *de facto* monopoly supplier of physical security. Conversely, if the weaker propose to club together to use the coercive machinery of the state to control contracts or redistribute resources, that is unjust. If Nozick is discontented to find that his views put him in nasty company, he should, I suggest, reflect on the possibility that the reason is that these are nasty views.[37]

NOTES

1. Robert Nozick, *Anarchy, State, and Utopia,* p. xi. In Part III all page references to *Anarchy, State, and Utopia* will be given in the text. Other references will be given in the standard way in the endnotes. I do not refer here to Nozick's *Philosophical Examinations* (Cambridge, Mass.: Harvard University Press, 1981), for it does not deal with the topics considered here.

2. Nozick, of course, is citing John Locke. For Locke's views, see his *Two Treatises of Government.*

3. Whether Nozick succeeds in making such a neat dichotomy is probingly challenged by Michael Neumann, "Side Constraint Morality," *Canadian Journal of Philosophy* 12, no. 1 (March 1982): 131–44.

4. See the essays in the following two volumes: Steven Sanders and David R. Cheney (eds.), *The Meaning of Life* (Englewood Cliffs, N.J.: Prentice-Hall, 1980); and E. D. Klemke (ed.), *The Meaning of Life* (New York: Oxford University Press, 1981).

5. Thomas Nagel has argued that Nozick's account is foundationless. See Thomas Nagel, "Libertarianism Without Foundations," *The Yale Law Journal* 85, no. 1 (November 1975): 136–49. This article is reprinted in *Reading Nozick,* ed. Jeffrey Paul (Totowa, N.J.: Rowman & Littlefield, 1981).

6. Nagel argues with considerable force that it is not sufficient to provide Nozick with a foundation for his entitlement theory. Ibid. See also Philip Pettit, *Judging Justice* (London: Routledge & Kegan Paul, 1980), pp. 94–97.

7. Bernard Williams, "The Minimal State," *Times Literary Supplement,* January 17, 1975, p. 47. The article is also reprinted in *Reading Nozick.*

8. Ibid., p. 46.

9. In Chapter 12 we shall critically examine that assumption.

10. For how unrealistic this is, see Bernard Williams, op. cit.

11. Ibid.

12. For the underlying methodological problems about the method of argument here, see Nozick's enticing but somewhat oracular remarks in *Anarchy, State, and Utopia,* pp. 227–79.

13. A recent (1983) striking example of this is the legislation brought in by the Social Credit government of British Columbia shortly after their defeat of the New Democrats, legislation reportedly deeply influenced by the extreme right wing libertarian think-tank, the Fraser Institute.

14. David Spitz, "Justice for Sale: A New Philosophy for *Laissez Faire*," *Dissent,* Winter, 1975, p. 89.

15. If these last two sentences seem like obscure sayings, note my discussion of Nozick's apoliticality in Chapter 10.

16. Sheldon S. Wolin, "Review of *Anarchy, State, and Utopia*," *The New York Times Book Review,* May 11, 1975, pp. 31–32.

17. Ibid., p. 32, and Steven Lukes, *Essays in Social Theory* (London: Macmillan Press, 1977), p. 194.

18. George Kateb, "The Night Watchman State," *The American Scholar,* 1975, p. 818.

19. Ibid., p. 819.

20. Ibid.

21. Ibid.

22. Ibid.

23. Ibid., p. 826.

24. Ibid. See as well Philip Pettit, op. cit., pp. 94–103.

25. Kateb, op. cit., p. 822.

26. Richard C. Edwards, Michael Reich, and Thomas E. Weisskopf (eds.), *The Capitalist System,* 2nd ed. (Englewood Cliffs, N.J.: Prentice-Hall, 1978), pp. 216–62; Ralph Miliband, *The State in Capitalist Society* (New York: Basic Books, 1969); Ralph Miliband, *Marxism and Politics* (Oxford: Oxford University Press, 1977).

27. In my "Capitalism, Socialism and Justice," in *And Justice For All,* eds. Tom Regan and Donald VanDeVeer (Totowa, N.J.: Rowman & Littlefield, 1982), I raise problems about how to determine an original acquisition. See also Steven Lukes, op. cit.

28. Kateb, op. cit., p. 824.

29. See the essays previously cited by Spitz and Nagel and see as well Brian Barry, "Review of *Anarchy, State, and Utopia,*" *Political Theory* 3, no. 3 (August 1975): 331–36.

30. Kateb, op. cit., p. 824.

31. Again see the need to appeal to considered judgments and the difficulties over not begging the question when we approach bedrock.

32. Brian Barry, op. cit.

33. Kateb, op. cit., p. 824.

34. G. A. Cohen, "Capitalism, Freedom and the Proletariat" in *The Idea of Freedom,* ed. Alan Ryan (Oxford: Oxford University Press, 1979).

35. Barry, op. cit., p. 332.

36. Ibid., p. 335.

37. Ibid., p. 335.

10

Nozick and Socialism:
Some Sociological Critiques

I

The moral criticisms of Nozick's account sketched in the last section of the previous chapter seem to me to be formidable. Indeed, I think they show that Nozick's libertarian theory, without some radical changes, could not possibly stand as an adequate moral and social theory. Nozick sees the importance of rights and liberty but his account, at the very least, has not got the right placement for them in an overall social theory.

Yet these arguments against Nozick do make an appeal to our considered convictions (as do Nozick's as well) and the contents of these considered convictions, as Steven Lukes and Richard Brandt, among others, have noted, and as we discussed in Part I, are hardly invariant among all human beings. Not all moral agents share Barry's, Kateb's, and Wolin's bedrock moral convictions. What if someone stayed within Nozick's narrower range of intuitions? How could we, or could we, show him to be mistaken?

Unlike Brandt or R. M. Hare, I am inclined to believe there is no way of dispensing with an appeal in moral theory to an interlocking cluster of considered judgments. It is an inescapable court of appeal when fundamental justificatory questions are raised in ethics and in normative political theory. But I am further inclined to believe—beliefs I argued for in Part I—that these considered judgments, when they are put in wide reflective equilibrium, can give us a kind of objectivity that would allow us in some measure to "argue out" these clashing intuitions—reason together about what it is we are to believe morally. Kateb and Barry engage in this enterprise. They seek to show what is sound in Nozick's intuitions and in turn to balance them against other intuitions. The point is to display, pruning here and there and modifying here and there, these diverse intuitions in a wider network of both intuitions (considered judgments) and social theory, a network which, when viewed from a more comprehensive perspective, gives us a more adequate conceptualization of the moral terrain.

However, such appeals, though they seem to me, and to some others as well, utterly realistic and sane, have not seemed so to some rather distinguished philosophers, for example utilitarians such as Brandt and Hare or neo-Hobbesians such as Gauthier and Narveson. Moreover, witness the repeated dismissive labelling of Rawls as an intuitionist because of his use of such a method with its appeal to considered convictions. Perhaps there should be, but in fact there is not, a consensus here among philosophers working in moral philosophy.

I also noted in the previous chapter the penchant among philosophers to look for something more fundamental in discussions of morality than a moral argument. I am deeply suspicious of this move on the part of philosophers. I suspect that it is an *ersatz* realism, a pseudo-toughmindedness, perhaps the irrational heart of rationalism. But, whether I am right or not in this reaction, it should be acknowledged that what I have tendentiously labelled as the reaction of an *ersatz* realism is very widespread. So I want to have a look at less moralistic criticisms of Nozick's radically conservative libertarianism.

Most Marxists, understandably enough, have shown very little interest in Nozick and sometimes when they have examined his views they have merely regarded it as a job, not very interesting or challenging in itself, of debunking yet another, for the moment fashionable, bourgeois ideology.[1] Some Marxist critics, however (G. A. Cohen for example), have taken Nozick with utter seriousness.[2] However, most of the left critiques, though not all, have not so much argued against Nozick on his own grounds (as have G. A. Cohen and Onora O'Neill), but have sought to show the utter unreality of Nozick's account—its lack of political sense or indeed (except as ideology) political relevance or any real understanding of our social world. They have tried to stick it with being utopian in the pejorative sense familiar to the Marxist tradition. In what they take to be his flight from reality, they also try to show that Nozick ignores important facts of social life and is held captive to, and vividly recreates, bourgeois ideological assumptions in such a way that he gives us a distorted picture of our social lives and of what we are and can become as human beings. He tries to show us that genuine liberty and a meaningful life requires the putting aside of what he regards as egalitarian myths and requires instead the quite unequivocal acceptance of full laissez-faire capitalist property rights. The left response is that in reality, and quite unwittingly, Nozick produces an apology for the enhanced power and control of the many by the few in which the capitalist class in free market relations can exercise an economic dictatorship over the working class. What Nozick sees as a defense of liberty and the rights of the individual, and what individuals, who do not understand the working of the capitalist system, will similarly see as defense of liberty and the rights of the individual, is in reality no such defense at all but a disguised defense of the privileges and power of the dominant class in capitalist society.

Sometimes ideology is in the eye of the beholder and the would-
be unmasker may unwittingly be donning a few masks himself. We
need to be wary of this in an age of ideology often parading as analysis.
Yet it is important to try to ascertain whether some or all of these left
critiques (Marxist and otherwise) stick.

In thinking them through, I think it is also important to take to
heart Thomas Scanlon's point—a point made at the end of a critical
article on Nozick—that a key value of Nozick's work consists in the
fact that it forces us, if we are at all reflective about it, "to consider
economic institutions not merely as mechanisms for the distribution
of goods, but also, like political institutions, as placing restrictions and
demands on us which raise questions of obligation. When things are
seen in this way it becomes apparent that questions of economic liberty
must be considered, along with political and civil liberty and fair
distribution, as conditions for the legitimacy of social institutions."[3]
But in doing this, as G. A. Cohen in effect reminds us, we must not
uncritically accept the persuasive definition of "economic liberty" given
by conservative libertarians.[4]

What I shall do in this chapter in bringing these considerations to
the fore is to state 28 theses which give expression to some criticisms
of Nozick and, in effect, of libertarianism generally that are less moralistic
than those we have considered in the previous chapter, though they
will also be criticisms which are less conceptual and less standardly
philosophical than the predominantly conceptual critiques I shall pursue
in the next chapter. The criticisms I shall articulate in these 28 theses,
I shall label, perhaps somewhat eccentrically, "sociological critiques."
By "sociological critiques" I mean critiques which have a considerable
empirical component turning on considerations about how society can
reasonably be expected to function. I do not mean by this to claim
that these theses are normatively neutral or that they are without their
conceptual side. In fact I do not know what it would be like for such
theses not to have their conceptual side, and the idea that there could
be *purely* normative utterances is also thoroughly problematical. In
these 28 theses, empirical considerations about how societies work or
can be made to work play a rather larger role than is typical in
philosophical discussions in, broadly speaking, what we used to call
the analytical tradition.

It it also true that in setting out these theses I do not pursue the
arguments in them to the bitter end. Sometimes an important claim
is little more than baldly stated. The strength of these theses, if indeed
they have any, is in their cumulative effect. They bring to bear a loosely
related cluster of considerations all of which have some plausibility.
Moreover, if several of them are plausibly true, they, given their relations,
increase each other's probability. Together, I believe, they provide a
persuasive critique of libertarianism.

II

1. Nozick assumes that the minimal state will be an impartial adjudicator in the conflicts of interests of the citizens of the state, protecting the rights of the citizens impartially. This is unrealistic. Contemporary states in capitalist societies are not neutral mediators of conflicting interests but preponderantly favor capitalist class interests. It is, of course, important in capitalist societies that people come to accept the ideology of state neutrality—that people believe that the state for the most part acts impartially to serve the interests of all its citizens and that its legal institutions protect the rights of everyone. But that is a myth. It is not such a neutral adjudicator, though it is vital for capitalist interests that it should be so seen. Rather, it protects the capitalist order. It helps through the schools to make the order seem legitimate and it, again through the schools and through various infrastructures such as the transport system and the road system, aids in an indispensable way in capital accumulation. With its monopoly on force (a feature of all states), it also has as well, in addition to its legitimation and accumulation functions, a coercive function. Where the internal devices of legitimation fail to work or work imperfectly, the coercive arm of the state comes forth to insure obedience and to make the society in question safe for capitalism. These state functions are, in our societies, functions in the service of capitalism.

The above was put cryptically and may strike some as overly assertive and perhaps as dogmatic. Such has not been my intention. I have tried to put briefly and without nuance what has been the subject of much investigation, discussion, argument and some confirmation.[5] At the very minimum, it should be said that Nozick has utterly ignored these and similar claims about the state's role in class domination and has simply naively and dogmatically, and without the slightest concern to get the sociology of it right (to get at the actual social realities), assumed the liberal notion that the state is, or at least readily can be, the impartial mediator of conflicts of interests and the protector of individual rights. Such a belief is innocent about state power and the actual workings of the capitalist order.

2. Allowing people within a Lockean natural rights context to do with their property what they will will lead to vast inequalities and to the control of the many by the few to the not inconsiderable detriment of the many. We should not accept the picture of the market as a collection of nearly equal and independent individuals trading among themselves in conditions of rough equality. That is a wildly ideological picture. We are too pervasively and intractably interdependent for something like that to be plausible even as a simplifying device. The appropriation of one thing by one person invariably effects others. The model of you having corn and me wheat and our freely trading back and forth only holds for some simple situations. The picture Nozick

operates with is that of a large number of small roughly equal entrepreneurs freely engaging in trade. But this is an idealized ideological
picture of the capitalist market in which, conveniently, the concept of
capital nowhere appears.

3. Nozick is utterly—or so one would judge from reading *Anarchy,
State, and Utopia*—innocent about power and particularly about the
ways a drive for power works in our societies. That is to say, he is
utterly innocent about the capitalist system. His account requires him
to assume that those bent on accumulating wealth, and with that wealth
unavoidably power, will restrain themselves when they reach the limits
set by the Lockean proviso.[6] But that is utterly unrealistic. Nozick just
assumes that in a free market society economic practices will not
generally require regulation to prevent massive injustices. But again
that is an unrealistic assumption. More than that, it is a morally dangerous
one as well. (Note that Nozick's assumption is an assumption also
made by Hayek and Friedman.)

4. Given population increases, the Lockean proviso cannot work.
Nozick gives us no account of what a just original acquisition of holdings
could come to in an industrial society. Indeed it would be hard to
understand what it could come to even in ancient Greece or in feudal
Europe, but in an industrial society such a notion is meaningless. In
most circumstances, there is nothing like "enough and as good left
over." The land is already for the most part held, productive facilities
are held, and what it could even mean to so speak of oil, coal and
iron reserves is totally unclear. How the original acquisitions were made
no one knows or can know, but what we do know of land and of
resource acquisition generally is not such as to make us at all sanguine
that things even approximating Nozick's just original acquisitons were
even remotely approximated. Again Nozick has given us a picture which
is both unrealistic and ideologically skewed.

5. Nozick assumes that contemporary capitalists, were they properly
informed, would want a genuinely free market society. That is simply
false.[7] The last thing they would want is a genuinely free market. The
capitalist order would then be very vulnerable. It would be a boom
and bust economy in which the poor would be driven to the wall. It
would become increasingly obvious to them that they would have
nothing to lose but their chains. The bourgeois state would not even
present the appearance of an illusory community. Revolution, or at
least extensive social strife, would be the order of the day. Such a
society would be too unstable for it to be the most optimal way to
maximize capital accumulation and expand and protect the capitalist
order. Moreover, we do not want workers who only produce, we also
want workers who consume. But impoverished workers could hardly
consume at a rate to satisfy the imperatives of capitalist expansion.
That point aside, big capital very much sees the advantge of not
competing. The thing is to divide up the markets in a stable and

cooperative way. There are genuinely competitive sectors of the economy, but in oil and steel and in big capital rather generally, such competition would be disastrous. It is the last thing such capitalists want. They want the illusion of laissez faire but not its reality.

6. It is thoroughly unrealistic and politically and intellectually unhelpful to talk, as Nozick does, of a state of nature, of rights in a state of nature, of moralized persons in a state of nature, of justifying the state in terms of consent and of taking the state of nature as our baseline for determining whether market activities harm people. This does not give us a good model for normative political theorizing. The social institutions that political theory is concerned with are fundamentally non-voluntary. We, as individuals, coming to consciousness, come to have our self-images with the socialization provided by these institutions. We, of course, have no choice about this socialization and we achieve whatever autonomy we are capable of within a fundamental human interdependence first experienced in a life definitely shaped by these institutions and always, in part, structured by them and perhaps later by other institutions as well. We are simply born into certain historically determinate social structures. It is with them, in determinate historical, cultural and socioeconomic contexts, that we must start in thinking about what is to be done and undone.[8] The relevant question is how, if at all, they are to be changed (radically altered or modified). There is no preinstitutional condition that we can contrast with our institutional condition to intelligibly ask if we should consent to an institutional condition.

We can indeed make thought experiments and we do form images of ourselves. We can, using such techniques, ask ourselves what it would be like if certain social conditions that now obtain did not obtain and what it would be like if certain social structures now unobtainable did obtain. And we can ask what would be our considered judgments in such situations. All of this is perfectly possible and indeed sometimes a desirable thing to do. But the farther we get from real life situations the more unreliable our intuitions tend to become about what would be desirable or what would be the right thing to do in such situations. Moreover, the factual assumptions we have to make are such that we can be less and less confident of what would be the probable consequences of them, should they obtain. Moral claims are often difficult enough in any case, but they are increasingly difficult as we move away from a world like the world we know into unfamiliar circumstances. (There is something roughly parallel here to Austin's remark that ordinary language tends to break down in extraordinary situations.) Moreover, how we will view things is going to be very deeply skewed by the institutions that in important ways form our social consciousness and structure our images of ourselves. We can carry out thought experiments, but the answers we will give ourselves—what will seem reasonable or even conceivable—will not be independent of who we are. The belief that by such thought experiments we can shed enough culture to know what it would be like to choose freely and impartially in a state of nature is utterly implausible.

7. Nozick, like Hobbes, reads into human nature a distinctive kind of human nature characteristic of a certain type of society during a certain historical epoch. That is to say, he makes people possessive individualists. Both within and without the state of nature, he has people deeply preoccupied with protecting their territory (their property, their individuality) and enhancing their self-esteem. He sees us, no matter what kind of culture we live in, as rather self-seeking creatures and not as creatures who are basically good, cooperative and loving or even as people who, under certain social conditions, are capable of standardly so acting.[9] He sees us instead, as individuals who are constantly trespassing each other's boundaries, violating each other' rights, and he sees us as needing protective agencies with the coercive power to mete out punishment and exact compensation. Individuals are conceived of as people who pervasively have bad intentions toward one another. And his concern with the state—that which has a monopoly of force in a given territory—is essentially a concern with punishment, deterrence and protection. He sees the state as an instrument for these tasks.

There are indeed all these negative features in human nature, but human beings have other more positive features as well. The mix will vary from society to society and from epoch to epoch and will not be unrelated to the productive wealth of the society and its general conditions of abundance. Nozick reveals a lack of imagination about human possibilities here. He has scant feel for possible future societies different from our own in certain fundamental respects. Even his meta-Utopia is *market society* writ large.

Boris Frankel, in this connection, claims that both Nozick and Rawls "base their expectations and regulations for a 'just' society on the *empirical* experience of human beings practising violence, egoism and hate within class societies."[10] But we should at least question, given the poverty of Nozick's conception of a just society, whether it is reasonable to erect a conception of justice from such a picture of the human condition. We should ask, in a way Nozick does not, whether his picture of the human condition is really a tough-minded one, telling it like it is and must be.

8. Nozick neglects the realities of class society in thinking about the justification of and the rationale for the minimal state. He forgets that "those who can hire protection will, to a large extent, be those who are generally involved in hiring labor. Protection appears along with and largely for an employing class."[11] He also forgets that those who hire protection, being an employing class, will do so with an eye to protecting the conditions which make the employment of labor possible. The ideology that Nozick unwittingly gives expression to

gives us to understand that protection and protection agencies appear on the scene exclusively for the protection of individual rights—indeed the individual rights of all classes. The reality of the situation is quite otherwise. Their main function is to protect the class interests of the dominant class. Nozick fails to understand the central function of the state in class societies. In such societies it cannot function neutrally and impartially, independently of one's class position, to protect everyone's Lockean rights: our rights to be free from force or fraud directed against our lives, health, liberty or possessions. Its central function is rather to protect dominant class interests and hegemony. That is its actual central function, though in ideology, as I remarked in number 1 above, it must be *seen* as a defender in an even-handed manner of the interests of everyone alike. This is necessary to give the state an aura of legitimacy. But that is ideology; its actual success, as a state, depends on its partisan service to the dominant class, while seeming to be an impartial protector of the rights of everyone alike. Nozick mistakes ideology for social reality. A dominant protective agency comes into existence, and stays in existence, when one group of people, with success, attain domination over another group of people.

9. The fact that x is entitled to y is not an independent fact or an independent truth (if fact here sounds odd to you) or an independent norm (if both fact and truth sound odd to you here). Such claims, Milton Fisk asserts, are relative to distinctive social perspectives. They are not society-independent absolutes, as Nozick takes them to be, something we could have in a state of nature. Nozick writes as if full capitalist property rights could obtain in a state of nature. (I mean by "full capitalist property rights" rights to complete control of holdings justly acquired in ways that do not violate the Lockean rights of others, rights to dispose of one's holdings however and to whomever one wishes, rights to accumulate holdings, and to accumulate from one's holdings, without limit.)[12] But there are many different kinds of property rights in many different societies. Such full capitalist property rights are not rooted in nature (whatever that means), in some "natural morality" or in reason, but in certain determinate forms of historically contingent social organization determined most fundamentally by certain historically contingent modes of production. Nozick just assumes, independently of such perspectives, that one is entitled to what one makes with the contracted labor of others, that one is entitled to all of one's inheritance, that one is entitled to one's full income and should not be required to transfer a part of it to others if it happens to be above the mean. But not all societies have organized things that way and not all societies have thought that things should be organized in that way. It is not self-evidently true that we should, or clear to the light of reason that we should, return to (if we ever had it), or bring into being, a society of full capitalist property rights. Nozick needs to give us some reason for thinking we should, in the light of such actual cultural differences. He needs to give us some reason for believing he

has not simply fastened onto a central element in the ideology of our tribe.

Nozick mistakenly thinks of the property rights he lists as absolute, inalienable rights when in reality the validity they have is relative to a certain group in a certain social system. His property rights are not human rights—or at least they have not been shown to be human rights—"belonging to human nature considered as invariant under social changes."[13] (I shall return to a fuller, less assertive and more dialectical discussion of this in the next chapter.)

10. Nozick also assumes, Milton Fisk argues, that in production, though agents work in different ways to produce a product, there is a natural division of that product among them. That natural division is "in terms of the marginal product of the various factors of production." But that is a very controversial claim within our own society and certainly is not something which all systems of property rights, including all systems of individual property rights, accept or take as unproblematical. Nozick needs to give us some reason why we should accept it. (I shall also return to this in the next chapter.)

11. There is a *status quo* bias built into libertarianism. It has taken as absolute the principle that people have a right to what they get by the free choice of others where the people making the choice and giving or selling have acquired what they have justly. By not qualifying this principle in the slightest and by not treating it as a principle holding *ceteris paribus* but instead giving such absolute weight, independently of the interests or needs involved, to what the individual holder would just *choose* to do, "the libertarian implicitly sanctions all the ways in which human beings have been interfered with that effect their choices."[14] Such a libertarian move simply ignores important background factors which effect and arguably distort choice. It forgets about capitalist socialization in the family, school and by the consciousness industry.

Suppose a worker (a) accepts a given wage as fair and (b) accepts the right of capitalists to set the wage and to determine whether he should be fired and to determine who should be hired. We need to ask whether such a worker makes such a choice because he has been taught in school from an early age that the system of private ownership is the best for everyone and has been given to understand repeatedly, in one way or another, through the mass media, that socialism is the road to serfdom. These are only a few of the many factors at work in conditioning the worker's choice. But such factors are ignored by Nozick, yet only if the choice is a choice that would be made under what Jürgen Habermas calls conditions of undistorted communication is it at all plausible to believe that we should hold that people have a right—a right not to be overridden—to what they get by the free choice of others, where the owner has justly acquired what he sells or gives away. It may be that in cases like the above, the entrepreneur, in getting control of the product, minus the wages the worker has accepted through his own choice, gets what he gets through indoctrination and manipulation. The worker makes the choices he makes because he has been indoctrinated in a certain way. Where this obtains it is anything but evident that people have a right to what they get by the free choice of others.

The factual claim made by the left—but not only by the left—is that this indoctrination and manipulation massively and pervasively occurs in capitalist societies in both subtle and not so subtle forms. To justify the principle "From each as he chooses, to each as he has been chosen" one would have to establish, at the very least, that under present and foreseeable conditions the free market system is the best system available to meet the needs of human beings and that people operating in it are not being extensively manipulated. Friedman and Hayek try something like that but Nozick doesn't. But establishing that quite contestable claim is a necessary but not a sufficient condition for validating "From each as he chooses, to each as he has been chosen." Only if the market system is so justified can choice generate such rights.[15]

12. What Nozick utterly fails to argue against or even to recognize as a serious difficulty for his view is the claim—indeed the familiar Marxist claim—that "a system of property rights can gain its validity only within a dominant form of practice and relative to a set of groups each defined by a certain role within that practice."[16] Within the capitalist system and for those committed to the capitalist system—that is, the owning class—such rights are acknowledged and fought for, though at great cost to industrial workers, farmers and the like. But Nozick has done nothing to show that these rights are valid universally or that the dominated groups within capitalist societies should accept them or regard such property rights claims as anything other than moral ideology.

13. Nozick argues that the lament that workers are exploited under capitalism is, given at least the present development of capitalism, a cover-up for the fact that workers are unwilling to take the risks of enterprise; for, after all, they by now have huge pension funds available which they could use to establish enterprises which could be firmly under worker ownership and worker democratic control. They just do not want to take the risks and the responsibilities of entrepreneurship and prefer instead the safe path of working for someone else at a fixed wage secured for them by strong unions. The cry that they are being exploited under such conditions is entirely empty except for its propaganda value.

This response on Nozick's part ignores the class nature of capitalist society where there is a well-entrenched capitalist class making a determined effort, through control of financial institutions (banks and the like) and with the aid of the state, to protect its own interests.

Workers' savings have been "drawn into the financial system of the class of private owners. The class has investment control over workers' savings. To deny it control over workers' savings would reduce the power of that class and its ability to react flexibly to changing economic conditions."[17] It is clearly not in the interests of the capitalist class to allow workers to amass capital from workers' sources to develop their own industries on anything like a mass scale. This would be resisted by the capitalists, with all their not inconsiderable power, as a deep threat to their very continued existence as a class. If it were more than mere tokenism, they would rightly see in such a movement a threat to the financial interests and industries they control. Were such a workers' movement to be initiated, the financial institutions that capitalists control and the state they control, at least in part, would be used to protect their interests. There is no possibility of building, on a larger scale, mini-socialist institutions within the overall framework of a capitalist organization of society.

14. Nozick believes that where, as in a welfare state, some redistribution of wealth takes place, the rich end up laboring for the benefit of the poor. But this, of course, is not so. In a market economy the rich are rich in large measure because they consume the labor of the poor in greater amounts than the poor consume the labor of the rich. (In thinking about this issue it is important not to confuse, as Nozick does, the freedom of contract with the freedom to enjoy the benefits of one's own labor. They are not identical notions. That A contracts B to make x for him, using A's capital, does not mean that x should be regarded as a fruit of A's labor, the benefit from which he can rightly enjoy.) It certainly appears that the rich do so consume the labor of the poor. To make his argument stick Nozick needs to show that what appears to be so in reality is not so.

15. Even if we assume that the theory of marginal productivity of wage labor is true—something which itself is very challengable—it is still possible to question the justice of the belief that unequal contribution always justifies unequal income. We should also ask how or indeed whether in any even remotely objective sense we can, except in a few obvious cases, measure, or in any other way ascertain, equal and unequal contributions. Does the person who tunes up motors or the person who orders parts contribute more to the automobile agency? There is no ascertaining such things.[18]

16. Nozick assumes what Von Mises, Hayek and Friedman argue for, namely the superior efficiency of free-market capitalism. There is no need for a critic of libertarianism to deny that capitalist firms in a capitalist system *sometimes* function efficiently or to deny that those firms that do not in most circumstances tend to lose out. But this efficiency is directed to maximizing the owners' rate of profit and to providing differential resources and differential life chances which greatly benefit him and the managers and professionals who help him maintain

control of the relations of production. While it benefits those people, it harms, or at least does not maximally benefit, the workers who labor in his firm. But there are alternative ways of organizing production—ways which can be efficient, perhaps even more efficient than free-market capitalism—which do not have those harmful side effects, though they would not benefit as much as would free market capitalism, the individuals who are owners and top managers. Indeed *some* of them would not benefit the owners, *qua owners,* at all; for, with some alternatives, they wouldn't remain owners for there would be no distinction, in that system, between owners and salaried employees. There would be neither. Instead there would be just workers who collectively owned and controlled their workplace. This does not mean, of course, that there would be no benefits accruing to former capitalist owners as persons. It might be that they would have the experience of living in a freer, juster and more humane society. Capitalist production to attain its greatest efficiency, as *capitalist production,* may have to organize hierarchically and unequally reward its workers. But it does not follow that only in this way can production be organized efficiently. Nozick simply assumes that it does, but that assumption requires justification.[19]

17. Nozick maintains that in a free society, which for him in contemporary conditions seems to be extensionally equivalent to a free-market capitalist society, there is no central distribution center deciding how things are to be doled out. Instead different people control different resources. That such a state of affairs could obtain in a socialist society—that people could control their own different resources—seems never to have entered his head; but the thing I want to emphasize here is that *something like* this central direction does obtain, and increasingly obtains, in capitalist society. This is hidden from us when we focus on market transactions and ignore production. There is indeed no official central planning and controlling agency in capitalism with authority over production and distribution, though something like this does happen with state intervention during wartime (and without loss of efficiency). But the general structure of economic organization in capitalist society, including its structured inequalities, is determined by members of the capitalist class who exercise authoritative control over the organization of production, and this is done in an increasingly organized and centralized way as capitalism develops. Those who say, as Nozick does, that capitalism operates by means of the choices of individuals in a free market are simply turning a blind eye to the role of coercive authority at work in the organization of the sphere of production.[20] Such authority (capitalist class organization) determines who shall work, how each shall work, what is to be made and how, how it is to be distributed and who owns the products of that production. This is qualified and mitigated by state intervention in the social welfare state (state capitalism), but on Nozick's model, as well as on Friedman's and Hayek's, of a capitalist system with full capitalist property rights,

it would not be so qualified. There would be full capitalist control over production, work organization and the very possibility of work. The general structure of economic organization would be in the control of the capitalist class who owned and controlled the forces of production.

18. Nozick (and Von Mises, Friedman and Hayek as well) believe that it is freedom which produces inequality in capitalist societies. You can't, they claim, have one without the other. You can't have both an egalitarian society and a free society. Believing this to be so, they opt for what they call a free society. But, it will be objected, the major obstacle to freedom is not the egalitarian-oriented redistributions but the organization of production relations in capitalist societies. They are the major determinates in such societies of the structure of opportunity and of liberty or lack thereof. In a capitalist society, relations of domination and subordination, and not liberty, prevail. Capitalism determines in area after area where people are and are not freely able to act without interference. This is not accidental to capitalism but is essential for its continued flourishing. Capitalism is not only the mortal enemy of equality it is the mortal enemy of liberty as well.[21]

19. Nozick's account (or for that matter Rawls's or David Gauthier's) ignores the seamy side of capitalist life and ignores questions about what it would take to get rid of it. There is little awareness of, or at least adverting to the fact, that, as Anthony Skillen points out, "most adults in our society spend most of their waking lives working to earn a living, or working domestically to make it possible for others to earn a living, that children spend their days at school preparing for such a life . . ."[22] And those who are inclined to think that there is nothing so bad about that, conveniently ignore the fact that "most people's work is a tedious and stultifying grind" and that beyond that there is in such work an undermining of self-respect and of initiative; there is pain, misery and lack of freedom through authoritarian work allocation and control of production.[23] That some of us are "free to pursue inquiry for its own sake as a profession rests on the fact that others lack it."[24] Moreover, it is a convenient ideological illusion to believe that this "drudgery of the masses working lives" is an inevitability, something that just must go with any industrial order.[25] If this were so, it would be the case that it would make no more sense to raise cries of injustice about such work, if it were fairly rotated (as it is not in our societies) than it does to complain that it is unjust that an earthquake occurred in a certain part of the world and injured people in a way that could not reasonably have been prevented. Terrible human ills follow from both earthquakes and work under capitalism, but it would be utterly mistaken to speak of injustice or wrongdoing here if things were as I described above. But this is an *ideological* response. It assumes falsely, in a way that is of considerable benefit to the capitalist order, that nothing—or at least nothing very substantial—can be done about such working conditions without making things still worse. The con-

ditions under which alienated labor takes place is not, like an earthquake, a natural catastrophe rooted in the nature of things.

20. Nozick's unexamined radical individualism and "philosophical reductionist perspective" is a thoroughly inadequate framework for examining political life and evolving a normative political theory. It is simply taken for granted that men "live separate existences" defined by an inviolable freedom and an absolute right to property. It is Nozick's largely unargued belief that no moral balancing is possible between such initially solitary beings and that, as a consequence, "voluntary consent" is an absolutely necessary prerequisite of each (every and any) step taken toward political relations: toward exchange, justice, the common pursuit of social goals, the compromising of freedom for utilitarian ends, and so forth.[26] But Nozick's background assumptions here are utterly unjustified and are, even on minimal reflection, quite evidently unrealistic.

21. Benjamin Barber maintains that philosophical analysis of the kind practiced by Nozick is not "fit for political theorizing or relevant to political reality."[27] Nozick, he believes, "uses apolitical concepts to move from apolitical premises to conclusions which are political in name only."[28] This is a dark saying which requires elucidation. It is his reductionism that Barber refers to here, namely the assumption, never examined by Nozick, that political discourse is replaceable by discourse about individual actions, choices, and intentions without loss of explanatory or justificatory power and indeed with a gain in both. To talk about states and social institutions, on Nozick's account, is just to talk about individuals. Politics can be fully explained in "philosophical categories untainted by politics."[29]

Here Nozick shares this general stance not only with Locke but with Hobbes (recall his resolutive-compositive method) and with Rawls. A central ruling assumption on Nozick's account is that even standing where we are in industrial societies in the twentieth century, we can intelligibly ask, not how the state should be organized, but whether there should be any state at all.[30] But in such a context, that is an unintelligible question. To think, as Nozick does, that that could be "the fundamental question of political philosophy" shows no political savvy or understanding at all. For us to try to think of ourselves as solitary individuals, hypothesized in some pre-political status, sufficient unto ourselves, shows no understanding of human nature or even of how individuals, if they would think with care, could conceive of themselves. To take *independence* rather than *interdependence* as the starting point for thinking about human beings and their obligations and sense of life shows at best arbitrariness and lack of reflection and incoherence at worst. If we try to take this utterly individualistic starting point, we need to answer the question "Why do people enter into political or community associations?" when the fact is that that is a pseudo-question that never should have been asked. The burden of proof then becomes ridiculously to ask why such atomic, anonymous individuals should enter into any political associations at all. "Individuals are taken for granted but society requires warrant; personal and property rights are self-evident but public purposes [stand] in need of proof. . . ."[31] But that this is a necessary or even a possible rest position is far from evident. We are reduced to the bare philosophical abstractions of talking about natural rights in a state of nature: "the *explanandum,* politics disappears in the *explanans,* philosophy."[32] Politics has been deconstituted into elements in terms of which it can never be understood. There is no possibility that sticking by these individualistic notions we could reconstitute political concepts in some rational reconstruction.[33] "*Anarchy, State, and Utopia* is to be criticized not for its [conservative libertarian] politics but for the absence of relevant politics altogether; not for its political inadequacies but for its inadequate conception of the political."[34]

Lest this be thought to be mere paradoxical posturing on Barber's part, let us note the evidence he provides of Nozick's apoliticality. Consider first Nozick's placement of freedom. It is embedded in *voluntary consent* and voluntary consent "is the test of all political justification, the sole criterion by which public claims are legitimated, the absolute measure by which each step away from anarchy [individual anarchism] is to be gauged and approved."[35] We can only justifiably cross each other's boundaries by the voluntary consent of the atomic, autonomous individuals involved. The model here of a free person is that of an utterly self-sufficient, independent person. Freedom is simply a matter of being unimpeded. What Nozick, preoccupied as he is with interference, does not at all recognize is "that men are frequently *self-interfering*—less enslaved by external obstacles than internal contradictions—and that self-interference, examined in the context of education, propaganda, advertising, and the manipulation of opinion, is a problem of major social and political import."[36] But his reductionist severely individualistic categories do not afford a framework in which we can come to grips with these problems.[37] In that way his framework is deeply apolitical. We need to be able to ask and answer: "What are the conditions of freedom for a man who is his own worst impediment?"[38] If we have any kind of adequate image of what humans are, we will not see ourselves as simply pitted in clearly delineated struggles against external interference, but we will see ourselves as well as engaged unendingly in all sorts of dubious, often unclearly understood interior struggles with ourselves, or as beings locked in struggles in which the division internal/external is not so clearly cut. Indeed, as Barber well puts it, "The conflict is not that of man against man, but of desire against need, need against conscience and conscience against custom, custom against reason, and reason, come full circle, against desire."[39] Struggles for enlightenment and emancipation, for what variously, and not incorrectly, have been called both rationality and freedom, are not simply struggles about voluntary consent. Seen against this rich political and human background, "voluntary consent ceases to function as a singular criterion for political justification. It becomes merely one more example, when it is implicated in practice, of the kind of controversy the art of politics is designed to resolve."[40]

22. Nozick sees what is private as being part of the realm of freedom and what is public as being coercive. The contrast for him is public power versus private rights, and what must be protected in a free society are private rights. We must protect the individual against the state. He ignores, and his categories have no ready way of accommodating, even the *possibility* of public-power-deployed-for-private-purposes in a way that can enhance liberty, and private-power-deployed-for-private-purposes in a way which is destructive of both liberty and well-being.[41] The state, in Nozick's view of things, is the cause of our ills. Multinational corporations and private enterprise generally are kept nicely out of sight.

23. Nozick sees, as we have just noted, the state as a perennial source of coercion and the illegitimate use of power, but he totally neglects how full capitalist property rights in a free-market society have a threatening potency for coercion. Nozick is wholly innocent of problems of power arising from the private sector. He fails, as does Friedman, to see how in market relations there can be, and frequently is, violence, deceit, corruption and terror. "He can count on the integrity of voluntary consent because he has discounted influence, blackmail, enticement, titillation and many other carrots by which men attenuate its vitality and corrupt the autonomy on which it depends."[42] Normative political theory should not take as its task the justifying of the authority of the state against the claims of individual anarchy. Rather it should be concerned principally with stating the conditions of the *legitimation* of power. A politically relevant social philosophy will, Barber claims, be concerned with that. There is no question of natural liberty set against the authority of the state, but there is a contrast between legitimate public power (something which is not a pleonasm), and illegitimate private power (also not pleonastic) parading as natural liberty.[43] Our interdependence is such that we will unavoidably come to use one another. The real moral question is how we do this and with what constraints. It is not for nothing that Kant stresses, again and again, that no man is to be treated *only* as a means. The thing is, Barber argues, in considering the ways in which people use each other, to avoid "private ways that are . . . arbitary and unjust" and to opt, instead "for a coercive state that (at least) uses men as justly and fairly as possible."[44] There is just no way of avoiding that it will sometimes be the case that some men are in some respects used as means to the welfare of others. Wars occur and sometimes people are conscripted to protect others. Life is such that we are continuously and unavoidably interfering with each other. Nozick to the contrary notwithstanding, there is no avoiding that. Faced with that reality, what

we should do, rather than try to avoid patterned principles of justice altogether, is to articulate and act in accordance with principles which interfere with the lives of human beings in the fairest and most humane way possible and which, even when coercion is necessary, show respect for persons.

24. The entitlement theory is the basis for Nozick's rights-respecting theory of justice. But there are in it unexamined premises of a quite questionable nature. Nozick is quite aware that what we are *entitled* to and what we *morally deserve* are two different things. Entitlement theories—think of Filmer—have typically been authoritarian and elitist. Nozick is no authoritarian, but, Benjamin Barber plausibly argues, "in place of the arbitrary power of an entitled political elite, he has in effect posited the equally arbitrary power of a natural elite—namely those contestants who turn out to be winners in the social Darwinest sweepstakes that masquerade as a free market place."[45] Here the arguments we made against meritocracy in Part III are relevant. Moreover, we must remember that in the free market it is not *right* but *power* that prevails. Nozick needs to show that his "original just acquisitions" give a title more tenability than titles based on conquest, royal lineage or scripture. All sorts of fraudulent and arbitrary claims have repeatedly been made in the guise of entitlements. How are these to be sorted out? Nozick, with his usual ignoring of things sociological, gives us not the slightest hint as to how to proceed here. But, if we would try to do it, we would see how very difficult this is. Our sense of difficulty here should make us rather wary of putting the kind of weight on entitlements that Nozick and his libertarian followers do. Moreover, when we look at entitlement theories historically and sociologically, we should conclude that the "prevailing theory of entitlement generally turns out to be the theory most conducive to prevailing power, justice being on the side of the holdings of the strongest."[46]

25. Nozick's severe individualism, methodological and otherwise, keeps him from acknowledging the force of the fact that "private acts often have public consequences which we may neither anticipate nor intend."[47] And it is this that makes it unreasonable, even if it were possible, to construe political acts as private acts. If we do, they lose their salient character. In paying Chamberlain a surcharge we merely give him the extra money (for each of us individually 25 cents) to see him play. In doing this we do not at all intend to set in motion a distributional pattern which will result in radically different income differentials with disproportionate power going to certain sectors of the society. But that may very well be less than accidentally the result from such individual actions. A politically responsive and responsible social philosopher must take these things into careful consideration. It is a reductionist illusion to think that because acts are private they are without public consequences.

26. The free market—the acceptance of full capitalist property rights—does not protect us from coercion. It does not, as Barber puts

it, "finally protect freedom against public power; it protects private power against public legitimacy."[48] As he remarks, "After all, John D. Rockefeller contracted freely and bilaterally with scores of smaller companies to buy them out; the gargantuan monopoly he created, however, was hardly a private affair."[49] *Private acts,* in many instances, have *public consequences;* we are very interdependent beings. In fact Rockefeller's acts, acts which may very well be perfectly legitimate on Nozick's entitlement theory, posed "a greater threat to the free market than the government which tried without much success to break it up."[50] The unintended consequences of adopting a social scheme, instantiating Nozick's theory of pure individual freedom, would not be to enhance freedom but to diminish it.

Nozick's abstract philosophical account shows a lack of political understanding. In reality, though not in Nozick's theory, our choices are between being "arbitrarily and heteronomously dependent or rationally and (within limits) autonomously dependent."[51] It is utterly unrealistic—unknowing of social reality—to think our choices are or can be between "absolute coercion and total non-interference," between political bondage and natural freedom. There is no "natural freedom," and our real choices are between socioeconomic bondage and socioeconomic freedom, between forms of social organization that make for greater or lesser freedom. Moreover, things are never likely to be black and white but grey on grey: social orders "can only be more or less justly coercive, more or less legitimately interfering, more or less rationally dependent."[52] And so too our freedom always admits of degrees.

27. Nozick's abstract individualism and corresponding state-of-nature theory fails to comprehend, and moreover lacks machinery to account for the fact that, as Steven Lukes puts it, "the identity of the individual is, in part, constituted by his social and cultural environment. . . ."[53] To try to abstract him from it, as Nozick tries to do, is "in a deep sense, incoherent."[54] If we really try to keep our individuals abstract, there is no way of making such "individuals" engage in the thought experiments essential to Nozick's project. Having no even partially determinate sense of the good (say a conception of Rawls's primary social goods), they will not be able to choose. Nozick's agents in "the state of nature" can choose because, unlike the abstract cultureless individuals they are supposed to be, they are actually (though unwittingly) given by Nozick the familiar, but historically and socially specific motivations, interests and behavior of possessive individualists. Thus Nozick, as Lukes puts it, "is involved in a double incoherence or absurdity," for "if, as is plausibly the case, the social context which actually serves to constitute the individuals of his theory is inconceivable without a state, then to try to image them independently of the state amounts to a further conceptual impossibility."[55] Moreover, the ideology of such an abstract individualism is dangerous, for while we can be

intellectually entranced by the abstract moral problems posed by "the freedom to choose" of the "pre-social, trans-social or non-social 'individuals,'" this, like all ideology, forms a "distorting lens" which is likely to distract from thinking clearly about the real and pressing problems of our actual social world, such as the hard problems posed by "the ever-growing role of the state within contemporary capitalism. . . ."[56] We need to know in what ways this harms us, whether it is essential to capitalism at this stage of its development and what, if anything, can and should be done about it. Moral philosophers should regularly repeat to themselves the truism that until we have some understanding of what can be done about some state of affairs and what the viable alternatives are, it makes little sense to talk about what should be done about it. But such realism is light years away from Nozick's purview.

28. There is in Nozick's account no discussion of how the "minimal state is to be controlled, and kept minimal."[57] With the utterly free operation of the market and particularly with human beings pictured as accumulating possessive individualists, it would appear at least that it would not be a minimal state for long. It seems almost astronomically unlikely that a free operation of the market system will not quickly run foul of the Lockean proviso.

III

These 28 theses (if that is the right word for them) pinpoint significant inadequacies which sometimes point to the fact that Nozick has either, on the one hand, not thought through carefully enough the moral implications of his views or, on the other, has appealed to too narrow a range of considered judgments. But even more frequently, and in ways which are not unrelated to the above inadequacies, they bring to light the fact that Nozick's empirical background assumptions are very uncritically and unreflectively held and that there is a kind of unworldly apoliticality to his account that is innocent of socio-political realities. It is for these latter reasons that I have labelled these critiques sociological critiques. They hardly count, nor are they meant to count, as a cumulative series of arguments that, by a single chain of reasoning, will crush Nozickian libertarianism; but together they raise very serious questions about it indeed, and they must weaken the confident libertarian claim that equality is the mortal enemy of liberty.

NOTES

1. Boris Frankel, "Review Symposium: Robert Nozick's *Anarchy, State, and Utopia,*" *Theory and Society* 3 (1976): 443–49; and Milton Fisk, "Property and State" in *Marx, Justice and Justification,* ed. David A. Crocker (The Red Feather Institute, 1978), pp. 1–18.

2. G. A. Cohen, "Capitalism, Freedom and the Proletariat" in *The Idea of Freedom,* ed. Alan Ryan (Oxford: Oxford University Press, 1979), pp. 9–25.

3. Thomas Scanlon, "Nozick on Rights, Liberty and Property," *Philosophy and Public Affairs* 6, no. 1 (Fall 1976): 24–25.

4. G. A. Cohen: "The Structure of Proletarian Unfreedom," *Philosophy and Public Affairs* 12 no. 1 (Winter 1983): 3–33; "Freedom, Justice and Capitalism," *New Left Review* 126 (March/April, 1981); and "Illusions about Private Property and Freedom," in *Issues in Marxist Philosophy,* eds. John Mepham and David Ruben (Sussex: Harvester Press, 1981).

5. Paul Sweezy, "The Primary Function of the Capitalist State," James Weinstein, "Corporate Liberalism and the Modern State," and James O'Connor, "The Expanding Role of the State," all in *The Capitalist System,* eds. Richard C. Edwards, Michael Reich, and Thomas E. Weisskopf, 1st ed. (Englewood Cliffs, N.J.: Prentice-Hall, 1972). The work of Miliband, Poulantzas, Laclau, Therborn, Offe, and Frankel is plainly relevant here.

6. Husain Sarker, "The Lockean Proviso," *Canadian Journal of Philosophy* 12, no. 1 (March 1982): 47–60.

7. Bernard Williams, "The Minimal State," *Times Literary Supplement,* January 17, 1975.

8. Some of Gerald Doppelt's critique of Rawls would also nicely apply here. See Gerald Doppelt, "Rawls' System of Justice: A Critique from the Left," *Nous* 15, no. 3 (September 1981): 259–308.

9. Boris Frankel, op. cit., p. 445.

10. Ibid.

11. Milton Fisk, op. cit., p. 3.

12. This conception will be discussed 'in the next chapter.

13. Milton Fisk, op. cit., p. 7.

14. Ibid., p. 10.

15. Alan Garfinkel and David Schweickart give us good reasons for thinking it is not so justified. See Alan Garfinkel, *Forms of Explanation* (New Haven, Conn.: Yale University Press, 1981), ch. 3; and David Schweickart, *Capitalism or Worker Control?* (New York: Praeger, 1980).

16. Milton Fisk, op. cit., p. 12.

17. Ibid., p. 14.

18. Ibid. See also David Schweickart, op. cit.; and Richard C. Edwards, Michael Reich, and Thoams E. Weisskopf (eds.), *The Capitalist System,* 2nd ed. (Englewood Cliffs, N.J.: Prentice-Hall, 1978), part 4.

19. Richard C. Edwards, et al., op. cit.; Samuel Bowles and Herbert Gintis, *Schooling in Capitalist America,* 2nd ed. (New York: Basic Books, 1976); and Richard C. Edwards, *Contested Terrain* (London: Heinemann, 1979).

20. See the references in the previous note and Harry Braverman, *Labor and Monopoly Capital* (New York: Monthly Review Press, 1974).

21. Richard Norman, "Does Equality Destroy Liberty?" in *Contemporary Political Philosophy,* Keith Graham, ed. (Cambridge, England: Cambridge University Press, 1982), pp. 83–109. See also the references in note 4.

22. Anthony Skillen, *Ruling Illusions* (Sussex: Harvester Press, 1977), p. 45.

23. *Work in America* (Report of a Special Task Force to the Secretary of Health, Education, and Welfare) (Cambridge, Mass.: MIT Press, 1973).

24. Skillen, op. cit., p. 46.

25. See the references in notes 19 and 20.

26. Benjamin Barber, "Deconstituting Politics: Robert Nozick and Philosophical Reductionism," *Journal of Politics* 39, no. 1 (1977), p. 3; and Garfinkel, op. cit.

27. Barber, op. cit., p. 7.

28. Ibid.

29. Ibid.

30. Ibid.

31. Ibid., p. 9.

32. Ibid.

33. Ibid., pp. 9–10.
34. Ibid., p. 10.
35. Ibid.
36. Ibid., p. 11.
37. Garfinkel, op. cit.
38. Barber, op. cit., p. 12.
39. Ibid.
40. Ibid.
41. Ibid., p. 13.
42. Ibid., p. 14.
43. Ibid.
44. Ibid., p. 15.
45. Ibid., p. 17.
46. Ibid.
47. Ibid., p. 19 and Garfinkel, op. cit.
48. Ibid., p. 20.
49. Barber, op. cit., p. 20.
50. Ibid.
51. Ibid.
52. Ibid., p. 21.
53. Steven Lukes, *Essays in Social Theory* (London: Macmillan Press, 1977), p. 193.
54. Ibid.
55. Ibid.
56. Ibid.
57. Ibid., p. 194.

11

Nozick and Socialism: Some Conceptual Critiques

I

I tried in the previous chapter to display some of the broadly sociological or sometimes factual-cum-theoretical reasons why Nozick's conservative libertarian analysis has been rejected, particularly by those writing from either a left or a liberal perspective. I have not tried in every case to get to the bottom of what is at issue. Indeed, often that could not be done by examining these criticisms in isolation, for sometimes one of them presupposes the acceptance of another. It is not infrequently the case that to say anything very decisive we would need to assess several of them as an ensemble. Moreover, Nozick's theory is itself an intricate one and is, for the most part, tightly knit. A point that might seem very vulnerable taken in isolation may seem less so when measured against the plausibility of a network of linked claims. In only some instances did I try to pursue in any detail whether there are resources in Nozick's account for an adequate response to these particular "sociological" criticisms. That is to say, only in some instances have I tried to ascertain whether these objections are decisively undermining of Nozick's version of conservative libertarianism. So there is more sorting out to be done here, but it does appear to me to be the case, from what we already have before us, that taken together these "sociological" objections have a very considerable force.

Earlier (in Chapter 9) I tried to show that certain straightforwardly moral arguments made it evident enough that such a libertarianism could not be an adequate moral theory or normative political theory. The sociological considerations displayed in Chapter 10 add considerable fuel to that fire. A libertarian moral theory is plainly defective if it makes such unrealistic assumptions about man and society and so conveniently ignores not terribly esoteric facts about our social lives which are very damaging to libertarianism.

In constructing a moral theory or a social philosophy, we want something that comes to grips with our actual moral condition, which helps make clear what it is, what the rationale for it is, gives us some understanding of how adequate that rationale is, and helps us see what we can and should do to ameliorate the human condition. What we do not want (or at least should not want) in doing moral philosophy is something which is simply a clever and intricate construction.

What Nozick does is repeatedly draw moral and normative political conclusions or construct abstract and, often in themselves, intriguing philosophical arguments, while ignoring social factors that are crucial for a serious examination of the situation. Nozick erects an intricate conceptual scaffolding to reach his conclusions but in doing so he ignores—and conveniently so for the capitalist course he is trying to defend—important facts about our social life and the functioning of our institutions and the overall functioning of the capitalist system. This includes, in reality, ignoring how the market functions in capitalist societies.[1] By ignoring this crucial background, a background which is essential in our time for serious moral and political argumentation, he is a desert-island philosopher *par excellence:* making things seem possible and worth worrying through that are not possible.

However, philosophers typically, though less obsessively so than in our very recent history, want to deploy conceptual arguments to refute other philosophers. The preferred mode of argumentation is to show that the philosopher in question or the philosophical account in question can be seen to be committed to both p and not-p, or that, through and through the position is crippled by multiple and not easily resolvable ambiguities or (even worse) by incoherencies which are not remediable within the confines of the theory in question. These are standard arguments within philosophy, as are arguments which start with a philosopher's basic assumptions and premises and show (or purport to show) that that philosopher cannot show what, on their basis, he claims to have shown. There is also the related procedure of *reductio ad absurdum* arguments or attempts to show that the position of the philosopher in question, if reasoned through, leads him to paradoxical or otherwise repugnant or absurd conclusions that he could not possibly embrace.

These are standard fare in philosophy, and many of the critiques of Nozick have taken such forms. Many, perhaps most, philosophers will tend to believe that such ways of arguing are superior to sociological or sociological-cum-moral critiques, for they turn, typically (or so it is thought) purely on the logic of the argument and/or on fairly evident considerations of plausibility. They are not, as the sociological ones, held hostage (so the claim goes) to arguments about what the facts really are or to tendentious interpretations of the facts and to ideologically infected social theories. The other side of that coin is that the more standard philosophical arguments often turn on a single thread of argument, a challengeable reading of a concept or proposition, or can be met by relatively minor alterations in the account criticized. It is also not true that all interpretations of our social life are tendentious, and sometimes what the social facts are can be reliably determined by anyone who will take the trouble to investigate them. The pervasive ideological nature of at least many social theories is indeed troublesome, but among social theories that is still very much a matter of degree (and the degree is important). Still, it is something that can be, and should be, constantly guarded against. We should also note in this connection that "being infected by ideology" does not distinguish the "philosophical approaches" from the "sociological ones," for the philosophical categories and constructions deployed, as is evident in Nozick's account, are as liable to be infected by ideology as the sociological ones and typically less consciously so. (Philosophers sometimes so conveniently deceive themselves that they can maintain that they do not know what ideology is. It is one thing, of course, to be quite unsure about the correct analysis of "ideology" and the extent of its application. It is another thing again to maintain that they have no idea what ideology is. That is at best self-deception.)[2]

The thing is that we do not need, and indeed should not try, to decide between these two modes of criticism: the sociological mode and the philosophical mode. They both have their very definite uses and characteristic strengths and weaknesses. In some contexts, and for some purposes, one mode is superior and in some contexts, and for some purposes, the other mode is superior. In any overall assessment of any developed social theory, it is fairly evident that both modes of criticism should be brought to bear.

Max Black, in a series of classic papers about the justification of induction, showed that it was perfectly silly to argue that deductive arguments were superior to inductive ones or vice versa.[3] They both have their distinctive and valuable uses, one cannot be assimilated to the other or replace the other or show itself to be more "ground floor" or fundamental than the other. It is mere rationalist prejudice to prefer deductive reasoning.

Similar things should be said for the two modes of criticism I have been discussing, though there is the important dis-analogy that while inductive and deductive modes of reasoning are always sharply distinct, what I have called the sociological mode of criticism and the philosophical mode tend to blend into each other. (And neither are always sharply distinct from moral arguments. The organization of this chapter and the previous two is a useful simplification.) So, while the sociological mode of criticism and the conceptual mode are plainly sometimes clearly distinct, they are, as modes of criticism, not always sharply distinct. Indeed philosophy and social science are not sharply distinct. This will be evident in many of the arguments deployed and examined in this chapter. They are paradigmatic philosophical arguments in social philosophy, yet they are not pure instances of the model of philosophical argument sketched above. They do carry out conceptual analyses and logical arguments but they also typically appeal to substantive considerations both moral and factual.

II

There are in the literature a myriad of different and often powerful standard philosophical criticisms of Nozick's account many of which are very perceptive indeed.[4] Since my general topic is equality and liberty and since I have been concerned here to articulate and defend an egalitarian conception of social justice which, I believe, requires a socialist order for its implementation, I will start with some arguments of the standard philosophical sort designed to show that Nozick has not made good his claim that egalitarianism is incompatible with liberty: that no patterned conception of justice can maintain a proper respect for human rights and that socialism leads us down the road to serfdom. Nozick has not shown, as he believes he has, that, if we desire to live in a free society, we must opt for laissez-faire capitalism. (It seems to me that it would have been somewhat more plausible for him to say that this obtains only for industrial societies. I have, in fact, taken that to be his intent.)

I shall start in my critical examination of this from some perceptive and closely reasoned arguments of the standard philosophical sort by two philosophers on the left (G. A. Cohen and Onora O'Neill) designed to show that patterns can preserve liberty, that equality and liberty need not be in conflict, and that it is not the case that a commitment to individual liberties requires, in an industrial society, acceptance of full capitalist property rights with an unrestricted free market and a ban on non-voluntary redistribution except where rectification for violation of past entitlements is in order.[5]

Nozick in his libertarian defense of laissez-faire capitalism will permit degrees of inequality far greater than any acceptable by liberal defenders of welfare state capitalism. Indeed there is no particular degree of equality/inequality that he believes must be maintained in a just society. Individual liberty is the central thing for him and in accordance with that he argues that what socialists and egalitarians consider just is in fact not just, and that, even if we persuasively define "justice" to fit such liberal preconceptions, individual rights cannot be protected on such a characterization of justice. The central thing to see, according to Nozick, is that socialism and egalitarianism are incompatible with liberty, with the protection of individual rights and with respect for persons. Cohen argues that Nozick's arguments fail here and that we have no sufficient reason to believe any of these things.[6]

Nozick's central argument, recall, was that patterned end-state principles of justice are morally speaking unacceptable. The principles of justice that a socialist or an egalitarian would have to espouse would have patterns, and these patterns would be upset in a free society where market relations were allowed to obtain and where people, where they did not violate the rights of other people, were allowed to do what they wanted with what was legitimately theirs. Patterns could only be maintained by constantly interfering with the lives of people. This would come to a not inconsiderable infringement of liberty and a violation of individual rights. A socialist society or any kind of egalitarian society, Nozick argues, no matter how humane, simply in virtue of having patterned principles of justice which it institutionalizes, cannot avoid trampling on liberty and violating the rights of individuals. His famous Wilt Chamberlain parable and his case of the part-time, after hours, entrepreneur in a socialist society (both described by us in Chapter 9) are designed to show that. Cohen, in turn, is out to show that nothing like this follows.

Cohen points out that Nozick makes two assumptions which are essential for his entitlement theory and for the conclusions he draws from the Wilt Chamberlain case and the entrepreneur case (as I shall call it). The assumptions are: (1) "Whatever arises from a just situation by just steps is itself just"[7] (page 151); and (2) "Whatever arises from a just situation as a result of fully voluntary transactions on the part of all legitimately concerned persons is itself just." One of Nozick's most firmly fixed considered judgments is that if an initial situation is just, future actions and transfers will be just if they are fully voluntary on the part of the contractors and if they make no one worse off than they already were at the time these initial just acquisitions were made or would have been if they had actually been alive at that time. This for him is a moral bedrock and he believes that most people (including egalitarians) on reflection would also find that it was one of their most deeply embedded considered judgments. Nozick thinks that if they do accept this considered judgment, he will then be able to show socialists and other egalitarians that they should abandon their socialism and egalitarianism. Their two convictions—their commitment to liberty and equality—are logically incompatible, and the libertarian one, they will come to see, is morally speaking more fundamental. That is to say, it is the one that should be overriding.

Cohen asks whether (2) is true. It is important to try to ascertain this in trying to judge the merits of Nozick's above argument. So we should ask whether it is really the case that liberty—Nozick's individual negative liberty—always preserves justice. The most obvious counter-example that comes to mind to show that it does not always do so is that of selling yourself, but only yourself—not any children of yours—into slavery. Number (2) would allow voluntary self-enslavement (as Nozick acknowledges he would), and most people, even strong anti-paternalists and defenders of liberty, such as J. S. Mill, do not think that a society which allows people to sell themselves into slavery is just. But Nozick doesn't run with the crowd here. He does not think there is anything wrong with selling yourself into slavery if an individual completely voluntarily chooses to so enslave himself, though Nozick quickly points out that there are "some things individuals may choose for themselves no one may choose for another" (page 331). Slavery is one of those things, but it would be paternalistic interference on our part, he argues, to forbid it for the person who voluntarily chooses to so sell himself and himself alone. His reaction here—his so running against the stream—shows how deep his commitment is to (2), i.e., to the proposition that whatever arises from a just situation as a result of fully voluntary transactions on the part of the legitimately concerned persons is itself just.

Nozick's reaction here reveals a difficulty in using moral arguments appealing to considered judgments as bedrock appeals in philosophical argumentation. We can continue to assert that slavery in any form, at least in societies such as ours, is intolerable, and Nozick can continue to deny it and unless we turn to some other grounds, than appealing so directly to considered judgments, we are deadlocked.

Other grounds are, however, available. We can see that this is so if we examine Cohen's careful scrutiny of the Chamberlain parable. He believes that when we do so we will come to see that (2) is false and that liberty—Nozick's individual "negative liberty"—does not always preserve justice. And we can do this without invoking any contestable considered judgments.

Cohen argues that contracting of the Chamberlain sort in an egalitarian society would, if it became widespread, seriously modify for the worse the lives of most people, including future generations. (Remember this is the society that Nozick allows us to start from in what he takes to be his devastating Chamberlain parable.) Notice that here we are arguing on Nozick's home turf, on his own grounds.

We can clearly see in the Nozick example what the fans think they are gaining. They love to see Wilt play basketball and they secure that chance for themselves at little extra cost to themselves and—or so they believe—without harmful side effects. But Cohen argues that the fans in the egalitarian society—a society they *ex hypothesi* prize and want to see remain secure—are mistaken about the consequences of their actions. (Notice here they are mistaken about a matter of fact.) Such actions are very likely to have unforeseen consequences which, by *their own standards and preferences,* they would not want to happen if they realized that they would be the consequences of their actions. They would not, Cohen claims, willingly pay the extra 25 cents and enter into such a contract with Chamberlain, if they foresaw that that might very well be the result.

The untoward consequences that Cohen has in mind are that such Chamberlain-like contracts will introduce an inequality *in power* into the previously egalitarian society and thus seriously damage the chances for the masses of people in that society to control their own lives in ways they, being egalitarians, very much want to control their lives. Inequalities in wealth, as is well known but frequently ignored, lead to inequalities in power, and inequalities in power lead to the undermining of the freedom of those people who have little power. To know whether a transaction is just, it is not sufficient to know that people would voluntarily agree to it; we need to know in addition whether they would agree to it knowing what the outcome would be.[8] (I refer here not just, or indeed even especially, to the outcomes for themselves but to resultant states of affairs that would effect social life generally.) Cohen's point is that egalitarians, under conditions of undistorted communication, would not agree to the Chamberlain surcharge. The possible outcome of a Chamberlain-like contract is too likely to be destabilizing to a society in which the relations of interdependence between people is that of equals and where a maximum freedom *for all* is prized. Where people are clear-headed about their situation, there would be the recognition that if the acquisition of holdings is not limited, some people will come to gain an unacceptable amount of power over others with the result that they will no longer live in a republic of equals—a condition they very much prize.

Some may think that such talk sounds paranoid or rhetorically exaggerated. Nozick does present both examples in such a way that they seem at first blush entirely innocent. A few chaps like Wilt making rather a wad or the existence of some minor entrepreneurship in a secure socialist society are not going to do any great harm. But surely if these cases are to have any polemical point they must be generalizable over a reasonable range of situations. What we can see is that if the outcomes of such transactions were to become reasonably widespread they would have the effect of making access to various resources which had previously been equal unequal. People with wealth could acquire things that people with considerably less wealth could not, people with wealth could command and control things that people with considerably less wealth could not. This would not be just a differential divvying up of goodies. It would have the effect that people would be unequal in political power; and thus in their relations with each other, given what political power is, they would no longer be people standing in relations of equality. They would no longer be equals. They would no longer live in a republic of equals.[9] Here a very fundamental principle of moral equality—a principle Nozick subscribes to—would be undermined.[10]

What we have here is an egalitarian society in danger of corruption. "Reflective people would have to consider not only the joy of watching Chamberlain and its immediate money price but also the fact, which socialists say they would deplore, that their society would be set on the road to class division."[11]

It is also important to recognize that it is not just, as Nozick would have it, the parties transacting but third parties as well who are effected. Nozick, with his atomistic individualism, misses the pervasiveness of our interdependence. Nozick thinks falsely that the third parties' shares have not changed. It is, of course, true that if you contract with

Chamberlain and put your 25 cents in the box and I, who care nothing for watching basketball games, do not, that you have parted with your 25 cents while I have not. But that is a simplistic way of looking at the situation. In reality "a person's effective share depends on what he can do with what he has, and that depends not only on how much he has but on what others have and on how what others have is distributed. If it is distributed equally among them he will often be better placed than if some have especially large shares."[12]

There is a distinction to be drawn between being interested in something or taking an interest in something, on the one hand, and that something's being in your interest or your having an interest in something, on the other. Sometimes people take no interest in what is in their interests, and sometimes people take an interest in something that is definitely not in their interest. We may be so ideologically bamboozled that we do not take an interest in things that are plainly in our interest, and the unborn can hardly take an interest in anything though it still may very well be the case that they have an interest in preventing a certain state of affairs with untoward effects from coming into existence.

The reasons why socialists and egalitarians generally, who are also lovers of liberty, would favor forbidding Chamberlain-type transactions in an egalitarian or even a roughly egalitarian society is that such contracts are likely to generate inordinate power in the hands of a few. We must remember, as Cohen nicely puts it, that in general, "holdings are not only sources of enjoyment but in certain distributions sources of power."[13]

Power, when it is the power of the capitalist class or economic power generally, is something that Nozick utterly neglects. He only gets exercised about power relations when he speaks of the power of the more-than-minimal state. This is a revealing characteristic which he shares with Hayek and Friedman. It is perhaps not an exaggeration to say that it is a characteristic of bourgeois apologetic.

III

In a memorable phrase, in talking about the entrepreneur case, Nozick remarks that a "socialist society would have to forbid capitalist acts between consenting adults (page 163). Concerning such a claim, Cohen makes a very important remark which I shall quote in full. It reminds us again of our sociological criticisms where, in appraising Nozick's theory, it became evident how very important it is to get as straight as possible certain background factors. Here what is important is the establishing of a set of reasonable claims about the nature and extent of malleability of human beings. Cohen makes it clear that Nozick's account turns on a popular but ungrounded assumption in our culture— an assumption we rather routinely make but which nonetheless has not been established and is not at all like those groundless beliefs that Wittgenstein points to that we can hardly not have. Cohen remarks of the possibility of capitalist acts between consenting adults:

> Socialism perishes if there are too many such acts, but it does not follow that it must forbid them. In traditional socialist doctrine capitalist action wanes not primarily because it is illegal, but because the impulse behind it atrophies, or, less Utopianly, because other impulses become stronger, or because people believe that capitalistic exchange is unfair. Such expectation rests on a conception of human nature, and so does its denial. Nozick has a different conception, for which he does not argue, one that fits many 20th century Americans, which is no reason for concluding it is universally true. The people in his state of nature are intelligible only as well socialized products of a market society. In the contrary socialist conception human beings have and may develop further an unqualified (that is, non 'instrumental') desire for community, an unqualified relish of cooperation, and an unqualified aversion to being on either side of a master/servant relationship. No one should assume without argument, or take it on trust from the socialist tradition, that this conception is sound. But if it is sound, there will be no need for incessant invigilation against 'capitalist acts,' and Nozick does not argue that it is unsound. Hence he has not shown that socialism conflicts with freedom, even if his unargued premise that its citizens will want to perform capitalist acts attracts the assent of the majority of his readers. How much equality would conflict with liberty in given circumstances depends on how much people would value equality in those circumstances. If life in a co-operative commonwealth appeals to them, they do not have to sacrifice liberty to belong to it.[14]

Looking at the logical possibilities, it is evident enough that socialism need not conflict with liberty. There could be a socialist or otherwise egalitarian community that did not interfere with peoples' lives, preventing them from doing what they wanted to do. Such a community is not a contradiction in terms—a conceptual impossibility. Whether it will come into being depends on what we are like and can plausibly become. Conceptual analysis will not settle that issue for us though it may help us to formulate what we want to investigate with sufficient precision so that we can do something with it. Nozick's easy *a priorism* blocks inquiry here.

Suppose, however, it is thoroughly utopian to claim people generally in a given society, particularly during the nascency of socialism, will want to maintain socialism. What then should we do? Should we force socialism on unwilling individuals who want to engage in capitalist acts?

Cohen remarks that three possibilities present themselves during that nascency period: (1) very few would lack enthusiasm for socialism, (2) very many would, and (3) some intermediate proportion would. It is (3) which poses the problem. Under (1) there is no need to prohibit the few who would wish to engage in capitalist acts. Their activity could do no damage. It is like allowing a few communist professors to teach in a society massively and stably either indifferent or hostile to communism and socialism. Let the chaps talk—would be the rational attitude on the part of the bourgeoisie in such a society— nobody is listening anyway. If anything their being at liberty to advocate their views and organize will only strengthen the system's self-image of itself. The same thing goes for a few would-be entrepreneurs in a solidly and stably socialist society. Let them strut their stuff, few will pay them any heed. There is no justification for prohibiting capitalist acts in such a circumstance.

Suppose instead (2) obtains. Suppose, as Cohen puts it, "that the disposition to perform capitalist acts is strong and widespread, so that 'socialism' is possible only with tyranny."[15] No socialist who understood what he was doing would try to institute socialism—say if he could somehow get the army under socialist control—when the masses of people were hostile to socialism and wanted capitalism. For socialists, that would be a time for determined and patient consciousness-raising. If socialist theory is near to the mark, the workers in that circumstance are so bamboozled by capitalist apologetic (ideology) that they do not take an interest, in certain important domains, in what is in their own interests. But again if socialist theory is close to being correct, capitalist modes of production will themselves create the conditions under which, prodded by constant socialist efforts at consciousness-raising, workers, and indeed the great mass of the people, will come to understand more clearly their own interests and become militant. To try to institute socialism "from above" before these conditions obtain is impossible. Since it is impossible, no reasonable question about its justifiability can arise. Again we see that it is not the case that socialism is morally impermissible because it is incompatible with respect for liberty and the rights of individuals.

It is (3) which is the difficult and interesting case. Of it, Cohen remarks:

> Could a socialist contain an amount of inclination to capitalism of such a size that unless it were coercively checked socialism would be subverted, yet sufficiently small that in socialist judgment socialism, with the required coercion, would still be worthwhile? Marxian socialists believe so, and that does commit them to a prohibition of capitalist acts between consenting adults in certain circumstances, notably those which follow a successful revolution. But why should they flinch from imposing the prohibition? They can defend it by reference to the social good and widened freedom it promotes.[16]

This seems to me exactly the right thing to say. Nozick would only have a plausible counter if he could establish the rightness of maintaining absolute side-constraints about individual liberty even in situations whereby, upon relaxing them, the extent of human liberty would be much greater than would otherwise be the case. But to opt for the lesser freedom here, even if only by way of omission, is surely mistaken.

Nozick wants to develop a theory which supports a free society. But such a side-constraint opting would, in such a circumstance, be undermining of a free society.

We need to remember that we are creatures who in complex and pervasive ways are interdependent. We cannot avoid interfering with each other in all sorts of ways. Imagine a family which tried to get along living in accordance with the absurd proclamation of Ayn Rand's character Howard Roark, "I do not recognize anyone's right to one minute of my life." But a society is scarcely more imaginable on that basis than is a family. (This does not mean that we have to view society, any society you like, as a *gemeinschaft*.) We are interdependent and our very humanness rests on this interdependence. We will, willy nilly, interfere with one another and our problem is to sort out when that interference is morally acceptable and when it isn't. (Recall here our discussion of Benjamin Barber's critique of Nozick in the previous chapter.) In no society can everyone just be at liberty to do their own thing regardless of its consequences to others.[17] Nozick, of course, does not think that we can, but he fails to take proper account of it. He also fails—and the points are related—to see that his restrictions on liberty reflect as much a moralized account of liberty as those of the socialists.[18] Sometimes there just are conflicts between various freedoms where we have to choose which freedoms to give pride of place. The socialist, as does Rawls in a different context, gives a coherent account of what to do in such circumstances, namely, in circumstances where no matter what you do freedom will in one way or another be restricted. In those circumstances the socialist will say that you should make those restrictions which will promote the widest extent of what Rawls calls basic liberties and, more generally, human well-being.

Nozick, as I just remarked, and as Cohen is well aware, will respond that to so act will violate certain side-constraints which are absolute. There are, Nozick believes, side-constraints that can never be rightly overridden no matter what the consequences. One of these "absolutes" is that contracts, legitimately made, ought never to be infringed no matter what the consequences of allowing their exercise. But, as we have seen, the obvious question in return is why make side-constraints so absolute and, even if some should be, why make this one about contracts so absolute? Arguing in the way Nozick does here has the look, at least, of bourgeois apologetics.

However, we should not let the issue drop there. Nozick's side-constraints are indeed very strong. Unlike Rawls, Nozick believes that "we may never limit one man's freedom in order to enhance the welfare or freedom of very many others, or even of everyone, him included, where we know he will benefit as a result at a future time" (page 256). By contrast, socialists and welfare state liberals, such as Rawls, Dworkin or Barry, are prepared in certain circumstances to restrict the liberty of some for the sake of others. In both cases a high priority is being given to liberty, but Nozick invokes side-constraints which he believes are absolutely overriding in any circumstance. Thus he regards it as totally impermissible to act as socialists and welfare state liberals are prepared to act in certain circumstances. For Nozick it is not a matter of maximizing freedom or anything else but of absolutely forbidding any act which restricts freedom. If this were the way we were to reason morally, it would entail that we not tax billionaires even the most modest sum to provide a milk subsidy at school for desperately impoverished, undernourished school children. Similarly, even if the exercise of certain legitimate freedoms would have the unintended consequence of leading to totalitarianism, we could not rightly interfere. And we could not move to limit the free market in any way at all, even if that were the only way of preserving it.

Again we have *reductio* arguments similar to those employed by Kateb and Barry—arguments we discussed in Chapter 9. But what if Nozick refuses to be reduced, does not take as a *reductio ad absurdum* what we take to be one? We are then back to considered judgments again. Conceptual analysis will not, in such instances, take us the whole way. I think this appeal to considered judgments is unavoidable and appropriate but some philosophers, hoping to escape all relativist challenges, want to avoid such an appeal. Like Norman Daniels, I believe that we should instead try to meet relativist challenges head on and to see if the careful use of the method of wide reflective equilibrium can meet that challenge or at least mitigate it.[19]

Nozick has a response of a certain kind, namely an appeal to a very fundamental defining condition of morality or, if you will, to a very high-level considered judgment, namely the "Kantian principle that individuals are ends and not merely means; they may not be sacrificed or used for the achieving of other ends without their consent" (pages 30–31). Strong side-constraints on action are corollaries of the individuals-are-inviolable axiom.

We have already stressed the unreality of the Kantian principle read in just this way. People are so thoroughly interdependent that they cannot avoid interfering with each other and in effect using each other (though putting it this way is misleading) in myriads of ways. The thing is to try to ascertain which ways are legitimate. (To say "None can be" is utterly self-defeating, for we cannot avoid interfering with each other.)

It is also important to recognize, as several commentators, including Cohen, have pointed out, that to invoke a conception of an overall social good, or of the public interest, in arguing against such a deployment of side-constraints, does not, as Nozick alleges, commit one to a belief in some mythical "*social entity* with a good that undergoes some sacrifice for its own good" (pages 32–33).

Nozick avoids what, in this context, is crucial morally by fastening on this mythical entity rather than (a) on the fact of our interdependence and (b) on the powerful claim that, when push comes to shove, numbers do count. For example, if we have two situations A and B, and if in situation A three people will be miserable and in situation B only one person will be miserable and each person will be equally miserable, then, *ceteris paribus,* it would be better for B to occur than A to occur if both can't be prevented and *the other* effects of preventing one or the other will be approximately the same. Indeed if I acted to prevent B rather than A in that circumstance, I would have done something that is wrong. It is claims like this that Nozick needs to face and it will not help to try to put them off by saying he is not interested in outcomes.

Until he faces them his remarks are hollow when he claims that (1) "there are only individual people, different individual people, with their own individual lives" and (2) that because of this—because there is no social entity—using "one of these people for the benefit of others, uses him and benefits the others. Nothing more." Such considerations are irrelevant. In arguing for redistribution under certain circumstances, we do not have to believe in a social entity. And in reasoning as we did about the above case, we were in effect appealing to a doctrine of the lesser evil. Where the suffering of each individual is the same, there is more suffering if three people suffer than if only one person suffers. (And do not let conceptual perplexities about how we determine "the same" in such contexts stand in the way of your recognizing the truth of such a claim.) But an appeal to that doctrine does not invoke a "social entity," whatever that means.

Nozick has given us no grounds for accepting such absolute side-constraints and so the socialist and the radical egalitarian need not be so constrained by them. He has done nothing to show that such egalitarians err in being willing, under certain circumstances, to restrict freedom in order to expand it (page 257).

However, we should also recognize that in arguing against Nozick as we have, we have been forced once again to appeal to considered judgments, though here to such basic ones that it is difficult to believe that anyone, who carefully thinks about them and takes them to heart, could possibly dissent from them. But we should also keep in mind Nozick's remark in his preface that he has reflected carefully on the counter-intuitive import of his views. Again, what if Nozick refused to be reduced? Have we simply reached bedrock here or would something like wide reflective equilibrium if carefully employed, possibly give us *lebensraum*? For wide reflective equilibrium to do that, it would entail capturing in a wider net Nozick's intuitions about the inviolability of persons. Nozick's intuitions would then be accounted for and many other *prima facie* conflicting intuitions as well in a single coherent account. Whatever we finally say about this, it is I think plain that conceptual analysis by itself will not carry us the whole distance.

IV

It is a central belief of Nozick's and indeed of all right-wing libertarians (as distinct from libertarian socialists such as Bakunin and Chomsky) that a commitment to individual liberties also requires a commitment to full capitalist property rights. The conservative libertarian belief is that in a society where there is no exclusive individual ownership of property, there can be no respect for individual liberty or at least not an adequate respect for the individual liberty.

It should first be noted, as A. M. Honoré has pointed out, that such a conception of individual property is a very distinctive western-style conception of ownership.[20] There are in other societies many systems of ownership which do not give the owner a right to his property which is exclusive, permanent and transmissible. This conception of full capitalist property rights is unique to our culture and indeed is not accepted in law without qualifications even in our societies.

Given this situation, it is indeed not unreasonable to suspect that Nozick's view of property and ownership is very ethnocentric. Such considerations apart, there is the powerful purely logical objection that there is a gap in Nozick's argument where Nozick argues that unless we have such individual property rights we cannot have a free society respecting individual liberty. The alleged gap is that to make the argument work Nozick must be able to show that individuals, through just initial acquisition or transfer, can become entitled to full (exclusive, permanent, transmissible) control over previously unheld resources. But what he has not been able to show is that rational agents or rational moral beings must accept this or even that this is the morally or rationally preferable view.

Onora O'Neill has succinctly and incisively argued that and I want to set out the central core of her argument.[21] Nozick, as we have seen, stands squarely in the Lockean tradition that individuals have a certain limited array of natural rights, namely the rights not to be harmed in life, health and liberty. Nozick thinks that he has shown, O'Neill argues, that if we have these rights that it follows that "individuals may justly acquire complete control over unlimited resources without needing the consent of all whose liberty will be restricted by these property rights."[22] Egalitarians and socialists to the contrary notwithstanding, we cannot Nozick argues, both be committed to individual natural rights and believe, as socialists, egalitarians and welfare state liberals must, that it can be just to limit or in any way regulate the legitimate holdings of individuals. Justice, if Nozick is right, is not only compatible with, but, at least in modern conditions, requires a laissez-faire capitalist order.

O'Neill accepts, for the sake of this discussion, Nozick's Lockean starting point, but argues that no such strong conclusions follow about the necessity of accepting full capitalist property rights. A person might quite consistently believe in certain forms of compulsory social sharing and still quite consistently believe that people have a natural right not to be harmed in life, health and liberty. Indeed, he might believe in such compulsory social sharing *because* he believes in those rights.

Nozick's theory of justice in order to count as an entitlement theory is committed to stating procedures by which individuals may justly acquire title to particular resources. The size of a person's legitimate holdings at a particular time, on an entitlement theory, is determinate in every case, but its being determinate in a certain way does not determine the holdings' justice. The justice of the holding depends, as we have seen, solely on the methods by which an individual acquires holdings. Individuals, on such an account, are connected in a sanctioned way—a way not to be violated—with *particular* holdings acquired by particular procedures.[23]

As can be seen from reflecting on the moral drawn from the Wilt Chamberlain parable and the entrepreneur case, Nozick's theory pre-supposes but, as O'Neill puts it, "does not demonstrate that it is wrong to interfere to restore disturbed patterns or end-states, and that such restorations are always redistributive and violate individuals' property rights. But it is just these property rights which have yet to be established."[24] Non-entitlement theories of distributive justice, Rawls' and my own included, also acknowledge that individuals have some sort of individual property rights. They recognize that individuals have some sort of claim to exercise some control over some resources. They have, that is, some entitlements. What they reject is the absolute entitlements of Nozick's full capitalist property rights. But that, even with *de facto* capitalism, let alone all societies seen over historical time and cultural space, is but one system of individual property rights among others. A. M. Honoré, as we have remarked, nicely documents this and O'Neill adverts to that fact in her argument. Nozick must show, to make his argument stick, *that the only morally justified liberty-respecting property rights are full capitalist property rights.* That that is so is anything but obvious and requires an argument. Welfare state liberals for example will deny that and maintain that the extent of individual property rights are limited in certain determinate ways and that pattern-restoring interference can maintain rather than violate the rights of individuals.[25] By contrast with Nozick, Friedman and Hayek, some welfare state liberals believe that there must be an upper limit on individual holdings or limitations on what individuals may do with their holdings or how or to whom they may transfer their holdings. These theories do not deny individual property rights but they provide a somewhat different theory of individual property rights. Unless Nozick can provide us with an argument for the moral superiority of *his* theory of individual property rights, he will simply have begged the question with the redistributionist. He believes that "individual property rights are rights to control resources in all ways, to dispose of them however and to whomever the owner wishes, or to accumulate them without limit."[26] But Nozick has done nothing to show that this is so. Yet, as O'Neill points out, it is this very "interpretation of property rights" which "must be established *before* the restoration of patterns or end-states by state action can be rejected as unjustified interference which violates individuals' rights."[27]

Nozick maintains that we lack a theory of property (page 171). Yet, as we have just seen, to establish the superiority of his entitlement account over the alternatives of his liberal welfare state opponents and his socialist opponents, Nozick needs to be able to show that property rights must be full capitalist property rights. This he has not done.

Rather than just stopping here with the remark that Nozick's case has not been established, O'Neill tries to patch together an argument from Nozick's account. It might at first blush seem plausible to try to move from Nozick's Lockean conception of initial just acquisition to full capitalist property rights.[28] If the former is justified, it might be argued, so is the latter. An initial acquisition is just, on such an account, if "title is acquired by mixing labour with unowned objects, provided that 'enough and as good' is left for others."[29] Nozick attempts to give a reading of this principle which shows that it is a justified and non-arbitrary principle of initial just acquisition. This reading, as O'Neill points out, involves both a streamlining and an extension of the principle.[30]

Locke's account, at first blush anyway, seems tolerably plausible where populations are thinly spread and the environment reasonably bountiful. It is in such situations that the "enough and as good" condition will perhaps not be violated. But that, to put it mildly, is hardly our world. Nozick attempts to get around this while keeping to what he takes to be the spirit of Locke. What Nozick takes to be a modern replacement of the "enough and as good" condition is the following: where appropriation leaves no further land or resources for the propertyless, they can be compensated for their loss, including their loss of liberty. This will be perfectly in accordance with his entitlement theory, if they are properly compensated. And they will be properly compensated if their overall position is not worsened by the acquisition (pages 175–179). If their situation is not worsened from what it was before the initial acquisitions occurred, the condition of "enough and as good" has been met and, if the other conditon is met, i.e., the owner mixes his labor with it or it is transferred from someone who justly acquired it, the acquisition is just.

So we can, according to Nozick, have situations in which resources of certain kinds have been entirely appropriated and yet the acquisitions are still just. The liberty of the person does not require any particular set of resources or opportunities but only equivalent resources and opportunities to those which existed before the appropriations began. Nozick believes that that is amply satisfied in capitalist societies.

I am inclined to think that even with this streamlining of Locke, many of the old difficulties remain. O'Neill, however, accepts, at least for the sake of present argument, this particular streamlining. Still, even accepting that, we have not shown, on Nozick's principles, "how one rather than another individual acquires a particular holding."[31] By itself "the 'enough and as good' proviso" does not show "that there would be anything unjust about reassigning holdings, provided that the 'general post' of holdings does not violate the proviso."[32] For Locke the answer to this is simple because his other criterion is that, if one is entitled to something as a just initial acquisition, one must have mixed one's labor with it. This is a necessary but not, of course, a sufficient condition for owning something previously unowned. That, if we accept that particular criterion, shows how, if the "enough and as good" condition also holds, a particular individual acquires a particular holding where the holding in question is of a previously unheld thing.

Still, why should we, or should we, accept mixing one's labor with something as being a necessary condition for something's being an initial just acquisition? How do we get complete ownership by contributing one factor in production? Even when the other alleged condition is satisfied, how do we get from "He works on it or makes something from it" to "He owns it," particularly in the sense of completely and exclusively owns it? There is certainly no logical entailment there.

O'Neill, in this general context, pushes home the following questions: Why should any rights accrue from mixing one's labor with something? "Why should not labouring be a way of losing one's labour, of improving what is 'in the common state'? Why, at best, should the labourer acquire more than a share in the final product in proportion to his contribution?"[33]

Locke could perhaps give a reasonable rationale for his claims concerning how we justly initially acquire something by appealing to his religious premiss that the earth is common property given to us by God to make the best advantage of and to improve. But Nozick will not, understandably, accept such religious premisses nor should he or we. After all they make thoroughly problematic cosmological and religious assumptions.

Locke needs to show how common property can become private property. Nozick, by contrast, must show how that which is unowned can become private property[34] (page 174). Locke argues from his religious premisses that property rights, as O'Neill aptly puts it, "are rights to use nature productively (improve it), not just use it" as one wills.[35] But Locke also assumed that one can improve only what one has a right to control. It is crucial for us to see that he needs to assume that to get from "A mixes his labour with X" to "A owns X." But that assumption is plainly false. As O'Neill points out "production can take place when producers do not have complete control of resources; and it can take place when they have no right to control resources."[36] Societies with very diverse social structures have not inconsiderable amounts of production which is collective and sometimes that production goes on, those production relations exist, without any claim or indeed sometimes without any claim at all to individual holdings. It is simply not true that we can improve only what we have a right to control. I might drive you off your land and take over your garden and grow much better vegetables than you do. But that does not mean that, since I have mixed my labor with it and have improved, it, I must have a right to control or own it. I have improved it but I have, in normal circumstances anyway, no right to control it.

Suppose Nozick tried, as some have, to modify this thesis by claiming that, instead of saying we can improve only what we have a right to control, we will assert alternatively that we will improve best what we have a right to control. But now we have made a utilitarian appeal, an appeal Friedman and Hayek could avail themselves of, but not Nozick, with his strictly rights-based anti-utilitarian theory. Yet consistent or not, sometimes Nozick hints at such a utilitarian justification (page 177). But, if that move is made, at least two things need be said. First, it is, to put it moderately, challengeable whether in all circumstances and in all societies one will improve best what one has a right to control. Moreover, even if one will improve best what one has a right to control, why should it be complete control rather than some control? Second, this utilitarian argument, even if accepted, would still not give one full capitalist property rights, for it would not give one the right to leave productive resources idle and it would not give one the right to destroy them.

How else, if Locke's arguments are abandoned, can Nozick justify full capitalist property rights? From reflecting on the general tenor of his account, one would expect him to say that any curtailment or abridgment of full capitalist property rights is a curtailment or abridgment of the liberty of the person.[37] But how do we, or do we, know this is so or have good grounds for believing this is so? "We could know," O'Neill remarks, "that such acts (full capitalist acts) were permitted by the right to liberty only on the basis of some other argument such as the 'enough and as good' proviso. . . ."[38] But Nozick is, as we have seen, fully aware that we cannot in our time literally appeal to that criterion. The Lockean proviso unstreamlined will not do. And, as we have seen, Nozick's replacement will not wash either. So we still need an argument to show that full capitalist property rights do not in themselves sometimes violate rights.[39]

We must not confuse liberty with license. I am not at liberty to go for a spin in your car without your permission. In every society there are certain things we are not free to do and certain things we are free to do. There is no society without socially sanctioned coercion which limits in various ways the freedom of human beings. It is not correct to characterize liberty (plain "negative liberty" if you will) as "doing what you wish without the interference of others." We must moralize the characterization to "doing what you wish without the *unjustified* interference of others." But then the central question becomes, how do we determine what is and what isn't *justified* interference with others? Nozick needs something like the "enough and as good" proviso and the "mixing your labor" proviso to get to the claim that any abridgment of full capitalist property rights abridges the liberty of the person: interferes *unjustifiably* in the living of his life. Indeed if a person cannot engage in such unqualified capitalist acts, he is interfered with. There can be no question about that. But his liberty is abridged and his rights are violated only if he is *unjustifiably* interfered with. But it is just that claim—the claim that he is unjustifiably interfered with—that Nozick needs an argument for.

V

Nozick, as we have seen, starts with the sparse Lockean account of natural rights, the rights not to be harmed in life, health, or liberty. He argues that if they are accepted then we are logically committed to laissez-faire capitalism, to full capitalist property rights and to his entitlement theory of justice. Onora O'Neill very directly and G. A. Cohen less directly have shown how these arguments are unsound.

However, even if they are somehow mistaken in all of their various finely spun arguments or even if it is the case that Nozick somehow by some inessential modification could elude them, there is still a more direct challenge made by A. M. Honoré to the effect that Nozick has just arbitrarily and ethnocentrically identified property rights with the historically and culturally contingent property rights of a certain phase of Western capitalistic society.[40] Nozick needs to give us some grounds for taking that system of property rights to be the norm or the preferred system for rational and informed persons with a sense of justice.

Honoré's underlying concern is to show that there is nothing in-consistent, incongruous or unreasonable about both believing in the legitimacy of individual private property and at the same time believing that "each member of a society is entitled to an equal or approximately equal standard of living."[41] To do this he must, of course, refute Nozick's arguments. Arguments we have already been at pains to refute. In particular he must refute Nozick's twin doctrines of the moral re-quiredness of full capitalist property rights and his argument for the minimal state.

If persons were to work in complete isolation, it might be true that they were entitled to keep exclusively and indefinitely for themselves whatever they made or produced.[42] Though, even here, as we have already seen, this is not beyond question. But, be that as it may, that condition is not met anywhere, for we are through and through inter-dependent social beings.[43] There are many systems of socially sanctioned private property rights which acknowledge this and are less individualistic than the fully capitalist property rights championed by Nozick. Nozick, Honoré points out, just complacently and uncritically presupposes in his reasoning, without making any attempt to justify his so proceeding, the system of ownership "conceived in Western society on the model of Roman law."[44] But there are both extant and coherently imaginable alternatives to it which have every appearance of being as morally respectable as the model of full capitalist property rights.[45] Some of these alternative systems come from economically simpler societies than our own, but there is, as Honoré puts it, "no special reason to think that our moral consciousness is superior to that of simple societies," so there is no good reason for rejecting them on that account and accepting full capitalist property rights.[46]

It is such an awareness that is behind the charge that Nozick's system is ethnocentric. Of course, it does not follow that, because there are diverse conceptions of private property, they are all equally justified or unjustified. Given such diversity, however, the burden of proof is on Nozick to show that his scheme is preferable or at least preferable in our socio-historical circumstances. Without such a justification, it is reasonable to believe that the person who, in such a circumstance, sticks with his own culture's scheme is being ethnocentric.

There are systems of property—private property—that grant entitlements to individuals but not entitlements of indefinite duration or exclusive right to that thing so as to deny access and use to everyone else or to grant that it be "transmissible *inter vivos* and on death, so that it can be sold, given, inherited, mortgaged and the like again without limit of time."[47] There can be systems that grant various combinations of those things. A system might, for example, grant exclusive use during an owner's lifetime but deny an entitlement to pass it on just as he wishes or even to pass it on at all. But a system with any of these restrictions falls short of being a full capitalist property rights system.

What we need to keep in mind here is that a system of full capitalist property rights, even if we grant its economic merits, is not self-evidently just.[48] Yet Nozick seems to treat it as such. We, of course, can challenge its economic merits as well. My point here is that, even granting these merits, there remain problems about its justice and, if there are problems about its justice in societies as wealthy as ours, questions of superior efficiency need not be decisive.

Nozick's rules about just acquisition, transfer and distribution are, as we have seen, based on an uncritical acceptance of the classical nineteenth-century conception of ownership in which ownership is permanent, exclusive and transmissible. But, as Honoré remarks, "this type of property system is neither the only conceivable system, nor the easiest to justify from a moral point of view, nor does it predominate in those societies which are closest to a 'state of nature.'"[49]

Primitive societies aside, modern law in western capitalist societies has evolved in ways that Nozick would not approve. Legal systems now typically allow for compulsory acquisition as in expropriation, when the government, acting through the courts, recognizes that it is in the general interest of people (the vast majority in the society) to expropriate some holding whether or not the owner agrees to sell. There are also sometimes rules which stipulate that when an owner neglects his property he may be deprived of it. The squatter, for example, may, in such a circumstance, rightly, in those systems, obtain it by a kind of "private expropriation."[50] It is not evident why or whether Nozick's severely individualistic model of property rights is superior to such extant systems—systems which are extant in complex societies.

Again we must beware of assuming, as Nozick does, that a rationale (a justificatory basis) can be reasonably decided on for acquiring or transferring property in abstraction from an historical and social context.[51] As several commentators have remarked, Nozick, with sociological naivete, simply reasons in a social and historical vacuum.[52] Aside from not being able to tell us when we have a just original acquisition, he assumes that "a just acquisition in 1066 or 1620 remains a just root of title in 1975."[53] But this is problematic. To bring this out, Honoré gives these examples:

Suppose, apart from any question of the justification for colonies, that in the nineteenth century Metropolitania occupied a deserted tract which it proceeded to colonize, building roads and irrigating the land. As a result a numerous indigenous population crowded in from the neighbouring areas. These people now claim to be free and to decide their own destinies. Whether or not colonization is in general thought a permissible form of "entitlement" the changed situation must surely change one's moral evaluation of Metropolitania's title to the formerly deserted tract. So with the Mayflowerite who bagged a large stretch of unoccupied land in 1620. If the situation is now that irrespective of title the tracts in question are occupied by people who have nowhere else to live surely the moral basis of the title of the Mayflowerite's successors must at least be open to debate. Once there was more than enough to go round, now there is not. And is the case very different if the thousands without property instead of occupying the colonies or tracts in question crowd the periphery and make claims on the unused resources inside: All this is intended to make the simple point that it is obtuse to suppose that the justification for acquiring or transmitting property could be settled once and for all at the date of acquisition or transfer. Legally it may be so, subject to the rules of lapse and expropriation. This is because of the need to frame rules of law in such a way as to ensure certainty of title. They are meant however to be applied in a context in which social and moral criticism may be directed against their operation and in which their defects may be corrected by legislation or similar means. Apart from positive law, can it seriously be maintained that the rules about what constitutes a just acquisition or transfer both express unchanging verities and, in their application to the facts of a given acquisition or transfer, are exempt from reassessment in the light of changed circumstances?[54]

To drive home his point that systems of ownership alternative to the full capitalist model are conceivable and morally intelligible, Honoré develops a neat Nozick-like parable.

Suppose that, in a "state of nature" a group of people live near a river and subsist on fish, which they catch by hand, and berries. There is great difficulty in catching fish by hand. Berries are however fairly plentiful. There are bits of metal lying around and I discover how to make one of them into a fishhook. With this invention I quadruple my catch of fish. My neighbours cannot discover the knack and I decline to tell them. They press me to lend them the fishhook or to give them lessons in acquiring the technique. I have however acquired western notions of property law and Lockean ideas about entitlement, I point out that I have a just title to the fishhook, since according to Nozick's version of Locke they are no worse off as a result of my invention. I am therefore entitled to the exclusive, permanent and transmissible use of the fishhook. My neighbours may try their hands at finding out how to make one, of course, but if they fail they may look forward to eating berries and from time to time a bit of fish while I and those persons whom I choose to invite to a meal propose to enjoy ourselves with daily delicacies. If they object that this is unfair I shall point out (though the relevance is not obvious) that they are not actually starving. Nor am I monopolizing materials. There are other pieces of metal lying around. They are no worse off than they were before and than they would have been without my find (in fact they are worse off relative to me). As to the parrot cry that they protect me and my family from marauders, wild animals and the like, so that I ought to share my good fortune with them, I reply that they have not grasped what is implied by a system of just entitlements. Are they saying that I am not entitled to the fishhook?[55]

A primitive interlocutor with our primitive Nozickian might press him as follows. I do not deny that you have a right to the fishhook. You found the materials simply lying around, unowned and unused; you invented and made the hook. I do not for a moment deny that it is yours. But I do deny that your right to it is exclusive, permanent and transmissible.

When our primitive Nozickian demurs, the interlocutor could plausibly respond by telling him to stop making *persuasive* definitions of "ownership" based on definitions in foreign books of a certain vintage and rooted in the practice of sophisticated societies bent on increasing production come what may. After all their society is a very different society in which their people are quite accustomed and generally quite willing to share fortunes and misfortunes. What may be fair and economically justified in laissez-faire societies need not apply to them in their situation. In their situation, given their system of property rights and their system of moral propriety—a system which functions quite well in their society—the Nozickian iconoclast has a right but not an unlimited right to his fishhook. His share, as the inventor, in the using of it is greater than that of any other individual in the society, but others have a right, though a more limited right, to its use too.

It is far from being certain that that society should accept the moral revolution of the Nozickian moral iconoclast as providing them with a morally superior system for that society in that historical situation. Indeed there seems to be no reason at all for advocating the Nozickian system.

The system of private property that our primitive Nozickian set himself against is *inherently distributive*. People have entitlements—there is individual ownership of property—but the holdings given by these entitlements are not exclusive, permanent and transmissible. *Distribution patterns emerge along with the entitlements, but there is no reason to think that they are unstable or that they will lead to a constant or even frequent interference with the liberty of people in that society.*

There is, however, in that society a *principle of sharing* which is not to be subverted by the recognition of either desert or the right, within limits, of people to choose with respect to, among other things, their economic priorities, and to have holdings. Such a system of private property compares, as Honoré puts it, rather favorably to our system of property ownership in terms of justice. It allows for entitlements and through them for contribution, desert and choice. While it acknowledges us as individuals—as separate persons with lives of our own—it also acknowledges, and gives prominent place to, "the interdependence of the members of the group" and recognizes "overtly that they cannot survive in isolation."[56] It also rejects a claim that is central to bourgeois individualism and to Nozick's vision of a moral community, namely it "rejects the notion that I do no harm to a member of my group if as a result of my effort I am better off, and he is no worse off than he would otherwise be."[57] There are circumstances—suppose I invent a cure for cancer and refuse to sell it to someone or give it to him when he has cancer—in which this bourgeois claim would not be true. By acting as a proper bourgeois, by reasoning in accordance with such bourgeois individualism and insisting on my "rights," I could very well harm my neighbor. The fishhook example is one case in point and my hoarding my cancer cure or only giving it to a few people I happen to like is another.

It is anything but evident whether a belief system which makes that rejection of bourgeois individualism is not morally superior to the Nozickian one which does not. At the very least the burden of proof is on the Nozickian system to show its moral superiority.

Though it would play havoc with his state-of-nature stance, Nozick could perhaps argue that while such a system of property rights will work well enough in primitive societies, in complex industrial societies such as our own, where the division of labor is well advanced, it is impossible.

This, we should start by noticing, is already to retreat in Honoré's direction from the grand abstractions of *Anarchy, State, and Utopia*.

Still, Nozick could argue: in modern industrial society, where the specialization of work is very extensive, it is indeed difficult to keep alive the notion that we all participate in a common enterprise. We are not at all in the position of a hunting and gathering society. Yet in reality in complex societies, with a very extensive division of labor, we are at least as interdependent as people in primitive societies. It is just that our common bonds are more hidden with such production relations and ways of living. Full capitalist property relations cannot replace the participatory property system of the more primitive societies we have described above and still give moral representation to the fact that we are both individual persons and persons who stand in need of each other and have a sense of responsibility for each other. In modern industrial societies we do stand in need of each other. The work process and our patterns of consumption, enjoyment and general navigation in the world massively and pervasively presuppose it. The bourgeois form of our relations, however, disguises it. We have in such a social world duties of mutual aid as well as duties not to harm each other. A stateless or relatively stateless system of participatory property law, such as we gestured at, can work in simple societies. To achieve similar moral effects in societies such as our own, Honoré argues, the community as a whole, through (at least in class-divided societies) its state apparatus, "must act as the surrogate of the participatory principles."[58] This means that we must tax the equivalent of the inventor of the fishhook in such complex societies and we must tax the great owners and controllers of the means of production. Honoré contends, in good liberal fashion, that if the state functions in this way as a surrogate for the participatory principles of the property ownership system of more primitive societies, rather than as a minimal state bent on protecting full capitalist property rights, it will provide us with a system of property which will support a social system in which "the economic advantages of specialization can be combined with a just or a juster distribution of the benefits derived from it."[59] We can have a society which is both fair and Pareto optimal. State intervention, in such a neo-participatory property system, will violate no rights (rights acknowledged within the system) and, subject to a reasonable reading, it will (as we have seen) violate no Lockean natural rights either. The burden of proof is on Nozick to show that his distinctive system of property rights is morally superior when it would seem at least that under the neo-participatory property system a greater justice in distribution would be achieved without violation of rights.

Nozick might respond that that system is not, after all, non-rights violating. In taxing people, in requiring the chap to share in that way his fishhook, the separateness, distinctiveness and individuality of the fishhook owner has been violated. The same is true for the taxed capitalist. They have not been treated as persons. They have been treated as a means only, as are people who are taxed to pay for soup kitchens so that others do not starve. But, as H. L. A. Hart has pointed out, this is absurd hyperbole.[60] If A's kidney is taken from him to give to B, if A is forced to serve B, whether he will or not, if A is forced to marry B, whether he will or not, then A's person is being violated. Things (at least in our society) that are very personal and very vital to A's life and conception of himself are being taken from him, but if some of A's income—quite clearly if it is a small bit—is taken from him in taxes in a democratic state, where he has his fair say in determining what the laws of that society are, it is absurd to say he is being treated *merely* as a means and that his person is not respected. Nozick's case against the more than minimal state and his defense of full capitalist property rights fails.

NOTES

1. Alan Garfinkel, *Forms of Explanation* (New Haven, Conn.: Yale University Press, 1981), ch. 3; and David Schweickart, *Capitalism or Worker Control?* (New York: Praeger, 1980).

2. Kai Nielsen, "A Marxist Conception of Ideology," in *Ideology, Philosophy and Politics,* ed. Anthony Parel (Waterloo, Ont.: Wilfred Laurier University Press, 1983), pp. 139–62.

3. Max Black, *Problems of Analyses* (Ithaca, N.Y.: Cornell University Press, 1954), pp. 157–225; and Max Black, *Models and Metaphors* (Ithaca, N.Y.: Cornell University Press, 1962), pp. 194–208.

4. *Some* of them have been collected together in the following volumes: Jeffrey Paul (ed.), *Reading Nozick* (Totowa, N.J.: Rowman & Littlefield, 1981); *Arizona Law Review* 19, no. 1 (1977); and *The Occasional Review* issue 8/9 (Autumn 1978).

5. G. A. Cohen, "Robert Nozick and Wilt Chamberlain: How Patterns Preserve Liberty" in *Justice and Economic Distribution,* eds. John Arthur and William H. Shaw (Englewood Cliffs, N.J.: Prentice-Hall, 1978), pp. 246–62; Onora O'Neill, "Nozick's Entitlements," *Inquiry* (Winter 1976), pp. 468–81.

6. Cohen, op. cit., p. 247.

7. Ibid., p. 248.

8. Ibid., p. 250.

9. Gerald Doppelt, "Rawls' System of Justice: A Critique from the Left," *Nous* 15, no. 3 (September 1981): 259–307.

10. See the discussion of moral equality in the first chapter. And see as well Thomas Nagel, *Mortal Questions* (Cambridge: Cambridge University Press, 1979), pp. 106–27.

11. Cohen, op. cit., pp. 351–53.

12. Ibid., p. 252.

13. Ibid., p. 253.

14. Ibid., p. 253–54.

15. Ibid., p. 255. Cohen adds a significant footnote here. "I add 'scare-quotes' because socialism, properly defined is incompatible with tyranny; but, contrary to what some socialists seem to think, that is no argument against those who say that the form of economy socialists favour requires tyranny" (p. 261). To put Cohen's point in a different way, we should know enough by now to realize that nothing substantial will be gained by a conventionalist's sulk.

16. Ibid., p. 255.

17. G. A. Cohen, "Capitalism, Freedom and the Proletariat," in *The Idea of Freedom,* ed. Alan Ryan (Oxford: Oxford University Press, 1979), pp. 9–25.

18. Ibid.

19. Norman Daniels, "Wide Relfective Equilibrium and Theory Acceptance in Ethics," *The Journal of Philosophy* 10, no. 1 (March 1980): 83–104; and "On Some Methods of Ethics and Linguistics," *Philosophical Studies* 37 (1980): 21–36.

20. A. M. Honoré, "Property, Title and Redistribution" in *Property, Profits and Economic Justice,* ed. Virginia Held (Belmont, Cal.: Wadsworth Publishing, 1980), pp. 84–92.

21. Onora O'Neill, op. cit., pp. 468–81.

22. Ibid., p. 468.

23. Ibid., p. 470.

24. Ibid., p. 471.

25. Ibid.

26. Ibid. See Nozick, *Anarchy, State, and Utopia,* pp. 281–82.

27. O'Neill, op. cit., p. 471.

28. I have talked throughout as if Nozick were a genuine descendent of Locke. This has been impressively challenged by Virginia Held, "John Locke on Robert Nozick," *Social Research* 43 (1976): 169–95; and Shadia Drury, "Robert Nozick and the Right to Property," in *Theories of Property,* eds. Anthony Parel and Thomas Flanagan (Waterloo, Ont.: Wilfred Laurier University Press, 1979), pp. 361–79.

29. O'Neill, op. cit., p. 472.

30. Ibid., p. 473.

31. Ibid., p. 475.

32. Ibid.

33. Ibid., p. 476.

34. Ibid.

35. Ibid., p. 478.

36. Ibid., p. 479.

37. Ibid.

38. Ibid.

39. Ibid. Husain Sarkar, "The Lockean Proviso," *Canadian Journal of Philosophy* 12, no. 1 (March 1982): 47–59.

40. A. M. Honoré, op. cit., pp. 84–92.

41. Ibid., p. 84.

42. Ibid., p. 85.

43. Ibid.

44. Ibid.

45. Ibid., p. 86.

46. Ibid.

47. Ibid.

48. Ibid.

49. Ibid. He documents this by reference to particular primitive societies in the latter part of his essay (pp. 88–91).

50. Ibid., pp. 86–87.

51. Ibid., p. 87.

52. Bernard Williams, "The Minimal State," *Times Literary Supplement,* January 17, 1975; Steven Lukes, *Essays in Social Theory* (London: Macmillan Press, 1977), pp. 191–95; Boris Frankel, "Anarchy, State and Utopia," *Theory and Society* 3 (1976): 443–49.

53. Honoré, op. cit., p. 87.

54. Ibid., pp. 87–88.

55. Ibid., p. 88.

56. Ibid., p. 89.

57. Ibid.

58. Ibid., p. 90.

59. Ibid.

60. H. L. A. Hart, "Between Utility and Rights," in *The Idea of Freedom,* ed. Alan Ryan, pp. 77–98.

12

Nozick and the Critique of Egalitarianism

I

In the previous three chapters I set out and then criticized Nozick's version of conservative libertarianism. I argued that there are moral, sociological and logical difficulties in Nozick's social philosophy that are quite insurmountable. Since Nozick's libertarianism is the most philosophically sophisticated version of right-wing libertarianism available to us, this conclusion, if my arguments have been near to the mark, is not an insignificant one.

The central thrust of what I have argued might very possibly be accepted and it might still be thought that the positive merits and defects of Nozick's own account aside, it still remains the case that he has made a devastating critique of egalitarianism—a critique that can survive the shambles of his own entitlement theory. In this chapter I shall be concerned to examine this critique of egalitarianism. I shall argue that it is not the devastating critique that many have taken it to be. It is for the most part very dependent on his entitlement theory and rather clearly reveals his own sociological naivete, narrow and ethocentric conception of human nature, inattention to the facts and a certain moral insensitivity. (Perhaps it is less moral insensitivity than being blinded by a theory?)

Robert Nozick in effect asks "*What's so hot about egalitarianism?*" and challenges its whole underlying rationale. Nozick notes that in cultures such as ours and among our moral philosophers there is a pervasive and indeed deeply embedded tendency to believe that any deviation from equality must be justified. Equality is the normative baseline and inequalities must be justified. He asks "Why ought people's holdings to be equal, in the absence of special moral reason to deviate from equality? (Why think there *ought* to be *any* particular pattern in holdings?) Why is equality the rest (or rectilinear motion) position of the system, deviation from which may be caused only by moral forces?" (pages 223–24).

One will be so committed to equality if one believes, as Rawls and I do, that human beings in the design of their social institutions have an equal right to concern and respect. We must not, that is, design our social life so that the interests of any human being are ignored. Rather, all interests must, as far as that is possible, be equally considered. *Prima facie* each person's interests must have equal consideration. It is only where it is not possible to avoid conflicts of interest—where both interests cannot be satisfied—that the interests of some may be rightly subordinated to the interests of others. One of the deep problems of moral philosophy is to try to determine a fair and a morally justified way of doing this. We start, or at least egalitarians start, from a baseline of an equal concern for the interests of everyone. (Nozick could, of course, still ask "Why take that as one's starting place?") The underlying rationale, or at least an evident underlying rationale, for that is the very deeply embedded belief that "all human beings have a natural right to an equality of concern and respect, a right they possess not in virtue of birth or characteristic or merit or excellence, but simply as human beings with the capacity to make plans and give justice."[1] This in effect is a moral ideal that everyone be treated equally as moral persons—a moral ideal that in spite of his anti-egalitarianism Nozick accepts. It is indeed an ideal reasonably widely rooted in people's moral sentiments that all human beings, great and small, virtuous and vicious, should be respected and cared for simply in virtue of the fact that they are human beings. Indeed this moral ideal is not infrequently rooted in an impersonal love for humankind. Where one does not have this sentiment, where the pull of it is not felt at all, it is difficult to imagine how it can be shown by some kind of argument or by appeal to evidence that we ought to have that sentiment or the ideal that it gives rise to.[2] But everything we reasonably commit ourselves to we do not commit ourselves to for a reason. Many things which are *consistent* with what it is to be rational are not *required* by any principle of rationality.[3]

Nozick rejects such a general natural right to an equality of concern and respect, though, as can be seen above, he does not deny it as an ideal, for he rejects any appeal to *general* rights to be in a certain state and only accepts *particular* rights grounded in our various entitlements flowing from our initial just acquisitions. "No neatly contoured right to achieve a goal—such as equality of respect—will avoid incompatibility with the substructure of particular rights which are the entitlements of just acquisitions" (page 238). Since these are, Nozick claims, the morally fundamental things and since such general rights-claims are incompatible with them, no general rights can exist. (We must not forget that ideals are one thing and rights another. Notice also how badly this fits with the claim that there are natural rights.)

This seems to me an arbitrary claim and, as well, a peculiarly private-property-hugging view for which no rationale is evident. Why should these particular rights be taken as fundamental, while general rights-claims, such as the one stated above, must be taken as dependent on them? Why shouldn't it be the case, alternatively, that only those particular rights-claims which are compatible with such a general principle of human rights be taken as genuine rights-claims, the rest being rejected as merely apparent rights or rights-claims? Why shouldn't a conception of human rights be taken as fundamental? And why rely on intuitions about particular situations when there are such conflicts about them and with other particular judgments, particularly when we have a general considered judgment which is so appealing?

Such general rights-claims, unlike the heterogeneous particular entitlements, afford a rationale for the existence of particular rights. So it seems much less arbitrary to take such general rights as fundamental. Nozick gives us no grounds for taking the particular rights as fundamental. He seems to be arbitrarily, and in a suspiciously ideological fashion, taking these particular property rights as the fundamental things morally.

II

Egalitarians believe that a greater equality in the conditions of life is desirable. We should not only seek a world in which there is as much happiness and as little pain as possible, we should also seek a world in which this is true for everyone. But to approximate this requires a greater equality in the conditions of life (including, of course, a greater equality of resources). One further reason, perhaps the fundamental reason, why this equality of condition is desirable is that it brings with it a greater moral autonomy and a greater self-respect for more people.

However, the moral iconoclast could quite naturally ask: Why should we care about that? Why should there be such a concern with each and everyone of us, particularly when, as Nietzsche shows and Nozick too avers, we are not in any factual sense all equals? There are, after all, very considerable differences in our moral sensitivity, our knowledge, our intelligence, our energy, our persistence, our concern for each other and the like. Why, then, should we be taken as all, in some moral sense, equally deserving of respect? Given our differences in moral sensitivity and concern for others, why should we be taken as moral equals? Why should there be an equality of moral concern for all human beings irrespective of what those human beings are like?

We can say that even to understand what morality is we must recognize that we cannot justifiably or justly treat A and B differently just because they are different *individuals*. If it is just that A be treated in manner y, then justice and morality, if not just logic, require that we treat B in manner y as well, unless there is some difference between them other than the bare fact that they are simply two different individuals. If there are no relevant differences between them we must treat them the same. But accepting this, as we indeed should, will not even begin to get us to the proposition that all human beings are to be treated with equal concern and respect, for it is a plain fact that they are not all alike. The differences between us are not inconsiderable. Yet Rawls, Dworkin and Nielsen stick to this principle of equal concern as something morally fundamental in the face of just as keen an awareness of the differences between human beings as that possessed by Nietzsche or Nozick. But why should one—or should one—do this? Why accept this egalitarian ideal? Perhaps it is, as Nietzsche believes, a cultural hangover from Judeo-Christian ideology. What is the justification for saying that all human beings have a natural right to an equality of concern and respect? Historically not everyone has thought that way, not everyone thinks that way today, and there surely are alternatives to so viewing things. Moreover, it is not clear that we have any good grounds for claiming the alternative views are irrational or less rational than egalitarianism. It is not evident that we can show that a Nietzschean morality or a Nozickian morality is *less rational* than an egalitarian one.

Even if we cannot show that *rationality* requires that there should be a concern for each and everyone of us just in virtue of the fact that we are human beings, it doesn't at all follow that there is anything irrational about that commitment. Even if we must say that we have no idea of how this moral belief could be justified, that does not mean that Nozick or Nietzsche is in any better position, because we can just as well ask, as we have in previous chapters, why we should treat full capitalist property rights as inviolable. Why should we be so committed to the protection of private property even when that protection causes widespread misery and makes possible exploitation and human degradation? And we can ask Nietzsche why we should sacrifice everything to the "higher man," to the attainment of certain ideals of human perfection among a small minority of mankind. Nozick and Nietzsche are in no better position to answer these questions in a non-question begging way than is the egalitarian who operates on a principle of an equal concern for the well-being of all human beings. And to most of us, at any rate, the egalitarian ideal is the more attractive.

I am not sure that we can justify fundamental ideals such as a belief that all humankind have a right to an equality of concern and respect. And I am not confident that we even need to try to, for it may very well be that there could be nothing more fundamental that we could appeal to for such a justification. *Perhaps* here we should say that justification comes to an end and that we simply have to make up our minds what kind of human being we want to be?

III

Still in the above remarks in defense of egalitarianism there was a rather heavy appeal to considered judgments, and Nozick might not unreasonably counter that we could not get those judgments into reflective equilibrium and that this should become evident when we face his specific arguments against egalitarianism. If we honestly do that, he might very well argue, we will not have such an easy way with dissenters. It is to these arguments that I shall now turn.

Most liberal and socialist thinkers, Nozick claims, just accept egalitarianism as an unexamined dogma, an article of faith. People who argue for egalitarianism assume (as Bernard Williams does for example) "that society (that is, each of us acting together in some organized fashion) should make provision for the important needs of all of its members." People need medical care. That being so, egalitarians reason, if medical care is available, people have a right to it and society has an obligation to provide it if it can. But why accept this commonly held belief? What argument is there for it? How can it be shown that people have some basic right to have their needs met—or at least their most fundamental needs met—where it is possible to do so?

Nozick, unlike Friedman, thinks that even the claims to equality of opportunity—a rather minimal goal for an egalitarian—are unjustified and indeed unjustifiable. Whatever we do to achieve it, we cannot, he claims, avoid using resources, and this will involve, quite unavoidably, "worsening the situation of some," namely of "those from whom holdings are taken in order to improve the situation of others" (page 233). But this, he says, appealing to his entitlement theory of justice, is plainly unjust, for "holdings to which these people are entitled may not be seized, even to provide equality of opportunity for others" (page 235). If they have justly acquired them, they are theirs and it is a fundamental violation of justice to take those things away from them. Here we can see, again, how absolutistic he is about property rights. And we can also see how very much his critique of egalitarianism at this point presupposes his own entitlement theory. Given the buffeting it has received in the previous chapters, it is essential that Nozick find some other grounds for his rejection of egalitarianism.

In this context the following passage from Nozick is crucial.

> The major objection to speaking of everyone's having a right to various things such as equality of opportunity, life, and so on, and enforcing this right, is that these "rights" require a substructure of things and materials and actions; and other people may have rights and entitlements over these. No one has a right to something whose realization requires certain uses of things and activities that other people have rights and entitlements over. Other people's rights and entitlements to *particular things* (*that* pencil, *their* body, and so on) and how they choose to exercise these rights and entitlements fix the external environment of any given individual and the means that will be available to him. If his goal requires the use of means which others have rights over, he must enlist their voluntary cooperation. Even to exercise his right to determine how 'something he owns is to be used may require other means he must acquire a right to, for example, food to keep him alive; he must put together, with the cooperation of others, a feasible package. [page 238]

How can Nozick justifiably be so absolutistic about the particular rights he stresses and in particular about the inviolability of property rights? We should not even grant Nozick that much, for as our discussion of Honoré's argument brought out in the previous chapter, Nozick is unwittingly appealing to one particular model of individual property rights here. There are, as we have seen, other models which have a principle of sharing and are inherently distributive. How can he be so confident that "No one has a right to something whose realization requires certain uses of things and activities that other people have rights and entitlements over"? (page 238) Suppose I am the first settler to come into an unoccupied country. I appropriate the really best land where two rivers come together and mix my labor with it. Others— let us call them "you"—come later and can only scratch out a rather marginal living in not very fertile land while I am slowly amassing great riches. Yet the Lockean proviso is not violated. I do not make you worse off than you already were. Moreover, it was just a matter of pure luck that I stumbled on this land before you did. Because of this good fortune on my part, my life and that of my children is substantially different than your condition of life and that of your children. But, according to Nozick, I have no duty or obligation to give up any of my holdings to make a more equal distribution, giving everyone more nearly equal life conditions. This is even true when it will not particularly hurt me to do so. The land is mine and I can stubbornly hold on to it if I want to even though I live in luxury and you in poverty. After all, I didn't make you worse off than you were before I acquired this land or you came into the country. And, after all, you came into this country, where I had already acquired a just acquisition, voluntarily.

To hold so stubbornly on to one's entitlements is not only, as Nozick would agree, ungenerous, it is, Nozick to the contrary notwithstanding, unfair and unjust. It was just by pure luck that I came on this land first. I am not even like the inventive chap with the fishhook. There is not even a question here of rewarding me for my superior industry and foresight. Moreover, while I have a right to my legitimate holdings, I also have a duty to relieve misery where I reasonably can and this duty to relieve misery here outweighs my right to do with my holdings what I like as long as I do not harm others. No particular property rights can justifiably be so absolute that they can override and outweigh the duties we have to *mutual aid* where, by not acknowledging that duty, extensive human misery would follow as a result. I have a very stringent duty to prevent that situation where I am in a position to do so and most particularly where no one else is. That this is so is even more obvious where my own well-being is also being equally catered to. My entitlements to property cannot override such a duty. Property rights—entitlements rights—are *prima facie* rights and they are de-feasible. People do indeed have rights to particular things but sometimes these rights can be rightly and justly overridden. Moreover, as we have seen, to the system of full capitalist property rights, there are alternative systems of individual property rights that can easily accommodate such considerations.

IV

We have a Lockean right not to be killed but we have, on Nozick's account, no positive right to life. Voluntary contractual arrangements aside, no one, not even the state, has a duty to help us, even in an affluent society, so that we will not starve, though it (the state as well as individual citizens) has a stringent duty not to kill us or take our property.

Here consider claims about a right to life or a right, where this can be had, to a share of the stock of goods in the world sufficient to maintain well-being, a right to respect, to the conditions productive of self-respect and to moral autonomy. My own sense of justice—my considered judgments concerning what is just and unjust—is such that where a particular entitlement concerning some holding of ours conflicts with these rights, there is at least a *prima facie* case for overriding that particular entitlement. If I am a David Rockefeller and my large holdings stand in the way of people moving out of conditions of misery and degradation, then these entitlements of mine should be overridden. This is true irrespective of whether or not my holdings were justly acquired.

In probing whether this is so, note that the above case is not like Nozick's case where we cannot share something (page 237). Though it has in common with his case, that to proceed in the manner I advocated, is to do what Nozick takes to be morally impermissible, since it makes the person with the better opportunities and the just entitlements somewhat worse off even though the person in question didn't volunteer to be worse off. But this is the fair thing to do in these circumstances. The worse off people have a legitimate complaint against me, if I am a David Rockefeller. I, who have plenty, will not share with others in order to relieve what is plainly extensive misery. I show, thereby, a thorough lack of concern for my fellow human beings. Moreover, it is not only that I lack certain desirable moral sentiments— Nozick might assent to that—it is also that I am neglecting the duties of *mutual aid* and my duty to *relieve distress*.

Nozick is, however, right about *some* particular entitlements. Suppose Frank is a child raised in a home with a swimming pool and Bill is a child raised in a hole without a swimming pool and suppose further that Frank is no more deserving of having a swimming pool than Bill. Still, it isn't unfair, says Nozick, that Frank can use it while Bill cannot. It is perhaps unfortunate that all families haven't a swimming pool who have members who want one, but the above situation with Frank and Bill is perhaps not unfair. That is to say, it is not unfair that Frank can use it and Bill cannot. At least it is not paradigmatically unfair.

But what is at least *prima facie* unfair is for one family of three to have five cars while another family of three, in the same general environment, say the same city, has none and its members must walk five miles each day to work. Duties to mutual aid and to relieve misery outweigh here full capitalist property entitlements. (Where is the cut-off point? When exactly is a person bald or elderly? We get on in our judgments about who is bald and who is elderly without an answer to this last question. Indeed, as Wittgenstein and Waismann help us see, we would not want such an answer. Why should the same thing not be said about the above moral case?) Again there is a reliance on considered judgments. But such a reliance is unavoidable. The crucial thing is whether they can be shown to be in wide reflective equilibrium.

V

There is another aspect of egalitarianism here, discussed by Nozick, which is linked to Rawls' discussion of self-respect and is less dependent, than are the above criticisms, on the validity of his entitlement theory.

Self-respect for Rawls is the most important of the various primary social goods. It is something which he takes to be very precious indeed. To have a perfectly just society we must have a state of affairs in which the conditions for an equality of self-respect obtains. It is something that a perfectly just society must make equally available to all. Such a commitment, according to Rawls, must be a part of any normative theory of justice which even approaches adequacy. Rawls also argues—and I have argued that even more uncompromisingly— that the attainment of such self-respect for the great mass of the people cannot be had in a non-egalitarian society.[4]

Nozick thinks this is all a mistake and tries to make short shrift of all this talk of an equality of self-respect. (He equates, questionably, self-respect with self-esteem and then proceeds to talk about the latter.)[5] Nozick thinks—and here he is typical of conservative social theorists—that the demand for equality is often rooted in envy. To maintain their self-esteem many people believe they need to level things, for the very idea that someone on various prized dimensions is better off than they are is a blow to their self-esteem. (Recall Nozick is equating it with self-respect.) But this leveling to preserve self-esteem cannot work, Nozick maintains, because "there is no standard of doing something well, independent of how it is or can be done by others" (page 241). When Banister first ran the four-minute mile there was reason for him to be proud. If it becomes routinely the case that almost any member of any high school track team can do it, then running a four-minute mile would not be a matter of pride. One might, say in Calgary, be proud of being fluently bi-lingual, but that would hardly be a source of pride in Montreal. One might be proud of one's ability to calculate rapidly when others were much slower at calculating, but surrounded by a group of super-calculators that same ability would no longer be a source of pride. One's sense of worth, Nozick contends, cannot only depend on facts about oneself, or facts about one's own characteristics, but it inescapably depends on facts about others as well.

It is very possible, Nozick contends, that certain inequalities in income or position of authority *rankle so,* not because the superior position is perceived not to be deserved, but just because it is perceived to be earned and deserved. It injures one's self-esteem, makes one feel less worthy as a person, to know that someone else has accomplished more or risen higher (page 241). Surely, this is a trait that is, to understate it, sometimes seen in human beings. Nozick argues that people "generally judge themselves by how they fall along the most important dimensions in which they differ from others" (page 243). They do not gain self-esteem from their common human capacities by comparing themselves to animals who lack them. They don't reason "I'm pretty good; I have an opposable thumb and can speak some language." "When everyone, or almost everyone, has some thing or attribute, it does not function as the basis for self-esteem. Self-esteem is based on differentiating characteristics; that's why it's self-esteem" (page 243).

VI

These claims are used against egalitarianism in the following way: If we level everything, income, authority, rank, prestige, power, the social status of people, so that we are all viewed as being the same or nearly the same, we will no longer have any basis for self-esteem. If everyone is really taken to be the same and is treated in the same way, we will have no grounds for being proud of our accomplishments and the basis for a sense of self-worth will be undermined. Far from enhancing self-respect, equality undermines self-respect. If we downgrade the importance of all those things which serve to distinguish people, we will undermine their sense of self-worth.

There is no way, Nozick continues, of equalizing self-esteem and reducing envy by equalizing positions along some dimension to which at that time envy is tied. If we make incomes more nearly equal, then something else, say, authority will be a source of envy. If, alternatively, we make authority more nearly equal, then charisma will be a source of envy. Nozick remarks that when we think of the varied attributes we can envy another's having, we will realize that the opportunities for differential self-esteem are vast and indeed unconquerable (page 245). Moreover, it cannot be right to reduce someone's situation in order to lessen envy and the unhappiness that flows from it. This is comparable to forbidding racially mixed couples from walking holding hands because the seeing of this causes distress in others. Perhaps morality can in certain circumstances rightly be enforced but prejudices surely cannot. Giving into envy like that is just giving into an irrational prejudice.

There are a number of ways in which such claims about envy can be either undermined or deflected, some of which have already been considered in this volume, while others will be considered in the next section. Perhaps most directly the following should be said. Nozick is utterly insensitive to the ways in which great disparities in wealth undermine self-respect (not just self-esteem), how it makes those severely deprived feel as if in reality they were not a part of the community. Indeed, this feeling of being outside, or hardly mattering at all, is very real when great disparities in condition of life obtain. This has a lot more to do with alienation than with envy. Moreover, even where they do feel envy, why shouldn't they be envious when it is plain that their disadvantaged state has nothing to do with achievement or lack of achievement? *Under such circumstances* envy is a perfectly understandable response.

VII

In arguing as he has above, Nozick, following a long line of anti-egalitarians, gives us a caricature of egalitarianism. Egalitarians do not wish to be rid of all human differentiations or differences. Egalitarians are concerned to secure equality in human rights, equality in conditions for a secure healthy life (well-being), equality in condition to obtain meaningful work, equality of power and authority in the control of one's life and in the determination of the direction in which society is going. They are not for, and the implementation of their theories would not result in, a grey world in which we are all socialized into being alike. (This is particularly true of Marx, as can be seen from his *The Critique of the Gotha Program,* where he stresses "To each according to his *needs,*" thereby stressing a concern for people's needs, needs which are different. In doing this Marx is acknowledging the vital importance of their individuality.) Egalitarians prize different qualities and capacities in people and show their admiration for this in various ways. People become natural authorities in various domains because of their abilities, including, of course, the knowledge they have and the perceptiveness and sensitivity they exhibit. We should listen to such people, admire them and follow their advice. There are many such different abilities and we mutually learn from each other. What the egalitarian rejects, Bakunin argued, is not natural authority— someone who has demonstrated his right to be listened to—but simply people who are in authority in virtue of a certain position in a hierarchy. Egalitarians seek a world without rank; they seek a world in which there are no bosses and bossed, no bowing and scraping, no deference merely to position. It is the world concretely and classically captured in passages of George Orwell's *Homage to Catalonia.*

Anthony Skillen challenges whether people, even in our possessive individualistic, competitive society, always gain their self-esteem and sense of self-worth from being able to distance themselves from others so that they are able to say to themselves over something "I'm the best," or "I'm the greatest."[6] That they react in this competitive manner, he admits, is often true. And this, he remarks, is hardly surprising in such an individualistic and competitive culture. A good bit of our socialization goes into building us that way. However, this says something more about a capitalist ethos than about all cultures. Such a generalization would be less true in some other cultures, e.g., China and Cuba, and in certain native American groups. There is also with most people, even in our culture, a sense of collective accomplishment and a pride and self-respect in that. Again its extent will vary from culture to culture. But it is something which is in all or almost all peoples. (Perhaps the Ik under their desperate circumstances are an exception.) Moreover, even in societies such as ours, there are personal sources of self-respect that are not comparative. Nozick is too obsessed with competitive sports examples. In his very examples he gives us a one-sided diet. You learn to cross-country ski well, you jog and feel your body come into better shape, you master a new language, you build a boat well. In the case of the boat, for example, it is either well built or it isn't; it either does what it was made to do efficiently or it doesn't. You need not compare it with the boats of others. You need not match your cross-country skiing with others. All you need to know is what are the standards for doing it well. It doesn't need to be a win or lose business. That need not come in at all. Many people can speak some foreign language well, many can cross-country ski well. If your cross-country skiing matches nicely those standards, you can take pleasure in your accomplishment and it can be, to the extent that it is tolerably difficult to achieve, a source of pride. Similar things can obtain for more important tasks. From doing them well or sometimes even doing them correctly one can gain a sense of self-worth. One need not endlessly be comparing oneself to others. There is simply the pride in a job well done as when a farmer looks out over his crops. It doesn't matter in the slightest that many other farmers have similarly excellent crops. There is still the pride of accomplishment in something that has taken work and has a point.

Suppose, to vary the examples, you have learned life-saving and mouth-to-mouth resuscitation. You have either learned these things or not and with them you can save someone's life. Such things are valued without point-scoring and they can be and are the source of self-respect. All the paraphernalia of winning and losing with which Nozick is so preoccupied is rather distinctive of bourgeois society and is expressive of its underlying ideology and way of organizing such a society. Unfortunately, it is true that for many people—Nozick sounds like one of them—their sense of self-esteem has, to a very considerable extent, evolved in the way Nozick says it has. But even in our societies it is not entirely so and in a society with a less competitive and individualistic socialization it perhaps need not be so at all. Nozick is very much a captive of his own culture here and confuses bourgeois man with man. He reads, that is, into human nature a particular kind of human nature which in reality is very much the product of a particular socioeconomic conditioning.[7]

VIII

Nozick next faces the socialist challenge about authoritarian work allocation and its effects on the self-respect of people. He puts it this way:

> Often it is claimed that being subordinate in a work scheme adversely affects self-esteem in accordance with a social-psychological law or fundamental generalization such as the following: A long period of being frequently ordered about and under the authority of others, unselected by you, lowers your self-esteem and makes you feel inferior; whereas this is avoided if you play some role in democratically selecting these authorities and in a constant process of advising them, voting on their decisions, and so on. [page 246]

Nozick remarks that there are too many exceptions to this to be a generalization that we could reasonably accept. Moreover, people in their subordinate positions should come "to face the facts of their existence" and consider whether or not they are not, after all, just inferior. Perhaps others just have superior talents and have a right to give them orders.

However, as Skillen shows, the exceptions Nozick cites, to disprove that generalization about work, are special cases.[8] Nozick ignores the statistically more standard cases which are the cases he must come to grips with if he is to disconfirm this sociological generalization. Here his sociological naivety is particularly evident. The standard statistically relevant case is that of the dominated classes in a capitalist society being, by the ideological instruments of that society, bombarded with and inculturated into myths about equal opportunity and social mobility only to face a harshly contrasting reality in which there is no such mobility or opportunity for them.[9] They are locked into jobs which are poorly paying, full of drudgery and in which they are simply told what to do; and in most cases they have no hope of finding a better one. Particularly, given the myths of mobility and success in the society, they readily develop a distinctive working class psychology with a pervasive sense of personal failure, a low sense of self-esteem and a lack of confidence—they pass these liabilities on to their children from generation to generation. This is the reality of work in North America.

Nozick hints—he doesn't quite come out and say it—that perhaps those people who accept such jobs and are content to remain in them are inferior (pages 246–47). The assembly line is the asylum for the unenterprizing! But this, aside from the fact that they are not so content, entirely ignores how people at a very early age are prepared for their place in society. Consider the sorting process in the elementary schools and its close relation to class and strata. And consider the even earlier conditioning a person gets in his family. The chance to do interesting, self-fulfilling, rewarding things is clearly connected with the length of time one remains in school, and the length of time one remains in school is clearly linked to the class or stratum one comes from.[10] There are exceptions to this of course. But in a sociological generalization about how people generally tend to respond, these few exceptions prove nothing at all.

NOTES

1. Ronald Dworkin, *Taking Rights Seriously* (Cambridge, Mass.: Harvard University Press, 1977), p. 182.
2. Kai Nielsen, "Reason and Sentiment," in *Rationality Today*, ed. Theodore F. Geraets (Ottawa, Ont.: The University of Ottawa Press, 1979), pp. 249–79.
3. Kai Nielsen, "On Needing a Moral Theory," *Metaphilosophy* 13, no.2 (April 1982): 97–116.
4. John Rawls, *A Theory of Justice* (Cambridge, Mass.: Harvard University Press, 1971), pp. 180–83, 234, 256, 440–46, 534–35, 543–47; and John Rawls, "A Kantian Conception of Equality," *Cambridge Review* 96, no. 2225 (February 1975): 94–99; Kai Nielsen, "Class and Justice," in *Justice and Economic Distribution*, eds. John Arthur and W. H. Shaw (Englewood Cliffs, N.J.: Prentice-Hall, 1978): 225–45; Kai Nielsen, "On the Very Possibility of a Classless Society," *Political Theory* 6, no. 2 (May 1978): 191–208; and Kai Nielsen, "Radical Egalitarian Justice: Justice as Equality," *Social Theory and Practice* 5, no. 2 (Spring 1979): 208–26.
5. David Sachs, "How to Distinguish Self-Respect from Self-Esteem," *Philosophy and Public Affairs* 10, no. 4 (Fall 1981): 346–60.
6. Anthony Skillen, *Ruling Illusions* (Sussex: Harvester Press, 1977), pp. 48–57.
7. My argument has been objected to in the following way: to support my argument that competitive individualism is primarily a function of acculturation, I point to the fact that many activities are not organized around winners and losers but allow a person to do something well or poorly as measured by the criteria of an art. What I fail to realize, it is claimed, is that the knowledge of an art is disruptive of my egalitarian premise—those who can, do, and are rewarded for their efforts; those who can't, don't, and are judged inferior. But my point is that there are a whole range of activities that in the very nature of the case need not have winners and losers. Moreover, these are activities, at least some of which, almost everyone can do and can find in them a source of self-respect. So it need not be the case that one must get one's self-respect from doing better than someone else. Self-respect need not be undermined in an egalitarian society. Indeed it is the only kind of society which will provide the conditions for its general availability.
8. Skillen, op. cit., pp. 50–53.
9. Samuel Bowles and Herbert Gintis, *Schooling in Capitalist America* (New York: Basic Books, 1976); h.a., *Work in America* (Cambridge, Mass.: MIT Press, 1973); Harry Braverman, *Labor and Monopoly Capital* (New York: Monthly Review Press, 1974); Richard C. Edwards et al. (eds.), *The Capitalist System* (Englewood Cliffs, N.J.: Prentice-Hall, 1978), pp. 24–28 and chs. 7 and 8; and Bryan Finnigan and Cy Gonick (eds.), *Making It: The Canadian Dream* (Toronto: McClelland & Stewart, 1972), chs. 2 and 3.
10. Samuel Bowles, "Schooling and the Reproduction of Inequality," *The Capitalist System*, pp. 315–29. See also pp. 274–91 of the same volume. See also Tom Christoffel et al. (eds.), *Up Against the American Myth* (New York: Holt-Rinehart Winston, 1970), pp. 320–47.

PART V

On Liberty Requiring Equality: A Final Word for Egalitarianism

INTERLUDE AND PROEM FOUR

Even Nozick and Hayek, in contrast with Nietzsche, believe in *moral* equality. But this, as we have seen, does not translate into anything like equality of condition or resource or even into an attempt to provide people with equal opportunities. It does argue for the protection of legal and political equality (taken in a formal sense) and, if this isn't redundant, the protection of civil liberties. The old egalitarianism, also accepting those equalities, in addition argues for, in a way that is totally unacceptable to libertarians, some minimal welfare floors to balance the harshest aspects of differences in wealth that obtain under capitalism (even a capitalist meritocracy) and to provide for stability in capitalist society. They also centrally stress, in a way some libertarians would not, equal opportunity, though, as we have also seen, they give a very distinctive reading to "equal opportunity," a reading which fits it nicely in a meritocratic framework. A just society, they stress, must give everyone an equal start at the starting post but it will not do anything to attain even a rough equality of result.

The equalities both libertarians and meritocrats accept are also a part of radical egalitarianism. Where radical egalitarianism essentially differs from libertarianism and the old egalitarianism is in what it adds, its placement of these equalities in an overall framework and in its priorities. (Though again, as we have seen, they do not take equality of opportunity as essentially just giving people an equal start at the starting post. They find a place for merit without meritocracy.)

I have been concerned in Parts III and IV to criticize these meritocratic and libertarian views, though I have also been concerned to carry forth from those views certain key ideas which I think must be incorporated into a radical egalitarianism and into any adequate conception of justice. From the old egalitarianism I take, though with a much diminished role, conceptions of merit and desert, and from the libertarians I take an acceptance of the importance of what I shall characterize in my final chapter as rights to non-interference. A morally acceptable egalitarianism must find a place for such an idea as well as for conceptions of merit and desert. (We should see here working, in the background, an appeal to anti-foundationalist coherence conceptions embedded in the appeal to considered judgments in wide reflective equilibrium.) It shall be a concern, though not a central concern, of my final chapter to incorporate these conceptions into my articulation of a radical egalitarian conception of justice.

In my final chapter, I shall return, though from an altered perspective, to some of the concerns of Parts I and II. I shall draw together some loose ends, provide a more comprehensive articulation and defense of a certain conception of an equality of condition, both as a goal and, in certain circumstances, as a right; and I shall also contrast my radical egalitarianism with liberal egalitarianism (this time Ronald Dworkin's articulation). In doing this I shall, of course, attempt to provide reasons for favoring radical egalitarianism. Finally, I shall criticize some remaining and persistent arguments purporting to show how equality undermines liberty, and in the course of doing that I shall conclude with arguments designed to show that liberty requires at least a rough equality of condition and that both liberty and equality can only be realized, if they can be instantiated at all, in a socialist society emerging under conditions of productive abundance and free from capitalist attack.

13

A Rationale for
Radical Egalitarianism

I

I have talked of equality as a right and of equality as a goal. And I have taken, as the principal thing, to be able to state what goal we are seeking when we say equality is a goal. When we are in a position actually to achieve that goal, then that same equality becomes a right. The goal we are seeking is an equality of basic condition for everyone. Let me say a bit what this is: everyone, as far as possible, should have equal life prospects, short of genetic engineering and the like and the rooting out any form of the family and the undermining of our basic freedoms. There should, where this is possible, be an equality of access to equal resources over each person's life as a whole, though this should be qualified by people's varying needs. Where psychiatrists are in short supply only people who are in need of psychiatric help should have equal access to such help. This equal access to resources should be such that it stands as a barrier to their being the sort of differences between people that allow some to be in a position to control and to exploit others; such equal access to resources should also stand as a barrier to one adult person having power over other adult persons that does not rest on the revokable consent on the part of the persons over whom he comes to have power. Where, because of some remaining scarcity in a society of considerable productive abundance, we cannot reasonably distribute resources equally, we should first, where consid- erations of desert are not at issue, distribute according to stringency of need, second according to the strength of unmanipulated preferences and third, and finally, by lottery. We should, in trying to attain equality of condition, aim at a condition of autonomy (the fuller and the more rational the better) for everyone and at a condition where everyone alike, to the fullest extent possible, has his or her needs and wants satisfied. The limitations on the satisfaction of people's wants should be only where that satisfaction is incompatible with everyone getting the same treatment. Where we have conflicting wants, such as where two persons want to marry the same person, the fair thing to do will vary with the circumstances. In the marriage case, freedom of choice is obviously the fair thing. But generally, what should be aimed at is having everyone have their wants satisfied as far as possible. To achieve equality of condition would be, as well, to achieve a condition where the necessary burdens of the society are equally shared, where to do so is reasonable, and where each person has an equal voice in deciding what these burdens shall be. Moreover, everyone, as much as possible, should be in a position—and should be equally in that position—to control his own life. The goals of egalitarianism are to achieve such equalities.

Minimally, classlessness is something we should all aim at if we are egalitarians. It is necessary for the stable achievement of equalities of the type discussed in the previous paragraph. Beyond that, we should also aim at a statusless society, though not at an undifferentiated society or a society which does not recognize merit. (We have seen in Part IV that that is detachable from any commitment to a meritocracy.) It is only in such a classless, statusless society that the ideals of equality (the conception of equality as a very general goal to be achieved) can be realized. In aiming for a statusless society, we are aiming for a society which, while remaining a society of material abundance, is a society in which there are to be no extensive differences in life prospects between people because some have far greater income, power, authority or prestige than others. This is the *via negativia* of the egalitarian way. The *via postiva* is to produce social conditions, where there is generally material abundance, where well-being and satisfaction are not only maximized (the utiliarian thing) but, as well, a society where this condition, as far as it is achievable, is sought equally for all (the egalitarian thing). This is the underlying conception of the egalitarian commitment to equality of condition.

II

Robert Nozick asks "How do we decide how much equality is enough?"[1] In the preceding section we gestured in the direction of an answer. I should now like to be somewhat more explicit. Too much equality, as we have been at pains to point out, would be to treat everyone identically, completely ignoring their differing needs. Various forms of "barracks equality" approximating that would also be too much. Too little equality would be to limit equality of condition, as did the old egalitarianism, to achieving equal legal and political rights, equal civil liberties, to equality of opportunity and to a redistribution of gross disparities in wealth sufficient to keep social peace, the rationale for the latter being that such gross inequalities if allowed to stand would threaten social stability. This Hobbesist stance indicates that the old egalitarianism proceeds in a very pragmatic manner. Against the old egalitarianism I would argue that we must at least aim at an equality of whole life prospects, where that is not read simply as the right to compete for scarce positions of advantage, but where there is to be brought into being the kind of equality of condition that would provide everyone equally, as far as possible, with the resources and the social conditions to satisfy their needs as fully as possible compatible with everyone else doing likewise. (Note that between people these needs will be partly the same but will still often be importantly different as well.) Ideally, as a kind of ideal limit for a society of wondrous abundance, a radical egalitarianism would go beyond that to a similar thing for wants. We should, that is, provide all people equally, as far as possible, with the resources and social conditions to satisfy their wants, as fully as possible compatible with everyone else doing likewise. (I recognize that there is a slide between wants and needs. As the wealth of a society increases and its structure changes, things that started out as wants tend to become needs, e.g. someone in the Falkland Islands might merely reasonably want an auto while someone in Los Angeles might not only want it but need it as well. But this does not collapse the distinction between wants and needs. There are things in any society people need, if they are to survive at all in anything like a commodious condition, whether they want them or not, e.g., they need food, shelter, security, companionship and the like. An egalitarian starts with basic needs, or at least with what are taken in the cultural environment in which a given person lives to be basic needs, and moves out to other needs and finally to wants as the productive power of the society increases.)

I qualified my above formulations with "as far as possible" and with "as fully as possible compatible with everyone else doing likewise." These are essential qualifications. Where, as in societies that we know, there are scarcities, even rather minimal scarcities, not everyone can have the resources or at least all the resources necessary to have their needs satisfied. Here we must first ensure that, again as far as possible, their basic needs are all satisfied and then we move on to other needs and finally to wants. But sometimes, to understate it, even in very affluent societies, everyone's needs cannot be met, or at least they cannot be equally met. In such circumstances we have to make some hard choices. I am thinking of a situation where there are not enough dialysis machines to go around so that everyone who needs one can have one. What then should we do? The thing to aim at, to try as far as possible to approximate, if only as a heuristic ideal, is the full and equal meeting of needs and wants of everyone. It is when we have that much equality that we have enough equality. But, of course, "ought implies can," and where we can't achieve it we can't achieve it. But where we reasonably can, we ought to do it. It is something that fairness requires.

The "reasonably can" is also an essential modification: we need situations of sufficient abundance so that we do not, in going for such an equality of condition, simply spread the misery around or spread very Spartan conditions around. Before we can rightly aim for the equality of condition I mentioned, we must first have the productive capacity and resource conditions to support the institutional means that would make possible the equal satisfaction of basic needs and the equal satisfaction of other needs and wants as well.

Such achievements will often not be possible; perhaps they will never be fully possible, for, no doubt, the physically handicapped will always be with us. Consider, for example, situations where our scarcities are such that we cannot, without causing considerable misery, create the institutions and mechanisms that would work to satisfy all needs, even all basic needs. Suppose we have the technology in place to develop all sorts of complicated life-sustaining machines all of which would predictably provide people with a quality of life that they, viewing the matter clearly, would rationally choose if they were simply choosing for themselves. But suppose, if we put such technologies in place, we will then not have the wherewithal to provide basic health care in outlying regions in the country or adequate educational services in such places. We should not, under those circumstances, put those technologies in place. But we should also recognize that where it becomes possible to put these technologies in place without sacrificing other more pressing needs, we should do so. The underlying egalitarian rationale is evident enough: produce the conditions for the most extensive satisfaction of needs for everyone. Where A's need and B's need are equally important (equally stringent) but cannot both be satisfied, satisfy A's need rather than B's if the satisfaction of A's need would be more fecund for the satisfaction of the needs of others than B's, or less undermining of the satisfaction of the needs of others than B's. (I do not mean to say that that is our only criterion of choice but it is the criterion most relevant for us here.) We should seek the satisfaction of the greatest compossible set of needs where the conditions for compossibility are (a) that everyone's needs be considered, (b) that everyone's needs be *equally* considered and where two sets of needs cannot both be satisfied, the more stringent set of needs shall first be satisfied. (Do not say we have no working criteria for what they are. If you need food to keep you from starvation or debilitating malnutrition and I need a vacation to relax after a spate of hard work, your need is plainly more stringent than mine. There would, of course, be all sorts of disputable cases, but there are also a host of perfectly determinate cases indicating that we have working criteria.) The underlying rationale is to seek compossible sets of needs so that we approach as far as possible as great a satisfaction of needs as possible for everyone.

This might, it could be said, produce a situation in which very few people got those things that they needed the most, or at least wanted the most. Remember Nozick with his need for the resources of Widner Library in an annex to his house. People, some might argue, with expensive tastes and extravagant needs, say a need for really good wine, would never, with a stress on such compossibilia, get things they are really keen about.[2] Is that the kind of world we would reflectively want? Well, *if* their not getting them is the price we have to pay for everyone having their basic needs met, then it is a price we ought to pay. I am very fond of very good wines as well as fresh ripe mangos, but if the price of my having them is that people starve or suffer malnutrition in the Sahel, or indeed anywhere else, then plainly fairness, if not just plain human decency, requires that I forego them.

In talking about how much equality is enough, I have so far talked of the benefits that equality is meant to provide. But egalitarians also speak of an equal sharing of the necessary burdens of the society as well. Fairness requires a sharing of the burdens, and for a radical egalitarian this comes to an equal sharing of the burdens where people are equally capable of sharing them. Translated into the concrete this does *not* mean that a child or an old man or a pregnant woman are to be required to work in the mines or that they be required to collect garbage, but it would involve something like requiring every able-bodied person, say from nineteen to twenty, to take his or her turn at a fair portion of the necessary unpleasant jobs in the world. In that way we all, where we are able to do it, would share equally in these burdens—in doing the things that none of us want to do but that we, if we are at all reasonable, recognize the necessity of having done. (There are all kinds of variations and complications concerning this—what do we do with the youthful wonder at the violin? But, that notwithstanding, the general idea is clear enough.) And, where we think this is reasonably feasible, it squares with our considered judgments about fairness.

I have given you, in effect appealing to my considered judgments but considered judgments I do not think are at all eccentric, a picture of what I would take to be enough equality, too little equality and not enough equality. But how can we know that my proportions are right? I do not think we can avoid or should indeed try to avoid an appeal to considered judgments here. But working with them there are some arguments we can appeal to to get them in wide reflective equilibrium. Suppose we go back to the formal principle of justice, namely that we must treat like cases alike. Because it does not tell us *what* are like cases, we cannot derive substantive criteria from it. But it may, indirectly, be of some help here. We all, if we are not utterly zany, want a life in which our needs are satisfied and in which we can live as we wish and do what we want to do. Though we differ in many ways, in our abilities, capacities for pleasure, determination to keep on with a job, we do not differ about wanting our needs satisfied or being able to live as we wish. Thus, *ceterus paribus,* where questions of desert, entitlement and the like do not enter, it is only fair that all of us should have our needs equally considered and that we should, again *ceterus paribus,* all be able to do as we wish in a way that is compatible with others doing likewise. From the formal principle of justice and a few key facts about us, we can get to the claim that *ceterus paribus* we should go for this much equality. But this is the core content of a radical egalitarianism.

However, how do we know that *ceterus* is *paribus* here? What about our entitlements and deserts? Suppose I have built my house with my own hands, from materials I have purchased and on land that I have purchased and that I have lived in it for years and have carefully cared for it. The house is mine and I am entitled to keep it even if by dividing the house into two apartments greater and more equal satisfaction of need would obtain for everyone. Justice requires that such an entitlement be respected here. (Again, there is an implicit *ceterus paribus* clause. In extreme situations, say after a war with housing in extremely short supply, that entitlement could be rightly overriden.)

There is a response on the egalitarian's part similar to a response utilitarians made to criticisms of a similar logical type made of utilitarianism by pluralistic deontologists. One of the things that people in fact need, or at least reflectively firmly want, is to have such entitlements respected. Where they are routinely overridden to satisfy other needs or wants, we would *not* in fact have a society in which the needs of everyone are being maximally met. To the reply, but what if more needs for everyone were met by ignoring or overriding such entitlements, the radical egalitarian should respond that that is, given the way we are, a thoroughly hypothetical situation and that theories of morality cannot be expected to give guidance for all logically possible worlds but only for worlds which are reasonably like what our actual world is or plausibly could come to be. Setting this argument aside for the moment, even if it did turn out that the need satisfaction linked with having other things—things that involved the overriding of those entitlements—was sufficient to make it the case that more need satisfaction all around for *everyone* would be achieved by overriding those entitlements, then, for reasonable people who clearly saw that, these entitlements would not have the weight presently given to them. They either would not have the importance presently attached to them or the need for the additional living space would be so great that their being overridden would seem, everything considered, the lesser of two evils (as in the example of the postwar housing situation).

There are without doubt genuine entitlements and a theory of justice must take them seriously, but they are not absolute. If the need is great enough we can see the merit in overriding them, just as in law as well as morality the right of eminent domain is recognized. Finally, while I have talked of entitlements here, parallel arguments will go through for desert.

III

I want now to relate this articulation of what equality comes to to my radically egalitarian principles of justice. My articulation of justice is a certain spelling out of the slogan proclaimed by Marx "From each according to his ability, to each according to his needs." The egalitarian conception of society argues for the desirability of bringing into existence a world, once the springs of social wealth flow-freely, in which everyone's needs are as fully satisfied as possbile and in which everyone gives according to his ability. Which means, among other things, that everyone, according to his ability, shares the burdens of society. There is an equal giving and equal responsibility here according to ability. It is here, with respect to giving according to ability and with respect to receiving according to need, that a complex equality of result, i.e., equality of condition, is being advocated by the radical egalitarian. What it comes to is this: each of us, where each is to count for one and none to count for more than one, is to give according to ability and receive according to need.

My radical egalitarian principles of justice, as we have seen, read as follows:

(1) Each person is to have an equal right to the most extensive total system of equal basic liberties and opportunities (including equal opportunities for meaningful work, for self-determination and political and economic participation) compatible with a similar treatment of all. (This principle gives expression to a commitment to attain and/or sustain equal moral autonomy and equal self-respect.)

(2) After provisions are made for common social (community) values, for capital overhead to preserve the society's productive capacity, allowances made for differing unmanipulated needs and preferences, and due weight is given to the just entitlements of individuals, the income and wealth (the common stock of means) is to be so divided that each person will have a right to an equal share. The necessary burdens requisite to enhance human well-being are also to be equally shared, subject, of course, to limitations by differing abilities and differing situations. (Here I refer to different natural environments and the like and not to class position and the like.)

Here we are talking about equality as a right rather than about equality as a goal as has previously been the subject matter of equality in this chapter. These principles of egalitarianism spell out rights people have and duties they have under *conditions of very considerable productive abundance.* We have a right to certain basic liberties and opportunities and we have, subject to certain limitations spelled out in the second principle, a right to an equal share of the income and wealth in the world. We also have a duty, again subject to the qualifications mentioned in the principle, to do our equal share in shouldering the burdens necessary to protect us from ills and to enhance our well-being.

What is the relation between these rights and the ideal of equality of condition discussed earlier? That is a goal for which we can struggle now to bring about conditions which will some day make its achievement possible, while these rights only become rights when the goal is actually achievable. We have no such rights in slave, feudal or capitalist societies or such duties in those societies. In that important way they are not natural rights for they depend on certain social conditions and certain social structures (socialist ones) to be realizable. What we can say is that it is always desirable that socio-economic conditions come into being which would make it possible to achieve the goal of equality of condition so that these rights and duties I speak of could obtain. But that is a far cry from saying we have such rights and duties now.

It is a corollary of this, if these radical egalitarian principles of justice are correct, that capitalist societies (even capitalist welfare state societies such as Sweden) and statist societies such as the Soviet Union or the People's Republic of China cannot be just societies or at least they must be societies, structured as they are, which are defective in justice. (This is not to say that some of these societies are not juster than others. Sweden is juster than South Africa, Canada than the United States and Cuba and Nicaragua than Honduras and Guatemala.) But none of these statist or capitalist societies can satisfy these radical egalitarian principles of justice, for equal liberty, equal opportunity, equal wealth or equal sharing of burdens are not at all possible in societies having their social structure. So we do not have such rights now but we can take it as a goal that we bring such a society into being with a commitment to an equality of condition in which we would have these rights and duties. Here we require first the massive development of productive power.

The connection between equality as a goal and equality as a right spelled out in these principles of justice is this. The equality of condition appealed to in equality as a goal would, if it were actually to obtain, have to contain the rights and duties enunciated in those principles. There could be no equal life prospects between all people or anything approximating an equal satisfaction of needs if there were not in place something like the system of equal basic liberties referred to in the first principle. Furthermore, without the rough equality of wealth referred to in the second principle, there would be disparities in power and self-direction in society which would render impossible an equality of life prospects or the social conditions required for an equal satisfaction of needs. And plainly, without a roughly equal sharing of burdens, there cannot be a situation where everyone has equal life prospects or has the chance equally to satisfy his needs. The principles of radical egalitarian justice are implicated in its conception of an ideally adequate equality of condition.

IV

The principles of radical egalitarian justice I have articulated are meant to apply globally and not just to particular societies. But it is certainly fair to say that not a few would worry that such principles of radical egalitarian justice, if applied globally, would force the people in wealthier sections of the world to a kind of financial hari-kari. There are millions of desperately impoverished people. Indeed millions are starving or malnourished and things are not getting any better. People in the affluent societies cannot but worry about whether they face a bottomless pit. Many believe that meeting, even in the most minimal way, the needs of the impoverished is going to put an incredible burden on people—people of all classes—in the affluent societies. Indeed it will, if acted on non-evasively, bring about their impoverishment, and this is just too much to ask. Radical egalitarianism is forgetting Rawls' admonitions about "the strains of commitment"—the recognition that in any rational account of what is required of us, we must at least give a minimal healthy self-interest its due. We must construct our moral philosophy for human beings and not for saints. Human nature is less fixed than conservatives are wont to assume, but it is not so elastic that we can reasonably expect people to impoverish themselves to make the massive transfers between North and South—the industrialized world and the Third World—required to begin to approach a situation where even Rawls' principles would be in place on a global level, to say nothing of my radical egalitarian principles of justice.[3]

The first thing to say in response to this is that my radical egalitarian principles are meant actually to guide practice, to directly determine what we are to do, only in a world of extensive abundance where, as Marx put it, the springs of social wealth flow freely. If such a world cannot be attained with the undermining of capitalism and the full putting into place, stabilizing, and developing of socialist relations of production, then such radical egalitarian principles can only remain as heuristic ideals against which to measure the distance of our travel in the direction of what would be a perfectly just society.

Aside from a small capitalist class, along with those elites most directly and profitably beholden to it (together a group constituting not more than 5 percent of the world's population), there would, in taking my radical egalitarian principles as heuristic guides, be no impoverishment of people in the affluent societies, if we moved in a radically more egalitarian way to start to achieve a global fairness. There would be massive transfers of wealth between North and South, but this could be done in stages so that, for the people in the affluent societies (capitalist elites apart), there need be no undermining of the quality of their lives. Even what were once capitalist elites would not be impoverished or reduced to some kind of bleak life though they would, the incidental Spartan types aside, find their life styles altered.

But their health and general well being, including their opportunities to do significant and innovative work, would, if anything, be enhanced. And while some of the sources of their enjoyment would be a thing of the past, there would still be a considerable range of enjoyments available to them sufficient to afford anyone a rich life that could be lived with verve and zest.

A fraction of what the United States spends on defense spending would take care of immediate problems of starvation and malnutrition for most of the world. For longer range problems such as bringing conditions of life in the Third World more in line with conditions of life in Sweden and Switzerland, what is necessary is the dismantling of the capitalist system and the creation of a socio-economic system with an underlying rationale directing it toward producing for needs—everyone's needs. With this altered productive mode, the irrationalities and waste of capitalist production would be cut. There would be no more built-in obsolescence, no more merely cosmetic changes in consumer durables, no more fashion roulette, no more useless products and the like. Moreover, the enormous expenditures that go into the war industry would be a thing of the past. There would be great transfers from North to South, but it would be from the North's capitalist fat and not from things people in the North really need. (There would, in other words, be no self-pauperization of people in the capitalist world.)

This can best be illustrated by examining the world food economy. Neo-Malthusians have led us to believe that with population explosions and diminished world food resources, we are on "lifeboat earth" that is fast approaching the very outer limits of its carrying capacity. This is pure fantasy. For the foreseeable future we have plenty of available fertile land and the agricultural potential adequately to feed a much larger world population than we actually have. Less than half of the available fertile land of the world is now being used for any type of food production.[4] Though it is well known that there are severe famine conditions in Africa, what is less well known is that African agriculture has been declining for the last 20 years.[5] Domestic food production in Africa is falling while food, formerly imported cheaply from the capitalist center, is now imported, from that same center, at prices that a very large number of people in Africa cannot afford to pay.[6] There is plenty of food around and much more could be produced. It is a matter, as Amartya Sen has argued, of its distribution and of people not having the money or other entitlements to obtain it.[7] While the cheap imports were still in the offing, African farmers were paid very little for their produce. Under such conditions larger numbers of them were driven, given the cheap food aid coming from the capitalist center (principally the USA), into rapidly growing large urban centers of societies trying to industrialize, where a proletariat was being formed. Where before we had agrarian societies, we came to have, in these

African countries, and elsewhere as well, a proletariat and a lumpen-proletariat living and working (when they have work) in conditions of incredible impoverishment.[8] They live in conditions not unlike those of Engels' description of the working class in Manchester in the nineteenth century. However, it is this proletariat in the periphery which provides a cheap, fantastically exploitable, pool of labor for the transnationals.[9]

Thus capitalism triggered the decline in African agriculture—it was not simply a natural occurrence, about which nothing can be done. What is in fact the case is that Africa has half the unused farmland in the world. If it were used, Africa could adequately feed itself and become, as well, a large exporter of food. Similar things should be said for the Indian subcontinent. When we look at the North/South imbalance it becomes tolerably plain that this is the result of the workings of a capitalist world economic system. A clear indicator of that is the world food economy. That could be corrected in a thoroughly humane way without any impoverishment of people in the affluent societies.[10]

V

Before I turn to a final consideration of how liberty is supposed to conflict with and indeed be undermined by such a radical egalitarianism, I want to relate my views to Ronald Dworkin's related but importantly distinct defense of equality. If his account is sound my conception would, in some important ways, have to be modified.

Ronald Dworkin defends a form of liberalism grounded in a doctrine of equality, grounded, that is, in what he calls an egalitarian morality "in firm contrast to the economics of privilege."[11] Unlike an older liberalism, it does not insist on government neutrality vis-à-vis moral issues. Indeed the state must in certain ways be interventionist. The government, in Dworkin's view, to be just, must treat people as equals: "it must impose no sacrifice or constraint on any citizen in virtue of an argument that the citizen could not accept without abandoning his sense of equal worth."[12] Someone committed to this principle will also believe that no government can rightly enforce a contentious and private morality.

This is a paradigmatic statement of liberal egalitarianism and it is a doctrine that stands in important contrast to my own. Dworkin puts his core claims thus:

> It [liberal egalitarianism] insists on an economic system in which no citizen has less than an equal share of the community's resources just in order that others may have more of what he lacks. I do not mean that liberalism insists on what is often called "equality of result," that is, that citizens must each have the same wealth at every moment of their lives. A government bent on the latter ideal must constantly redistribute wealth, eliminating

whatever inequalities in wealth are produced by market transactions. But this would be to devote *unequal* resources to different lives. Suppose that two people have very different bank accounts, in the middle of their careers, because one decided not to work, or not to work at the most lucrative job he could have found, while the other single-mindedly worked for gain. Or because one was willing to assume especially demanding or responsible work, for example, which the other declined. Or because one took larger risks which might have been disastrous but which were in fact successful, while the other invested conservatively. The principle that people must be treated as equals provides no good reason for redistribution in these circumstances; on the contrary, it provides a good reason against it.[13]

These are very distinct liberal egalitarian principles, principles which are at home in a welfare state capitalist order. I shall turn in a moment to a contrast with radical egalitarianism and to a renewed critique of liberal egalitarianism, but I want first to flesh out more fully Dworkin's views. "Treating people as equals," he tells us, "requires that each may be permitted to use, for the projects to which he devotes his life, no more than an equal share of the resources available for all. . . ."[14] This indeed perspicuously captures something I also sought to capture in a different way with my second principle of justice. But then he turns to the question of how to compute whether a person actually has had an equal share. To compute on balance how much any person has consumed of his share, we must take "into account the resources he has contributed as well as those he has taken from the economy."[15] Dworkin remarks:

> The choices people make about work and leisure and investment have an impact on the resources of the community as a whole, and this impact must be reflected in the calculation equality demands. If one person chooses work that contributes less to other people's lives than different work he might have chosen, then, although this might well have been the right choice for him, given his personal goals, he has nevertheless added less to the resources available for others, and this must be taken into account in the egalitarian calculation. If one person chooses to invest in a productive enterprise rather than spend his funds at once, and if his investment is successful because it increases the stock of goods or services other people actually want, without coercing anyone, his choice has added more to social resources than the choice of someone who did not invest, and this, too, must be reflected in any calculation of whether he has, on balance, taken more than his share.[16]

However, Dworkin, no more than I, will take a libertarian turn and allow as just, or even morally acceptable, the results of an efficient market to define or determine what we are to take as equal shares of community resources. It perhaps is the mechanism to appeal to if people actually start "with equal amounts of wealth and have roughly equal levels of raw skills."[17] But people in real life, Dworkin hastens to add, do not start with such equalities; many, indeed most, are disadvantaged, and indeed sometimes severely disadvantaged in all sorts of ways, many of which are not by any stretch of the imagination by things for which they stand at fault. Given these facts "some people who are perfectly willing, even anxious, to make exactly the choices about work and consumption and saving that other people do may end up with fewer resources, and no plausible theory of equality can accept this as fair."[18] Because of such considerations a liberal egalitarian cannot accept "the market results as defining equal shares."[19]

Dworkin's liberal egalitarian principles of economic justice give abstract expression and a rationale for the liberal welfare state conception that we must use the state—indeed the capitalist state—to redress certain social imbalances along with a reliance on the market. Without such state intervention the market will be a serious source of injustice. However, we also need the market, Dworkin argues, to get a certain kind of fairness. People in a just society should have "at any point in their lives, different amounts of wealth insofar as the genuine choices they have made have been more or less expensive or beneficial to the community, measured by what other people want for their lives."[20] To ascertain what they should have here, the market is, Dworkin would have it, an indispensable mechanism. So his first principle of justice is market-oriented. The second principle of justice is welfare-statist. It "requires that people not have different amounts of wealth just because they have different inherent capacities to produce what others want, or are differently favored by chance."[21] The first is ambition-sensitive (some might say desert-sensitive); the second refuses to be endowment-sensitive and compensates for the luck of the draw. This means "that market allocations must be corrected in order to bring some people closer to the share of resources they would have had but for these various differences in initial advantage, luck and inherent capacity."[22]

In practice, Dworkin is aware, these two principles will sometimes conflict and we will have to engage in tradeoffs and compromises. There is no way we can ascertain "which aspects of any person's economic position flow from his choices and which from advantages or disadvantages that were not matters of choice. . . ."[23] There is no way of attaining a perfectly just system of redistribution. We have to muddle along choosing social policies and social programs that we think will "bring us closer to the complex and unattainable ideal of equality, all things considered, than the available alternatives, and be ready constantly to reexamine the conclusion when new evidence or new programs are proposed."[24]

Dworkin does not, however, believe that in all circumstances we should attempt to provide complete equality of resources, and he thinks our deeply embedded belief that we should treat people as equals, as being of equal worth, does not commit us to insisting on an equality of resources no matter what. In certain circumstances it is perfectly reasonable, and indeed not unjust, for a government "to devote special resources to the training of exceptionally talented artists or musicians, beyond what the market would pay for services these artists produce, even though this reduces the share others have."[25] We need not, and indeed should not, make insidious judgments about the intrinsic worth of people here. Rather, what is involved in the justified making of such choices is the belief that it is a very good thing indeed to have a community with a lively cultural tradition. It provides an environment within which people may live more imaginatively and this is surely a non-trivial part of human flourishing. Where it is unavoidable we should allow some inequalities of resources to achieve that. And by so acting we are not overriding the principle that people must be treated with equal concern. However, Dworkin believes that there are important limits to the sacrifices we can expect of people for the good of the community. The community, not to violate the principle of equal concern, at a minimum, must offer the opportunity, for those for whom sacrifices are asked, to develop and lead a life each individual can regard as valuable both to himself and to the community.[26] There is a "floor beneath which people cannot be allowed to drop for the greater good."[27] To try to ascertain what this is, Dworkin contends, we need to ascertain "the minimal grounds on which people with self-respect can be expected to regard a community as their community, and to regard its future as in any sense their future."[28]

The underlying liberal egalitarian ideal, an ideal to which Marxists and radical egalitarians should also ascribe, is that *everyone's life matters equally, that everyone's interests are equally important.*[29] The crucial differences between liberal and radical egalitarians would come over an interpretation of what this would come to and over what kind of social arrangements are necessary for anything like egalitarian conditions of life to be a genuine possibility.

This can be seen if we reflect about the role Dworkin assigns to the market and to insurance programs. In my conception of things they would have a very reduced role. We need a market in a socialist society to efficiently allocate consumer durables, but that is all we need a market for. Work will no longer be so allocated, when the socialist society is sufficiently fully developed so that radical egalitarian principles can be instituted. Labor power in any socialist society will not be sold as a commodity in a labor market and there will, plainly, be no individual investment. There are other ways of giving people a range of choices about where they will work and on what. And there are also other efficient ways of allocating work in a socialist society. It will not only be the case that labor power will no longer be a commodity in a socialist society, but banks as well will no longer play the role they play in capitalist society. In the kind of social structures that radical egalitarianism requires for even the approximate realization of its principles of justice, we cannot have the labor and banking institutions we now have. In such a society market mechanisms will simply work for the efficient allocation of consumer durables.

By contrast Dworkin assumes the stable background of capitalist institutions. People invest conservatively, imaginatively or disastrously and the resources they command at various times in their lives will vary with the decisions they make. In his social world, as he is anxious to acknowledge, investment will have an impact on the resources of the community as a whole. Such matters, he claims, must be taken into consideration in the egalitarian calculation; while on my account such considerations do not even arise. In a socialist society, or at least a fully developed socialist society, there will be no such capitalist acts. And, if we have egalitarian sentiments, we will not long for their return.

Dworkin sets aside questions about equality of power, but it is fairly evident that there will be nothing approaching either an equality of welfare, something Dworkin does not advocate, or an equality of resources, something he does defend, without a rough equality of power.[30] Within capitalist society—even liberal welfare state capitalist society—nothing like this is even remotely possible. Or so it has been one of the burdens of this book to argue.

Doesn't such a radically egalitarian socialist conception of justice give insufficient scope to the market, missing the element of fairness here that Dworkin stresses? Should it not be the case that people should have different amounts of wealth at various times in their lives depending on whether their choices have been more or less expensive or beneficial to the community in which they live? Suppose we have two M.D.s one of which goes to an outlying district in short supply of medical care to work as a general practitioner, the other stays in the metropolis working entirely in plastic surgery designed to take the wrinkles from the faces of the middle aged. By any non-arbitrary criterion the former doctor does the most good. Should he not have more wealth because of his greater contribution? (In reality, as things now stand, the reverse would be the case.) Isn't the same even more obviously true for anyone who works hard at something which is valuable to the community as over against someone who has quite deliberately made the minimum contribution all his life and, where he could, went as a freerider? Was Lenin being too puritanical and plainly unfair when, echoing the Bible, he said: "He who does not work, neither shall he eat?"

Here we are brought back to our discussion of desert. I allowed there for some role, though a diminished role, for contributions according to desert. This is particularly true where there is a need to develop the productive forces to enhance productivity so that the springs of social wealth would flow very fully. But we must not forget that the ambitious, the not so ambitious, and the nonambitious all not infrequently have children and the multiple advantages of differential wealth will surely flow to these children quite undeservedly. And the correcting of this is obviously not just a matter of disallowing inheritance.

Presumably, Dworkin, like Rawls, would be anxious to keep the wealth differentials sufficiently in control so that power differentials undermining equal liberty would not emerge. I have already argued that that is impossible to attain in a capitalist society. But that point aside, the differences of wealth, even for a portion of one's life, would give advantages to children and spouses that are plainly unfair. Still, that notwithstanding, it also remains the case that the need to adjust resources constantly here would, as the libertarians stress, be harmful to liberty. If the wealth differentials are small, there really will not be much of a problem, for they then would not lead to the unequal life prospects of the children involved. But allowing the market the scope Dworkin gives to it, will allow considerable wealth differentials which will unfairly disadvantage many children. But how then do we reward people for what they have done or at least suitably acknowledge what they have contributed? Affording greater wealth is not the only effective way to acknowledge merit. What we need to recognize is that there are ways, particularly in a society of full-abundance (the sort of society in which radical egalitarian principles could be more than heuristic ideals), to reward desert and to be ambition-sensitive. There is the reward of more interesting work in a more interesting environment, the recognition of ability, the respect and the like shown by one's fellows that goes with accomplishment. (Remember we are talking about a society in which the general level of material wealth is high.) In a wealthy society principles of marginal utility will quickly come into play when the greater wealth is not considerable enough to be transformed into greater power and control. In short, in such circumstances, more wealth will not be prized enough to drive people to excel.

Finally, even if I am too optimistic here and human nature is more entrenchedly Hobbesian than I am inclined to believe, we still have the points made by Hampshire and Rawls about the luck of genetic and social roulette. We can hardly say, if we keep those facts firmly in mind, that anyone is more intrinsically deserving than anyone else. Desert remains a pragmatic criterion, and where that is taken to heart we should in a society of *vast productive wealth* make trade-offs here in efficiency, *if* necessary, to achieve greater fairness. We should, that is, go for a lesser efficiency, where the difference is not great, to achieve a greater fairness. That is to say, we might need to become less ambition-sensitive than we otherwise would be so that we can sustain a greater equality of condition.

VI

I think it is important to recognize that Dworkin and I are providing rival elucidations and conceptions of a common concept of equality.[31] That common concept is what Dworkin calls "*the abstract egalitarian thesis*" that from "the standpoint of politics, the interests of the members of the community matter, and matter equally."[32] Dworkin would probably think that I am defending a distinct conception of that commonly shared concept, a conception which he would call equality of welfare and which he contrasts with his own conception of the shared concept of equality, namely equality of resources. Part of the dispute here turns on different views about what people's basic and comprehensive interests are. Welfare egalitarians, as Dworkin views the matter, believe that people's most comprehensive interests lie in their welfare according to some criterion of desire-satisfaction or some other psychological state.[33] It is also vital to ascertain what follows from supposing that people's interests matter equally.

Whatever conception of interests we take, we are very likely to come to believe that among our interests there is a set of highest-order interests, namely "interests which we have, not in virtue of any judgment about what other interests these serve, but rather as the tests . . . of all our other interests."[34] What is particularly vital, morally speaking, is the satisfaction of these highest order interests which must, from the moral point of view, be met equally; that is to say, the central aim of a perfectly just society is to assure as far as possible that these interests, as well as all the interests crucially instrumental to them, be met both as maximally as possible and as extensively as possible.

I am uneasy with calling my account either what Dworkin calls an equality of welfare or an equality of resources.[35] It seems to me to have some features of both as well as features which are not neatly forced into either typology. My two principles of radical egalitarian justice can be taken as giving a reading of what it is to have our highest order interests satisfied equally as far as social arrangements can do anything to help us to satisfy them. These principles direct us to the achievement of the most extensive total system of equal basic liberties and opportunities attainable. These include equal opportunities for meaningful work, for self-determination and political and economic participation. This respects the value of such things for everyone, and commits us to organizing society in such a way as to attain them, as much as possible, both equally and maximally. This in turn points to the fact that moral autonomy and the good of self-respect are fundamental values. It is a fundamental aim of an egalitarian society that we construct a world in which these values are equally available to everyone.

There is also a commitment to an equality of resources, for my second principle of justice seeks, after certain conditions are met, to divide the common stock of means, that is to say, our resources, so that each person over a lifetime will have a right to an equal share. But this has caveats which are desert-sensitive, namely that in the dividing due weight must be given to just entitlements. Thus, if there is a piece of land that I have cultivated and made bear fruit that contributes to the commonwealth and I have not acquired it by way, directly or indirectly, of robbery or fraud, I have a *prima facie* valid claim to it and *ceterus paribus* my claim must be honored. There can, of course, be a just overriding of it, say if my having it honored so disturbs the balance of power in my community that I am on the way to gaining power and control over others. But often nothing like this is even remotely in the offing, and where that obtains I have a just entitlement that should be honored even if it means that the dividing up of the resources will not be exactly equal. But the commitment to equality there will jealously guard such departures from equality so as to assure that the departures are not so wide as to allow the formation of classes or elites that will again control the lives of others or have a greater share of the power to determine the direction of the society than others. The thing to aim at is a classless and statusless society. (The reading I gave to "statusless" in Chapter 3 is vital to retain here.) Similarly, radical egalitarians do not make the error of the Eisenackers, so deftly criticized by Marx, of seeking to divide up the common stock of means equally.[36] It is essential, before any such division takes place, that provisions are made to provide for public goods (schools, hospitals, recreation areas, highways and the like), that provision is made to preserve the society's productive capacity and that resources are husbanded so that they are not simply squandered on the present generation.

What Dworkin calls the welfare role of equality comes out in my making allowances for differing unmanipulated needs and preferences. The satisfaction of our basic needs, needs which are pan-human, is essential for the realization of our highest-order interests. That, as far as possible, they be met and met equally is essential to radical egalitarianism and, I would think, to any tolerably adequate reading of abstract egalitarianism where the assumption is that everyone's life matters equally, that everyone's interests are equally important. The radical egalitarian conception of justice sets out to do its part as far as institutional design can contribute toward everyone's having "as good a life as possible, a life that has in it as much of what a life should have."[37] But this means that one—that is, anyone taking an egalitarian moral point of view—would not only want everyone to have his basic needs maximally met, to the extent this is possible, but to have a world in which everyone, as far as that is possible, could have as much as possible of whatever it is that he needs that is compatible with this being true for everyone equally.

What of people with expensive tastes? I would like, in a world of utter abundance, to have, not infrequently, very good wines with the appropriate dinners. There would be many an evening when I would like a bottle of Roderer Cristal with Coquilles St. Jacques. Yet should an egalitarian society, concerned with the interests of everyone alike, set out to meet those expensive tastes of mine? Certainly not at the expense of anyone's needs or under conditions which would render impossible the equal compossible satisfaction of preference. But where it is possible to satisfy these expensive tastes while all others will continue to have their compossible preferences equally satisfied as well, as much as any institutional design can provide the conditions for that, then those expensive tastes should be satisfied. The underlying aim should be to give as many people as possible as much as possible of what they on reflection want. Only scarcity should make us puritanical about those things, though practical mechanisms for approximating this should come from an equal division of resources (subject to the above-mentioned constraints). But the point of such an equal division of resources is to structure social organization to optimize situations where everyone stands an equal chance of having as good a life as possible. And in a world where the rationale for objective intrinsic goodness is problematic, the giving everyone as much as possible of what, each on reflection, and with a good knowledge of the causes of his desires, and the consequences of getting what he desires, would want, is a pretty good approximation of affording for everyone as good a life as possible.

I think it would be a mistake to label my view as what Dworkin calls a welfarist view. Need, on my account, remains a primitive notion. I do not claim to be able to unpack it in terms of wants and I do recognize that it is a complex concept. I do think, however, that we know enough about what our salient needs are to use it, in contexts like the present, unanalyzed. But such an employment of needs by me—and a similar thing should be said of interests—does not commit me to the welfarist view that we in general aim, as an overriding goal, at maximizing happiness or the satisfaction of desire or any other psychological state. Moreover, I am not committed to the belief that an egalitarian is trying to achieve a situation where we are all equally in some such state, e.g., happiness, which is to be maximized equally for everyone. My view does talk about giving everyone as much as possible of whatever it is that he or she on reflection wants, but it also talks of providing equally for our needs and of equally distributing benefits and burdens subject to certain specified qualifications.

Dworkin makes it quite plain that his egalitarianism does not commit him to anything like equality of result.[38] What I have been arguing is that, given the need to have an egalitarian society, we must have, for it to obtain, something approximating an equality of power. Furthermore, an equality of power is a necessary condition for there being an equality of condition. In turn, a rough equality of condition, with something like the qualifications spelled out above, is a necessary condition for the realization of Dworkin's abstract egalitarian thesis. Let me put the essential point alternatively, the very idea of what it is to be an egalitarian commits Dworkin, as it commits me, to the belief that an egalitarian moral point of view requires the belief that the interests of all the members of the human community matter and matter equally. But where there is not something like an equality of result or of condition, it *cannot* be the case that the members of the human community are being so treated that their interests matter equally. What

Dworkin calls the abstract egalitarian thesis really does commit him, his disavowals to the contrary notwithstanding, to trying to bring into existence an equality of condition.

VIII

It has been repeatedly argued that equality undermines liberty. Some would say that a society in which principles like my radical egalitarian principles were adopted, or even the liberal egalitarian principles of Rawls or Dworkin were adopted, would not be a free society. My arguments have been just the reverse. I have argued that it is only in an egalitarian society that full and extensive liberty is possible.

Perhaps the egalitarian and the anti-egalitarian are arguing at cross purposes? What we need to recognize, it has been argued, is that we have two kinds of rights both of which are important to freedom but to rather different freedoms and which are freedoms which not infrequently conflict.[39] We have rights to *fair terms of cooperation* but we also have rights to *non-interference.* If a right of either kind is overridden our freedom is diminished. The reason why it might be thought that the egalitarian and the anti-egalitarian may be arguing at cross purposes is that the egalitarian is pointing to the fact that rights to fair terms of cooperation and their associated liberties require equality while the anti-egalitarian is pointing to the fact that rights to non-interference and their associated liberties conflict with equality. They focus on different liberties.

What I have said above may not be crystal clear, so let me explain. People have a right to fair terms of cooperation. In political terms this comes to the equal right of all to effective participation in government and, in more broadly social terms, and for a society of economic wealth, it means people having a right to a roughly equal distribution of the benefits and burdens of the basic social arrangements that effect their lives and for them to stand in such relations to each other such that no one has the power to dominate the life of another. By contrast, rights to non-interference come to the equal right of all to be left alone by the government and more broadly to live in a society in which people have a right peacefully to pursue their interests without interference.

The conflict between equality and liberty comes down to, very essentially, the conflicts we get in modern societies between rights to fair terms of cooperation and rights to non-interference. As Joseph Schumpeter saw and J. S. Mill before him, one could have a thoroughly democratic society (at least in conventional terms) in which rights to non-interference might still be extensively violated. A central anti-egalitarian claim is that we cannot have an egalitarian society in which the very precious liberties that go with the rights to non-interference would not be violated.

Socialism and egalitarianism plainly protect rights to fair terms of cooperation. Without the social (collective) ownership and control of the means of production, involving with this, in the initial stages of socialism at least, a workers' state, economic power will be concentrated in the hands of a few who will in turn, as a result, dominate effective participation in government. Some right-wing libertarians blind themselves to that reality, but it is about as evident as can be. Only an utter turning away from the facts of social life could lead to any doubts about this at all. But then this means that in a workers' state, if some people have capitalistic impulses, that they would have their rights peacefully to pursue their own interests interfered with. They might wish to invest, retain and bequeath in economic domains. In a workers' state these capitalist acts in many circumstances would have to be forbidden, but that would be a violation of an individual's right to non-interference and the fact, if it was a fact, that we by democratic vote, even with vast majorities, had made such capitalist acts illegal would still not make any difference because individuals' rights to non-interference would still be violated.

We are indeed driven, by egalitarian impulses, of a perfectly understandable sort, to accept interference with laissez-faire capitalism to protect non-subordination and non-domination of people by protecting the egalitarian right to fair terms of cooperation and the enhanced liberty that that brings. Still, as things stand, this leads inevitably to violations of the right to non-interference and this brings with it a diminution of liberty. There will be people with capitalist impulses and they will be interfered with. It is no good denying, it will be said, that egalitarianism and particularly socialism will not lead to interference with very precious individual liberties, namely with our right peacefully to pursue our interests without interference.[40]

The proper response to this, as should be apparent from what I have argued throughout, is that to live in any society at all, capitalist, socialist or whatever, is to live in a world in which there will be some restriction or other on our rights peacefully to pursue our interests without interference. I can't lecture in Albanian or even in French in a standard philosophy class at the University of Calgary, I can't jog naked on most beaches, borrow a book from your library without your permission, fish in your trout pond without your permission, take your dog for a walk without your say so and the like. At least some of these things have been thought to be things which I might peacefully pursue in my own interests. Stopping me from doing them is plainly interfering with my peaceful pursuit of my own interests. And indeed it is an infringement on liberty, an interference with my doing what I may want to do.

However, for at least many of these activities, and particularly the ones having to do with property, even right-wing libertarians think that such interference is perfectly justified. But, justified or not, they still plainly constitute a restriction on our individual freedom. However, what we must also recognize is that there will always be some such restrictions on freedom in any society whatsoever, just in virtue of the fact that a normless society, without the restrictions that having norms imply, is a contradiction in terms.[41] Many restrictions are hardly felt as restrictions, as in the attitudes of many people toward seat-belt legislation, but they are, all the same, plainly restrictions on our liberty. It is just that they are thought to be unproblematically justified.

To the question would a socialism with a radical egalitarianism restrict some liberties, including some liberties rooted in rights to noninterference, the answer is that it indeed would; but so would laissez-faire capitalism, aristocratic conceptions of justice, liberal conceptions or any social formations at all, with their associated conceptions of justice. The relevant question is which of these restrictions are justified.

The restrictions on liberty proferred by radical egalitarianism and socialism, I have argued, are justified for they, of the various alternatives, give us both the most extensive and the most abundant system of liberty possible in modern conditions with their thorough protection of the right to fair terms of cooperation. Radical egalitarianism will also, and this is central for us, protect our civil liberties and these liberties are, of course, our most basic liberties. These are the liberties which are the most vital for us to protect. What it will not do is to protect our unrestricted liberties to invest, retain and bequeath in the economic realm and it will not protect our unrestricted freedom to buy and sell. There is, however, no good reason to think that these restrictions are restrictions of anything like a basic liberty. Moreover, we are justified in restricting our freedom to buy and sell if such restrictions strengthen, rather than weaken, our total system of liberty. This is in this way justified, for only by such market restrictions can the rights of the vast majority of people to effective participation in government and an equal role in the control of their social lives be protected. I say this because if we let the market run free in this way, power will pass into the hands of a few who will control the lives of the many and determine the fundamental design of the society. The actual liberties that are curtailed in a radically egalitarian social order are inessential liberties whose restriction in contemporary circumstances enhances human well-being and indeed makes for a firmer entrenchment of basic liberties and for their greater extension globally. That is to say, we here restrict some liberty in order to attain more liberty and a more equally distributed pattern of liberty. More people will be able to do what they want and have a greater control over their own lives than in a capitalist world order with its at least implicit inegalitarian commitments.

However, some might say I still have not faced the most central objection to radical egalitarianism, namely its statism. (I would prefer to say its putative statism.) The picture is this. The egalitarian state must be in the redistribution business. It has to make, or make sure there is made, an equal relative contribution to the welfare of every citizen. But this in effect means that the socialist state or, for that matter, the welfare state, will be deeply interventionist in our personal lives. It will be in the business, as one right-winger emotively put it, of cutting one person down to size in order to bring about that person's equality with another person who was in a previously disadvantageous position.[42] That is said to be morally objectionable and it would indeed be deeply morally objectionable in many circumstances. But it isn't in the circumstances in which the radical egalitarian presses for redistribution. (I am not speaking of what might be mere equalizing upwards.) The circumstances are these: Capitalist A gets his productive property confiscated so that he could no longer dominate and control the lives of proletarians B, C, D, E, F, and G. But what is wrong with it where this "cutting down to size"—in reality the confiscation of productive property or the taxation of the capitalist—involves no violation of A's civil liberties or the harming of his actual well-being (health, ability to work, to cultivate the arts, to have fruitful personal relations, to live in comfort and the like) and where B, C, D, E, F, and G will have their freedom and their well-being thoroughly enhanced if such confiscation or taxation occurs? Far from being morally objectional, it is precisely the sort of state of affairs that people ought to favor. It certainly protects more liberties and more significant liberties than it undermines.

There is another familiar anti-egalitarian argument designed to establish the liberty-undermining qualities of egalitarianism. It is an argument we have touched upon in discussing meritocracy. It turns on the fact that in any society there will be both talents and handicaps. Where they exist, what do we want to do about maintaining equal distribution? Egalitarians, radical or otherwise, certainly do not want to penalize people for talent. That being so, then surely people should be allowed to retain the benefits of superior talent. But this in some circumstances will lead to significant inequalities in resources and in the meeting of needs. To sustain equality there will have to be an ongoing redistribution in the direction of the less talented and less fortunate. But this redistribution from the more to the less talented does plainly penalize the talented for their talent. That, it will be said, is something which is both unfair and an undermining of liberty.

The following, it has been argued, makes the above evident enough.[43] If people have talents they will tend to want to use them. And if they use them they are very likely to come out ahead. Must not egalitarians say they ought not to be able to come out ahead no matter how well they use their talents and no matter how considerable these talents are? But that is intolerably restrictive and unfair.

The answer to the above anti-egalitarian argument is implicit in a number of things I have already said. But here let me confront this familiar argument directly. Part of the answer comes out in probing some of the ambiguities of "coming out ahead." Note, incidentally, that (1) not all reflective, morally sensitive people will be so concerned with that, and (2) that being very concerned with that is a mentality that capitalism inculcates. Be that as it may, to turn to the ambiguities, note that some take "coming out ahead" principally to mean "being paid well for the use of those talents" where "being paid well" is being paid sufficiently well so that it creates inequalities sufficient to disturb the preferred egalitarian patterns. (Without that, being paid well would give one no relative advantage.) But, as we have seen, "coming out ahead" need not take that form at all. Talents can be recognized and acknowledged in many ways. First, in just the respect and admiration of a fine employment of talents that would naturally come from people seeing them so displayed where these people were not twisted by envy; second, by having, because of these talents, interesting and secure work that their talents fit them for and they merit in virtue of those talents. Moreover, having more money is not going to matter much—for familiar marginal utility reasons—where what in capitalist societies would be called the welfare floors are already very high, this being made feasible by the great productive wealth of the society. Recall that in such a society of abundance everyone will be well off and secure. In such a society people are not going to be very concerned about being a little better off than someone else. The talented are in no way, in such a situation, robbed to help the untalented and handicapped or penalized for their talents. They are only prevented from amassing wealth (most particularly productive wealth), which would enable them to dominate the untalented and the handicapped and to control the social life of the world of which they are both a part.

To the very elitist remark that they, being talented, *should* so dominate and control, there is—Kantian responses about treating persons as ends and never only as means aside—the response that our various citizenship roles are such that all people of normal intelligence can perfectly well play them.[44] This is most evident where they are given a sane education and decent media (neither of which we actually have now but would have in a properly socialist society). This, incidentally, and harping back to Chapter 2, is the sort of contingent connection that Nietzscheans neglect. Returning, however, to the main line of my argument, for people so socialized (and perhaps even for people not so socialized), the crucial decisions there are not so complicated that they cannot collectively make them, relying on interchange with each other. This is particularly true where they are given reasonable information, intelligibly presented and where they live in a democratic environment where there is what Jürgen Habermas calls a genuine public sphere. There is no reason why such people cannot play the decisive roles here as equals in determining the overall direction of their societies. What is essentially at issue is not so complicated that such people cannot understand it. There is no need here for mandarins or the personages of democratic elite theory. There are no good grounds for giving the talented control and domination here. Indeed the very idea of there being those—say a Henry Kissinger or Zbigniew Brezinski— "talented to manage social life" is an anomalous idea anyway. But even if it were not, there is no need to put such people into such managerial employment and a very good reason for not doing so, namely because of the fundamental belief in the *moral* equality of persons, i.e., the belief that we are to treat all human beings as members of a Kantian kingdom of ends. This is a deeply entrenched belief widely, but not quite universally, shared (at least in theory) across the political spectrum. It is as much a part of Nozick's moral repertoire as Cohen's.

There is another reason why no injustice has been done in not giving the talented elite control of society. If such control were given, the elite group would in time in a previously egalitarian society come to gain power through greater wealth or greater institutional power. They could, however, without having such power, have, and rightly so, greater prestige than the plain man because of their talents, but that prestige would not put them into a position to control or dominate. It would not be an avenue to wealth and power. In such a society, their talents would still be recognized and rewarded and the talented would continue to live in an environment where they could optimally exercise them and would be able to do so in security and comfort. (Indeed their optimality here might very well be enhanced.) Moreover, the respects in which they are not rewarded, namely in wealth, power, and control over people, are not relevant to their talents or at least to talents which should be rewarded (e.g., not talents for exploiting people). And while there has been a slight diminution in their freedom springing from these specific and limited overridings of the right to non-interference, it has been more than compensated for by the overall enhancement of liberties linked to the full realization of the right to fair cooperation. Here, if you will, we have a kind of "utilitarianism of liberty": more freedom, *ceterus paribus,* is better than less freedom. But calling something "utilitarian," in all circumstances, is not a way of showing that it is mistaken. However, the general and, of course, central thing to see here is that radical egalitarianism does not penalize the talented for their talents or rob them of their liberty.

Some anti-egalitarians will say that even if all the above egalitarian responses are well taken there is still a plain sense in which equality undermines liberty. It makes absolutely all resources (including transferable parts of your own body) social resources and available for redistribution in the interests of equality. But this is plainly an intolerable attack on the integrity of the person and thus on liberty.[45] The first thing to be said in response is that there is nothing in my account of radical egalitarianism that would allow such an onslaught on the integrity of the person. And a similar thing should be said for Rawls and for

Dworkin. My first principle of justice protects the basic liberties of all persons and certainly your basic liberties would be assaulted if, without your permission, one of your two good eyes were taken to place in the sightless sockets of someone who had lost, albeit from no negligence of his own, both his eyes. And I also spoke, in my second principle of radical egalitarian justice, of giving due weight to the just entitlements of individuals. But it is surely one of our just entitlements that we have sovereignty over our own bodily parts. It is simply wild to think of them as some of the common stock of means or as social resources or community assets to be so divided that each person should have a right to an equal share. No egalitarian, radical or otherwise, has ever reasoned in that way.

What if it is said, in response, that that is simply due to the fact that egalitarians have been sufficiently muddled, and perhaps commonsensical, not to push their analysis to its logical limit? Egalitarians want to achieve the most extensive maximal liberty equally possible for everyone in a society, indeed finally in a world order, and equality of material wealth where it is also the case that people's other compossible needs are equally met. If this is being adhered to and these conditions are met or reasonably approximated, we should limit liberty, even a basic liberty, where such a limitation is necessary to strengthen and make more extensive the system of equal basic liberties. (In order for this not to be Draconian, it must at least be plausible to believe that these conditions are actually met.)

This has the unsettling side that it is the case that in some specific circumstance some basic liberty of an individual could be at risk. There are a number of things that could be said in response here, but one very salient one, for a world that is anything like the one we know, is that a person's sense of the integrity of his person is so tightly tied up with a sense of the inviolability of his body that any such seizure of his bodily parts would be perceived as such a deep attack on this person that any social system which allowed it could not be a system of the most extensive maximal equal liberty possible.[46]

Some anti-egalitarians would say, shifting now to another argument, that egalitarianism undermines liberty because it is in effect *authoritarian*.[47] It assumes someone, the government or an egalitarian secular mandarin, has the right to divy up resources in such a way as maximally and equally to answer to the needs of everyone alike. But by whose *authority* are such actions taken? Egalitarians, the argument goes, just assume that someone has the authority to do this but no one has any such authority. *Perhaps* there would be such an authority if everyone had *unanimously* agreed that resources are to be divided up equally or even (though this is less likely) if they had all agreed to settle such fundamental moral issues by majority vote or a two-thirds majority vote or something of the sort. But it is perfectly evident that none of these agreements obtain in the real world or are even in the offing.

There is no such consensus among our contemporaries. Moreover, it is simply not true, that as a matter of fact, everyone has an equal concern for everybody's interests. In no literal sense is it true that even in a single society every person in that society matters, and matters equally, to every other person in the society. Moreover, it is absurd to think that anything like that obtains, could obtain, or even should obtain, if it could. We typically care much more about our family, friends and close associates than we do about total strangers and it is both natural and appropriate that this should be so. But, the argument goes, to give egalitarianism the requisite moral authority, there would have to be something like this kind of consensus. But there plainly isn't and (more arguably) should not be. Moreover, we can't, even if we had such a majoritarian consensus, rely on the majority, for such fundamental issues are not vote issues. We cannot rightly railroad a dissenting minority.

I think that the moral authority for abstract egalitarianism, for the belief that the interests of everyone matters and matters equally, comes from its being the case that it is *required by the moral point of view*.[48] What I am predicting is that a person who has a good understanding of what morality is, has a good knowledge of the facts, is not ideologically mystified, takes an impartial point of view, and has an attitude of impartial caring, would, if not conceptually confused, come to accept the abstract egalitarian thesis. I see no way of arguing someone into such an egalitarianism who does not have that attitude of impartial caring, who does not in this general way have a love of humankind.[49] A hard-hearted Hobbesist is not reachable here. But given that a person has that love of humankind—that impartial and impersonal caring— together with the other qualities mentioned above, then, I predict, that that person would be an egalitarian at least to the extent of accepting the abstract egalitarian thesis. What I am claiming is that if these conditions were to obtain (if they ceased to be just counterfactuals), then there would be a consensus among moral agents about accepting the abstract egalitarian thesis.

Whether that consensus would be extendable to my specific formulations of radical egalitarian principles of justice would depend on how cogent my arguments are for them. It would, I believe, be highly unlikely that such detailed and specific philosophical conceptualizations of a concept could have such a consensus. It would be both unrealistic and involve *hubris* to expect such arguments could be air-tight and would ever garner such a consensus. One thing we can be very confident about indeed is that any fairly complicated philosophical thesis, no matter how carefully argued, of any general import, is going to contain some error or other. (Only some technical arguments of narrow scope and import will get past.) What can perhaps be reasonably hoped— and this is a maximal hope—is that a philosophical thesis is gesturing in the right direction. I have that hope for my radical egalitarian principles. Even more realistically, it is perhaps not unreasonable to hope that there just might, when, at some later date, the claims of the radical egalitarian tradition have been thoroughly sifted, emerge a significant consensus about some form of what I have called radical egalitarianism. But I think it is altogether more reasonable to expect such an informed moral consensus concerning the spare abstract egalitarian thesis. That might very well come to be seen as encapsulating a central feature of informed contemporary moral commitment. The more specific egalitarian claims will, I suspect, remain more controversial, though this does not mean that all claims are equally valid.

Someone might respond that, all the above not withstanding, egalitarianism is still authoritarian, arrogating to itself an authority to divy up resources that it does not have. For, after all, I still appealed to a battery of counterfactuals, and until there is some *actual* extensive consensus, where these counterfactuals cease to be just counterfactuals, one would, in insisting on an egalitarian social order, just be pushing dissenters into line.

What I have to say here by way of response, is what, I believe, should be said for any abstract moral (normative ethical, not meta-ethical) thesis or theory. I am not trying—and I take it that no philosophical moral theory is trying to do anything of the sort—to force or impose any egalitarian social order on anyone. What I have tried to do is argue for a moral and political thesis, trying like anyone else, who sets out a systematic conception of the good, the right and the just, to argue that this is a standard that rational moral agents would accept, and use to guide their lives, if my arguments are cogent and I have not made very many significant mistakes about the facts— or indeed any really crucial mistakes. I have only added one weaker condition, a condition that many moralists would not appeal to, since they think that somehow they can get morality out of rationality, namely the condition that in addition the moral agents in question must have an impartial attitude of impersonal caring for humankind.[50] They must believe, that is, that from the moral point of view, everyone matters and matters equally. In that distinct way they care and not just about their peers or about the people of their culture but about everyone just in virtue of the fact that they are human beings. Without such an attitude I think there is no arguing people into egalitarianism, but with it there is.

I am also *not* saying that the case for socialism rests on the case for egalitarianism. Workers, if they have a clear sense of what is in their own interests, will see the evident desirability of socialism over capitalism, though this may not be sufficient to give them the revolutionary motivation to risk their necks and those of their families in the struggle to achieve it. However, particularly to rootless intelligentsia with an anomalous class position, the recognition of the moral cogency of egalitarianism, and particularly of radical egalitarianism, will also reveal, for the reasons I have argued for in this book, that socialism has a deep rationale rooted in part in this egalitarianism. But just as there is no justifiable forcing of socialism on people, it should be even more evident that there is no justifiable forcing on people (even if this were possible) of something as complex and controversial as radical egalitarianism. It is utterly counter-productive to try to impose either socialism or radical egalitarianism from above. To be achievable, to be translatable into a social organization, either must emerge out of a real mass movement with wide popular support. If, in a world of considerable material abundance, we also had conditions of undistorted discourse, we would, I predict, also get or sustain a socialist structuring of society which would carry through with it, as a corollary, generalized egalitarian commitments. But before egalitarianism would be a justifiable part of an actual political program, it would have to have mass support and even then, for it to have the moral authority I have claimed for it, it would have to sustain the more rigorous kind of consensus of which I have spoken. I have claimed that, if examined carefully, it would be seen, by those with a good grasp of the tradition of moral theory, to have that authority. But that is quite different from saying I now have the authority to start divying up things or that there is any "egalitarian clerisy" who has that authority.

However, I do not want to be misunderstood here. To accept the above, let me repeat, is certainly not to say that workers should wait until that moral authority is established to struggle for their emancipation. What is minimally necessary to vindicate the socialist position is a good knowledge of what the social world is like, a firm sense of proletarian interests and an awareness, which is both vivid and steadfast, of some moral commonplaces about the wrongness of oppression, exploitation, domination and the wrongness of the existence of great wealth in the midst—when we see things globally—of massive poverty, malnutrition and starvation when none of that is necessary, i.e., impossible to eradicate without bringing into existence a still worse world. What is vital for proletarian emancipation is that the proletariat come to see those things and see them vividly and steadfastly.

Someone might perfectly well accept all these claims about proletarian emancipation and the evils of capitalism while remaining puzzled and perhaps even sceptical about egalitarianism. I think because of that, as a tactic, a practical socialist program should not be linked to a defense of radical egalitarianism. But what I have tried to show, in a more abstract way, is that the capitalist order in our epoch is a morally unacceptable order, because, among other things, it is a very unjust social order. I have also attempted to show that a capitalist apologetic is utterly mistaken in maintaining that equality undermines liberty and that a free society could not be a radically egalitarian society. With that apologetic broken, one of their principal arguments against socialism fails.

NOTES

1. See the debate between Robert Nozick, Daniel Bell and James Tobin, "If Inequality Is Inevitable What Can Be Done About It?" *The New York Times,* January 3, 1982, p. E5. The exchange between Bell and Nozick reveals the differences between the old egalitarianism and right-wing libertarianism. It is not only that the right and left clash but sometimes right clashes with right.

2. Amartya Sen, "Equality of What?" *The Tanner Lectures on Human Values,* vol. 1 (1980), ed. Sterling M. McMurrin (Cambridge, England: Cambridge University Press, 1980), pp. 198–220.

3. Henry Shue, "The Burdens of Justice," *The Journal of Philosophy* 80, no. 10 (October 1983): 600–601; 606–8.

4. Harriet Friedman, "The Political Economy of Food: The Rise and Fall of the Postwar International Food Order," in *Marxist Inquiries,* eds. Michael Burawoy and Theda Skocpol (Chicago: University of Chicago Press, 1982), pp. 248–86.

5. Ibid.

6. Ibid.

7. Amartya Sen, *Poverty and Famines: An Essay on Entitlement and Deprivation* (Oxford: Clarendon Press, 1981).

8. Friedman, op. cit.

9. Ibid.

10. Kai Nielsen, "Global Justice, Capitalism and the Third World," *Journal of Applied Philosophy,* forthcoming.

11. Ronald Dworkin: "Why Liberals Should Believe in Equality," *New York Review of Books* (February 1983), pp. 32–35; "What is Equality?" *Philosophy and Public Affairs* (Summer 1981 and Fall 1981); and "In Defense of Equality," *Social Philosophy and Policy* 1, no. 1 (Autumn 1983): 24–40.

12. Dworkin, "Why Liberals Should Believe in Equality," p. 32.

13. Ibid.

14. Ibid.

15. Ibid.

16. Ibid.

17. Ibid. Dworkin's right-wing critics have not, as might be expected, let that claim go uncontested. See Jan Narveson's two critical essays in *Social Philosophy and Policy* 1, no. 1 (Autumn 1983): 1–23 and 44–44.

18. Dworkin, "Why Liberals Should Believe in Equality," p. 33.

19. Ibid.

20. Ibid.

21. Ibid.

22. Ibid.

23. Ibid.

24. Ibid., p. 34.

25. Ibid.

26. Ibid.

27. Ibid.

28. Ibid.

29. Dworkin, "In Defense of Equality," pp. 24–40. Some Marxists may deny that saying, on the contrary, that the interests of the proletariat are more important than the interests of the bourgeoise. It is simply not the case, Marxists typically argue, that everyone's interests are equally important. In class struggle the interests of the proletariat trump the interests of people in any other class. I think this is true as a tactic in the struggle for proletarian emancipation and to finally end class rule. But this is true only as a tactic. After all, proletarian emancipation, and the ending of class rule, is designed to bring about a classless society in which it is finally actually possible in some meaningful way to consider the interests of everyone alike: to regard all people as brothers and sisters in a world in which everyone's life matters equally.

30. The phrases "equal power" or "equality of power" strike some as odd. Certainly it does not make sense to think of power as a commodity which could be distributed in different proportions, including equal proportions, and which would still retain the same character however distributed. Moreover, it is natural enough to think that if we ever had genuinely equal relations between people, that would do away with power altogether and hence with equal power. There would, where equality reigns, no longer be any power brokers: there would no longer be relations between people, at least in the social dimensions of our lives, characterized by domination and submission. But talk of equality of power is meant to mark that and to mark the further fact that everyone is to have, where what I have called equality of power obtains, equal say in how social decisions are to be made and carried out. See Richard Norman, "Does Equality Destroy Liberty?" in *Contempoary Political Philosophy*, ed. Keith Graham (Cambridge: Cambridge University Press, 1982), pp. 99–100. I should add that Norman's article is a truly excellent essay on the topic of this book.

31. That Dworkin is fully aware of that is shown in the first few pages of his response to Narveson. Dworkin, "In Defense of Equality," pp. 24–27.

32. Ibid., p. 24.

33. Ibid., p. 25.

34. Ibid., p. 26.

35. His most extensive explications of those conceptions occur in his two part essay "What is Equality?" *Philosophy and Public Affairs* (Summer 1981 and Autumn 1981).

36. Karl Marx, *Critique of the Gotha Programme* (New York: International Publishers, 1938).

37. Dworkin, "In Defense of Equality," pp. 25–26.

38. Dworkin, "Why Liberals Should Believe in Equality," pp. 32–34.

39. Richard W. Miller, "Marx and Morality," in *Marxism,* eds. J. R. Pennock and J. W. Chapman, Nomos 26 (New York: New York University Press, 1983), pp. 9–11.

40. Ibid., p. 10.

41. This has been argued from both the liberal center and the left. Ralf Dahrendorf, *Essays in the Theory of Society* (Stanford, Cal.: Stanford University Press, 1968), pp. 151–78; and G. A. Cohen, "Capitalism, Freedom and the Proletariat" in *The Idea of Freedom: Essays in Honour of Isaiah Berlin,* ed. Alan Ryan (Oxford: Oxford University Press, 1979).

42. The graphic language should be duly noted. Jan Narveson, "On Dworkinian Equality," *Social Philosophy and Policy* 1, no. 1 (autumn 1983): 4.

43. Ibid., p. 1–24.

44. Steven Lukes, *Essays in Social Theory* (London: Macmillan Press, 1977), pp. 30–51.

45. Narveson, "On Dworkinian Equality," p. 19.

46. Dworkin, "In Defense of Equality," pp. 38–39.

47. Jan Narveson, "Reply to Dworkin," *Social Philosophy and Policy* 1, no. 1 (Autumn 1983): 42–44.

48. Some will argue that there is no such thing as a moral point of view. My differences with him about the question of whether the amoralist can be argued into morality not withstanding, I think Kurt Baier, in a series of articles written subsequent to his *The Moral Point of View,* has clearly shown that there is something reasonably determinate that can, without ethnocentrism, be called "the moral point of view."

49. Richard Norman has impressively argued that this is an essential background assumption of the moral point of view. Richard Norman, "Critical Notice of Rodger Beehler's *Moral Life,*" *Canadian Journal of Philosophy* 11, no. 1 (March 1981): 157–83.

50. Again, for how crucial this background assumption is, see the reference to Richard Norman cited in the previous footnote and see J. M. Findlay, *Values and Intentions* (London: George Allen & Unwin Ltd., 1961).

Index